POLITICS AND ENVIRONMENT

A Reader in Ecological Crisis

POLITICS AND ENVIRONMENT

A Reader in Ecological Crisis

Edited by

WALT ANDERSON

San Fernando Valley State College

GOODYEAR PUBLISHING COMPANY, INC.
Pacific Palisades, California

© 1970 by GOODYEAR PUBLISHING COMPANY, INC.
Pacific Palisades, California

Library of Congress Catalog Card Number: 76-110815

Current printing (last number):

10 9 8 7 6 5 4 3 2

Printed in the United States of America

This book is for my son Daniel
and for the world in which he'll live.

CONTENTS

FOREWORD:
WHAT KIND OF LEGACY?

There was a special adventure to being a young boy in northwestern Wisconsin. There was the adventure of exploring a deep green pine forest, crunching noisily through the crisp leaves and pine needles on a sharp fall day, or taking a cool drink from a fast running trout stream or a hidden lake.

I grew up in that kind of place. It was the village of Clear Lake, a community of 700 persons. A short walk from my house was the edge of town, and the edge of town was Wisconsin farm and forest land that stretched north to Lake Superior and west to the Minnesota border.

There was never any reason to believe that the rest of the world wasn't as clean and comfortable as northwestern Wisconsin. It is easy to believe that the other children of Clear Lake felt that the legacy they had inherited in rich land, clean air, and safe water was one every boy and girl in the nation had.

It is certain that those same children soon grew up to know that northwestern Wisconsin was an isolated part of America where the devastation of exploding population and irresponsible pollution was slow in coming.

For myself, I was shocked to see the debilitation of the country's natural resources. It wasn't necessary to leave Wisconsin to see what was happening. Rivers and lakes, especially in the southern part of the state, were rapidly being poisoned by industrial wastes and antiquated septic systems. As a resident of Madison where I served as a state senator and as governor, I saw the steady deterioration of the lakes around the city that were one of the major attractions of the state capital. As in other cities around the country action was taken to stop the dumping of raw sewage into the lakes, but increased population, septic tank systems that seep into the water table, and pesticide and silt runoffs continue to feed the relentless deterioration.

Wisconsin's stirring of interest in the condition of the environment was similar to the stirring throughout the nation as people began to see that it was in the public interest to be concerned. The devastation of the environment was easily observable to anyone traveling back and forth across the country. The chaos of crowded, industrial America was everywhere: cities choked by smog; cities without sufficient space to dump garbage; storm sewers that dump raw sewage into lakes and rivers during heavy rains; inadequate recreational facilities; unrestricted and unplanned development and construction; filling of swamps and wetlands; and the rapidly increasing use of deadly, persistent pesticides.

The nation's capital itself stands as an example of the desecration of the environment. Washington is a nonindustrial city of broad avenues and vast expanses of green. In that, it is unique among major American cities. But, as in all other American cities, the pressures caused by a rapidly growing and crowded metropolis are evident. Urban growth is spilling out from the decaying central city and is chewing up the once beautiful forest lands of surrounding Maryland and Virginia. The bulldozer is working continuously, totally wiping out areas that were rich in wildlife. The historic Potomac River, described by early explorers as "teeming" with fish and wildlife, is little better than an open sewer. It is totally unsafe for swimming and questionable for fishing. The streets of the city and suburbs are jammed with traffic, and a haze of pollution hangs in the air with many tons a day added by airplanes alone. Recreation space is scarce, and the District of Columbia is running out of room to dump its garbage.

Just flying into the New York City area provides a terrifying look at what we have done to our environment. An ever-present cloud of industrial smoke and automotive exhaust haze floats, not only over the city, but over nearby New Jersey and Connecticut as well. The ugly sprawl of unplanned suburbia can be seen in all directions, and the traffic jams on the streets and freeways nearly defy description. Metropolitan New York offers us a glimpse into the future, and the future doesn't look good.

What is happening to the Great Lakes offers still another prediction of things to come. The lakes represent the largest collection of fresh water bodies in the world. Lake Erie, the sewer of Cleveland, Detroit, Buffalo, and Toledo, is now almost a dead lake. Lake Michigan is on the way, with scientists warning that its phosphate level is rapidly approaching a critical point that could set off an explosive growth of algae and weeds that may never be stopped. Even Lake Superior, the cleanest of the Great Lakes, where a boatsman can still dip a cup of drinking water directly from the lake, is threatened.

The problems that arise in attempts to halt just the pollution of the Great Lakes are good examples of the kinds of things one runs into when attempting to grapple with the whole cancerous pollution problem. Sportsmen who so want to see the waters stay pure for fishing and boating frequently object when they are told to have self-contained toilets installed in their boats. Industrial firms who rely on fresh, clean water argue that converting to nonpolluting mechanisms is too expensive and makes it impossible for them to compete with industries in other areas where such rules do not exist. Farmers want clean streams for their livestock, but they often ignore the fact that the pesticides they use on their crops run off into the streams to poison farm animals, fish, and wildlife. There is concern about the threat to the environment, but it is the concern that someone else should clean up what he is doing first. That kind of attitude clearly won't solve the dilemma. The commitment must be nationwide—hopefully, worldwide.

This country's use of herbicides and defoliants in Vietnam is another example of a dangerous threat to the entire ecology of that Southeast Asian nation. Two zoologists made a study of the ecological effects of the Vietnam war in the spring of 1969. They found, in addition to the massive bomb cratering that is turning much of the countryside into areas resembling the surface of the moon, that there is heavy damage to areas treated with herbicides to defoliate the trees and plants. Some of the damage appears to be permanent.

Because of the necessity for the occasional jettisoning of herbicides and spraying accidents, not all the defoliation was along the suspected

jungle trail hiding places of the Viet Cong. In one residential area between Saigon and the U. S. Air Base at Bien Hoa, the scientists examined diseased mango trees and talked to a trained biologist who claimed
that the trees had suffered defoliation three years previously and had
not flowered or produced fruit since that time.

In a preliminary report of their experiences the zoologists described
the defoliants as having a "ghastly effect of denuding the country of
growth," and related that "we consider the ecological consequences of
defoliation very severe."

With all the almost indifferent normal destruction of the natural resources of the world going on, it is particularly horrifying to read of
wholesale, premeditated destruction of plant life in vast sections of
Vietnam. No one apparently knows how long it takes for the destroyed
areas to return to normal. Some of the military testing of chemical-
biological warfare weapons has had similar disastrous effects.

There is a small island called Gruinard off the remote northwest
coast of Scotland where the British tested deadly Anthrax germs during
World War II. That island is still infected, and scientists believe it will
stay that way for at least 100 years. The same is true of a plot of land
on the Dugway Proving Grounds in Utah, and one in Alaska.

Fortunately the awareness of the magnitude of the threat facing the
environment of the world is growing. Congress recognizes the seriousness of the threat, but has not given it the urgent attention it deserves.
The problem is being dealt with in piecemeal fashion. Some limitations
on chemical-biological testing are discussed; a few water quality and air
pollution bills pass, the threat of persistent pesticides is argued, and
legislative bans considered.

What fails to be realized is that the threat to the environment is the
number one crisis facing this nation and the world. What is done or is
not done will determine the kind of nation or world we leave to the
citizens of tomorrow, and may well decide the future of the human race.
The environment should receive at least the same attention that is given
national defense or the space race. Nothing can possibly be more basic
to life than the necessity for clean air and water. There is a distinct
possibility that the money spent for national defense ultimately will
serve the cruel irony of protecting national resources that are unworthy
of defense.

It is difficult not to think about the kind of world the children of
America inherited fifty years ago in comparison with the world the
children of today face. Most children now live in crowded suburbs,
miles away from any kind of forest or clean body of water. They are

being cheated of their legacy, and their children may have no legacy at all.

It may well be that the youth of the world will have to take the responsibility of insuring their own legacy. Former Interior Secretary Stewart L. Udall has made the suggestion that since it will be their world, "young people may start picketing polluters and campaign against ugliness."

There is heartening evidence that the awareness is beginning. Just recently a group of high school juniors in Ashland, Wisconsin, took a major step to show their concern for the growing threat to the ecology of Lake Superior when they demonstrated in support of action at Duluth's Pollution Enforcement Conference. They also revealed future plans to confront dumpers of industrial wastes that are slowly polluting the relatively clean lake.

The Ashland students do not represent an isolated example. They are part of the newly aware generation—young people who are taking a no-nonsense look at society and the world as it is. They are painfully aware that the world they inherit is their responsibility, because for too long the generations before them have shown that "progress" was an excuse for irresponsibility.

What is most refreshing is that they are seeing the world in a new perspective. A student at a Washington, D. C., university had an interesting response when he was told that a congressional proposal to bring a complete halt to any federal program which damaged the environment might be unconstitutional. In a puzzled, quick reaction he retorted: "Isn't polluting our rivers unconstitutional?" His question demands an answer. The time has long passed when the institutions of our society—government, industry, the universities—can profess a concern for environment and yet do nothing.

The answer to that question won't come without a tough political fight that will require government to become a trustee of the environment for all people, industry to make pollution control a part of the industrial process, and the universities to devote their immense resources to developing new bodies of knowledge and new technology to insure the survival of man. Only in this way can we assure in the crucial final third of the 20th century that there will be quality as well as quantity in American life.

The responsibility for seeing that the tough political fight will be successful belongs to the youth, who clearly have the most to lose in a world raped of its resources. The goals can be accomplished if youth make the same efforts they have made in bringing about a new direction in the country on foreign commitments, on defense expenditures, on human rights and human conditions, and on the crisis of urban life. It obviously is of the utmost urgency that the New Politics and the conservation of our natural resources become joined in a responsible effort to make the world a livable place.

The necessity of fast action was expressed by biologist Barry Commoner, chairman of the St. Louis Committee for Environmental Information, who warned, "We don't really know what the long-term effects of various types of environmental deterioration will be, and the kids are the guinea pigs."

Gaylord Nelson
United States Senator

POLITICS AND ENVIRONMENT

A Reader in Ecological Crisis

● INTRODUCTION

Political scientists, in the continuing process of defining and defending the territorial boundaries of their discipline, have somehow managed to avoid confronting as a totality the most pressing complex of political issues of our time—those which can be called environmental. It is quite common, for example, for college courses in *geography* to deal with overpopulation, but when I first assigned Paul Ehrlich's *The Population Bomb* as supplementary reading in an introductory American government class, that was generally regarded as an interesting but rather far-out exercise, although most of the national issues with which we were dealing . . . from urban renewal to foreign aid . . . were closely connected to population problems, and so were the issues which most personally involved myself and the students: the politics of the exploding state public higher education system of which we were all a part.

Today there are many signs of a new national awareness of environmental issues. The cause of this awakening is not hard to locate: it is

1

simply that the consequences of years of *un*awareness have suddenly become so evidently disastrous that it is no longer possible—at least no longer possible for everybody—to continue to ignore the problem. By consequences I mean inescapably evident human creations such as the smog in most American cities, the pollution of our major rivers and lakes, and the disappearance of large segments of our native wildlife and open land. Each of these has roused certain segments of the population to awareness of an environmental problem and to consideration of some form of political action as a possible solution. The conflict between interest groups which represent differing points of view on an environmental issue—as, for example, between the auto industry and the state of California on the issue of smog control, between the Santa Barbara Chamber of Commerce and the oil industry on the issue of offshore drilling, or between conservationists and industrialists or developers on any number of issues—has become an increasingly familiar kind of political conflict; it will undoubtedly become more familiar still as technology continues to develop, as population continues to grow, and as the returns on man's years of carelessness toward the environment continue to come in.

A variation on Frederick Jackson Turner's frontier thesis might be useful as a way of looking at the situation in which the human race now finds itself.[1] Turner's idea was that the existence of the frontier had been vastly influential in the development of America's political institutions, economy, and national character—and that the disappearance of the frontier, around 1890, was thus an historical event of major importance. "The frontier," he said, "has gone, and with its going has closed the first period of American history."

Turner's thesis was put forth in 1893; today, in the light of another 70-odd years of American history, we can add that, at the same time as the geographic frontier was disappearing, another frontier—the technological one—was opening up. Just as westward expansion dominated the past century, so has technological progress dominated our own—and much of it has been carried out in the same aggressive, exploitative, and short-sighted style of action. The frontiersman, clearing the forests and slaughtering the buffalo, gives way in a smooth historical transition to the developer bulldozing the hills and the industrialist dumping wastes into the streams. But the days when land and resources could be used in that spirit of limitlessness are coming to an end; the second frontier is disappearing also, and its going may be no

---

[1] I am not sure whether the frontier thesis is in or out of fashion at the moment; personally I accept it as a valid observation.

less a landmark in American history—and no less disturbing to the national consciousness—than the one of which Turner spoke in 1893.

Along with the technological expansion in this century there has been an expansion of the American economy and its population; these three are, of course, interrelated factors in the single process which has taken place: the development of a gigantic mass-production economy, kept alive and growing by mass merchandising through mass media. Each year the population (number of consumers) increases, and each year the health of the economy is measured in terms of the *increase* in gross national product.

But such an enormous growth in the number of one living species (man) and such an enormous utilization of natural resources have many kinds of ecological consequences. Consider, for example, one of the less-noticed aspects of this development: packaging. The packaging of food and manufactured goods has become an important industry in itself, especially because of the intimate connections between packaging and merchandising; manufacturers have found that the commercial success of a product may be determined by its container rather than by its quality, and consumers have shown a preference for goods packaged in attractive, convenient individual containers. This has been particularly evident in the growing popularity of disposable bottles. The result has been a great increase in the number of packages produced, in relation to the amount of goods. This is healthful from the standpoint of the gross national product. From an ecological standpoint, however, it presents certain problems: one is that the raw material for the packaging has to come from somewhere, raising the question of whether this is the best utilization of natural resources. The second problem is that the disposable container has to be disposed of somewhere. The Department of Health, Education and Welfare predicts that by 1976 every American will be disposing of 136 more pounds of packaging waste than he did in 1966—the volume of packaging waste is growing more than twice as much as could be expected on the basis of population increase alone. The latter problem is one that we can clearly identify as political because it is left to political units such as cities to devise ways of getting rid of the wastes, and the process of doing so is one that invariably effects the local ecology. The city of Berkeley, California, for example, has dealt with the problem in what seemed for a long while to the municipal government to be a quite satisfactory manner: they used garbage as a fill to create new usable land along the San Francisco Bay shoreline. This in turn contributed to a new problem, the gradual reduction in the size of the Bay.

It is now, because of this and similar activities, down to about 60 percent of its original size, and the state of California, after extensive political wrangling, has passed a bill to preserve what is left. Here we can see, by following only one line of cause and effect, that a certain kind of technological and economic progress, related to population growth, has contributed to the severity of a problem involving conflict between different political entities (Bay area cities and counties), between interest groups (developers and conservationists), and between political factions over how it should be solved. And it also has had a major impact upon the natural ecology of San Francisco Bay.

Technology and population growth together have brought the human race to the point where we must now realize that we cannot decide whether or not to manipulate the world environment; we do manipulate it. What we must now decide is what forms the manipulation will take, what will be our policy for environmental control.

One policy—the prevailing one—is that of taking minimal responsibility for a given manipulation of the environment: the consequences of packaging practices, the use of insecticides, the effusion of industrial wastes into air and water, and so forth. This policy has various kinds of consequences, ranging from mildly unpleasant (minor eye irritation from smog) through enormously damaging and just possibly reparable (the pollution of rivers and lakes) to complete and irreversible (the extinction of species).

The contrasting basic policy available is one of accepting full responsibility for environmental manipulation and devising comprehensive programs and techniques—which would have to be based on such considerations as the ecology of continents and the effects of varying environmental conditions on the human mind and body—for controlling, limiting, and planning such manipulation. Undoubtedly, much of such planning would take the form of governmental action on the national and even international level. This is a consideration which is likely to dismay those people—among whom I include myself—who hope that the future evolution of government will be toward decentralization. But, given the reality of human numbers and the reach of modern technology, I do not see how environmental disasters are likely to be averted by the decision-making of small governmental units. Furthermore, it is now imperative that those whose basic sentiment is that man ought to begin to learn to leave nature alone—another group with which I have considerable sympathy—realize that the same realities of population and technology now make it necessary for leave-alone policies to be supported by legislation, administration, and enforcement—as, for example, American wilderness areas have to be legislated into existence by the government and then protected.

One difficulty which we encounter as we begin to move into an era of environmental responsibility is that traditional political subdivisions which exist are frequently virtually irrelevant as organizations for handling environmental problems. For example, rivers have frequently provided the boundaries between governmental entities, and yet a river system—including its entire watershed—is a natural ecological whole; one of the most common kinds of political-environmental conflict today is between nations, states, or smaller governmental entities divided by water boundaries over water problems: pollution control, use of water, or diversion of streams. Various kinds of special-purpose regional and international agencies are being formed to deal with environmental problems, but they face—and will continue to face—tremendous conflicts with existing governmental units. And, as everyone who has ever moved among the bureaucracies knows, governmental units have survival instincts of their own.

A similar kind of problem faces those who would study, as academic specialists, the processes and consequences of environmental change. The academic establishment, like the governmental establishment, is made up of discrete entities which have no necessary relationship to problems requiring solution. Academicians often make valiant attempts to do "interdisciplinary research," but unfortunately an *anschluss* of compartments seldom adds up to what is needed: a wide breadth of vision, an impatience with rubrics, and a willingness to try to confront a problem in its own terms.

In my opinion, the parochialism of governmental organization and academic disciplines is not merely a condition which makes it difficult to solve the problems; it is, rather, a condition which has helped to cause the problems. Viewed from the kind of long perspective which is necessary for ecological problems, the vast problem-solving machinery of intellect, technology, and government which we have built begins to appear as unwieldy and maladaptive as the body of a dinosaur.

As I write this, the successful landings on the moon by American astronauts are being widely celebrated as inspiring triumphs of the human intellect, monumental proof that man *does* have the capacity to solve problems. However, I am afraid the program's place in history is more likely to be quite the reverse: a tragic example of 20th century man's incapacity to make rational decisions about major issues. The technological sophistication of the moon landings was indeed impressive, but the fact that the program was given priority over such unglamorous national needs as water and air pollution and population control indicates that at the level of decision-making our technology is in fact highly immature.

This shortsightedness in technological decision-making at the direc-tive—which usually means the governmental—level, is an especially discouraging reality to confront when we consider the necessity for such large scale decision-making as the only way out of many of the major crises into which technological progress has already gotten us. I have said earlier that I believe some programs at the national and international level appear to be necessary to deal with modern en-vironmental problems. Yet, although that need does exist, I am not at all sure that modern national governments are capable of meeting the challenge. I offer this as unthinkable thought number one about politics and environment.

It does seem unthinkable that our governments—especially the gov-ernment of the United States—may be in fact incapable of averting ecological disasters; this would mean that the human race, far from having mastered nature, has only advanced to the point where it can create situations leading to catastrophes, at which point we must abandon all pretenses of control and let nature work things out how-ever it can. Surely we are farther along than that. But are we? Con-sider, as an example, the matter of overpopulation. The problem has been caused by technological progress, chiefly medical, and the prob-lem has not been solved. In spite of the recent awakening of many people to the seriousness of the problem, it is still not being solved. Furthermore, most demographic information indicates that even if we do suddenly decide to mobilize all our technology toward birth control and increased food production, there will still be millions of deaths from disease, starvation, inadequate housing, and other consequences of overpopulation within the coming generation. The term most writers use for this—a "death-rate solution"—is certainly no euphemism, but even it tends to conceal the reality of what will happen—which is simply that nature will step in to clean up in a tragic and painful way the enormous mess that men have made by refusing to confront the ecological consequences of one kind of scientific-technological prog-ress.

Many people with whom I have discussed this problem deal with it, if they deal with it at all, by expressing their confidence that the scientists will "come up with something" before it is too late; they talk of something they have read about food from the sea, or mention the possibility of exporting surplus population to another planet. All of this is evidence of a remarkably blind and passive faith in the capacity of the experts to deal with problems, and it is evidence that the old human credulity which led the masses to follow blindly kings and emperors has not at all disappeared from modern society; it has only been subtly transferred, and now, although we are critical and demanding of our elected leaders, we trustingly place our futures and our lives in the keeping of anonymous experts.

There are alternatives to this kind of credulity: for one, we can begin to realize that there can be vast consequences not only to "controversial" and "political" decisions, but also to decisions which are represented as simply "administrative," "neutral," "technical," "matters for expert competence." For another, we can begin to insist that, until the consequences of actions are *truly* known and understood, there frequently must be decisions made *not* to build, *not* to alter, *not* to innovate. This I offer as unthinkable thought number two. I first encountered it in a remarkable passage in a *Ramparts* article written a few years ago by Gene Marine. The author talked about the Great Swamp area of New Jersey, a wildlife refuge and natural flood-control area that was being threatened by the proposal to build New York's fourth jetport there. He had been, he implies, attracted to the thought that the new airport might be built somewhere else. Then:

Shortly after visiting the Great Swamp, I was in the 42nd Street office of attorney David Sive, who is representing the Sierra Club in another case; after discussing that other case, we fell to talking about the airport, and after a moment Sive leaned forward with a soft smile.

"Did you ever think," he asked me curiously, "that you might be asking the wrong questions? I mean—suppose we simply didn't build the airport?" The question was so simple that it was minutes before I took it in. Ridiculous, of course. But . . . .

"Suppose we simply didn't build the airport?" Does any resident of New York or its surrounding area really want more people, more crowding, more conversion of land to buildings? Does New York *need* to double the number of people who fly in or out?

Based in San Francisco, I can choose from more than a dozen non-stop flights to New York every day, most of them with at least some empty seats. Within limits, I can as easily take one flight as another, go on Wednesday instead of Tuesday, even fly to Washington and shuttle to New York without the demands of my work being seriously affected; and this is certainly true of many, probably most, air travelers.

If a fourth jetport is not built, perhaps some factories will move. Some are moving anyway; Revlon, the cosmetic firm which operates three plants in New Jersey, has just opened its fourth—in Arizona. There will be fewer jobs. But in the long run, the people will go where the jobs are anyway. Certainly some human families will suffer; but human families will suffer far more if we go ahead and build all the jetports and the canals and the freeways, and fill in the swamps and dam the canyons. . . .

There are, of course, tomorrow's bigger jets. They will carry more people into the same airports—and they may need longer runways, but they don't need new airports. And even if they did, why not carry the argument further? Do we *need* bigger jets?

The problem is not just the jetport; there is, for example, California's massive water plan, which in its final form will alter the distribution of water from virtually every river in the state. There are a lot of local, political reasons for opposing it, but aside from those—suppose Los Angeles simply doesn't get any more water?

The Engineers immediately answer, in panic or derision, with projections of population growth; we *must* have the water, because we will have the people. But if there is no fourth jetport, New York will not have 65 million air travelers in 1980. And if there is no California Water Plan, and water shortage becomes a serious problem, then the people will not go to Los Angeles, and some of the people who are there will leave.

Is that bad? [2]

The dangerousness of the present situation and the unthinkability of some of the concepts which may help us get out of it exist within the context of our prevailing structure of ideas about the uses of science and technology, the self-regulating qualities of a pluralistic, interest-group society, and the relationship between man and his environment. These ideas are being challenged on many fronts. There have been any number of well-grounded criticisms of the bases of technological decision-making, of the assumptions of interest-group liberalism and its attendant economics, of the ways that men sense and comprehend the place of humanity in nature. It is necessary now that we begin to understand that these criticisms, which might have seemed to be separate approaches to separate problems, are in fact naturally interrelated; and we must begin to pull together the fibers of many inquiries. We urgently need to develop a new ecological consciousness, a way of thinking and feeling about the needs and priorities and possibilities of human life in the world environment which will enable us to make rational decisions about the use of technology.

This is of course another way of making the commonplace observation that social progress has not kept pace with technological progress, but it carries the observation to specifics; we must, as an act of survival, develop institutional arrangements, levels of ecological conceptualization, and human values at least commensurate with our capacity to damage the environment.

[2] Gene Marine, "America the Raped," Part 2, RAMPARTS, May 1967, p. 45. Reprinted by permission. The series of articles has been expanded and issued in book form: AMERICA THE RAPED (New York: Simon & Schuster, Inc., 1969).

Much of this work will have to be done in political terms, and so I come back finally to politics and its attendant discipline of political science. Politics has in the past been defined—by political scientists— as a matter of who gets what, when, and how; that was the kind of definition which was acceptable so long as we were allowed to believe that goods and services were created and exchanged in a kind of ecological vacuum. Today, if we are to accept and handle wisely our technological abilities, we must realize that politics is the making of decisions by human beings about the manipulation and utilization of the natural environment; it is an interaction among life forms which directly or indirectly affects other life forms. Increasingly and inevitably, politics *is* ecology.

THE POLITICS OF POPULATION

The most serious single problem confronting the human race today is the amazing increase in the size—and in the rate of growth—of the human population. It is estimated that it required one million years for the human race to double its population prior to 6000 B.C. By the middle ages, doubling time was approximately one thousand years. By the nineteenth century, the rate of population growth had increased to the point where world population would double in approximately 200 years. Today, as a result of further scientific progress and the cumulative effect of population growth itself, the doubling time of the world's population is about 35 years. There are three to three and one-half billion people on the planet today; by the end of this century, unless something—either very fortunate or very disastrous—intervenes, there will be six to seven billion.

Population growth is a part of many current political issues. In the United States we can see its effects in our overcrowded schools and colleges, with their impersonal processing of students and their continual building needs which place heavy burdens upon taxpayers; in the explosive urban ghettos, abandoned by the middle classes in their flight to the ever-spreading suburbs; in the exploitation of land space by developers with the resulting pressure on, and corruption of, public officials; in the disappearance of wilderness, and the pollution of air and water. In other countries the political-population problems are even more serious: what many of the "emerging" nations are emerging into is a future of greater misery and deprivation than they know already, and international organizations cannot continue much longer to avoid—as they have in the past—the touchy religious and cultural obstacles to international cooperation for population control.

One of the men who has worked hardest to awaken the American public to the realities of overpopulation is Paul Ehrlich, professor of biology at Stanford University. In his book *The Population Bomb* and in numerous articles, speeches, and scientific papers, he has advocated an immediate and vast mobilization of public opinion and technology to arrest population growth. His basic argument is that population growth is a function of two things—the birth rate and the death rate—and that if we do not lower the birth rate, then nature will inevitably restore the balance by increasing the death rate. The "death-rate solution" predicted by Ehrlich and others will most likely be the result of plagues and famines. Ehrlich's article in this section argues further that the battle is probably already lost—that we have already passed the point in history when the death-rate solution might have been averted.

There are, of course, many people who do not agree with Ehrlich's views. The population problem is now a political issue, and there are many shadings of opinion about it—but, like other environmental issues, it does not lend itself to easy liberal-conservative compartmentalization. There are many people of all political persuasions who still believe that some sudden increase in our ability to use land and produce food will avert famines; there are many more who oppose birth control on a variety of ideological grounds. The best-known source of such opposition is the Catholic Church, but it is by no means the only one, and the two short articles which follow Ehrlich's essay give examples of two lesser-known sources: the fear of some blacks that birth control programs can become a subtle form of genocide, and the theory that population is a source of national strength. The first article is by an editorial writer for the Pittsburgh *Post-Gazette,* the second by a prominent Roman Catholic layman who is a professor of economics at Oxford University. Both articles deal with attitudes which boil down to the simple proposition that numbers mean power —political, military or economic—and this attitude is relevant to the fact that many national governments today are still following a policy of *encouraging* population growth.

There are other—and still subtler—forms of resistance to an all-out campaign against population growth, and these are most evident in capitalist systems. In the United States many entrepreneurs—from real-estate speculators and contractors to heavy industrialists and retail merchants—are profiting from population growth and expecting to continue to do so. These do not constitute an organized and articulate source of opposition comparable to the Catholic Church, but nevertheless they do help to create a climate of opinion in which population growth is seen as good rather than dangerous; in American chamber of commerce prose the word "growth" is used often and with reverence.

As the issue of population receives more attention some surprising new political alignments can be expected. One indication of this is already apparent: many women's political organizations are already taking positions in favor of population control measures, including legalization of abortion. And beyond this political alignment it can be expected that there will in the future be profound sociological effects resulting from population control as attitudes toward marriage, sexual behavior, and family alter, and as more women begin to demand social recognition and status for roles other than wife and mother.

The fourth selection on population deals with the problem of world food supply. The authors, William and Paul Paddock, are brothers, both of whom have been able to view international food problems at close hand—one as an agronomist and consultant on tropical agricultural development, the other as a career foreign service officer with a lifetime spent mainly in Africa and Asia. The Paddocks predict that a world food crisis—the beginning of the time of famines—will be upon us by 1975, and offer an American policy for dealing with it. I do not expect that the policy advocated by the Paddocks will ever be put into practice: it contains the flaw of viewing nation-states as individual organisms which can survive or perish separately, and it requires a kind of single-minded conviction that is seldom seen in the doings of American diplomacy. But the proposal, however unrealistic it may be, still brings us into contact with a very possible world emergency which, if it does develop, will demand the formulation of some kind of a policy.

Not all authorities agree that there will be a world food crisis by 1975. Some agree there will be one, but allow for more time: former Secretary of Agriculture Orville Freeman has estimated that world food demand will pass world supply, leading to "a breakdown of the world food economy with consequences that would range from catastrophic famine in many areas to an elemental struggle for the control of food resources," in 1984. Others, such as Lester R. Brown and Gail W. Finsterbusch (see page 253), believe new techniques in agriculture will support population growth and avoid famine. But even the prospect of a miraculous breakthrough in food production is hardly a cause for optimism, because it means that population growth can continue until it meets other obstacles: depletion of natural resources and of supplies of basic goods such as paper; further overcrowding of schools, hospitals, urban living space, highways and recreational areas; continued deterioration of the environment through the many kinds of pollution which multiply along with human numbers. The most basic question about population growth is this: should technology be used to make further population growth possible, or should it be used to prevent further population growth? When we are prepared to formulate issues in such terms as these, the era of environmental responsibility may begin.

WORLD POPULATION: A BATTLE LOST?

Paul R. Ehrlich

The facts of human population growth are simple. The people of the Earth make up a closed population, one to which there is no immigration and from which there is no emigration. It can be readily shown that the Earth's human population will remain essentially closed—that no substantial movement of people to other planets is likely and that no substantial movement to other solar systems is possible. Now, a closed population will grow if the birthrate exceeds the death rate, and will shrink in size if the death rate is greater than the birthrate.

Paul R. Ehrlich, *"World Population: A Battle Lost?"* *Reprinted from* STANFORD TODAY, *Winter 1968, Series I, No. 22, with the permission of the publishers, Stanford University.* © *1968 by the Board of Trustees of the Leland Stanford Junior University.*

Over the past half-century or so a massive increase in man's under-standing and utilization of death control has resulted in a rapid rise in the rate of growth of the human population. So, we have a closed, growing population. And, intriguing as the prospect may be to certain irresponsible politicians, economists, and religious leaders, we will not achieve an infinite population size. Sooner or later the growth of the human population must stop.

On the "later" side it has been possible to compute when physical limitations, notably the problem of dissipating the heat produced by human metabolic processes, will put an end to growth in the solar system. We are forever barred from exporting a significant part of our population to the stars, so the theoretical maximum for the solar sys-tem coincides closely with the extreme possible numerical peak for *Homo sapiens,* estimated by some to be one billion billion people. This peak would be reached, at the current growth rate, in far under 1,500 years. Indeed, if we are confined in large part to the planet Earth (and there is every reason to believe we will be), the end will be reached in less than 1,000 years. For those interested in such long-range thinking there is one more cheery datum—the rate of increase of the population is itself accelerating!

On the "sooner" side we must face considerably less certainty. A fantastic world effort over the next decade at changing the attitude of people toward family size and developing, promoting, and distributing birth control technology might conceivably arrest population growth at two to three times its present level—if nothing untoward intervenes. On the other hand, it is quite within our power to reduce the popula-tion size to zero tomorrow, should we opt for thermonuclear war. But, later or sooner, one thing is certain. The human population *will* stop growing. This halt must come through either a decrease in the birth-rate, or an increase in the death rate, or both. A corollary of this is that anyone or any organization opposing reduction in the birthrate is automatically an agent for eventually increasing the death rate.

Since we need have only an academic interest in theoretical limits on the size of the human population, I am going to examine the very real crisis we face this instant. It is shockingly apparent that in the battle to feed humanity our side has been routed. In 1966 the popula-tion of the world increased by some 70 million people, and there was no compensatory increase in food production. Indeed, in areas such as Africa and Latin America there has actually been a decrease in food production over the past two years. According to the United Nations Food and Agriculture Organization, advances in food production made in developing nations between 1955 and 1965 have been wiped out by agricultural disasters in 1965 and 1966. All this means that last year, on the average, each person on earth had 2 percent less to eat. The reduction is, of course, not uniformly distributed. Starvation already is a fact in many countries. Only 10 countries, including the United States, grew more food than they consumed—all other populous countries, including Russia, China, and India, imported more than they exported.

Agricultural experts state that a tripling of the food supply of the world will be necessary in the next 30 years or so, if the 6 or 7 billion people who may be alive in the year 2000 are to be adequately fed. Theoretically such an increase might be possible, but it is becoming increasingly clear that it is totally impossible in practice. A few months ago I would have told you that *if* we had ideal conditions of research, development, and international cooperation we might triple our food production by then—if we started immediately. I would then have examined the possibility of meeting such assumptions. You would have been treated to the history of the unsuccessful attempts of the International Whaling Commission to control the hunting of whales, as a sample of the kind of international cooperation we can anticipate. I would have explained why the idea that our food supply can be dramatically increased by harvesting the sea is a gigantic hoax. Then I would have told you about some of the unhappy physical and social barriers in the way of attempting to produce much more food on the land.

All of this, however, now seems to me to be beside the point. There is not going to be any massive tooling up to meet the food crisis. There is not going to be any sudden increase in international cooperation. Even if there were a miraculous change in human attitudes and behavior in this area, *it is already too late to prevent a drastic rise in the death rate through starvation.* In a massively documented book, William and Paul Paddock predict that the time of famines will be upon us full-scale in 1975. The U.S. Department of Agriculture estimates that America can continue to feed the developing countries until 1984. Which estimate is more correct will depend in part on the validity of the assumptions on which they are based, and in part on such things as the weather. My guess is that the Paddocks are more likely correct, but in the long run it makes no difference. Millions of people are going to starve to death, and soon. There is nothing that can be done to prevent it. They will die because of short-sighted governmental attitudes. They will die because some religious organizations have blocked attempts over the years to get governmental and United Nations action under way to control human birthrates. They will die because scientists have managed to persuade many influential people that a technological rabbit can always be pulled out of the hat to save mankind at the last moment. They will die because many people, like myself, who recognized the essential role of overpopulation in the increasing woes of *Homo sapiens,* could not bring themselves to leave the comforts of their daily routine to do something about it. Their blood will be distributed over many hands.

But then, what good can a partitioning of guilt do? Perhaps some people will recognize their culpability and mend their ways—too late. What's done is done, to coin a phrase. We must look to the survivors, if there are to be any. We must assume that the "time of famines" will not lead to thermonuclear Armageddon, and that man will get another chance, no matter how ill-deserved. What I'd like to consider now is what we can do today that would improve the probability of man's making the most of a second chance, should he be lucky enough to get one.

Of course, the most important thing that we must do is to educate people and change many of their attitudes. We must, for example, alert people to the possible environmental consequences of attempting continually to increase food production. They must be made aware of subtle biological properties of our environment which, if ignored, may lead to very unsubtle future calamities. For instance, one of the basic facts of population biology is that the simpler an ecological system (or ecosystem) is, the more unstable it is. A complex forest, consisting of a great variety of plants and animals, will persist year in and year out with no interference from man. The system contains many elements, and changes in different ones often cancel one another out. Suppose one kind of predator eating small rodents, say foxes, suffers a population decline. There may be a compensatory increase in the population of another predator, perhaps wildcats. Such compensation may not be possible in a simpler system. Similarly, no plant-eating animal feeds on all kinds of plants, and the chance of a population explosion of a herbivore completely defoliating a mixed woodland is virtually nil.

Man, however, is a simplifier of complex ecosystems, and a creator of simple ecosystems. For instance, he persists in creating systems which consist almost entirely of uniform stands of a single grass— wheat fields and corn fields are familiar examples. Any farmer can testify to the instability of these ecosystems. Without human protection such an ecosystem rapidly disappears.

Plans for increasing food production invariably involve large-scale efforts at environmental modification. And the more we have manipulated our environment, the more we have been required to manipulate it. The more we have used synthetic pesticides, the less we have been able to do without them. The more we have deforested land, the more flood control dams we have had to build. The more farmland we have subdivided, the more pressure we have created to increase the yield on the land remaining under cultivation and to farm marginal land. This trend has been enhanced by an unhappy historical factor. The Earth has come largely under the control of a culture which traditionally sees man's proper role as dominating nature, rather than living in harmony with it. It is a culture which equates "growth" and "progress" and considers both as self-evidently desirable. It is a culture which all too often considers "undeveloped" land to be "wasted" land. Unquestionably people's attitudes toward their physical environment need changing if we are to make the grade—attitudes which unfortunately are among the most basic in Western culture. And, unfortunately, the state of our physical environment is just part of the problem.

Perhaps more important than recent changes in our physical environment are those in our psychic environment. Unhappily, we cannot be sure of these latter changes—although riots, the hippie movement, and increased drug usage are hardly cheery signs. We can't even be sure of how much of an individual's reaction to these environmental changes will be hereditarily conditioned, and how much of it will be a function of his culture.

Man clearly has gone a long way toward adapting to urban environments and despoiled landscapes. We badly need to understand the effects of this adjustment, especially in terms of group behavior, and to be able to predict the effects of further changes in man's perceptual environment. It is important to note that our perceptual systems have evolved primarily to react to stimuli representing a sudden change in our environment—a lion's charge, a flaring fire, a child's cry. Long-term changes often are not noticed. We tend not to perceive a friend's aging, or the slowing of our reflexes. If the transition from the Los Angeles of 1927 to that of 1967 had occurred overnight Angelenos surely would have rebelled. But a gradual 40-year transition has permitted southern Californians actually to convince themselves that the

Los Angeles basin of 1967 is a suitable habitat for *Homo sapiens*.

It is clear that man's present physical and psychic environment is far from optimum, and that permitting today's trends to continue is likely to lead to further rapid deterioration. We also know that we will have a dramatic increase in the death rate in the near future, an increase we can do nothing about. What then should be our course of action?

I think our first move must be to convince all those we can that the planet Earth must be viewed as a space ship of limited carrying capacity. It must be made crystal clear that population growth must stop, and we must arrive at a consensus as to what the ideal size of the human crew of the Earth should be. When we have determined the size of the crew, then we can attempt to design an environment in which that crew will be maintained in some sort of optimum state. The sociopolitical problems raised by such an approach are, of course, colossal. People within cultures have different ideas on how close they want to live to their neighbors, and cross-cultural differences in feelings about crowding are obvious. The only way I can think of for achieving a consensus is for people to start voicing opinions. So here goes.

I think that 150 million people—rather than our present population of 200 million—would be an optimum number to live comfortably in the United States. Such a number is clearly enough to maintain our highly technological society. It is also a small enough number that, when properly distributed and accommodated, it should be possible for individuals to find as much solitude and breathing space as they desire. With a population stabilized at such a level we could concentrate on improving the quality of human life at home and abroad. And, what a pleasure it would be to work toward an attainable goal instead of fighting the miserable rearguard action to which runaway population condemns us.

After all, what do we gain from packing more and more people into the United States? Those encouraging population growth in the hope of keeping our economy expanding must realize the consequences of such advocacy. Some men would doubtless accumulate considerable wealth, and would be able to retreat from riot-torn cities to the increasingly smoggy countryside in order to live. If thermonuclear war does not solve their children's problems permanently, what kind of a world will those children inherit? Will their heritage include social disorder and unemployment on an unprecedented scale? Will they have to wear smog masks as a matter of routine? Will they enjoy mock steaks made from processed grass or seaweed? Will they have to be satisfied with camping under plastic trees planted in concrete? Will they accept regimentation and governmental control at a level previously unheard of? Will they fight willingly in small wars and prepare diligently for the big one? Above all, will they be able to retain their sanity in a world gone mad?

Let's suppose that we decide to limit the population of the United States and of the world. How could such limitation be accomplished? Some biologists feel that compulsory family regulation will be necessary to retard population growth. It is a dismal prospect—except when viewed as an alternative to Armageddon. I would like to suggest four less drastic steps which might do the job in the United States. I suggest them in the full knowledge that they are socially unpalatable and politically unrealistic.

The first step would be to establish a Federal Population Commission with a large budget for propaganda which supports reproductive responsibility. This Commission would be charged with making clear the connection between rising population and lowering quality of life. It would also be charged with the evaluation of environmental tinkering by other governmental agencies—with protecting us from projects such as the FAA's supersonic transports or from the results of the Army Engineers' well-known "beaver complex" (which some predict will only be satiated when every gutter in the country has a dam thrown across it). Commission members should be distinguished citizens, as free as possible from political or bureaucratic meddling.

The second step would be to change our tax laws so that they discourage rather than encourage reproduction. Those who impose the burden of children on society should, whenever they are able, be made to pay for the privilege. Our income tax system should eliminate all deductions for children and replace them with a graduated scale of increases. Luxury taxes should be placed on diapers, baby bottles, and baby foods. It must be made clear to our population that it is socially irresponsible to have large families. Creation of such a climate of opinion has played a large role in Japan's successful dealing with her population problem.

Third, we should pass federal laws which make instruction in birth control methods mandatory in all public schools. Federal legislation should also forbid state laws which limit the right of any woman to have an abortion which is approved by her physician.

Fourth, we should change the pattern of federal support of biomedical research so that the majority of it goes into the broad areas of population regulation, environmental sciences, behavioral sciences, and related areas, rather than into shortsighted programs on death control. It is absurd to be preoccupied with the medical quality of life until and unless the problem of the quantity of life is solved. In this context we must do away with nonsense about how important it is for "smart" people to have large families in order to keep *Homo sapiens* from being selected for stupidity. It is far from established that the less intelligent portion of our population is out-reproducing the more intelligent. Even if a reproductive disparity did exist, the worst consequence over a period of a few generations only would be a slight lowering of average intelligence—a slight and *reversible* lowering. *Quantity is the first problem.* If we can lick that one perhaps we will buy the time for scientists in fields such as biochemical genetics to solve some of the problems of quality. If we don't solve the quantity problem, the quality problem will no longer bother us.

All of these steps might produce the desired result of a reversal of today's population growth trend. If they should fail, however, we would then be faced with some form of compulsory birth regulation. We might, for instance, institute a system which would make *positive* action necessary before reproduction is possible. This might be the addition of a temporary sterilant to staple food, or to the water supply. An antidote would have to be taken to permit reproduction. Even with the antidote freely available, the result of such a program would be a drastic reduction in birthrates. If this reduction were not sufficient, the government could dole out the antidote in the proper quantities. If we wished to stabilize the American population at its present level, each married couple could be permitted enough antidote to produce two offspring. Then each couple who wished could be given a chance in a lottery for enough antidote for a third child—the odds carefully computed to produce the desired constancy of population size. At the moment, the chances of winning would have to be adjusted to about two out of five, assuming that all couples wanted to play the game.

An attempt to institute such a system is interesting to contemplate, especially when one considers the attitude of the general public toward such a relatively simple thing as fluoridation. I would not like to be the first elected official seriously to suggest that a sterility agent be added to our reservoirs. Perhaps it might seem that we can start such a program by treating the wheat we ship to India, or fish meal we ship to South America. Or can we? As you doubtless realize, the solution does not lie in that direction. For one thing, saying that the population explosion is a problem of underdeveloped countries is like telling a fellow passenger "your end of the boat is sinking." For another, it is naïve to think that Indians or Brazilians are any more anxious to be fed fertility-destroying chemicals with their daily bread than are Americans. Other people already are suspicious of our motives. Consider what their attitude would be toward an attempt to sterilize them en masse.

If we can solve the population problem at home then we will be in a position to make an all-out effort to halt the growth of the world's population. Perhaps we can shorten the time of famines and lay the groundwork for avoiding a second round of population-food crises. Our program should be tough-minded. We should remember that seemingly charitable gestures such as our grain exports to India have actually harmed rather than helped Indians in the long run. I think that we should:

(1) Announce that we will no longer ship food to countries where dispassionate analysis indicates that the food-population unbalance is hopeless.

(2) Announce that we will no longer give aid to any country with an increasing population until that country convinces us that it is doing everything within its power to limit its population.

(3) Make available to all interested countries massive aid in the technology of birth control.

(4) Make available to all interested countries massive aid for increasing yield on land already under cultivation. The most important export in this area should be trained technicians, not fertilizer. We need to establish centers in the country where technicians can be trained not only in agronomy, but also in ecology and sociology. Many of the barriers to increased yields are sociological, and all increase should be made in a manner which minimizes environmental deterioration.

(5) Accept the fact that if we can use our power to further military goals, then it can be used for the good of mankind as well. Extreme political and economic pressure should be brought on any country impeding a solution to the world's most pressing problem. A good place to start would be closing our diplomatic channels to the Vatican until that organization brings its policies into line with the desires of the majority of American Catholics. Much of the world will be horrified at our stand, but as a nation we're clearly willing to go against world opinion on other issues—why not on the most important issue?

Well, perhaps if we get on the ball and set a good example the United States can lead the way in focusing the world's attention on the cause of its major sickness rather than upon the symptoms. Perhaps we can shift our efforts from the long-term pain-depressing activities to the excising of the cancer. The operation will require many brutal and callous decisions. The pain will be intense, but the disease is so far advanced that only with radical surgery does the patient have any chance of survival.

THE BLACKS CRY GENOCIDE

Ralph Z. Hallow

Not long ago a family planning center in Cleveland was burned to the ground after militant Negroes had labeled its activities "black genocide." More recently, the anti-poverty board of Pittsburgh became the first in the nation to vote down OEO appropriations to continue Planned Parenthood clinics in six of the city's eight poverty neighborhoods. The move resulted from intense pressure and threats of violence by blacks—all males—who have kept the genocide issue boiling since one of the clinics was threatened with fire bombing last fall. Although a coalition of women, black and white, has succeeded in rescuing the program, national officers of Planned Parenthood-World Population fear the Pittsburgh example may encourage black opponents to lay siege to similar programs in other cities. Organized opposition can be found in cities from California to New York, and summer could bring the violence which militant critics of the clinics have threatened.

Although concerted opposition to the Planned Parenthood Association (PPA) programs in the ghettos has centered in Pittsburgh, the issue has been gaining national currency through articles published in *Muhammad Speaks,* the newspaper of the Black Muslims. The author of the articles is Dr. Charles Greenlee, a respected black physician in Pittsburgh who first raised the issue nearly two years ago. Dr. Greenlee contends that the birth control information and "propaganda" of federally financed family planning programs are carried into the homes of poor blacks by "home visitors" and public assistance workers, who allegedly coerce indigent black women into visiting the clinics. Greenlee says, and welfare officials deny, that the

Ralph Z. Hallow, "The Blacks Cry Genocide," THE NATION, *Apr. 28, 1969. Reprinted by permission.*

intimidation takes the form of implicit or explicit threats that welfare payments will be cut off if the recipient has more children. Thus it is argued, the free clinics constitute "genocide," a conscious conspiracy by whites to effect a kind of Hitlerian solution to the "black problem" in the United States.

Dr. Greenlee's formula for leading his people out of white America's cul-de-sac is: black babies equal black votes equal Black Power. Recognizing this logic, he said recently on a local television panel discussion, the white power structure is using the neighborhood clinics to "decimate the black population in America within a generation." The Planned Parenthood national office sent a black representative to sit on the panel. The two top white executives of PPA in Pittsburgh decided their presence on the panel would only lend credence to Dr. Greenlee's charges. But, they point out, the neighborhood community action committees have representatives, including blacks, on the local PPA board.

Also arguing PPA's side of the question was Mrs. Frankie Pace, a resident of the city's largest black ghetto, the Hill District, where most of the "action" occurred during the civil disorders last April. Mrs. Pace believes that most black women in poor neighborhoods not only want the clinics but also desperately need such help because they are often ignorant of scientific methods of birth control. (Health department and welfare workers in nearly every U.S. city report that they still occasionally encounter indigent women who believe that urinating after intercourse prevents conception.)

The television panel illustrated the new alliances that have grown up over the "black genocide" issue. Seated next to Dr. Greenlee was Msgr. Charles Owen Rice, who for more than thirty years has enjoyed the reputation of being the liberal's liberal. Always a champion of the cause of labor and more recently of peace and an end to the war in Vietnam, he has nevertheless enunciated a position on birth control that is closer to that of the Vatican than to the more liberal one held by a significant number of priests and lay Catholics in America. He said during the panel discussion that the term "black genocide" is not too strong; for, he observed, it is "passing strange" that no clinics exist in the city's two mostly white poverty neighborhoods. Local PPA officials point out, however, that the predominantly Catholic populations in those neighborhoods have rejected the establishment of clinics in their communities.

PPA supporters also suggest it was no accident that William "Bouie" Haden was the only black leader to whom the Catholic

diocese of Pittsburgh recently gave a $10,000 annual grant—to help
run the United Movement for Progress, Haden's black self-help group.
Haden, a fiery though not so young militant, was quick to pick up
Dr. Greenlee's charges of "black genocide" and to force the temporary
closing last summer of one of the clinics on his "turf," the city's
Homewood-Brushton district. Although about seventy irate black
women forced Haden to back off from the issue for a time, in early
February he led the forces which, through skillful parliamentary
maneuvering, got a divided and confused anti-poverty board to vote
down an appropriation to continue the clinics. Although Haden's
enemies flaunt his long criminal record, most observers recognize him
as a sincere and effective leader who did much to keep Homewood-
Brushton cool during the disorders last April.

In spite of his leadership abilities, Haden has only piecemeal support for his "black genocide" charges. Family planning supporters
point out that it was the black women in the poverty neighborhoods
who demanded that PPA set up a network of neighborhood clinics
under the hegemony of the city's anti-poverty board. The women
claimed that the PPA center in the downtown area was inaccessible to
the indigent whose welfare allowances made no provision for baby-
sitting fees and bus fares.

To complicate the issue still further, supporters of family planning
programs in the ghettos include such eminent black men of the Left
as Bayard Rustin and Dr. Nathan Wright, Jr., who was chairman of
the Black Power conference. Writing on "Sexual Liberation" in the
Newark *Star-Ledger*, Dr. Wright said the poor—both black and white
—are discriminated against sexually and should seek the help of
Planned Parenthood.

The term "family planning" is slightly euphemistic; except in the
states where it is prohibited, birth control counseling is offered even
to unmarried girls under 18, provided there is parental consent and
usually if the girl has had one child. Women in the 15-to-19-year age
group account for the highest percentage of illegitimate births (40.2
percent for whites and 41.9 for blacks), according to U.S. Public
Health Service figures for 1964. Here again, defenders of birth control
argue that the clinics help to alleviate one of the grossest hypocrisies
practiced by our male-dominated legislatures. Lawmakers, they say,
hand down so-called moral standards for American women in defiance
of the sexual practices actually prevailing in the society. If young
women from enlightened middle-class families are still undergoing
unwanted pregnancies and are forced to seek expensive or dangerous

abortions, how much worse must it be for the teen-age daughters of the indigent?

Everywhere the statistics are on the side of family planning—at least for those who view them in unideological terms. In New Orleans, for example, where the largest family planning program in the United States has been operating, an indigent female population of 26 percent accounted for 56 percent of all births, 88 percent of illegitimate births and 72 percent of stillbirths. Nationally, the infant mortality rate of blacks is twice that of whites. The United States ranks fifteenth in the world in infant mortality, and there is a surfeit of evidence relating the problem directly to poverty. A study by the U.S. Department of Health, Education and Welfare found that the most effective way to reduce infant mortality is to offer family planning. Finally, of the 5.3 million indigent women in the United States, only 850,000 receive family planning services, and only 30 percent of those who do are nonwhite.

All this, however, means nothing to the black militant and his white allies who believe that Black Power and "poor" power (and the consequent redistribution of wealth they would bring) are threatened by free family planning clinics whose representatives actively seek out black women. Caught in the middle is the indigent American woman who wishes to have the same freedom to choose sex without conception that her middle-class counterpart enjoys.

WORLD POWER AND POPULATION

Colin Clark

There are many obvious things which we take for granted, of which however it is necessary to remind ourselves occasionally; not only in order to obtain a better understanding of our situation; but also because what is obviously true today has an awkward way of ceasing to be true tomorrow.

Let us begin with one of these obvious statements. The United States is a world power. What precisely do we mean by this? It means

Colin Clark, "World Power and Population," NATIONAL REVIEW, *150 East 35th Street, New York, New York 10016, May 20, 1969. Reprinted by permission.*

that statesmen all over the world, planning their countries' foreign policies, have to take into account what the United States may think or do; indeed further, that the United States is in a position to influence, by methods ranging from tactful suggestions to open threats, events anywhere in the world. (It is of course by no means implied that it is either wise or expedient for the United States always so to intervene; or that past decisions to intervene, or not to intervene, have always been soundly judged.) In this sense, it is clear, the United States is a world power, and Mexico is not—important though Mexico's foreign policy decisions may be to her immediate neighbors.

It is another well-known fact that the United States now has a population of 202 million, and Mexico under 50 million. The facts of world power and of population are inescapably connected. Americans sometimes like to think that it is their advanced industrial technology, rather than the size of their population, which makes them a world power. Switzerland has an industrial technology comparable with that of the United States; Soviet Russia comparable with that of Mexico. Soviet Russia is a world power, and Switzerland is not. Some people have yielded to the superficial theory that, in these days of nuclear and other advanced weaponry, size of population has ceased to matter. Indeed, it probably matters more than before, as the historical table below will show. The technical ability to produce advanced weapons

Populations Required for World Power Status

(millions)

1670 (Minimum 1 million)

Turkey	25
France	20
Russia	16
Spain-Portugal	7
England	6
Poland	5
Netherlands	1

1770 (Minimum 6 Million)

Russia	33
Turkey	30
France	24
Austria	20
U.K.	14
Spain	9
Prussia	6

1870 (Minimum 27 million)

Russia	78
Germany	41
Austria-Hungary	40
U.S.A.	39
France	36
U.K.	31
Italy	27

1970 (Minimum 100 Million)

China	670
India	550
USSR	245
U.S.A.	205
Indonesia	120
Pakistan	110
Japan	100

is only one element in a country's ability to become a world power. Equally necessary are the very large economic resources needed to produce and maintain them. The size of a country's population also plays an important part in its ability to exert economic, political or cultural influence in the world; or indeed, to construct adequate defenses or retaliatory measures against nuclear warfare or, if the worse comes to the worst, to recover from its consequences.

Looking at the world situation in four succeeding centuries, it is indeed possible to specify the "ante" (if one may use a card player's word) required for entering the grim contest of world politics.

It is true that many idealistic Americans, up to 1917, thought that it was possible and desirable, while being militarily prepared, to stay outside the "world power game." But later generations have concluded that a powerful country may owe a real duty to the rest of the world to enter world politics on certain occasions; or indeed that those who think that they can stay out of the world power game are in some danger of becoming subjugated to those who actively play it.

The reader will see that this excludes countries which have largely or completely isolated themselves from dealings with other countries, such as seventeenth-century India, China or Japan; or are ruled by another country, as was eighteenth- and nineteenth-century India; or are in a state of internal political confusion, as were nineteenth-century China and Turkey.

It is true that seventeenth-century military equipment was vastly simpler than that of the present century. But it must be remembered also that the economic ability to produce it was relatively even more retarded. So we get the paradoxical result that in the seventeenth century two nations of small population, economically advanced by the standards of the time, Sweden and the Netherlands, were able to create, respectively, the most powerful army and navy of their times, and to be leading world powers. (The Dutch indeed were then wealthy enough to be able to obtain as large an army as they wanted by hiring Germans at sixpence a day.) The Swedish Empire, which covered a large part of Northern Europe, was effectively brought to an end by Peter the Great of Russia in the early eighteenth century. The Dutch had to retreat from New York, and lost their position as a world power, when confronted by a temporary Anglo-French alliance in the time of Charles II.

The table for 1970 is admittedly somewhat forward-looking. There may be statesmen now who, in planning their foreign policy, do not think that they need take into account what China, Indonesia or Japan might think about it. But they will be imprudent if they do not do so.

It cannot be denied, however, that the "ante" is increasing rapidly, at least fourfold per century. We really should be asking ourselves what the position will be in a hundred, or even in fifty, years' time.

Population changes, in spite of all the superficial talk about "population explosion," do not come suddenly. A demographic change, whether in an upward or downward direction, takes more than a century to work out all its consequences; and those who recommend or try to bring about such changes should bear in mind that they are carrying some responsibility for events at least a century into the future. The present size of the American population has been achieved, in the superficial sense of the word, by the present generation of Americans, and by those of the recent past. But the decisions which really made the difference were those of the nineteenth-century immigrants who had the courage to leave their homelands, and of the hardy Midwestern pioneers who brought up large families under austere circumstances.

From the point of view of becoming a world power it is of importance to build up a population, and to preserve it in a political union. If it had not been for the hundreds of thousands of Americans who fought and died to preserve the Union in 1861-65, or had they been unsuccessful, there can be no doubt that the political face of the world now would be immeasurably different from what it is—and, almost certainly, for the worse. It may be that in a generation's time (though there is hardly any sign of it at present) Latin Americans, Africans, even Southeast Asians may have succeeded in welding what are now weak and quarreling states into genuine political unions, which will become world powers. Within our grasp in the past two decades— though we have in fact failed to grasp it—has been the shining opportunity of creating a real political union of Western Europe, which could have played a vital part in helping to preserve a peaceful and civilized world. Responsibility for this failure will be placed by future historians, I think, upon inaction by British governments between 1945 and 1957, under Attlee, Churchill and Eden. These were the critical years during which, with British participation, a Western European political union could have been easily achieved; and it is permissible to speculate that, under these circumstances, France would have resisted the temptation to rock the boat, to which she succumbed under de Gaulle.

We cannot speculate any further on these political possibilities. But we can to some extent foresee demographic trends; and the conclusions are disquieting.

In the first place, the reader may have noticed that the population given for China in the table is considerably lower than is generally supposed. The United States Government's official advisers on this subject estimated the Chinese population at just over 600 million (somewhat higher than the Chinese census of that date) for 1953; but subsequently they have accepted unquestioningly the Chinese claim that population has been growing 2 percent per year or more, bringing it to 850 million by 1970. It was the same group of advisers who persistently overestimated the population of Soviet Russia in the 1950s; and they are almost certainly wrong again. It is true that information about Chinese population, fertility and mortality, is extremely scanty, scattered and indirect. But some scientific analysis is possible. During the troubled period of the 1940s, population had been declining. For 1953, I estimate it at 560 million, a little below that given by the census. The rate of growth never reached anything like that officially claimed of 2.2 percent per year. During the comparatively undisturbed 1950s, I estimated it at 1.1 percent per year. Agricultural chaos and near-famine prevailed after "The Year of the Great Leap Forward" in 1958, and the rate of population growth probably fell to .05 percent per year or less. There was some recovery of agriculture during the mid-1960s, due in part to some restoration of small private plots. In 1966 further chaos supervened in the form of the Cultural Revolution. The estimate of 670 million for 1970 is indeed probably on the high side. If China's future has in store a prolonged spell of ordered government and agricultural improvement, we will then see a rapid increase in population, at 2 percent per year or even more. But it has not happened yet.

Meanwhile, if present rates of growth persist, India's population will overtake that of China in the early 1980s.

Of the other world powers mentioned in the table, we know that population is growing at over 2 percent per year in Pakistan. Independent critics consider that the recent census of Indonesia was reasonably accurate; and there are clear signs of agricultural recovery there. Population growth in Indonesia can be estimated at over 2 percent per annum.

In Japan, on the other hand, while the number of births still exceeds the number of deaths (present deaths being on the average those of the considerably smaller generation born some sixty years ago), the number of births now taking place falls considerably short of those required to replace the present generation of parents. Unless this situation is radically and permanently altered, the Japanese population must ultimately age and decline.

But what of Soviet Russia and the United States? There has been a decline in the size of family in Soviet Russia, and throughout Eastern Europe (with the exception of Rumania). In Hungary and Bulgaria the number of births is below replacement level. Though material for complete analysis is lacking, the same is now almost certainly true of Soviet Russia also. Though the process is starting later than in Japan, the consequence is none the less inevitable.

But what of the United States? It is generally known that a heavy fall in births began in 1961, and indeed the social and propagandist pressures for its continuance are being maintained with unabated force.

There are many people who reassure themselves with the shallow fallacy that, so long as the number of births exceeds the number of deaths, they need not seriously concern themselves about a check to population growth. They fail to realize the elementary fact that the deaths now occurring (with a few exceptions) represent the passing of the generation born sixty to seventy years ago, when the United States had a very much smaller population. The critical question is the extent to which the number of children now being born suffices to replace, or enlarge, the numbers of their parents of the present generation. The indications now are that within a year or so American births will fail to replace the parents, and that the United States also, within a measurable time, will enter the cycle of population decline.

To measure, from information contemporarily available, whether the number of children being born suffices to replace their parents is, in fact, a complex mathematical problem. (The problem is easy enough when one is dealing with the past generation, when the total offspring born to the generation can readily be counted; but it is very much harder when analyzing the fertility of the generation which is still in the process of reproduction.) America has many highly skilled demographers. But, without exception, they are fervently committed to the advocacy of population restriction and they all seem unable or unwilling to measure or to criticize the consequences of the reduction of births which has already taken place.

An attempt may be made to describe in non-mathematical language the various successive methods which have been devised for making, from contemporary information, a true estimate of fertility. The reader with some familiarity with this subject must however be warned that methods believed until recently to be reliable are now known to be unreliable, and have been replaced; demographic science has been advancing rapidly.

It is easy to see that the crude birthrate, or number of births per thousand of population, does not tell you very much. The first refinement, devised in the nineteenth century, was to measure the annual number of births per head of the female population aged between fifteen and 45, the generation actually concerned in reproduction. This method was further refined in the 1930s, by the calculation of "net reproduction rates." This ingenious method took account of the number of contemporary births to mothers under twenty, to mothers aged twenty to 24 etc. and then added them up to obtain, as it were, a snapshot picture of the reproduction of a generation, but based on a single year's evidence. Allowance was made for the proportion of children (now very small) who were expected to die before reaching maturity, to give an estimate, called the "net reproduction rate," of the extent to which a generation was failing to maintain, maintaining or enlarging itself.

The defect in this method is that it implicitly assumes, as the discerning reader may have observed, that ages at marriage do not significantly change. One effect of the war years in the 1940s was that there was an acceleration of marriage in many countries, and the tendency to the reduction of the age of marriage has persisted, for other reasons. When the age of marriage is changing, the method of net reproduction rates completely breaks down.

The next step forward was taken by the American demographer, Whelpton, who introduced into his methods of calculation the sensible assumption that parents, having had a child, were less likely to have another in the immediate future. He divided all the women of reproductive age into "cohorts" i.e., the generation born in each succeeding year, and then analyzed their reproductive performance, taking all their past offspring into account, to measure the extent to which they were replacing themselves. Whelpton's method made it clear that it was the cohorts born between 1900 and 1910 who were the least reproductive—and this is not all to be blamed on the Great Depression, because most of them reached marriageable age during the 1920s. The cohorts born during the two subsequent decades showed considerably higher reproductivity.

But Whelpton's method has two drawbacks. The first is that his curves require extrapolation, a difficult mathematical procedure at best, and always likely to lead to error. The second and more serious objection is that it conceals an underlying assumption that families know in advance how many children they are going to have and how they are going to be spaced, and that therefore the observation of their record over a limited number of years makes it possible to predict their final totals. While this is true for most times, it breaks down in a period of violent change of reproductivity, such as has occurred since 1961.

About the same time, a quite different method was pioneered by Karmal in Australia, namely the method of "marriage-duration specific fertilities." This takes account of another obvious fact, that most children are born in the early years of marriage. If the duration of the parents' marriage is registered at the time of the child's birth (not all countries do this), and the number of marriages is also recorded, it is possible to sum the specific fertilities for each year of duration of marriage. These can then be extrapolated, without serious risk of error, to predict the expected total offspring of the marriages of recent years. Unfortunately the American system of registration does not lend itself to this method. Furthermore, American statistics of marriages are incomplete; and in any case made much more difficult to handle by the high proportion of divorces and re-marriages, as compared with other countries.

The best method now available for analyzing contemporary information in order to estimate the final reproductivity of a generation was devised in 1953 by Henry, of the Institut National des Etudes Démographiques in Paris, the method of "probability of family enlargement." Unlike Whelpton's cohort method, this method does not make the assumption that parents plan their offspring and their spacing in advance, but rather the opposite, namely that they change their minds drastically from year to year. It is a method of considerable mathematical elegance. In non-mathematical language it can best be described as a method of analyzing succeeding drop-outs. Out of each generation, in the first place, a certain small proportion will die before reaching maturity, and these can be counted. At the next stage we need not, if we do not wish to, or if we do not have the information, calculate those who drop out of the race without marrying. We make our next count for those who fail to have even one child—less than 10 percent. Of those who have had one child, however, some 20-30 percent or more drop out without having a second child. These in their turn show a 35-40 percent drop-out without having a third child. After the third child the drop-out proportion remains curiously constant for subsequent children; but it must be remembered that we now are dealing with a greatly reduced number of parents, and the contribution of these few large families to the total of reproduction is not very great.

The application of Henry's method required some detailed tables showing the distribution over past years of first births which might be expected to produce a second birth this year, of second births likely to produce a third birth, etc. The official tabulations of births by order unfortunately are always considerably delayed, and it is not therefore possible to make complete calculations fully up to date. Use is therefore made of the recognized demographic device of taking "standard rates" of the numbers and time distribution of first births expected to the rising generation, of second births expected to those who have already had a first, etc., and then of comparing actual births with those predicted from the "standard rates." To bring it up to date, this method requires a limited extrapolation, unlikely to lead to serious error, of the numbers of recent births of given order. (*See Table.*)

Percentage by Which Current U.S. Number of Births Exceeds Number Required to Replace Parental Generation

1959	32	1964	22
1960	33	1965	14
1961	32	1966	10
1962	27	1967	8
1963	25	1968	2

Unless there is a very drastic reversal of trend, the number of American births will very shortly fall below replacement rate. And this has happened in less than a decade from the time when they were providing for a one-third increase in the size of the generation.

The advent of oral contraceptives may have played a part in this extraordinary movement. But other forces must have been at work. In the first place, oral contraceptives were not abundant in 1961. Secondly, a marked downward movement began at almost exactly the same time in many other countries, including Soviet Russia where, so far as is known, oral contraceptives are not available.

In France and England, however, the downward movement started later, in 1965, and has been more moderate, and births in those countries are still 15–20 percent above replacement rate.

We conclude by looking back at our world power table. It is of course always possible that powerful political confederations will be formed in time in Europe, Latin America, Africa and Southeast Asia, to create a new balance of power in the world. But at present, it does not look probable, on the face of it. As far as we can see it now, the prospects for fifty years hence are of a world in which both the United States and Soviet Russia have fallen out of the race, a world dominated by the Asian countries, with India and China in the lead, and Pakistan and Indonesia as the runners-up.

PROPOSAL FOR THE USE OF AMERICAN FOOD: "TRIAGE"

William and Paul Paddock

I propose a course of action which I believe to be a feasible procedure to achieve maximum benefits from the distribution of our food stocks, both for the United States and for the world as a whole. It is my alternative to an unplanned escalation of food aid, an alternative to an aimless frittering away of this precious food resource. It requires no new law but can be carried out under the existing Food for Peace bill.

To summarize:

(a) The exploding populations in the hungry nations combined with their static agricultures make famines, in many, inevitable. Their future contains a mounting increase of civil tensions, riots and military take-overs as the growing scarcity of food forces prices higher and higher.

(b) The timetable of food shortages will vary from nation to nation, but by 1975 sufficiently serious food crises will have broken out in certain of the afflicted countries so the problem will be in full view. The Time of Famines will have begun.

(c) The stricken peoples will not be able to pay for all their needed food imports. Therefore, the hunger in these regions can be alleviated only through the charity of other nations.

(d) Only bulk food can alleviate this hunger, which means grain. Yet the only grain available in sufficient quantity is wheat, except insofar as corn is sent to certain parts of Latin America and Africa. Only four countries produce enough wheat to play a major role in the Time of Famines, countries I term "The Granary."

(e) However, three of these countries, Canada, Australia and Argentina, have in the past given only small amounts of food as charity to the hungry nations, and it is unlikely they will do more in the future. They will sell their stocks on the international market to anyone with cash in hand. Whatever these three countries may give to the needy will be only a token gesture.

(f) This leaves the United States as the sole hope of the hungry nations.

(g) Yet the United States, even if it fully cultivates all its land, even if it opens every spigot of charity, will not have enough wheat and other foodstuffs to keep alive all the starving.

THEREFORE, the United States must decide to which countries it will send food, to which countries it will not.

THE THESIS OF "TRIAGE"

"Triage" is a term used in military medicine. It is defined as the assigning of priority of treatment to the wounded brought to a battlefield hospital in a time of mass casualties and limited medical facilities. The wounded are divided on the basis of three classifications:

(1) Those so seriously wounded they cannot survive regardless of the treatment given them; call these the "can't-be-saved."

(2) Those who can survive without treatment regardless of the pain they may be suffering; call these the "walking wounded."

(3) Those who can be saved by immediate care.

The practice of triage is put into effect when the flow of wounded fills the tents of the battlefield hospitals and when it becomes impossible for the available medical staff to give even rudimentary care to all. Furthermore, the number allowed to be sorted into the third group for immediate treatment must be limited by the number of doctors available. The marginal cases must then also be selected out into the other two groups.

It is a terrible chore for the doctors to classify the helpless wounded in this fashion, but it is the only way to save the maximum number of lives. To spend time with the less seriously wounded or with the dying would mean that many of those who might have lived will die. It would be a misuse of the available medical help.

Call triage cold-blooded, but it is derived from the hard experience of medical humaneness during a crisis. In fact, if there is time before the battle starts, the medical staff prepares in advance the facilities to sort out these three groups.

TRIAGE APPLIED TO THE TIME OF FAMINES

President Johnson has proposed "that the United States lead the world in a war against hunger." On the battlefields of this forthcoming war the practice of triage will be vital because choices must be made as to which wounded countries will receive our food.

The leadership in Washington comprises the medical staff. The stricken ones in need of medical attention (American food aid) are the hungry nations. To provide maximum effective treatment the medical staff must divide them into the three classifications of triage:

(1) Nations in which the population growth trend has already passed the agricultural potential. This combined with inadequate leadership and other divisive factors make catastrophic disasters inevitable. These nations form the "can't-be-saved" group. To send food to them is to throw sand in the ocean.

(2) Nations which have the necessary agricultural resources and/or foreign exchange for the purchase of food from abroad and which therefore will be able to cope with their population growth. They will be only moderately affected by the shortage of food. They are the "walking wounded" and do not require *food* aid in order to survive.

(3) Nations in which the imbalance between food and population is great but the *degree* of the imbalance is manageable. Rather, it is manageable in the sense that it can give enough time to allow the local officials to initiate effective birth control practices and to carry forward agricultural research and other forms of development. These countries will have a chance to come through their crises provided careful medical treatment is given, that is, receipt of enough American food and also of other types of assistance.

The stocks of American food will be limited. Therefore, the extent of aid to the nations in the third group must be limited proportionately.

Call it a sieve. Adjust the size of the openings to the amount of food available to be shipped. The smaller the openings (of food), the fewer can be treated.

Unfortunately, it is not that simple. The size of a nation can itself be the determining factor against it or for it. If the available food is sent to the few big, politically important nations, then nothing will be left over for the smaller ones. Or vice versa. Thus, strictly on the basis of size and without regard to any other factors the decision might be to send food to:

Brazil but not to Central America
Central America but not to Brazil
Nigeria but not the rest of West Africa
India but not Africa and Latin America

Decisions that take into account all the assorted, highly complex factors affecting differently each nation cannot be made within a vacuum. Political, economic and psychological factors must be considered. This calls for the careful analysis by experts studying the actual food capacity of the United States as set against the food needs and *survival capabilities* of the individual nations.

One delusion must be fought. Because each of these nations is hungry it is easy to jump to the conclusion that all internal problems can be solved by sending in enough food. Unfortunately, the affected nations have an assortment of wounds from an assortment of causes in addition to the food shortage. Ceylon has its language division. Sudan has its racial conflict. Bolivia has its class schism. Many have stifling corruption and graft.

In certain cases no amount of food can prevent political and social upheavals and continued, steady degeneration. Food sent to these will by itself not heal the wounds, wounds already festered.

Nor can the national interests of the United States be excluded, whether political, military or economic. American officials when applying triage decisions and shipping out *American* food are surely justified in thinking beyond only the food requirements of the individual hungry nations. They are justified, it seems to me, in considering whether the survival of a specific nation will:

(a) Help maintain the economic viability and relative prosperity of the United States during the Time of Famines.

(b) Help maintain the economic stability of the world as a whole.

(c) Help create a "better" world after the troubles of the Time of Famines have ended.

No nation lives on an island all alone. Each is a part of the whole. Thus, if two nations are equal in their need for American food to increase their chances for eventual self-sufficiency but there is not enough food to send to both, then, assuredly, the one must be chosen which is better able to contribute to the foregoing three goals.

And when overall demand for food in the hungry world catches up with the American capacity to produce food (the Department of

Agriculture officially forecasts this will be by 1984 and I maintain it will occur by 1975), then America's own consumption of food will have to be curtailed or altered in order to maintain the same level of food aid. For instance, curtailment of meat. Every pound of grain-fed meat that a person eats takes four to twelve pounds of feed grain.

Now is the time to recognize the implications of this. For when such shortages and/or high prices do force the American public to change their diet, it is certain that our citizens will become dead serious about this food, food which they will forgo in order to feed distant foreigners. When this happens, I take for granted that American public opinion will demand that this food be distributed in a manner which will give them their "money's worth." But unless we begin *now* to concentrate our food aid on those who can be saved during the Time of Famines, our future efforts may be ineffective. By the next decade today's savable nations may have passed beyond the point of help.

What will Americans consider to be their "money's worth"? What will be a legitimate return on the food they are sending to others?

The ultimate answer, I am sure, will be stated in terms of American economic and political aims. Some can criticize this as selfish, as unhumanitarian and as unChristian. Yet the continued stability and relative prosperity of the United States during the coming decades are, surely, the single most important guarantee to insure:

—that the world as a whole, and especially the selected hungry nations themselves, will survive the Time of Famines without sinking into chaos, and
—that the world will evolve into that "better" life which we hope will come to all peoples afterwards; a "better" life (both spiritual and material) is difficult to visualize as coming to fruition without the support of American capital goods which today nearly equal all those possessed by the rest of mankind.

Therefore, I emphasize the following pertinent aspects which American officials must consider when they make their decisions as to which countries will receive our food:

(1) *Ignore the prospect that if food is withheld from a country it will "go communist."*

If a nation needs food aid to survive, then its political stability does, to a degree, depend upon that food. Like Samson's hair, when the food aid is cut off weakness will result. Assuming that the Cold

War with Russia and/or China continues throughout the 1970's at its present heat (and that can be only an assumption), it is hard to see any one of these hungry nations being so vital to the United States that disaster would overwhelm our interests if it does, in fact, "go communist."

Cuba, for instance, has been a worrisome irritant to us, but not a disaster. One constantly hears the threat that India will "go communist" unless we send in ever larger amounts of food; maybe so, but a nation in the chaos of famine poses no threat of disaster to us. In any event, the drag of such deficient countries on the already weakened economies and food stocks of either Russia or China might even, in the end, be a benefit to us. One can develop a case that Cuba has been a debit, on balance, to Russia, not an asset whether economically or in international diplomacy.

(2) *Ignore the short-range political changes in these countries.*

My own guess is that the single greatest weakness of Washington in its conduct of foreign affairs since the last war has been its pusillanimous dashing to and fro, like a mouse in a cage, whenever a government is overthrown by revolution, by assassination or by correct election. Aid is rushed in or pulled out. Diplomatic recognition is quickly given on a silver platter or fitfully held back. Perhaps this is a part of the United States' becoming accustomed to its new role as the dominant world power. Whatever the reason, this has been a major cause in preventing stable foreign policies with a single nation or with a continent. During the Time of Famines revolution and turmoil will be the order of the day in most of the affected countries. To help pull a nation through the Time of Famines Washington itself must remain stable in its policies toward that nation.

(3) *Take into consideration the quality of local leadership.*

In times of stress do people retrogress? In applying the thesis of triage, that is, in selecting one country but not another to receive American food (and other forms of technical assistance), the quality of a nation's leadership must be taken into account. Without effective leaders the populace will indeed retrogress. Thus, whenever the rare quality of imaginative leadership is found, then surely it is the duty of outsiders, such as the American government, the international organizations and others, to give support in whatever manner can be extended. This support can be in the form of trade benefits or military assistance or whatever. And food—unless the nation is hopelessly in the "can't-be-saved" category or, hopefully, in the "walking wounded."

(4) *Give maximum* NON-FOOD *aid to those nations where we wish short-range political advantages.*

If we do not have enough food to supply a nation or if we have already decided it is a "walking wounded" case, then we still will have at hand the full range of our non-food resources and technical assistance with which to help it. If administered wisely this often ought to be enough to help maintain those leaders and governments whom we wish to stay in power.

(5) *Favor nations which have raw materials required by the American and the world economy.*

Some countries produce agricultural and mineral materials which have a strategic value in today's industrial economy, while other countries do not. If a choice must be made between two equally de-serving hungry nations then, certainly, the importance of keeping production lines open for a key product must be the deciding factor.

(6) *Favor nations which have military value to the United States.*

"Strategic military value" is an elusive and transitory factor amid the kaleidoscope shiftings of international politics. But it cannot be ignored by the decision-makers.

EXAMPLES OF HOW TO APPLY TRIAGE

The clearest way to understand a theory is, of course, to apply it to specific examples. So now I present certain nations most of whom, I am sure, will make strident calls during the coming decade for American food and assistance above the levels they may already be receiving.

To bring home the painful responsibility of the official when he must himself sign the paper that will give one applicant nation priority over another, I provide a blank space where the reader can insert his own considered view of what the decision should be.

Afterwards, I give my own opinion and I recognize that my presen-tation of each "case" is colored by that opinion. Nevertheless, the adverse facts I state must be faced up to by the American official judging the case; and the local officials anxious to present only their country's good points must refute these same adverse facts.

Libya. Probably, no area has received so much aid attention as Libya, not only from the United States but also from Great Britain and others. The succession of foreign aid and technical assistance teams and advisers that have gone to Libya since the war form a case study of this whole subject. In varying degrees this help did have an effect, but seldom beyond the propping up stage. It did not result in creating the forces which would develop the nation, nor was this ever even in prospect. The resources of the country were then too paltry, the population increases too steady.

Then, glory be, oil spouted forth and now the nation has an income that ought to be able to cover its needs.

I was in and out of Libya a few times before the oil was discovered and when it was a most backward country. What it is like now with all the excitement the oil has engendered I can only dimly visualize. Yet now the oil is gushing out in sufficient quantity to support the country if the leadership and the public keep their "rising expectations" down to the level for which the oil can pay—but, on the contrary, the "rising expectations" are spiraling upward like an unchecked hot air balloon.

The population is spiraling upward just as fast. So far, there is no birth control program and its population growth is the second highest in all Africa. The United States has not sent food to Libya for several years and now, fortunately, the resources are at hand, namely the oil, with which Libya can buy abroad the food it needs.

Yet with a doubled population within nineteen years one foresees the demand for Food for Freedom supplies that probably will come from Libya. When it does, should the answer be "yes"?

Can't-Be-Saved ☐
Walking Wounded ☐
Should Receive Food ☐

India. India is the example that cuts across all the political and economic guide rules I have been using for the other nations. Also, more than in any other country, if the United States should today cut off its food aid, or even curtail it, immediate turmoil and possible catastrophe would result.

Today India absorbs like a blotter 25 percent of the entire American wheat crop.

No matter how one may adjust present statistics and allow for future increases in the American wheat crop, for future shipments of rice and corn to India and for a possible increase of India's own production of grains, today's trends show it will be beyond the resources of the United States to keep famine out of India during the 1970's. Indian agriculture is too antiquated. Its present government is too inefficient to inaugurate long-range agricultural development programs. Its population tidal wave is too overwhelming; more than 11,500,000 are added each year to the current half-billion population.

Thus far, the Indian leadership, beginning with Nehru, appears to have botched just about every effort at progress in local food development and population control that has been offered to it.

Of all the national leaderships the Indian comes close to being the most childish and inefficient and perversely determined to cut the country's economic throat. But, except for a degree of graft, it is not an evil leadership like those of some other nations. It is not looting the country or threatening rapine on its neighbors. It is just childish. There is little reason to believe that future American help will result in a more responsible Indian leadership than our past help has effected.

So the famines will come. Riding alongside will surely be riots and other civil tensions which the central government will be too weak to control.

Throughout the past decade the American shipments of food to India have escalated planlessly each year. We have committed our resources to the country's short-term emergencies, *not* to long-range development. Step by step we have so added to our responsibility that now Washington cannot afford, it fears, to let that country sink. To save the "investment" of $6.5 billion we have already put into India, to save the nation from breaking up into civil disorder, to save it from "going communist," we are rushing in more and more food. We have drifted along until now it is too late to make decisions on the basis of what is the best use of our food capacity for filling worldwide needs. India is moving quickly toward taking so much of our available food that, if continued, our food aid to other countries must soon be slashed.

Although I emphasize the planlessness it is important to repeat that a planned disposal of our surpluses was never the intent of the P.L. 480 law, nor has it been a governing instruction for the officials of this program. They were charged with the quite different task of just getting rid of the food. The result in India, therefore, is that our officials were not required to sit back and ask, "Do we have enough food to save India? Could all the world save India? Is India worth this food if other countries are to be lost?" Under triage such decisions would have to be made.

In retrospect it is hard to see any positive, direct advantage the United States has received from its $6.5 billion of aid to India, other than the negative one of, so far, bolstering a sort of stable nation.

Although the vituperative blasts against all things American that the Indian representative used to shout in the United Nations are now muted, the present government continues to work actively against many American policies in the assorted chancelleries of the world. Yet this has done little harm, one way or another, to the United States.

If we cut off the food to India we are not losing a reliable friend. Nor do we gain an enemy able to do us serious hurt.

On the other hand, we do condemn a segment of the human race to disastrous suffering, people who, in the end, may be as worthy to receive our limited food aid as other, perhaps equally neuter, nations.

Can't-Be-Saved ☐
Walking Wounded ☐
Should Receive Food ☐

Pakistan. On the surface Pakistan suffers from the same troubles, the same malaise, as the rest of the undeveloped world. It is indeed a candidate for mass starvation in the 1970's. Its population of 115,000,000—which will double in twenty-five years—makes effective aid from the United States a stupendous job and one which must perforce divert our energies and resources away from many smaller nations.

Birth control programs are not yet intensive, but they have had a firm background in the efforts since 1953 of the Family Planning Association of Pakistan to popularize family planning. Also, since 1958 they have had the strong support of President Ayub Khan who has made them a part of the national development plan and even included his advocacy in his election platform manifesto. This fifteen-year history, combined with Ayub's type of government, may indeed have an effect on the birth rate within the next couple of decades.

Most important of all, Pakistan has a unique asset now working for it: it is one undeveloped country whose top leadership seems to have faced up to the problem of feeding the exploding population. So far, apparently, the effort is concentrated primarily on expanding the wheat production of West Pakistan, thus for the most part letting the rice of East Pakistan and other types of crops remain in their time-worn ruts. Nevertheless, it is so unusual for the key men in an undeveloped country to give full support to even one part of the agriculture that Pakistan is today special. And, of course, success with the wheat crop may spill over and favorably affect the rest of the agriculture.

The interest in wheat was generated by successful development of new wheats in Mexico. These are of a dwarf variety designed especially for the application of fertilizer; they do not fall over and lodge even when too much fertilizer is put on. Since parts of West Pakistan have climates similar to those of Mexico (and the local populace is accustomed to eating this type of wheat), the introduction of the new Mexican wheats was, technologically, relatively easy.

Nevertheless, despite the optimism of everyone connected with this program, can even maximum success meet the food demands of an additional 115,000,000 persons rolling in on the tide of the next twenty-five years? This wheat may in time be the salvation of West Pakistan, but it is doubtful that East Pakistan will receive similar hope until its own agriculture is accelerated. In fact, the true moment of crisis will come for Pakistan when the one half of the nation retains hope of adequate food but the other half sinks without hope into famine. It is hard to see how West Pakistan, even with the most sincere sacrificing of its own food stocks, can itself transport enough wheat to East Pakistan to save that region, a thousand miles away across a hostile, equally hungry India or three times as far by sea.

Through the years Pakistan has been, next to India, the largest recipient of American aid. Yet the leaders of all parties blithely ignore this in their active opposition to most American international policies and they ignore the omens that their nation must continue to be dependent on this aid.

Politically and militarily Pakistan has value to the United States because of accumulated activities and installations resulting from CENTO and SEATO. Actually, however, it is about as queasy an ally as France is to NATO.

If the United States continues to send food to this elephant-sized, apathetic "ally," it may be possible to keep East Pakistan quiescent for a decade or so and thus, perhaps, give West Pakistan enough time to press forward birth control and to increase food production in order to prevent at least that part of the nation from foundering. As for East Pakistan it must surely sink into famine unless drastic and comprehensive programs for agriculture are immediately started; this the national leadership, the majority of whose background is in the West, seems unable to initiate.

Although one can say that the saving of a half a loaf, namely West Pakistan, is better than giving up the entire loaf, nevertheless the size of American food shipments, directed to the nation as a whole, would probably have to remain at the present gigantic scale.

Can't-Be-Saved ☐
Walking Wounded ☐
Should Receive Food ☐

My own opinion as to the triage classification of these sample nations is:

Libya	Walking Wounded
India	Can't-Be-Saved
Pakistan	Should Receive Food

IN THE END THE RESPONSIBILITY LIES WITH AMERICA'S OFFICIALS

The weakness of triage lies in its implementation by a democratic government like that of the United States. The democratic process does not lend itself to thinking through coldly and logically a complex problem such as American food versus the world's hungry, trying to formulate a practical program before the crisis strikes and then sticking with it through several administrations. The strength of triage is that it satisfies what I assume will be the demands of:

(a) *The humanitarians:* to save the maximum number of lives during the Time of Famines.

(b) *The patriots:* to safeguard the economic stability of the United States.

(c) *The diplomats:* to safeguard the political, economic and strategic interests of the United States on all continents.

(d) *The realists:* to keep our goals within the limits of our resources.

Equally important, triage fits existing legislation. It gives a jumping-off point for the leaders in Washington to begin their analysis of what our government will do with our foodstuffs that soon will be forthcoming from the land under the new Food for Peace concept of "turning the farmers loose." Today's India has alerted one and all to the magnitude of the problem created by the population explosion in the face of static agriculture.

Washington may dally and shuffle and procrastinate, but the Moment of Truth will come the morning when the President must make a choice whether to save India or to save Latin America, when he must sign a piece of paper to send available food to one of two neighboring countries but not to the other, though both are equally friendly to the United States, both equally worthy of help.

Let us hope that before this Moment of Truth arrives there has been wide discussion of this problem in the press, in church councils, in Congress and in the departments of the government. The many-faceted problems of the choices of triage, the most far-reaching problem of the coming generation, cannot be resolved on the spur of the hour or, worse, on a fluctuating day-to-day, crisis-to-crisis basis.

This is so because during this discussion in the open forum of a democracy, the following compromises must be reached:

(a) The humanitarians must come to realize it will be impossible to save everyone, that choices must be made, that logical, thought-out choices are themselves the essence of humanitarianism.

(b) The patriots must come to realize that the economic stability of the United States is weakened, not strengthened, by a policy of isolationism.

(c) The diplomats must come to realize that although the Time of Famines will last for several decades it will indeed end some day; and when it does end then the interests of the United States will be served best by independent friends, not subordinate retainers.

(d) The realists must accept the policy of utilizing our resources to the maximum, not the minimum, in behalf of the hope, the quite practical hope, of a "better" world when the Time of Famines gives way to the Next Age.

Finally, everyone—the Bolivians, the Indians, the Gambians, the Zambians, the Trinidadians, and most of all, the Americans—must realize that when a 10,000-ton freighter loaded to the scuppers with Food for Peace wheat sails out of New York or Baltimore or Seattle or Buffalo or Houston a specific component of American wealth is shipped out, wealth in the form of 200 tons of nitrogen, 41 tons of phosphorus and 50 tons of potassium. Multiply these figures by the approximately 14,600 freighter loads shipped out from 1954 to July 1965 and one see that the portion of our soil's fertility thus lost forever is a significant part of our national resources, resources which we are denying to our children and grandchildren.

Also carried within the freighter is American wealth in the form of the farmers' labor, the depreciation of the tractors, the consumption of the diesel fuel, the use of the transportation system which moved the wheat to the ports and the labor that loaded the ships. The ship-loads of food (and currently we are rushing to India 1,000,000 tons a month, or three to four ships *each day*) are not a gift which "has cost nobody nothing." They are as real as the gold in Fort Knox.

When we pour out this wealth we ought to get something in return for it. Let us make certain that what we get from our future shipments is a "better" world for our children. They are the ones who will suffer if we fail to obtain a fair return on this forfeiture of national resources.

Triage would seem to be the most clean-cut method of meeting the crisis. Waste not the food on the "can't-be-saved" and the "walking wounded." Send it to those nations which, having it, can buttress their own resources, their own efforts, and win the fight through to survival.

THE VARIETIES OF POLLUTION

The four articles in this section by no means exhaust the varieties of pollution of the environment. There is also thermal pollution, the increase in the temperature of bodies of water because of the disposal of water which has been used as a cooling agent, particularly in electric-power plants. According to the Federal Water Pollution Control Administration, waters above 93 degrees Fahrenheit are uninhabitable for most species of fish; many rivers in the U.S. reach a temperature of 90 degrees Fahrenheit or better now during summer months as a result of natural heat, and future increases in the number of plants generating electric power—particularly nuclear plants, which have an extremely high heat waste—will create an increasingly dangerous source of thermal pollution.

Another form of pollution not touched on here is noise pollution; it is a very real political issue, especially in communities adjacent to jet airports, and one which will undoubtedly escalate in the era of supersonic transports. Visual pollution, the sheer clutter of landscape, highway, and city views with gadgetry, junk and advertising devices, had for awhile a high-level opponent while Mrs. Lyndon Johnson was advocating highway beautification. Both noise and visual pollution have difficulty being taken seriously by Americans; until ways of measuring the detrimental emotional effects of certain kinds of environmental deterioration are perfected, we will undoubtedly continue to group these issues as "aesthetic," and, hence, relatively trivial.

Even when the effects of pollution are clearly physical and quite accessible to the techniques of empirical measurement, reaction time to pollution dangers is often amazingly slow. The late Rachel Carson's book *Silent Spring* is rightly regarded as one of the classic studies of environmental alteration; the chapter from it which is included in this section, "Elixirs of Death," deals with the dangers of the various kinds of insecticides—particularly DDT—which have been developed and put into agricultural use. *Silent Spring* was first published in 1962, and it was widely praised and widely read—but farmers continued to buy and use DDT until it was prohibited by Secretary of Health, Education and Welfare Robert Finch in 1969. Seven years is a dangerously long period of elapsed time for a response to a threat to the ecology, however, and the DDT ban was clearly short of a final solution to the problem: it did not ban the manufacture of DDT by American firms, nor did it, of course, remove the danger of other pesticides already in use or still to be developed. We can expect many political battles yet between the advocates and the enemies of pesticides.

Another form of pollution—and one about which relatively little is known—is nuclear: the results from the testing of nuclear weapons, and, increasingly more critical, the results from the generation of electrical power by atomic energy. I have pointed out the danger of thermal pollution from atomic power plants; the article by Barry Commoner, a biologist at Washington University in St. Louis, addresses itself to the nuclear pollution problem. It should be noted that one of the problems about pollution control is that so many things remain unknown or subject to dispute; this is particularly true of nuclear pollution, and, as Commoner's article shows, many of the assumptions about the results of various uses of nuclear power are subject to change.

Air pollution is probably the form of environmental deterioration of which the greatest number of Americans are to some extent aware; it is both "aesthetically" unpleasant and the cause of measurable damage to animal and plant life, and to property. However, the fact that it offends many people in many ways has not led to its being immediately eliminated; as is shown in the study by Robert U. Ayres, a Washington-based research scientist, there are many sources of air pollution, and steps toward ending it run into a multitude of technological, administrative and political obstacles.

The sheer accumulation of solid physical wastes which results from modern habits of packaging of food and other consumer goods would seem to be the most obvious pollution of all; yet even it has tended to become for most people a completely unnoticed process. Public services which are taken entirely for granted pick up garbage, take it somewhere out of sight, and for most of us that also means out of mind; only on those occasions when the system breaks down— as it has, for example, as a result of strikes in New York and London —does the enormity of the amount of garbage present itself to public view. Even then, I suspect that the problem is generally perceived as a temporary deficiency in the system of getting rid of garbage—and that there is little inclination to consider possible ways of reducing the production of garbage. This latter possibility is not raised in the article by Charles Einstein, a San Francisco journalist, but Einstein does give a vivid picture of one city's various solutions to the problem of getting rid of its garbage.

Finally, in discussing pollution, a couple of perhaps obvious generalizations should be made: one is that all pollution is either directly or indirectly a result of technological progress. This is even true of the sewage, human wastes, which becomes a disposal problem for many cities; certain kinds of progress have created both the cities and the population growth which crowds them. A second generalization is that pollution inevitably creates political conflict involving interest groups. It costs money to eliminate pollution, and industries often find it necessary to fight pollution control as an act of economic survival.

ELIXIRS OF DEATH

Rachel L. Carson

For the first time in the history of the world, every human being is now subjected to contact with dangerous chemicals, from the moment of conception until death. In the less than two decades of their use, the synthetic pesticides have been so thoroughly distributed throughout the animate and inanimate world that they occur virtually everywhere. They have been recovered from most of the major river systems and even from streams of groundwater flowing unseen through the earth. Residues of these chemicals linger in soil to which they may have been applied a dozen years before. They have entered and lodged in the bodies of fish, birds, reptiles, and domestic and wild animals so universally that scientists carrying on animal experiments find it almost impossible to locate subjects free from such contamination. They have been found in fish in remote mountain lakes, in earthworms burrowing in soil, in the eggs of birds—and in man himself. For these chemicals are now stored in the bodies of the vast majority of human beings, regardless of age. They occur in the mother's milk, and probably in the tissues of the unborn child.

All this has come about because of the sudden rise and prodigious growth of an industry for the production of man-made or synthetic chemicals with insecticidal properties. This industry is a child of the Second World War. In the course of developing agents of chemical warfare, some of the chemicals created in the laboratory were found to be lethal to insects. The discovery did not come by chance: insects were widely used to test chemicals as agents of death for man.

The result has been a seemingly endless stream of synthetic insecticides. In being man-made—by ingenious laboratory manipulation of the molecules, substituting atoms, altering their arrangement—they differ sharply from the simpler insecticides of prewar days. These were derived from naturally occurring minerals and plant products—compounds of arsenic, copper, lead, manganese, zinc, and other minerals, pyrethrum from the dried flowers of chrysanthemums, nicotine sulphate from some of the relatives of tobacco, and rotenone from leguminous plants of the East Indies.

What sets the new synthetic insecticides apart is their enormous biological potency. They have immense power not merely to poison but to enter into the most vital processes of the body and change them in sinister and often deadly ways. Thus, as we shall see, they destroy the very enzymes whose function is to protect the body from harm, they block the oxidation processes from which the body receives its energy, they prevent the normal functioning of various organs, and they may initiate in certain cells the slow and irreversible change that leads to malignancy.

Yet new and more deadly chemicals are added to the list each year and new uses are devised so that contact with these materials has become practically worldwide. The production of synthetic pesticides in the United States soared from 124,259,000 pounds in 1947 to 637,666,000 pounds in 1960—more than a fivefold increase. The whole-sale value of these products was well over a quarter of a billion dollars. But in the plans and hopes of the industry this enormous production is only a beginning.

A Who's Who of pesticides is therefore of concern to us all. If we are going to live so intimately with these chemicals—eating and drinking them, taking them into the very marrow of our bones—we had better know something about their nature and their power.

Although the Second World War marked a turning away from inorganic chemicals as pesticides into the wonder world of the carbon molecule, a few of the old materials persist. Chief among these is arsenic, which is still the basic ingredient in a variety of weed and insect killers. Arsenic is a highly toxic mineral occurring widely in association with the ores of various metals, and in very small amounts in volcanoes, in the sea, and in spring water. Its relations to man are varied and historic. Since many of its compounds are tasteless, it has been a favorite agent of homicide from long before the time of the Borgias to the present. Arsenic is present in English chimney soot and along with certain aromatic hydrocarbons is considered responsible for the carcinogenic (or cancer-causing) action of the soot, which was recognized nearly two centuries ago by an English physician. Epidemics of chronic arsenical poisoning involving whole populations over long periods are on record. Arsenic-contaminated environments have also caused sickness and death among horses, cows, goats, pigs, deer, fishes, and bees; despite this record arsenical sprays and dusts are widely used. In the arsenic-sprayed cotton country of southern United States beekeeping as an industry has nearly died out. Farmers using arsenic dusts over long periods have been afflicted with chronic arsenic poisoning; livestock have been poisoned by crop sprays or weed killers containing arsenic. Drifting arsenic dusts from blueberry lands have spread over neighboring farms, contaminating streams, fatally poisoning bees and cows, and causing human illness. "It is scarcely possible . . . to handle arsenicals with more utter disregard of the general health than that which has been practiced in our country in recent years," said Dr. W. C. Hueper, of the National Cancer Institute, an authority on environmental cancer. "Anyone who has watched the dusters and sprayers of arsenical insecticides at work must have been impressed by the almost supreme carelessness with which the poisonous substances are dispensed."

   Modern insecticides are still more deadly. The vast majority fall into one of two large groups of chemicals. One, represented by DDT, is known as the "chlorinated hydrocarbons." The other group consists of the organic phosphorus insecticides, and is represented by the reasonably familiar malathion and parathion. All have one thing in common. As mentioned above, they are built on a basis of carbon atoms, which are also the indispensable building blocks of the living world, and thus classed as "organic." To understand them, we must see of what they are made, and how, although linked with the basic chemistry of all life, they lend themselves to the modifications which make them agents of death.

   The basic element, carbon, is one whose atoms have an almost infinite capacity for uniting with each other in chains and rings and various other configurations, and for becoming linked with atoms of other substances. Indeed, the incredible diversity of living creatures from bacteria to the great blue whale is largely due to this capacity of carbon. The complex protein molecule has the carbon atom as its basis, as have molecules of fat, carbohydrates, enzymes, and vitamins. So, too, have enormous numbers of nonliving things, for carbon is not necessarily a symbol of life.

   Some organic compounds are simply combinations of carbon and hydrogen. The simplest of these is methane, or marsh gas, formed in nature by the bacterial decomposition of organic matter under water. Mixed with air in proper proportions, methane becomes the dreaded "fire damp" of coal mines. Its structure is beautifully simple, consisting of one carbon atom to which four hydrogen atoms have become attached:

$$
\begin{array}{ccc}
H & & H \\
 & \diagdown \, \diagup & \\
 & C & \\
 & \diagup \, \diagdown & \\
H & & H
\end{array}
$$

Chemists have discovered that it is possible to detach one or all of the hydrogen atoms and substitute other elements. For example, by substituting one atom of chlorine for one of hydrogen we produce methyl chloride:

$$
\begin{array}{ccc}
H & & Cl \\
 & \diagdown \, \diagup & \\
 & C & \\
 & \diagup \, \diagdown & \\
H & & H
\end{array}
$$

Take away three hydrogen atoms and substitute chlorine and we have
the anesthetic chloroform:

$$
\begin{array}{ccc}
H & & Cl \\
 \diagdown & & \diagup \\
 & C & \\
 \diagup & & \diagdown \\
Cl & & Cl
\end{array}
$$

Substitute chlorine atoms for all of the hydrogen atoms and the result
is carbon tetrachloride, the familiar cleaning fluid:

$$
\begin{array}{ccc}
Cl & & Cl \\
 \diagdown & & \diagup \\
 & C & \\
 \diagup & & \diagdown \\
Cl & & Cl
\end{array}
$$

In the simplest possible terms, these changes rung upon the basic
molecule of methane illustrate what a chlorinated hydrocarbon is. But
this illustration gives little hint of the true complexity of the chemical
world of the hydrocarbons, or of the manipulations by which the
organic chemist creates his infinitely varied materials. For instead of
the simple methane molecule with its single carbon atom, he may work
with hydrocarbon molecules consisting of many carbon atoms, arranged in rings or chains, with side chains or branches, holding to
themselves with chemical bonds not merely simple atoms of hydrogen
or chlorine but also a wide variety of chemical groups. By seemingly
slight changes the whole character of the substance is changed; for
example, not only what is attached but the place of attachment to the
carbon atom is highly important. Such ingenious manipulations have
produced a battery of poisons of truly extraordinary power.

DDT (short for dichloro-diphenyl-trichloro-ethane) was first synthesized by a German chemist in 1874, but its properties as an insecticide were not discovered until 1939. Almost immediately DDT was
hailed as a means of stamping out insect-borne disease and winning
the farmers' war against crop destroyers overnight. The discoverer,
Paul Müller of Switzerland, won the Nobel Prize.

DDT is now so universally used that in most minds the product
takes on the harmless aspect of the familiar. Perhaps the myth of the
harmlessness of DDT rests on the fact that one of its first uses was the
wartime dusting of many thousands of soldiers, refugees, and prisoners, to combat lice. It is widely believed that since so many people

came into extremely intimate contact with DDT and suffered no immediate ill effects the chemical must certainly be innocent of harm. This understandable misconception arises from the fact that—unlike other chlorinated hydrocarbons—DDT *in powder form* is not readily absorbed through the skin. Dissolved in oil, as it usually is, DDT is definitely toxic. If swallowed, it is absorbed slowly through the digestive tract; it may also be absorbed through the lungs. Once it has entered the body it is stored largely in organs rich in fatty substances (because DDT itself is fat-soluble) such as the adrenals, testes, or thyroid. Relatively large amounts are deposited in the liver, kidneys, and the fat of the large, protective mesenteries that enfold the intestines.

This storage of DDT begins with the smallest conceivable intake of the chemical (which is present as residues on most foodstuffs) and continues until quite high levels are reached. The fatty storage depots act as biological magnifiers, so that an intake of as little as 1/10 of 1 part per million in the diet results in storage of about 10 to 15 parts per million, an increase of one hundredfold or more. These terms of reference, so commonplace to the chemist or the pharmacologist, are unfamiliar to most of us. One part in a million sounds like a very small amount—and so it is. But such substances are so potent that a minute quantity can bring about vast changes in the body. In animal experiments, 3 parts per million has been found to inhibit an essential enzyme in heart muscle; only 5 parts per million has brought about necrosis or disintegration of liver cells; only 2.5 parts per million of the closely related chemicals dieldrin and chlordane did the same.

This is really not surprising. In the normal chemistry of the human body there is just such a disparity between cause and effect. For example, a quantity of iodine as small as two ten-thousandths of a gram spells the difference between health and disease. Because these small amounts of pesticides are cumulatively stored and only slowly excreted, the threat of chronic poisoning and degenerative changes of the liver and other organs is very real.

Scientists do not agree upon how much DDT can be stored in the human body. Dr. Arnold Lehman, who is the chief pharmacologist of the Food and Drug Administration, says there is neither a floor below which DDT is not absorbed nor a ceiling beyond which absorption and storage ceases. On the other hand, Dr. Wayland Hayes of the United States Public Health Service contends that in every individual a point of equilibrium is reached, and that DDT in excess of this amount is excreted. For practical purposes it is not particularly important which of these men is right. Storage in human beings has been well investigated, and we know that the average person is storing potentially harmful amounts. According to various studies, individuals with no known exposure (except the inevitable dietary one) store an average of 5.3 parts per million to 7.4 parts per million; agricultural workers 17.1 parts per million; and workers in insecticide plants as high as 648 parts per million! So the range of proven storage is quite wide and, what is even more to the point, the minimum figures are above the level at which damage to the liver and other organs or tissues may begin.

One of the most sinister features of DDT and related chemicals is the way they are passed on from one organism to another through all the links of the food chains. For example, fields of alfalfa are dusted with DDT; meal is later prepared from the alfalfa and fed to hens; the hens lay eggs which contain DDT. Or the hay, containing residues of 7 to 8 parts per million, may be fed to cows. The DDT will turn up in the milk in the amount of about 3 parts per million, but in butter made from this milk the concentration may run to 65 parts per million. Through such a process of transfer, what started out as a very small amount of DDT may end as a heavy concentration. Farmers nowadays find it difficult to obtain uncontaminated fodder for their milk cows, though the Food and Drug Administration forbids the presence of insecticide residues in milk shipped in interstate commerce.

The poison may also be passed on from mother to offspring. Insecticide residues have been recovered from human milk in samples tested by Food and Drug Administration scientists. This means that the breast-fed human infant is receiving small but regular additions to the load of toxic chemicals building up in his body. It is by no means his first exposure, however: there is good reason to believe this begins while he is still in the womb. In experimental animals the chlorinated hydrocarbon insecticides freely cross the barrier of the placenta, the traditional protective shield between the embryo and harmful substances in the mother's body. While the quantities so received by human infants would normally be small, they are not unimportant because children are more susceptible to poisoning than adults. This situation also means that today the average individual almost certainly starts life with the first deposit of the growing load of chemicals his body will be required to carry thenceforth.

All these facts—storage at even low levels, subsequent accumulation, and occurrence of liver damage at levels that may easily occur in normal diets, caused Food and Drug Administration scientists to declare as early as 1950 that it is "extremely likely the potential hazard of DDT has been underestimated." There has been no such parallel situation in medical history. No one yet knows what the ultimate consequences may be.

Chlordane, another chlorinated hydrocarbon, has all these unpleasant attributes of DDT plus a few that are peculiarly its own. Its residues are long persistent in soil, on foodstuffs, or on surfaces to which it may be applied. Chlordane makes use of all available portals to enter the body. It may be absorbed through the skin, may be breathed in as a spray or dust, and of course is absorbed from the digestive tract if residues are swallowed. Like all other chlorinated hydrocarbons, its deposits build up in the body in cumulative fashion. A diet containing such a small amount of chlordane as 2.5 parts per million may eventually lead to storage of 75 parts per million in the fat of experimental animals.

So experienced a pharmacologist as Dr. Lehman has described chlordane in 1950 as "one of the most toxic of insecticides—anyone handling it could be poisoned." Judging by the carefree liberality with which dusts for lawn treatments by suburbanites are laced with chlordane, this warning has not been taken to heart. The fact that the suburbanite is not instantly stricken has little meaning, for the toxins may sleep long in his body, to become manifest months or years later in an obscure disorder almost impossible to trace to its origins. On the other hand, death may strike quickly. One victim who accidentally spilled a 25 percent industrial solution on the skin developed symptoms of poisoning within 40 minutes and died before medical help could be obtained. No reliance can be placed on receiving advance warning which might allow treatment to be had in time.

Heptachlor, one of the constituents of chlordane, is marketed as a separate formulation. It has a particularly high capacity for storage in fat. If the diet contains as little as 1/10 of 1 part per million there will be measurable amounts of heptachlor in the body. It also has the curious ability to undergo change into a chemically distinct substance known as heptachlor epoxide. It does this in soil and in the tissues of both plants and animals. Tests on birds indicate that the epoxide that results from this change is more toxic than the original chemical, which in turn is four times as toxic as chlordane.

As long ago as the mid-1930's a special group of hydrocarbons, the chlorinated naphthalenes, was found to cause hepatitis, and also a rare and almost invariably fatal liver disease in persons subjected to occupational exposure. They have led to illness and death of workers in electrical industries; and more recently, in agriculture, they have been considered a cause of a mysterious and usually fatal disease of cattle. In view of these antecedents, it is not surprising that three of the insecticides that are related to this group are among the most violently poisonous of all the hydrocarbons. These are dieldrin, aldrin, and endrin.

Dieldrin, named for a German chemist, Diels, is about 5 times as toxic as DDT when swallowed but 40 times as toxic when absorbed through the skin in solution. It is notorious for striking quickly and with terrible effect at the nervous system, sending the victims into convulsions. Persons thus poisoned recover so slowly as to indicate chronic effects. As with other chlorinated hydrocarbons, these long-term effects include severe damage to the liver. The long duration of its residues and the effective insecticidal action make dieldrin one of the most used insecticides today, despite the appalling destruction of wildlife that has followed its use. As tested on quail and pheasants, it has proved to be about 40 to 50 times as toxic as DDT.

There are vast gaps in our knowledge of how dieldrin is stored or distributed in the body, or excreted, for the chemists' ingenuity in devising insecticides has long ago outrun biological knowledge of the way these poisons affect the living organism. However, there is every indication of long storage in the human body, where deposits may lie dormant like a slumbering volcano, only to flare up in periods of physiological stress when the body draws upon its fat reserves. Much of what we do know has been learned through hard experience in the antimalarial campaigns carried out by the World Health Organization. As soon as dieldrin was substituted for DDT in malaria-control work (because the malaria mosquitoes had become resistant to DDT), cases of poisoning among the spraymen began to occur. The seizures were severe—from half to all (varying in the different programs) of the men affected went into convulsions and several died. Some had convulsions as long as *four months* after the last exposure.

Aldrin is a somewhat mysterious substance, for although it exists as a separate entity it bears the relation of alter ego to dieldrin. When carrots are taken from a bed treated with aldrin they are found to contain residues of dieldrin. This change occurs in living tissues and also in soil. Such alchemistic transformations have led to many erroneous reports, for if a chemist, knowing aldrin has been applied, tests for it he will be deceived into thinking all residues have been dissipated. The residues are there, but they are dieldrin and this requires a different test.

Like dieldrin, aldrin is extremely toxic. It produces degenerative changes in the liver and kidneys. A quantity the size of an aspirin tablet is enough to kill more than 400 quail. Many cases of human poisonings are on record, most of them in connection with industrial handling.

Aldrin, like most of this group of insecticides, projects a menacing shadow into the future, the shadow of sterility. Pheasants fed quantities too small to kill them nevertheless laid few eggs, and the chicks that hatched soon died. The effect is not confined to birds. Rats exposed to aldrin had fewer pregnancies and their young were sickly and short-lived. Puppies born of treated mothers died within three days. By one means or another, the new generations suffer for the poisoning of their parents. No one knows whether the same effect will be seen in human beings, yet this chemical has been sprayed from airplanes over suburban areas and farmlands.

Endrin is the most toxic of all the chlorinated hydrocarbons. Although chemically rather closely related to dieldrin, a little twist in its molecular structure makes it 5 times as poisonous. It makes the progenitor of all this group of insecticides, DDT, seem by comparison almost harmless. It is 15 times as poisonous as DDT to mammals, 30 times as poisonous to fish, and about 300 times as poisonous to some birds.

In the decade of its use, endrin has killed enormous numbers of fish, has fatally poisoned cattle that have wandered into sprayed orchards, has poisoned wells, and has drawn a sharp warning from at least one state health department that its careless use is endangering human lives.

In one of the most tragic cases of endrin poisoning there was no apparent carelessness; efforts had been made to take precautions apparently considered adequate. A year-old child had been taken by his American parents to live in Venezuela. There were cockroaches in the house to which they moved, and after a few days a spray containing endrin was used. The baby and the small family dog were taken out of the house before the spraying was done about nine o'clock one morning. After the spraying the floors were washed. The baby and dog were returned to the house in midafternoon. An hour or so later the dog vomited, went into convulsions, and died. At 10 P.M. on the evening of the same day the baby also vomited, went into convulsions, and lost consciousness. After that fateful contact with endrin, this normal, healthy child became little more than a vegetable—unable to see or hear, subject to frequent muscular spasms, apparently completely cut off from contact with his surroundings. Several months of treatment in a New York hospital failed to change his condition or bring hope of change. "It is extremely doubtful," reported the attending physicians, "that any useful degree of recovery will occur."

The second major group of insecticides, the alkyl or organic phosphates, are among the most poisonous chemicals in the world. The chief and most obvious hazard attending their use is that of acute poisoning of people applying the sprays or accidentally coming in contact with drifting spray, with vegetation coated by it, or with a discarded container. In Florida, two children found an empty bag and used it to repair a swing. Shortly thereafter both of them died and three of their playmates became ill. The bag had once contained an insecticide called parathion, one of the organic phosphates; tests established death by parathion poisoning. On another occasion two small boys in Wisconsin, cousins, died on the same night. One had been playing in his yard when spray drifted in from an adjoining field where his father was spraying potatoes with parathion; the other had run playfully into the barn after his father and had put his hand on the nozzle of the spray equipment.

The origin of these insecticides has a certain ironic significance. Although some of the chemicals themselves—organic esters of phosphoric acid—had been known for many years, their insecticidal properties remained to be discovered by a German chemist, Gerhard Schrader, in the late 1930's. Almost immediately the German government recognized the value of these same chemicals as new and devastating weapons in man's war against his own kind, and the work on them was declared secret. Some became the deadly nerve gases. Others, of closely allied structure, became insecticides.

The organic phosphorus insecticides act on the living organism in a peculiar way. They have the ability to destroy enzymes—enzymes that perform necessary functions in the body. Their target is the nervous system, whether the victim is an insect or a warm-blooded animal. Under normal conditions, an impulse passes from nerve to nerve with the aid of a "chemical transmitter" called acetylcholine, a substance that performs an essential function and then disappears. Indeed, its existence is so ephemeral that medical researchers are unable, without special procedures, to sample it before the body has destroyed it. This transient nature of the transmitting chemical is necessary to the normal functioning of the body. If the acetylcholine is not destroyed as soon as a nerve impulse has passed, impulses continue to flash across the bridge from nerve to nerve, as the chemical exerts its effects in an ever more intensified manner. The movements of the whole body become uncoordinated: tremors, muscular spasms, convulsions, and death quickly result.

This contingency has been provided for by the body. A protective enzyme called cholinesterase is at hand to destroy the transmitting chemical once it is no longer needed. By this means a precise balance is struck and the body never builds up a dangerous amount of acetylcholine. But on contact with the organic phosphorus insecticides, the protective enzyme is destroyed, and as the quantity of the enzyme is reduced that of the transmitting chemical builds up. In this effect, the organic phosphorus compounds resemble the alkaloid poison muscarine, found in a poisonous mushroom, the fly amanita.

Repeated exposures may lower the cholinesterase level until an individual reaches the brink of acute poisoning, a brink over which he may be pushed by a very small additional exposure. For this reason it is considered important to make periodic examinations of the blood of spray operators and others regularly exposed.

Parathion is one of the most widely used of the organic phosphates. It is also one of the most powerful and dangerous. Honeybees become "wildly agitated and bellicose" on contact with it, perform frantic cleaning movements, and are near death within half an hour. A chemist, thinking to learn by the most direct possible means the dose acutely toxic to human beings, swallowed a minute amount, equivalent to about .00424 ounce. Paralysis followed so instantaneously that he could not reach the antidotes he had prepared at hand, and so he died. Parathion is now said to be a favorite instrument of suicide in Finland. In recent years the State of California has reported an average of more than 200 cases of accidental parathion poisoning annually. In many parts of the world the fatality rate from parathion is startling: 100 fatal cases in India and 67 in Syria in 1958, and an average of 336 deaths per year in Japan.

Yet some 7,000,000 pounds of parathion are now applied to fields and orchards of the United States—by hand sprayers, motorized blowers and dusters, and by airplane. The amount used on California farms alone could, according to one medical authority, "provide a lethal dose for 5 to 10 times the whole world's population."

One of the few circumstances that save us from extinction by this means is the fact that parathion and other chemicals of this group are decomposed rather rapidly. Their residues on the crops to which they are applied are therefore relatively short-lived compared with the chlorinated hydrocarbons. However, they last long enough to create hazards and produce consequences that range from the merely serious to the fatal. In Riverside, California, eleven out of thirty men picking oranges became violently ill and all but one had to be hospitalized. Their symptoms were typical of parathion poisoning. The grove had been sprayed with parathion some two and a half weeks earlier; the residues that reduced them to retching, half-blind, semiconscious misery were sixteen to nineteen days old. And this is not by any means a record for persistence. Similar mishaps have occurred in groves sprayed a month earlier, and residues have been found in the peel of oranges six months after treatment with standard dosages.

The danger to all workers applying the organic phosphorus insecticides in fields, orchards, and vineyards, is so extreme that some states using these chemicals have established laboratories where physicians may obtain aid in diagnosis and treatment. Even the physicians themselves may be in some danger, unless they wear rubber gloves in handling the victims of poisoning. So may a laundress washing the clothing of such victims, which may have absorbed enough parathion to affect her.

Malathion, another of the organic phosphates, is almost as familiar to the public as DDT, being widely used by gardeners, in household insecticides, in mosquito spraying, and in such blanket attacks on insects as the spraying of nearly a million acres of Florida communities for the Mediterranean fruit fly. It is considered the least toxic of this group of chemicals and many people assume they may use it freely and without fear of harm. Commercial advertising encourages this comfortable attitude.

The alleged "safety" of malathion rests on rather precarious ground, although—as often happens—this was not discovered until the chemical had been in use for several years. Malathion is "safe" only because the mammalian liver, an organ with extraordinary protective powers, renders it relatively harmless. The detoxification is accomplished by one of the enzymes of the liver. If, however, something destroys this enzyme or interferes with its action, the person exposed to malathion receives the full force of the poison.

Unfortunately for all of us, opportunities for this sort of thing to happen are legion. A few years ago a team of Food and Drug Administration scientists discovered that when malathion and certain other organic phosphates are administered simultaneously a massive poisoning results—up to 50 times as severe as would be predicted on the basis of adding together the toxicities of the two. In other words, 1/100 of the lethal dose of each compound may be fatal when the two are combined.

This discovery led to the testing of other combinations. It is now known that many pairs of organic phosphate insecticides are highly dangerous, the toxicity being stepped up or "potentiated" through the combined action. Potentiation seems to take place when one compound destroys the liver enzyme responsible for detoxifying the other. The two need not be given simultaneously. The hazard exists not only for the man who may spray this week with one insecticide and next week with another; it exists also for the consumer of sprayed products. The common salad bowl may easily present a combination of organic phosphate insecticides. Residues well within the legally permissible limits may interact.

The full scope of the dangerous interaction of chemicals is as yet little known, but disturbing findings now come regularly from scientific laboratories. Among these is the discovery that the toxicity of an organic phosphate can be increased by a second agent that is not necessarily an insecticide. For example, one of the plasticizing agents may act even more strongly than another insecticide to make malathion more dangerous. Again, this is because it inhibits the liver enzyme that normally would "draw the teeth" of the poisonous insecticide.

What of other chemicals in the normal human environment? What, in particular, of drugs? A bare beginning has been made on this subject, but already it is known that some organic phosphates (parathion and malathion) increase the toxicity of some drugs used as muscle relaxants, and that several others (again including malathion) markedly increase the sleeping time of barbiturates.

In Greek mythology the sorceress Medea, enraged at being supplanted by a rival for the affections of her husband Jason, presented the new bride with a robe possessing magic properties. The wearer of the robe immediately suffered a violent death. This death-by-indirection now finds its counterpart in what are known as "systemic insecticides." These are chemicals with extraordinary properties which are used to convert plants or animals into a sort of Medea's robe by making them actually poisonous. This is done with the purpose of killing insects that may come in contact with them, especially by sucking their juices or blood.

The world of systemic insecticides is a weird world, surpassing the imaginings of the brothers Grimm—perhaps most closely akin to the cartoon world of Charles Addams. It is a world where the enchanted forest of the fairy tales has become the poisonous forest in which an insect that chews a leaf or sucks the sap of a plant is doomed. It is a world where a flea bites a dog, and dies because the dog's blood has been made poisonous, where an insect may die from vapors emanating from a plant it has never touched, where a bee may carry poisonous nectar back to its hive and presently produce poisonous honey.

The entomologists' dream of the built-in insecticide was born when workers in the field of applied entomology realized they could take a hint from nature: they found that wheat growing in soil containing sodium selenate was immune to attack by aphids or spider mites. Selenium, a naturally occurring element found sparingly in rocks and soils of many parts of the world, thus became the first systemic insecticide.

What makes an insecticide a systemic is the ability to permeate all the tissues of a plant or animal and make them toxic. This quality is possessed by some chemicals of the chlorinated hydrocarbon group and by others of the organophosphorus group, all synthetically produced, as well as by certain naturally occurring substances. In practice, however, most systemics are drawn from the organophosphorus group because the problem of residues is somewhat less acute.

Systemics act in other devious ways. Applied to seeds, either by soaking or in a coating combined with carbon, they extend their effects into the following plant generation and produce seedlings poisonous to aphids and other sucking insects. Vegetables such as peas, beans, and sugar beets are sometimes thus protected. Cotton seeds coated with a systemic insecticide have been in use for some time in California, where 25 farm laborers planting cotton in the San Joaquin Valley in 1959 were seized with sudden illness, caused by handling the bags of treated seeds.

In England someone wondered what happened when bees made use of nectar from plants treated with systemics. This was investigated in areas treated with a chemical called schradan. Although the plants had been sprayed before the flowers were formed, the nectar later produced contained the poison. The result, as might have been predicted, was that the honey made by the bees also was contaminated with schradan.

Use of animal systemics has concentrated chiefly on control of the cattle grub, a damaging parasite of livestock. Extreme care must be used in order to create an insecticidal effect in the blood and tissues of the host without setting up a fatal poisoning. The balance is delicate and government veterinarians have found that repeated small doses can gradually deplete an animal's supply of the protective enzyme cholinesterase, so that without warning a minute additional dose will cause poisoning.

There are strong indications that fields closer to our daily lives are being opened up. You may now give your dog a pill which, it is claimed, will rid him of fleas by making his blood poisonous to them. The hazards discovered in treating cattle would presumably apply to the dog. As yet no one seems to have proposed a human systemic that would make us lethal to a mosquito. Perhaps this is the next step.

So far . . . we have been discussing the deadly chemicals that are being used in our war against the insects. What of our simultaneous war against the weeds?

The desire for a quick and easy method of killing unwanted plants has given rise to a large and growing array of chemicals that are known as herbicides, or, less formally, as weed killers. . . . The question that here concerns us is whether the weed killers are poisons and whether their use is contributing to the poisoning of the environment.

The legend that the herbicides are toxic only to plants and so pose no threat to animal life has been widely disseminated, but unfortunately it is not true. The plant killers include a large variety of chemicals that act on animal tissue as well as on vegetation. They vary greatly in their action on the organism. Some are general poisons, some are powerful stimulants of metabolism, causing a fatal rise in body temperature, some induce malignant tumors either alone or in partnership with other chemicals, some strike at the genetic material of the race by causing gene mutations. The herbicides, then, like the insecticides, include some very dangerous chemicals, and their careless use in the belief that they are "safe" can have disastrous results.

Despite the competition of a constant stream of new chemicals issuing from the laboratories, arsenic compounds are still liberally used, both as insecticides (as mentioned above and as weed killers, where they usually take the chemical form of sodium arsenite. The history of their use is not reassuring. As roadside sprays, they have cost many a farmer his cow and killed uncounted numbers of wild creatures. As aquatic weed killers in lakes and reservoirs they have made public waters unsuitable for drinking or even for swimming. As a spray applied to potato fields to destroy the vines they have taken a toll of human and nonhuman life.

In England this latter practice developed about 1951 as a result of a shortage of sulfuric acid, formerly used to burn off the potato vines. The Ministry of Agriculture considered it necessary to give warning of the hazard of going into the arsenic-sprayed fields, but the warning was not understood by the cattle (nor, we must assume, by the wild animals and birds) and reports of cattle poisoned by the arsenic sprays came with monotonous regularity. When death came also to a farmer's wife through arsenic-contaminated water, one of the major English chemical companies (in 1959) stopped production of arsenical sprays and called in supplies already in the hands of dealers, and shortly thereafter the Ministry of Agriculture announced that because of high risks to people and cattle restrictions on the use of arsenites would be imposed. In 1961, the Australian government announced a similar ban. No such restrictions impede the use of these poisons in the United States, however.

Some of the "dinitro" compounds are also used as herbicides. They are rated as among the most dangerous materials of this type in use in the United States. Dinitrophenol is a strong metabolic stimulant. For this reason it was at one time used as a reducing drug, but the margin between the slimming dose and that required to poison or kill was slight—so slight that several patients died and many suffered permanent injury before use of the drug was finally halted.

A related chemical, pentachlorophenol, sometimes known as "penta," is used as a weed killer as well as an insecticide, often being sprayed along railroad tracks and in waste areas. Penta is extremely toxic to a wide variety of organisms from bacteria to man. Like the dinitros, it interferes, often fatally, with the body's source of energy, so that the affected organism almost literally burns itself up. Its fearful power is illustrated in a fatal accident recently reported by the California Department of Health. A tank truck driver was preparing a cotton defoliant by mixing diesel oil with pentachlorophenol. As he was drawing the concentrated chemical out of a drum, the spigot accidentally toppled back. He reached in with his bare hand to regain the spigot. Although he washed immediately, he became acutely ill and died the next day.

While the results of weed killers such as sodium arsenite or the phenols are grossly obvious, some other herbicides are more insidious in their effects. For example, the now famous cranberry-weed-killer aminotriazole, or amitrol, is rated as having relatively low toxicity. But in the long run its tendency to cause malignant tumors of the thyroid may be far more significant for wildlife and perhaps also for man.

Among the herbicides are some that are classified as "mutagens," or agents capable of modifying the genes, the materials of heredity. We are rightly appalled by the genetic effects of radiation; how then, can we be indifferent to the same effect in chemicals that we disseminate widely in our environment?

NUCLEAR POLLUTION: THE MYTH OF OMNIPOTENCE

Barry Commoner

We have been living under a vast and potentially fatal illusion: that we can enjoy the enormous benefits of modern technology without risk to the integrity of human life and the environment. This illusion is evident from the following statements, selected more or less at random from numerous similar ones:

Chemical herbicides are being used in Vietnam to clear jungle growth and to reduce the hazards of ambush by Vietcong forces . . . They are not harmful to people, animals, soil or water. (Letter from Dixon Donnelley, Assistant Secretary, Department of Defense, September 28, 1966)

. . . the general public is not now, nor in the immediate future, facing a lead hazard. (Report of American Medical Association's Committee on Occupational Toxicology, 1966)

. . . no evidence is presently available that there is a danger of anyone being poisoned by pesticide residues in food. (Testimony of E. M. Mrak, former Chancellor, University of California, Congressional Hearings, Interagency Coordination in Environmental Hazards [Pesticides], August 20 and 21, 1963)

There has been no instance of radiation injury to any worker in a commercial atomic power plant. Nor has there been any instance in which these plants have affected public health and safety . . . atomic power plants make good neighbors. ("The What and Why of Atomic Power," *Atomic Industrial Forum*, 1966)

The continuance of the present rate of H-bomb testing by the most sober and responsible scientific judgment . . . does not imperil the health of humanity. (President Eisenhower, October 2, 1956)

Barry Commoner, "The Myth of Omnipotence," ENVIRONMENT, *March 1969. Reprinted by permission.*

In order to substantiate my view that such claims are illusory, I should like to discuss, in some detail, certain recent observations regarding the environmental hazards of nuclear energy.

THE HIDDEN COSTS OF NUCLEAR POWER

Despite claims such as the one cited above, it is my view that there are risks—to the environment and to human life—associated with the considerable benefits of nuclear power. These costs have thus far been nearly successfully hidden from public view.

We can usefully begin our consideration of this problem with a question: Is nuclear power a paying proposition? A more elegant way to put the question is this: Can nuclear power produce more good than it costs? Whether we ask this question in the direct language of profit and loss, or in the more abstract language of social welfare, the question is crucial. For, sooner or later, every human endeavor—if it is to continue—must pass this simple test: Is it worth what it costs?

It might appear that the question has already been answered. The power industry, long accustomed to meticulous cost accounting, has given the answer in the increasingly frequent decision to build new plants for nuclear fuels rather than fossil ones. Apparently, many utilities have decided that nuclear power plants will yield the best available margin between costs and profits.

I should like to suggest, however, that these calculations are not complete—and that certain costs represented by environmental hazards have not yet been taken into account. Until these costs are considered, not only by the industry, but also by the scientific community and the public at large, we cannot know whether nuclear power—either as a simple business proposition, or as a great social enterprise—will be worth what it costs. And I believe that if we proceed with present development plans in the absence of a full evaluation of *all* the costs and benefits, we risk the future, not only of the industry itself, but of the nation's entire power system—in which nuclear sources loom so large. For if we develop the industry without a full appreciation of what it really costs us, we may find—at some future time when we become aware of the full price—that we are unwilling to pay the bill. If that should happen, the development of nuclear power and the nation's reliance on it will come to be regarded as a tragic and costly mistake.

Some may be surprised at my suggestion that such a gross error could possibly be made in an industry which embodies all the skills of modern technology. Yet, the brief, if spectacular, history of nuclear technology already records an error at least as gross and shocking. I refer to the explosions of nuclear weapons in the atmosphere. Who is prepared to deny that atmospheric nuclear testing would have been banned, not in 1963, but before it began if the nation had known in the 1950's what President Johnson told us in a televised address, October 12, 1964:

The deadly products of atomic explosions were poisoning our soil and our food and the milk our children drank and the air we all breathe . . . Radio-active poisons were beginning to threaten the safety of people throughout the world. They were a growing menace to the health of every unborn child.

That this was indeed a technological mistake, and not a public deception, is evident from the record of the government's estimates of the biological risks from fallout. These estimates made in the fifties were in error because crucial data (for example on the effects of radioactive iodine) were lacking. A prudent regard for past mistakes in using the enormous power of nuclear technology demands that we remain alert to possible future mistakes.

How shall we calculate the balance sheet for nuclear power? On the income side, matters are relatively simple. In a given part of the country a kilowatt hour of power brings a definite financial return, and the social good that comes of it is widely known and appreciated. What of the costs? Some of them are about as well known as the income. The cost of building a reactor is readily calculable, as are the costs of maintenance and repair. But the costs due to environmental pollution are largely hidden and need to be brought to light if they are to be properly evaluated.

Unfortunately, our experience with the nuclear power industry is too brief to give us most of the data needed for an estimate of such hidden costs. But we can at least begin to define them by looking at our experience with the chief competitive form of power production—electric generators driven by fossil fuels.

We now know that a coal-burning power plant produces not only electricity, but also a number of less desirable things: smoke and soot, oxides of sulfur and nitrogen, carbon dioxide, a variety of organic compounds, and heat. Each of these is a *non*-good and costs someone something. Smoke and soot increase the householder's laundry and cleaning bills; oxides of sulfur increase the cost of building maintenance; for organic pollutants we pay the price—not only in dollars, but in human anguish—of some number of cases of emphysema and lung cancer.

Some of these costs can be converted to dollar values. The U.S. Public Health Service estimates the overall cost of air pollution at about $60 per person per year. A reasonable assessment of the overall costs of air pollution to power production from fossil fuels is about one third. This means that we must add to the cost of such power production, for each urban family of four, about $80 per year—an appreciable sum relative to the annual bill for electricity.

The point of this calculation is obvious: The *hidden* costs of power production, such as air pollution, are *social* costs; they are met, not by a single producer, but by many consumers. To discover the true cost of electric power we need to look for and evaluate all the hidden social costs represented by environmental pollution—the dirty linen, so to speak.

At first glance nuclear power appears to be a good way of reducing the hidden costs of pollution. Nuclear power is "clean" in the sense that it avoids environmental pollution from smoke, soot, and noxious chemicals. But nuclear power generates one *new* type of pollutant—radiation—and we need to discover what hidden costs it carries.

The problem of containing radioactive emissions from nuclear processes have been a major concern of nuclear engineers. Every nuclear plant is carefully designed to restrict the release of radiation, which must meet certain government standards. Moreover, apart from occasional accidents, largely due to experimental or previously untried reactors, these standards are apparently being met by operating nuclear power plants. (One exception, the Pathfinder reactor, is noted below.) On these grounds, one might conclude that the problem of radioactive contamination from the nuclear power industry is under excellent control and that there is no need to look further for the "dirty linen."

Speaking as a biologist, I must dispute this claim. A biologist cannot be satisfied with the statement that the radioactive pollutants released by a given nuclear power plant meet design specifications and government standards. He must ask, what radiation is released; how does it move through the web of life; what risks to the integrity of life does it involve; and what are their ultimate costs?

To specify this issue more precisely, let me discuss the problem of the release of radioactive iodine 131 from nuclear power plants. This is one of the inevitable products of nuclear reactions, whether in a bomb or a power plant. Iodine 131 is a short-lived atom; in a matter of a few weeks any of it released into the environment decays of its own accord. However, iodine is an essential part of the hormone produced in the thyroid gland, so that an animal—or child—exposed to even low concentrations of iodine 131 quickly builds the atom into the substance of its thyroid gland. When iodine 131 is incorporated into the thyroid gland and then decays, it leaves behind it, in the cells of that gland, microscopic tracks of severe molecular damage—which may in time lead to harmful biological changes, among which the most serious is thyroid cancer.

Because iodine 131 is a short-lived man-made radioactive element, in the absence of nuclear tests or reactor accidents the environment ought to be totally free of iodine 131—but it is not. Investigators at the University of Nevada who studied the iodine 131 content of cattle thyroids during a several year period (1959-61) in which there were only rare environmental intrusions of iodine 131 from nuclear tests, found that cattle thyroids always contained *some* iodine 131— about one picocurie per gram of thyroid. They concluded:

This constant level in the absence of testing indicates that all the I-131 in the biosphere is not from nuclear explosions. Some other process[es] must be producing I-131 at a reasonably constant rate and in copious quantities. The principal known source of I-131 that could contribute to this level is exhaust gasses from nuclear reactors and associated fuel processing plants.[1]

The most recent results, reported by the U.S. Public Health Service for the period January-March, 1968, are much more striking. In this period of time, in which there were no nuclear explosions capable of nation-wide dispersal of radioactive iodine, such radioactivity was found in cattle thyroids in Georgia, Iowa, Kansas, Louisiana, North Carolina, Oklahoma, South Carolina, South Dakota, Tennessee, and Texas. Average concentrations ranged from 1 to 68 picocuries of radioiodine per gram[2] in the thyroid gland.

Other studies show that when radioiodine appears in the thyroid glands of cattle it also enters the thyroid glands of people. If, as it appears from the available data, this radioactivity is a product of nuclear reactors, then, to evaluate the hidden costs of nuclear power we must determine the hazard to human health represented by iodine 131 taken into human thyroid glands.

[1] C. Blencoe, AEC Contract No. AT (04-3) 34, *Report* TID 17229, 1963, and *Report* CONF-244-1, 1962.
[2] A curie is a measure of the activity or strength of radioactive material. It is expressed in terms of particles emitted per second, or disintegrations per second. One gram of radium has an activity of one curie, and represents a very large quantity of radioactivity. A picocurie is one-millionth of a millionth of a curie.

The government's radiation-control agency, the Federal Radiation Council (FRC), has worked out the relevant radiation protection standards. These are based on a general agreement within the scientific community that *each* increment of radiation, however small, carries with it *some* risk of biological harm.

For iodine 131 the most recent FRC guide states that the average lifetime exposure to the thyroid should not exceed ten rads. One can calculate that if the environment is sufficiently contaminated with radioiodine to deposit a constant level of one picocurie per gram in cattle thyroids, then human beings will be exposed, in a lifetime, to about 0.2 rads of radiation—about one fiftieth of the present FRC guide level. If, as indicated by the more recent results, the radioiodine levels of cattle thyroids are sometimes greater than 50 picocuries per gram, then in these instances human exposures probably have exceeded the present FRC guide level, if only for a time.

Some will take comfort from these numbers, but I do not. In 1967 the Atomic Energy Commission (AEC) projected for 1980 a national level of nuclear power production more than a hundred times greater than the 1960-61 output; for the year 2000, the AEC projects more than a thousandfold increase over the 1960-61 level. In simple economic terms this means that if we are to stay within the present FRC radiation protection guide, the nuclear power industry will need to include in its projected costs of future power development at least a twentyfold improvement (and in view of the most recent cattle thyroid data, probably a much greater improvement) in the technique for restricting the release of iodine 131 into the environment. Obviously this will add to present projections of the cost of producing nuclear power, if indeed such an improvement is technically feasible.

So far I have dealt only with the cost in money—the price of a considerable improvement in the control of iodine 131 released from reactors. But the FRC tells us (in its Staff Report No. 2, of September, 1961) that there is a human cost associated with the acceptance of its guideline—ten rads of radioactive exposure to the thyroid. It states that "*any* radiation exposure involves some risk." There is indeed some risk associated with a ten rad exposure. One calculation suggests that a ten rad dose to the thyroid would increase the national incidence of thyroid cancer about tenfold; another estimate suggests only a 50 percent increase.[3] In any case, if we accept as the

[3] C. W. Mays, *Environment,* Aug. 1966.

price of nuclear power that citizens of the U.S. shall accumulate a radiation exposure of ten rads to their thyroids for however long that industry endures, we must reckon with the knowledge that some people, at some time, will pay that price with their health.

The foregoing evidence shows that, despite assurances, human beings are being subjected to a risk from iodine 131 radiation resulting from the operation of nuclear reactors in the U.S. generally. It is useful to discuss, as well, how this problem relates to a specific reactor, and to pollutants other than iodine 131.

The New York State Electric & Gas Corporation proposes to operate an 830-megawatt nuclear power plant (Bell Station) on the shore of Cayuga Lake. Construction to prepare the site has already begun. In the past year scientists and citizens in Ithaca and the surrounding area have become concerned with the possible environmental hazards that might arise from the operation of Bell Station. Their efforts have resulted in two detailed studies of the problem[4], and we now know a good deal about this particular situation.

If the Bell Station is licensed to operate by the AEC, it will be permitted to release into lake water and the air a certain amount of various radioactive nuclides including tritium, cobalt 58 and 60, strontium 90, iodine 131, and krypton 85. The Ithaca group has calculated the radionuclide concentration that would develop in the water of Cayuga Lake (which would receive the plant's discharge) and concludes that "Concentrations of strontium 90, which could exist in Cayuga Lake after several years of discharge at maximum permissible concentrations, greatly exceed those recommended by the National Technical Advisory Subcommittee for Public Water Supplies and Agricultural Uses," (a committee reporting to the Federal Water Pollution Control Administration). The Ithaca group also points out that Cayuga Lake currently supplies drinking water to a number of nearby communities and private residences.

A newsletter issued by the Citizens Committee to Save Lake Cayuga in November, 1968, also points out that existing reactors of the type proposed for Bell Station (a boiling-water reactor manufactured by the General Electric Company) are known to operate with releases of radiation to the environment which represent appreciable fractions of the total permissible amounts. For example, in 1967 the Humboldt Bay reactor in California released 900,000 curies of noble and activation gases (57 percent of the permissible annual amount),

---

[4] A. W. Eipper, et al., "Thermal Pollution of Cayuga Lake by a Proposed Power Plant," (Ithaca, N.Y.: 1968); E. Abrahamson, et al., "Radioactivity and a Proposed Power Plant on Cayuga Lake," (Ithaca, N.Y.: 1968).

0.64 curie of halogens (including iodine 131) and particulates (11 percent of the permissible amount), and 3.1 curies of liquid effluents (17 percent of the permissible amount). The meaning of these numbers can be inferred from the facts that one curie represents the amount of radioactivity emitted by one gram of radium, and that before the advent of nuclear power, the total world supply of refined radium was less than ten grams. It is also relevant that the Humboldt Bay reactor never operated at full power during 1967 and that the Pathfinder reactor, another boiling-water reactor, exceeded its yearly limit of radioactive release despite being operated below full power and was forced to shut down in October, 1967.

The official Bell Station Preliminary Safety Analysis report issued by the New York State Electric and Gas Corporation states that: ". . . there is reasonable assurance that Bell Station can be constructed and operated at the proposed site without endangering the health and safety of the public."

In view of the evidence I believe that this statement must be regarded as an example of the illusion that the benefits of nuclear power can be enjoyed without risk to man and his environment.

THE HAZARDS OF NUCLEAR TESTS IN NEVADA

One unfortunate feature of an illusion is that it tends to propagate further illusions. In the early 1950's when the AEC conducted a long series of test nuclear explosions at the Nevada Test Site, the nation was assured that ". . . these explosives created no immediate or long-range hazard to human health outside the proving ground."[5] Some of the evidence for the illusory nature of this statement is already well-known: Every teenager who has grown up in the U.S. in the period of the Nevada tests carries in his bones a burden of strontium 90, which generates a potential hazard of bone cancer and leukemia that will not be fully evaluated until many more years have passed. Some members of this generation, particularly in Utah, have absorbed in their thyroids sufficient iodine 131 from Nevada tests to necessitate a medical survey in this area, which has already detected an increased incidence of abnormal thyroid nodules.

Perhaps the most remarkable illusion about fallout has been the conviction that the intensely radioactive material which has been deposited *within* the guarded confines of the Nevada Test Site is also "no immediate or long-range hazard to human health outside the

[5] *Thirteenth Semi-Annual Report of The Atomic Energy Commission,* Jan. 1953, p. 124.

proving ground." This view is based on the assumption that the fall-out hazard arises only from the contamination of food and water (as it does in the case of strontium 90 and iodine 131). Since there is practically no farming in and around the Nevada Test Site, it is assumed that the heavy deposit of radioactivity in the area does not represent a health hazard.

We now have serious reasons to doubt this assumption, for there is evidence that fallout radiation can reach people directly from the soil, in the form of very small dust particles, without passing through the food chain. For example, Dr. Robert Pendleton's recent work in Utah shows that fallout radioisotopes are associated with soil particles which become airborne as dust during harvest operations. The dust particles are very small, in the aerosol range (less than five microns in diameter—less than five-thousandths of an inch). Particles of this size tend to accumulate in the lungs. When a person breathes air containing large dust particles, the particles tend to get trapped in the nose and throat and do not reach the lungs. However, particles in the aerosol range are too small to be trapped in the nose and throat and lodge in the lungs themselves. There they form local radioactive "hot spots," increasing the risk of radiation-induced disease such as cancer. Pendleton regards the radiation exposure to farmers in Utah resulting from such dust heavy enough to be of real concern.

These observations in Utah also raise serious questions about the situation in Nevada. The fallout which reaches Utah is only a small proportion of the total radioactivity produced by nuclear explosions in Nevada. Because of the direction of the prevailing winds most of the fallout that leaves the site immediately after a test goes northeast toward Utah. However, most of the fallout produced by an explosion settles out much closer to the site of the explosion—in and around the Nevada Test Site itself. Therefore, there is a great deal of radioactivity from test explosions in the soil of the test site. It might be reasoned that the fallout that comes down near the site of an explosion must, for that reason, be associated with rather large particles which cannot later be blown about as dust. However, there is no reason to expect that such radioactivity will *remain* attached to large soil particles. Chemical and physical changes in the particles, due to weathering action, readily break up the originally large fallout particles into smaller ones that become airborne in desert winds.

Therefore, the possibility of dispersal of test site radioactivity in windborne dust must be considered very seriously. Some of the relevant evidence is the following:

A recent study of changes in the soil at the Trinity Site (the location of the original nuclear explosion in New Mexico in 1945) shows that there has been considerable soil movement due to wind. The report states that "the action of wind on an arid area is a major factor in soil movement."[6] The report shows that at the Trinity Site about four to six inches of soil have been removed by wind action in a twenty-year period. This means that about one-fourth inch of soil, with considerable radioactivity, has been carried off by wind each year.

A study of the Sedan shot at the Nevada Test Site[7] provides direct evidence that considerable fallout radioactivity at the site is in the form of readily airborne dust. Studies of radioactive dust that deposited on plants at various distances down wind from the explosion showed that "Most of the activity (i.e., radioactivity) deposited on plants in all four study areas was attributable to particles (or aerosols) smaller than those we were able to measure microscopically, i.e., less than five microns diameter." Furthermore, the report shows that an appreciable part of the fallout dust on plants down wind from the shot is removed, apparently by wind action, as time goes on. Thus, this report shows that the Sedan shot produced radioactive aerosol particles and that these can be carried away from the close-in area by wind long after the explosion has taken place.

Pendleton finds that radioactivity is carried by wind from the Nevada Test Site even though no tests are underway. It has been observed that the radioactivity of airborne dust increases sharply in Salt Lake City when there is a strong wind from the southwest. Winds from other directions do not show this effect. This means that winds traveling from Nevada to Salt Lake City carry dust-borne radioactivity.

The largest concentration of population close to the Nevada Test Site is in Las Vegas, a distance of about 65 miles. It would be of interest to know how much of the huge amount of radioactivity deposited on the soil of the site over the years has been carried by wind into Las Vegas. To what extent have radioactive dust particles lodged in the lungs of residents of Las Vegas? To my knowledge, there have been no reported studies of this problem, but I know of one relevant observation: A recent traveler was detained as he passed through a radiation-monitored gate at Kennedy Airport. It

[6] *AEC Research Report* COO-1296-1, 1965.
[7] W. S. Martin, "Interception and Retention of Fallout by Desert Shrubs," *Health Physics* 2:1341.

was found that the dust in his trouser cuffs was sufficiently radio-active to trigger the monitors. The trousers had been worn, not long before, on bird walks in the desert around Las Vegas.

Like the oil spilled from a broken trailer, the lead shed from a moldering wall, or the asbestos flaking from building materials and brake linings, the intensely radioactive soil at the Nevada Test Site does not necessarily remain in its original location. It is a funda-mental law of nature that with time a substance originally concen-trated in a local place must spread into the surrounding environment. It is illusory to expect that pollutants can evade this law.

TECHNOLOGY AND THE MYTH OF OMNIPOTENCE

No optimistic assurances, no government guideline, can give us release from a profound fact of modern life—that the environment exacts a price for the technological intrusions upon it.

The powerful illusion that we can avoid payment of this price is fostered by the enormous accomplishments of technology. Tech-nology is widely credited with many of the good things in modern life: rising agricultural productivity, new sources of power, auto-mated industries, enormously accelerated travel, a vast increase in the volume and speed of communication, spectacular improvements in medicine and surgery. Technology has greatly magnified the wealth that is produced by human labor; it has lengthened our lives and sweetened the fruits of living. All this encourages a faith that tech-nology is an undiluted good.

In a sense, this faith is justified. The modern automobile, or the nuclear reactor, is indeed a technological triumph. In each is em-bodied the enormous insights of modern physics and chemistry, and the exquisite skills of metallurgy, electronics, and engineering. Our success is in the construction of these machines; our failure is in their operation. For once the automobile is allowed out of the fac-tory and into the environment, it is transformed. It then reveals itself as an agent which has rendered urban air carcinogenic, burdened human bodies with nearly toxic levels of carbon monoxide and lead, embedded pathogenic[8] particles of asbestos in human lungs, and contributed significantly to the nitrate pollution of surface waters. Similarly, the design and construction of a nuclear reactor epitomizes all the skills of modern science and technology. However, once it

[8] Carcinogenic means cancer-producing; pathogenic means disease-producing.

begins to operate, it threatens rivers and lakes with its heated waters and human bodies with radiation.

We have already paid a large price for our illusions. For the advantages of automotive transportation, we pay a price in smog-induced deterioration and disease; for the powerful effects of new insecticides, we pay a price in dwindling wildlife and unstable ecological systems; for nuclear power, we risk the biological hazards of radiation; by increasing agricultural production with fertilizers, we worsen water pollution.

Because of our illusions we have become *unwitting* victims of environmental pollution. Most of the technological affronts to the environment were made, not out of greed, but out of ignorance. We produced the automobiles that envelop our cities in smog—long before anyone understood its harmul effects on health. We synthesized and disseminated new insecticides—before anyone learned that they also kill birds and might be harmful to people. We produced synthetic detergents and put billions of pounds into our surface waters— before we realized that they would not be degraded in disposal systems and would pollute our water supplies. For a number of years we spread radioactive fallout across the globe—before we learned that the resulting biological risks made it too dangerous to continue. We have unwittingly killed thousands of sheep in testing our chemical weapons and have triggered unanticipated earthquakes with our nuclear tests. We are now, in Vietnam, spraying herbicides on an unprecedented scale—with no assurance that we know their long-term effects on the life of that unhappy land.

We have come a long way from the days when man could move only as fast as his legs could carry him, when his house was close to the earth and his food was only what he himself could pluck or kill. Man knew then that he was dependent upon nature and was a part of it. We pride ourselves on the technological marvels that make our cities the tallest, our travel the swiftest, our living conditions the most comfortable and our weapons the deadliest of any man has created. Bemused by our own accomplishments, we forget that like our primitive ancestors, we are dependent on the rest of nature.

Primitive man lived by his understanding of nature, but his impact on it was small. We also must live by our understanding of nature, but our impact on it is great and is growing rapidly. We have stressed the web of processes in the living environment at its most vulnerable points, and there is now little leeway left in the system. Unless we learn to match our technological power with an increased understanding of what it is doing to the natural world, we may stress the living environment to the point of collapse, and find that it will no longer support us.

We are still in a period of grace. In that time, let us hope, we can overcome the myth of omnipotence, and learn that the proper use of science is not to conquer the world, but to live in it.

AIR POLLUTION IN CITIES

Robert U. Ayres

It does not seem so long ago that the earth's atmosphere was assumed to be essentially inexhaustible in relation to the foreseeable demands upon it. Los Angeles' smog and London's dirty fogs were considered exceptional, anomalous local situations but, in general, it seemed obvious that there was no actual scarcity of air.[1] On the contrary, air was one of the classic examples (cited by generations of economists) of a good which is free because there is more of it available than could possibly be sold at any finite price.

The above view has rapidly been supplanted by a different and (hopefully) more realistic picture. Today the air—especially the air above cities—is increasingly seen as a scarce and valuable resource whose price is zero not because it is in oversupply but for the more complicated reason that there exists no social institution of ownership or exchange which would permit an economic balance to be struck between incompatible uses through the operation of a competitive free market. If it were not for this "market failure," a party wishing to use the air as a medium for dispersal and disposal of gaseous wastes, for instance, would have to pay some price for this service. Similarly, an individual wishing to utilize the air for breathing would also pay an appropriate price (just as one pays for food).

Robert U. Ayres, "Air Pollution in Cities," NATURAL RESOURCES JOURNAL, *January 1969. Reprinted by permission.*

[1] For instance, in the report of the President's Materials Policy (i.e., Paley) Commission in 1952, there is no mention at all of air. The same is true of H. Brown, J. Bonner, and J. Weir, "Man's Natural and Technological Resources" (1957); and the monumental "Resources in America's Future" (1962) by Landsberg, Fischman, and Fisher.

The first use is incompatible with the second: that is, the utility of the air for breathing is reduced if the atmosphere is used as a sink for residuals of combustion or industrial processes.

A decade or two ago the atmosphere was generally thought of as an immense—virtually limitless—but passive reservoir of air in much the same way that the oceans are reservoirs of water. Currently, however, a more sophisticated ecological notion is coming to the fore. The important element in the air is oxygen, without which life cannot exist. Water is constantly being removed from the ocean as vapor and returned to it again as rain or runoff, but water never changes its basic chemical form. However, oxygen is highly reactive. Oxygen in the air is converted to CO_2 by the metabolic processes of animals (as well as by the combustion of fossil fuels), while CO_2 is essential for plants which fix the carbon but release most of the oxygen. Normally the two processes would be in equilibrium, the oxygen-consuming and oxygen-producing activities being adjusted to one another.

Modern (urban) civilization affects this balance in several ways. In the first place, the combustion of fossil fuels—coal, petroleum products, and natural gas—is producing "extra" carbon dioxide and using up oxygen at a staggering rate.

In the United States in 1965 about 1.3 billion tons of fossil fuels were consumed for all purposes along with 2.74 billion tons of atmospheric oxygen—to yield 3.77 billion tons of CO_2 plus immense tonnages of assorted by-products.[2] In comparison, human respiration requires about 60 millions tons of atmospheric oxygen (for the population of the United States) and produces 98 million tons of CO_2. Based on biomass, the sum total of all animals—mainly cattle—would require less than five times as much oxygen as the human population alone, or somewhere in the neighborhood of 0.3 billion tons and produce 0.5 billion tons of CO_2 at most. Thus industrialization has multiplied the natural rate of oxygen consumption and CO_2 production by factors of 10 and 7½ respectively in North America. Similar, albeit smaller, multipliers exist in other parts of the world.

There are other factors which may also be tipping the balance in the direction of less oxygen and more CO_2, viz., erosion, deforestation and defoliation of large stretches of countryside, the plowing of grasslands for crops—which leaves the ground bare for part of the year—

[2] Carbon and oxygen combine in the ratio of 12 to 32, since the atomic weights are 12 and 16 respectively; coal and natural gas contain approximately 75 percent carbon by weight and petroleum contains about 85 percent carbon.

and the spread of cities and paved areas over sizable areas of productive land. There is evidence also that water pollution may be causing reduced phytoplankton (algae) production in coastal waters.[3] It is far from certain that all the above effects are in the direction of reduced oxygen supply, however. Fertilization of surface waters by organic waste disposal often results in increased algae harvests, and there is even some evidence that higher levels of atmospheric CO_2 stimulate photosynthesis and therefore the oxygen "cycle" and may tend to be self-regulating.[4] Nevertheless, the atmosphere is clearly a finite and extremely valuable resource which is probably being used up or degraded considerably faster than it is being regenerated. It is hardly the unlimited reservoir it was generally imagined to be as recently as a decade or two ago.

As indicated above, the primary use of this resource—to support animal life—is being compromised by other secondary uses of the atmosphere which are not "rationed," as they would be if all such uses were governed by a free competitive market, but are available at no charge to all. The capability of the atmosphere to satisfy all demands put upon it is being exceeded. This is especially so in urban areas where the density of population, as well as commercial and industrial activity, are the greatest.

In the remainder of this paper I shall discuss successively major sources of pollution of the air over cities, physical effects, economic costs, and alternative pollution control policies and technologies.

SOURCES OF POLLUTION

As hinted above, the single most important source of air pollution is energy conversion, especially where the combustion of fossil fuels is involved. It is convenient to consider the problem in four segments: (1) utility electric power generation, (2) transportation (especially

[3] See Winsten, "DDT Reduces Photosynthesis by Marine Phytoplankton," *Science* 1474 (1968): 159.

[4] There is also the possibility that higher levels of CO_2 may result in higher worldwide temperatures, through the well-known "greenhouse effect," which, in turn, may cause shifts in precipitation patterns. The climatic effects of a temperature rise (or fall) are matters of speculation at present. However, mechanisms have been proposed which might suggest quite drastic effects, not excluding a possible new ice-age (resulting from increased precipitation in the form of snow over the arid land areas of northern Canada and Siberia). *See* Conservation Foundation, "Implications of Rising Carbon Dioxide Content of the Atmosphere" (1963).

automotive), (3) industry, and (4) households and commerce in general.

The fuel requirements of each sector are notably different, as shown in the table below.[5]

Sources of Energy Used by Various Sectors
(in person)

	Utility	Trans-portation	Industry	Households and Commercial
Coal	55		29.4	0.4
Petroleum	6	99.85	22.8	38.8
Natural gas	22		39.3	42.8
Utility electricity	[a]	0.15	8.5	14.4
Other	17			3.6
	100	100	100.0	100.0

[a] Not applicable.

In the case of electric power production, minimum cost per British thermal unit BTU) is of paramount importance: thus, natural gas is dominant in the west and southwest, water power in the upper northwest, coal in the midwest and east, and residual oil imported from Venezuela on the east and Gulf coasts. Natural gas is comparatively clean and contributes very little in the way of unwanted emissions (other than CO_2) except for minor quantities of oxides of nitrogen. Coal and residual oil, on the other hand, both normally contain a considerable amount of sulfur (~ 2.5 percent) which burns to form sulfur dioxide (SO_2) and sulfur trioxide (SO_3).

Electric utilities produced an estimated 13.6 million tons of sulfur oxides in 1965, plus 3.7 million tons of oxides of nitrogen, 2.5 million tons of carbon monoxide, and 2.4 million tons of particulates (soot).[6] Oxides of sulfur are toxic in themselves; they also combine with water to form acids (H_2SO_3 and H_2SO_4) which are highly irritating to lungs and bronchial passages as well as to plants, painted surfaces, bare

[5] W. A. Vogely and W. E. Morrison, "Patterns of Energy Consumption in the United States 1947–65 and 1980 Projected," presented at the World Power Conference, Oct. 1966.

[6] R. Ayres and A. Kneese, "Environmental Pollution" in *New Resources in an Urban Age,* edited by Perloff (1969).

metal and—not least—stone (especially limestone or marble, which are rapidly eroded in the presence of atmospheric sulfur oxides).

In the transportation sector, the prime consideration is that the fuel be liquid, for ease of storage and handling. Thus, petroleum products account for all but 0.15 percent of the total (over 300 mil-million tons in 1965) and about 90 percent of this is gasoline—the fuel used by conventional spark-ignited (Otto-cycle) internal combustion engines for automobiles and all except the largest trucks—the remainder being jet fuel (similar to kerosene) and diesel oil.[7]

All of these products are distillates and therefore relatively free of inherent contaminants such as sulfur. However, in order to prevent pre-ignition and "knocking" in internal combustion engines without sacrificing engine performance (by reducing compression ratios) or utilizing more costly aromatics such as xylene and toluene, it is standard practice to add a small quantity of tetraethyl lead to increase the so-called "octane number." However, on a national basis, this amounts to 200,000 tons of lead per year (one sixth of all annual lead production), practically all of which appears as very fine particles in automotive exhausts and is dispersed into the air. Its subsequent pathway through the ecosphere is, at present, largely unknown in detail, although presumably accumulation must be taking place in soil, in plants and animals, and in surface waters.

In addition to additives such as lead, the internal combustion engine is so inefficient that prior to the 1968 model-year as much as 10 percent of the fuel used in automobiles, or 20 million tons on a national basis in 1965, was wasted and dissipated in the atmosphere unburned or partially burned. Carbon monoxide is produced by uncontrolled vehicles, i.e., those without smog-control devices, at the rate of about one pound (equivalent to 7.5 cubic feet of gas) for each two pounds of fuel burned.[8] Assuming the lethal concentration of CO is somewhere in the range of 200 parts per million or 0.02 percent, and assuming each automobile in a city drives 10,000 miles per year and obtains 14.7 miles per gallon—the national average figures[9]—each car will produce roughly 2500 pounds of carbon monoxide in a year, while trucks produce considerably more. This adds up to a national total in the neighborhood of 100 million tons for 1965. This is enough to contaminate nearly one hundred million cubic

[7] W. Vogely and W. Morrison, op. cit.

[8] See President's Science Advisory Comm., *Restoring the Quality of Our Environment* (Nov. 1965).

[9] See Automobile Manufacturing Association, "Automobile Facts and Figures" (1966).

feet of air to the point of lethality. If we further assume an urban population density of 10,000 per square mile with one car or truck for every two persons, a little arithmetic indicates that such a community produces enough carbon monoxide each year to poison *the entire atmosphere above itself*. Clearly, if the carbon monoxide simply accumulated without being dispersed or oxidized to CO_2, cities could not co-exist with automobiles.

Fortunately, due to natural processes, the half-life of carbon monoxide in the atmosphere is apparently fairly short, but peak concentrations as high as 140 parts per million (ppm) have been observed over city streets during periods of heavy traffic.[10] Levels of 40 ppm are thought to be sufficient to have an adverse effect on physiological and mental functions and may be contributory causes of many accidents.

Oxides of nitrogen (NO and NO_2) are also produced by the high-temperature, high-pressure combustion processes characteristic of internal combustion engines—about 5.7 million tons in 1965.[11] These are toxic in themselves, and, together with unburned hydrocarbons, are the main ingredients in the photochemical mixture which constitutes Los Angeles-type "smog."

In addition to gaseous emissions, automotive vehicles are significant sources of particulates. Minor quantities originate in the engine exhausts; others come from mechanical wear, especially rubber from tires and asbestos particles from brake linings. The latter are not directly by-products of combustion, although they are produced mainly because the kinetic energy of vehicular motion is converted into heat as the vehicle is slowed down or brought to a stop.

Although people living in densely populated cities travel by automobile somewhat less than people living in suburbs or smaller towns, the differences on the average are not great. Only in New York City is a significant fraction of total passenger-miles attributed to railroads or rapid transit. Generally speaking, it can be assumed that local trips (50 miles or less) are distributed geographically roughly in proportion to population—which means most of them occur in urban areas—although longer trips would be more likely to utilize intercity or rural routes. However, automobile trips over 100 miles in length account for only 20 percent of total automobile passenger-miles and, presumably, a comparable fraction of overall emissions.[12]

[10] Subpanel on Air Pollution, "Report on the Automobile and Air Pollution: A Program for Progress" (1967).

[11] R. Ayres and A. Kneese, op. cit.

[12] Automobile Manufacturing Association, op. cit.

Industrial processes, especially metallurgy, cement and glass manufacture, and refractories, plus space-heating in households and other buildings, account for the remaining fossil fuel consumption in the United States. All three types of fuel are significantly represented. Thus 188 million tons of coal were used in industry in 1965, of which 96 million were first carbonized, yielding 77 million tons of coke plus coal gas, coal tar, and coal tar derivatives.[13] Low sulfur coal is necessary to produce metallurgical quality coke and the output of low sulfur Pennsylvania and West Virginia sources by the coking industry is mostly tied up by long-term contracts. Coal is no longer used to an appreciable extent for space heating purposes. Thus industry and households together contribute less than electrical utilities to the overall sulfur problem—8.4 million tons of SO_x from these sectors was estimated for 1965. In addition, these sectors yielded 7 million tons of nitrogen oxides (NO_x) and 7 million tons of particulates (soot) and were the major single source of both.[14] Smoke control is, of course, particularly difficult in small heating plants for homes or apartments.

Residuals contributing to urban air pollution arise from two other principal sources: (1) production and processing wastes, and (2) consumption wastes. In the first category one must include such major items as evaporative losses in natural gas production, petroleum refining and petrochemicals, ore beneficiation, and so forth. In the second category must be included not only "final" goods whose ultimate disposal results in combustion (e.g., trash burning), but also a large number of "intermediate" products which never appear physically in a product for final consumption and which are actually dissipated and dispersed into the environment in normal usage. Among this category of products are many which contribute in a major way to air pollution, such as cleaners, solvents, pesticides, explosives, aerosol propellants, and so forth.

Fortunately, a number of the most obnoxious airborne industrial wastes, such as the fluorides which arise from the processing of phosphate rock into "superphosphate" fertilizer, and the sulfur oxides associated with copper, zinc, or lead ore reduction, are not produced in heavily populated areas. Petroleum refining, too, is sometimes restricted to fairly remote locations, although there are also large refineries to serve the local market in most metropolitan areas. Chemical plants in general, however, tend to be situated in or near cities and

[13] R. Ayres and A. Kneese, op. cit.
[14] Id.

these are among the most prolific producers of evil-smelling,[15] corrosive, and irritating fumes.

Among the dissipative intermediates, solvents are the most noteworthy contributors to urban air pollution. This category includes turpentine, benzene, xylene, naphtha, methyl-, ethyl-, and isopropyl alcohols, glycol ethers, acetone, methyl-ethyl-ketone, carbon disulfide, carbon tetrachloride, vinyl chloride, and various other chlorinated hydrocarbons. Most of these substances have a variety of basic chemical uses, so that one cannot simply add up the total quantities produced and assume that it all contributes to air pollution. Nevertheless, this is the ultimate fate of very large tonnages of dry-cleaning agents, paint-removers, diluents and thinners used in many fast-drying paints, varnishes, and lacquers, among others. The function of a solvent is to selectively separate and remove solid substances from places where they are not wanted and/or to permit solids to be deposited easily and uniformly in places where they are needed. The solvent itself may or may not be deliberately thrown away (i.e., allowed to evaporate) after such use, but even if it is distilled and re-used, there is bound to be some loss. If the cycle is repeated frequently, as in commercial dry-cleaning plants, the cumulative loss will be large.

The disposal of "final" goods, such as garbage, household trash, demolition wastes, and junk, may or may not contribute to air pollution, depending on how it is handled. Garbage and trash—about 4 pounds per capita per day, or 150 million tons per year, nationally—are largely ($\sim$80 percent) combustible,[16] whence refuse collection costs can be significantly reduced by incineration at the point of origin. However, local incineration is extremely inefficient and there is virtually no way to control smoke production, in particular. Many cities haul trash and garbage to central locations for processing. Again, to reduce bulk, open burning has been practiced at many such sites—with concomitant ill-effects on the surrounding area. Incineration in enclosed furnaces under controlled conditions is somewhat more efficient, but even so, a significant fraction of the fly ash (and all of the SO_x and NO_x) tends to escape into the atmosphere. Detailed statistics on emissions from refuse incineration are not currently available, but it is clear from materials-balance considerations that if only 100 million tons are burned annually in an uncontrolled manner, of which 20 percent is incombustible, then somewhere in the

---

[15] Particularly, the mercaptans (RHS) including hydrogen sulfide.
[16] Aerojet General Corp., "California Waste Management Study," *Report No. 3056 to the State of California Department of Public Health* (1965).

neighborhood of possibly several million tons of soot is being injected into the atmosphere annually. In New York City about 75 tons of particulates a day are attributed to municipal refuse burning and a further 61 tons a day are attributed to dwellings and apartment houses —of which a significant fraction is also due to incineration.[17] All in all, probably half of all particulates (soot) come from this source.

EFFECTS

This is not the place for a detailed explanation of the physical, physiological and socio-psychological effects of air pollution. It may be of interest, however, to summarize briefly the multitude of ways in which externally induced changes in the chemical composition of its atmosphere may affect the inhabitants of a city.

To begin with, there are direct effects on people, ranging in severity from the lethal to the merely annoying. Fatalities are not, as a rule, traceable individually to the impact of air pollution, primarily because most of the effects are synergistic. Thus, air pollution is an environmental stress which, in cooperation with a number of other environmental stresses, tends to increase the incidence and seriousness of a variety of pulmonary diseases, including lung cancer, emphysema, tuberculosis, pneumonia, bronchitis, asthma, and even the common cold. Statistical studies suggest that most or all of these are definitely correlated with long-term exposure to polluted air.[18] The most dramatic proof of the lethal capabilities of air pollution is the sharp rise in death rates (mainly from the elderly or those already suffering from one or more of the above complaints) during each major air pollution "episode" in a major city. Oft-cited examples include the Meuse Valley, Belgium 1930 (60 deaths); Donora, Pennsylvania 1948 (20 deaths); London 1952 (3500-4000 deaths); New York City 1965 (400 deaths).[19]

For every actual fatality attributable to the effects of pollution, there are many persons who are affected to the point of physical illness and a larger number who may not require medical treatment but who suffer significant annoyance, such as coughing, wheezing, pains in the chest, smarting eyes, and so forth. Finally, there is a still broader class, which probably includes nearly everybody living in an

---

[17] R. Ayres and A. Kneese, op. cit.

[18] They also may be correlated with smoking, malnutrition and other forms of stress. This makes statistical analysis extremely difficult.

[19] See Goldsmith, "Effects of Air Pollution on Health," *Air Pollution* 1, 2d ed. (1968).

urban area, who object to the soot, bad smells, and other visible or sensory manifestations of pollution. Unfortunately, there are no good yardsticks to measure the disutility experienced by each group or the number of people who belong in each classification. However, one rather significant point deserves emphasis. The disutility arising from minor discomfort and essentially aesthetic objections to air pollution is probably the most underestimated and certainly the fastest-growing component of the total problem. This arises from two inter-related factors: (1) the rising level of education on the part of the population and even more rapid rate of increase in the means and possibilities of communications, all of which results in an explosive increase in the level of awareness and general perception of the pollution problem as compared with a few decades ago, and (2) the fact that comfort and aesthetic satisfaction are "superior goods," as many economists have pointed out, and the demand for them grows nonlinearly with general prosperity and affluence, which are themselves rapidly increasing. Here lies the explanation of the superficially paradoxical fact that a generation ago belching smokestacks were welcomed, as indicators of full employment, whereas today they are more likely to be taken as symbols of technological obsolescence and management irresponsibility.

Direct effects on humans have parallels in the animal and plant worlds. Animals of economic importance (livestock) are not co-located to any appreciable extent with cities and can safely be overlooked in the present context. Effects on pets (dogs, cats and birds) almost certainly exist, although they have not been much documented. To the extent that the effects are chronic, perhaps resulting in discomfort and life-shortening for the animal, the disutility to humans may not be very great in most cases. In fact, since more kittens and puppies are born than are needed to satisfy the demand for pets, replacements of nonpedigreed animals can be had at virtually zero price.[20]

As far as plants are concerned, much the same situation holds. Crops are mostly some distance away from cities, and hazards are likely to be rather special in nature (e.g., fluorides from superphosphate plants, or sulfur oxides from copper smelters). However, there are some districts where truck crops—mostly fruits and vegetables—are grown in close juxtaposition to major cities. This is particularly true of Connecticut, Long Island, New Jersey, eastern Pennsylvania,

[20] Pets are valued highly once they become "part" of a family, but their value declines later on as they become elderly and decrepit.

and Delaware, and of southern California between San Diego and Santa Barbara where citrus growers still exist in considerable abundance. Agricultural damage in the citrus belt of southern California seems to be due mainly to oxidants, such as ozone and peroxy-acyl-nitrate,[21] which are produced by the interaction of unburned hydrocarbons, oxides of nitrogen, and strong sunlight. In the mixed truck-farming region of the Middle Atlantic states (potatoes, tomatoes, leafy vegetables, green peas, sweet corn, apples, peaches, dairy and poultry farming), the major cause of damage seems to be sulfur which often causes leaf-spotting and discoloration—reducing the market value of the product—and sometimes stunted growth or worse. In suburban gardens and city parks, there are deleterious effects on shrubs, flowers, and shade trees.

As with direct effects on human health, it is difficult to unambiguously trace a given symptom or a case of stunted growth to a particular air pollutant. Again, air pollution must be considered an environmental stress, along with drought, extremes of temperature, or pest outbreaks. Very often—in fact, probably in the majority of instances—a healthy organism can withstand a single moderate stress but not two or three different stresses at the same time. Another way of looking at the matter is to say that exposure to constant stress from air pollution tends to weaken the plants' resistance to other environmental stresses, such as cold winters or dry, hot summers. Thus part of the excess mortality associated with events of the latter type should be attributed to the abnormal stress of air pollution, just as part of the excess mortality which might follow a very severe air pollution "episode" might fairly be attributable to the extra cold winter or an extra wet spring. Again, there are no satisfactory methods of allocating the observed damages among a number of synergistically interacting multiple causes, nor can the damages themselves be adequately measured and reduced to economic terms.

A third category of effects comprises damage to property. Here again, sulfur and oxidants are perhaps equally potent. As noted previously, sulfur oxides combine with water to form sulfurous acid (H_2SO_3) and the much more corrosive sulfuric acid (H_2SO_4). These acids will damage virtually any exposed mental surface and will react especially strongly with limestone or marble (calcium carbonate). Sulfur oxides will also cause discoloration, hardening and embrittle-

---

[21] Brandt and Heck, "Effects of Air Pollution on Vegetation," *Air Pollution* 1, 2d ed. (1968).

ment of rubber, plastic, paper, and other materials. Oxidants such as ozone will also produce the latter type of effect. Of course, the most widespread and noticeable of all forms of property damage is simple dirt (soot), which has some secondary effects of its own. Thus, if shirt collars can be worn twice, the shirt itself will last approximately twice as long as if the shirt requires laundering after only one day— since a shirt's useful life is essentially measured in terms of the number of washings it undergoes, rather than the number of days it is worn.[22] Of course, airborne dirt also affects other clothing, furniture, carpets, drapes, exterior paintwork, and automobiles. It leads to extra washing, vacuum cleaning, dry-cleaning, and painting; and, of course, all of these activities do not entirely eliminate the dirt, so that people also must live in darker and dirtier surroundings.

A final category comprises bio-climatic and ecological effects. On the urban scale, it is known that there are distinct, measurable differences between the climate in a city and in its environs. Thus temperatures and humidity are higher, precipitation and cloud cover are slightly more frequent, fog is much more common (especially in winter), and so forth.[23] These differences are almost certainly due in part to the large amount of waste heat generated in cities and very likely also owe a debt to the concentration of particulates (which can serve as condensation nuclei for fog, for instance) and possibly some of the other residuals which are commonly dispersed in the air over cities.

On the continental scale, of course, one must begin to worry seriously about major perturbations to the climate which might be caused by the (apparently) rising level of atmospheric CO_2, as noted earlier. If, as has been suggested, the "greenhouse effect" leads to higher temperatures and results in melting the massive accumulations of ice in Greenland and Antarctica, one obvious consequence would be a distinct rise in the sea-level and a considerable problem for low-lying coastal cities. The rise would occur gradually, over centuries, permitting either evacuation or the building of dikes and protective walls, but in either event the consequences would be quite important for many urban dwellers. On the other hand, it has also been suggested that higher temperatures might trigger a new ice age

----

[22] Our grandfathers' generation got around this difficulty by utilizing detachable collars, but this frugal custom has disappeared in the United States. It still survives, to some degree, in coal-burning London—where the celluloid "white collar" was once the universal badge of a clerical—and hence middle-class—job.

[23] See Lowrey, "The Climate of Cities," *Scientific American* (Aug. 1967).

which would have precisely the opposite effect. If this were to happen, a number of seaports would be stranded, like gasping fish, away from deep water.

COSTS

The notion of pollution "cost" is somewhat more elusive than it might at first appear to be. Although one may be forced by practical considerations to take a very simplistic view of the matter in the end, it seems worthwhile to mention some of the underlying difficulties in the concept. Quantitative national estimates of the cost of air pollution are relatively few and, with rare exceptions, not very illuminating.[24]

The usual approach is to add up dollar expenditures, such as extra cleaning or hospital bills, which would not be necessary if there were no pollution, plus lost future income and call these the "cost" of pollution. There are two immediate and cogent objections to this procedure, however. The first is that many, if not most, of the most important disutilities of pollution are not reflected by any such dollar expenditures. Clearly, hospital or burial costs, or even the present value of lost future income, are a poor measure of the value of a human life.[25] In the very large number of cases where the disutilities are sensory and aesthetic, no dollar value at all is allowed by such a measure.

Clearly, what is wrong here is that the real benefits which air pollution has deprived us of—life, health, and clean fresh air—are provided free. But they are free *not* because they exist in oversupply,[26] but because there exists no market in which they can be exchanged and priced. We have, at present, no satisfactory way of attaching a dollar sign to the loss of a free benefit. However, it is misleading and quite incorrect to assume explicitly or implicitly that the loss should be counted as zero.

[24] This literature has been reviewed and summarized in the presentation by A. V. Kneese, "How Much is Air Pollution Costing Us?" National Conference on Air Pollution (Washington, D.C.: Dec. 12-14, 1966).

[25] The absurdity of this measure is clear if we note that according to it men are "worth" 70 percent more than women at age 20, but men and women have equal expectations at age 60, with the relative values reversed by age 70. Again, by this measure, an individual is "worth" much more if he dies slowly and agonizing in a hospital than if he dies at home in his sleep.

[26] The population explosion notwithstanding. Each individual only has one life to live, some threescore and ten years (give or take a few) in length.

The second fundamental objection to equating pollution costs with dollar expenditures which would not otherwise be made is the elementary fact that, in an exchange economy, an expense to one individual results in an income to another. Thus the extra cleaning costs noted previously result in extra income for the laundry. There is no *a priori* way of balancing the utilities and disutilities resulting from such a transaction since they depend upon the alternatives which exist for each party. For the person forced to spend more of his income on cleaning than he otherwise would, the welfare loss to him is the difference between the amount of satisfaction he would have received from spending a few cents per day in other ways *vis-à-vis* the satisfaction received from spending it on laundry.

For the economy as a whole, the question is more complicated: it boils down to the comparison of alternative patterns of expenditure and forms of employment for capital and certain categories of labor. If unskilled labor is in short supply, the use of it in a laundry is wasteful of resources, but if it is in over-supply, the alternative might be unemployment. There is no easy universal formula for measuring the marginal social utility of money spent on a particular good or service. Each case would have to be judged on its merits.

However, in a society such as the United States where neither labor nor capital is fully utilized under normal circumstances, it seems likely that, *ceteris paribus,* extra costs imposed by pollution do have some compensating economic benefits in creating employment for otherwise hard-to-employ workers. This is not to say that other forms of socially useful employment may not be found in the future, but at the present time it is probable that money now spent on extra laundry, cleaning, and maintenance produces more jobs for unskilled and semi-skilled labor than alternative modes of expenditure (e.g., on durable goods) would do. This being so, the sum total of dollar expenditures would have to be reduced by the net (dollar) benefits thereby produced to arrive at an estimate of net dollar costs.[27]

The fact is that any change in the pattern of consumption and expenditure has its effect on production and prices also. The example given above postulated that a change in expenditure patterns might result in a reduced demand for certain types of labor which are currently in oversupply.[28] Similarly, in another sphere, it must be pointed

[27] It is not impossible that the dollar benefits actually exceed the dollar costs, although this may seem a bit far-fetched at first.
[28] Of course, in principle, the reverse could also happen, which would be no less important (but with opposite implications) if true.

out that the economic distortion resulting from the fact that residuals can be disposed of into the environment without cost—or at too little cost—implies that certain products and services are probably being sold too cheaply, whereas others may be more expensive than they would be if *all* goods and services—including those provided by the environment—were exchanged only in a free competitive market.[29]

Electric power is a good case in point. It is produced as cheaply as it is in certain areas only because the electric utilities are allowed to use the air as a place to dispose of smoke and excess heat, without cost. If an economic price were charged for this service, the cheapest means of producing electric power might involve a different technology, and it might conceivably be more expensive.[30] Since electric power is an input to essentially all other industries, production costs would rise in other sectors of the economy. If aluminum production, for instance, depended to any extent on electric power from coal or oil-burning plants (which it does not), the price of aluminum would, in turn, have to be raised. This would affect the price of kitchenware, aircraft, and other products.

Speaking generally, the effects of air pollution on the economy include the sum total of all distortions[31] and implicit readjustments of the above type. To estimate these quantitatively would involve first knowing what the entire economy would be like if these distortions did not exist. A rather elaborate analysis of each industry would be required to estimate what its production costs would be on the basis of an altered set of input costs, including hypothetical payments for environmental services. From the revised set of prices (based on existing demand and elasticities), a new set of demands would have to be derived. From these, in turn, further revisions in calculated prices would be made. Thus, by iteration, a picture of the hypothetical

---

[29] In this context, the availability of assimilation capacity for residuals is a service rendered by the environment, for which an appropriate price should be paid, while the provision of unwanted residuals (such as soot or gaseous effluents) constitutes a disservice for which there should be a compensation corresponding to a negative price.

[30] Actually, it would necessarily be more expensive under the altered ground rules only *if* the present technology were the cheapest one available. This is probably not the case in most big cities, however, since nuclear plants are now cheaper than almost any existing fossil fuel plants, except where coal or oil is available locally. New facilities are overwhelmingly nuclear and if all doubts regarding safety and radioactive waste disposal were resolved, most existing fossil fuel plants in big cities would be replaced by nuclear power plants.

[31] Again, this refers to the fact that certain economic services rendered by the environment are exchanged at zero price, which would not be the case in a perfectly operating free competitive market.

undistorted economy could be derived—assuming one had a reasonable method of assigning virtual prices to the environmental services which are currently free.[32]

Assuming full employment (or making any other reasonable assumption about labor utilization), the GNP of the hypothetical "undistorted" economy could be computed by a linear programming model and compared with the actual one. However, this does not necessarily bring us closer to a realistic estimate of the cost of air pollution, since what counts is the *welfare* output—i.e., the total satisfaction provided—by the two economies. Once more we are reminded that welfare or satisfaction includes many things which are not bought or sold in a competitive market, and it is entirely possible, although not necessarily true, that the "undistorted" economy would produce fewer material goods or a smaller GNP, but greater welfare than our present one.

In summary, the overall costs of air pollution would be the sum of three terms, as follows:

disutility or losses of non-market ("free") benefits (life, health, aesthetics)	+	disutility or net direct dollar expenditures (e.g., laundry, medical costs, etc.)	+	disutility (or utility) of net indirect dollar costs (or benefits) to society (e.g., employment, distorted prices, etc.)

Of these three terms, the first has implicitly been assumed to be zero, although most analysts realize that this is unrealistic. The second term has been computed although the existing studies still leave much to be desired.[33] The third term has been ignored completely, possibly because first-order approximations may well be negative (i.e., beneficial to society in dollar terms) and no economist has wished to appear to say that "air pollution is good for you," however qualified that statement would be. Actually the numerical comparison of dollar costs and benefits appears to be unimportant in comparison with the glaring omission of the first term of the three: the physical and psychic losses for which we have no convenient dollar price tags. It is not acceptable to say that these kinds of losses are not zero, or even to say that they are large but inherently unquantifiable. The problem remains, however,

[32] This problem is discussed in Ayres and Kneese, "Production Consumption, and Externalities" to be published in *The American Economic Review* (1969).
[33] The best estimates are those by R. Ridker, "Economic Costs of Air Pollution: Studies in Measurement" (1965).

to estimate them quantitatively *in terms of dollars,* which is the only existing available measure of utility (or disutility).

Fortunately it is not quite accurate to say that there exists no marketplace in which the services and/or disservices provided by air pollution are exchanged. Literally speaking, this is so, but there is one market where the impact of these services/disservices is felt and can be measured: real estate. To quote Ridker,

If the land market were to work perfectly, the price of a plot of land would equal the sum of the present discounted stream of benefits and costs derivable from it. . . . Since air pollution is specific to locations and the supply of locations is fixed, there is less likelihood that the negative effects of pollution can be significantly shifted onto other markets. We should, therefore, expect to find the majority of effects reflected in this market, and can measure them by observing associated changes in property value.[34]

To the above, it should be added that the real estate market, like others, is very imperfect. In this case, the crucial flaw is the lack of perfect information on the part of purchasers. It would have been equally accurate and more appropriate to say that the price of a plot of land reflects the sum of present values of *anticipated* (i.e., perceived) future benefits and costs derivable from it. The point of this remark is that the vast majority of real estate buyers have essentially no knowledge at all of the more acute medical effects of air pollution—which are still being argued in highly abstruse terms even among doctors. Hence, it is apparent that the latter are not being taken into account in land prices. What the real estate market primarily reflects is the tangible, experiential aspects of pollution: more rapid deterioration and extra cleaning and maintenance costs, the milder medical symptoms, such as shortness of breath and smarting eyes, plus bad smells and dirt. Ridker assumed—justifiably, no doubt—that these problems would be closely correlated with sulfur dioxide emissions. Eight "sulfation zones" were identified in St. Louis, and it was found by survey that average property values varied by about $250 per lot, per zone, other things remaining equal.[35]

Assuming an annual discount rate[36] of 6–8 percent, this presumably can be interpreted to mean that the marginal utility of a shift from one sulfation level to the next is about $15-$20 for a lower middle-class or middle-class city-dweller. The marginal utility of a

[34] R. Ridker, "Strategies for Measuring the Cost of Air Pollution," *The Economics of Air Pollution* (1966).

[35] Id.

[36] The "discount rate" is equivalent to the average annual increase in value of alternative investments. To find the present value of a dollar-benefit to be received some years in the future one asks "what is the dollar amount which, if we invested it at 6-8%, would equal the specified amount at the appropriate time?"

shift from the highest to the lowest sulfation level was evidently about $150 to $200 per year, on the basis of the rather narrow spectrum of tangible disservices (maintenance, odor, soot) mentioned above.

The amount which a fully knowledgeable real estate buyer would add to this to allow for the more serious, but rarer conditions, such as lung cancer and emphysema—whose link with air pollution is apparent statistically but not causally—is much harder to estimate. It has been observed that a human life is worth more to society than the simple discounted present value of future earnings, and acknowledged, also, that its value must nevertheless be finite, rather than infinite.[37] Limited guidance may perhaps be derived from the upper range of awards of juries in cases of accidental injury or death in cases where the negligent party is insured and can be presumed to have unlimited resources. Such awards nowadays often run above $250,000.

In the future, better information may come from sophisticated polling techniques, designed to elicit "willingness to pay." It is well known that simple questions, like "what would you be willing to pay to avoid (or gain) so and so," yield misleading answers.[38] However, there are methods of reducing, if not eliminating, some of these secondary interactions between the pollster and the person being polled. It is possible that more meaningful answers can be obtained to questions like "would you accept a 1-in-10 chance of dying within 5 years in exchange for X thousand dollars?" Indeed, there are several professions—such as bullfighting and auto-racing—which offer opportunities (but not certainties) of large rewards in exchange for very high risks of injury or death. By analyzing data from polls, together with actual statistics for risky professions, it should be possible to cast much more light into this area of ignorance.

Whether by these methods, or others, only when the problem of putting a dollar value on illness and death has been grappled with, will it be possible to estimate the costs of pollution and the benefits of pollution control.

ALTERNATIVE CONTROL POLICIES AND TECHNOLOGIES

This topic is a broad one which can only be skimmed in an overview such as this. As regards basic policies, there is a continuum of

[37] Notwithstanding the irreplaceable uniqueness of each personality and each soul.

[38] Since the person queried actually pays nothing to have his opinion recorded, he can make very extreme statements in the hope of indirectly influencing policy makers.

possibilities, depending largely on where the policy-maker stands with respect to one basic philosophical issue: the value of the free market as a method of allocating resources and incomes in our society. If the free market is deemed to be a mechanism worth preserving and improving, then the appropriate method of minimizing the disutilities[39] arising from air pollution is to recognize the fact that most of them arise from market failures and thus to attempt to eliminate these failures or find means of compensating for them. If, on the other hand, the free market *per se* is not felt to be important, then there is no basic objection to strictly pragmatic *ad hoc* responses, even though the latter may perpetuate or worsen the fundamental market failures. As a matter of observation, existing approaches to the problem of control tend to be of the latter type.

A classic market-preserving approach essentially attempts to eliminate externalities by "internalizing" them. On the government level this approach leads to regional compacts and "super agencies." In the private sector, however, the standard method of internalization—merger—is not available in most cases.[40]

The next alternative is to eliminate the effect of the market imperfections (if not the imperfections themselves) by attaching prices to *all* services—and disservices—which, are now rendered "free" by the atmosphere. This means dollar exchanges, positive or negative as the case warrants, would be imposed for:

(1) private use of air as an input for any purpose,

(2) private use of the assimilative capacity of the atmosphere, for any purpose,

(3) inadvertent or unwanted material inputs *from* the air.

A formal scheme for incorporating such exchanges in the general equilibrium theory of economics has been described elsewhere.[41] In practice, the charges for air used for breathing would be very low since the quantity available greatly exceeds any possible near-term demand for this purpose. Charges for oxygen used for combustion might be the same, per unit, but would be greater in total. Charges

[39] As distinguished from *effects,* which are strictly physical.

[40] The most extreme example would be public ownership of all sources of pollution (which essentially means all productive facilities and all energy-converting devices). This eliminates externalities as such, by merging the producers and consumers into one unit, but it also eliminates competition—another important feature of the free market—and has a very serious problem with respect to its "internal" operation, including the question of allocation of resources. Thus public ownership essentially begs the question rather than solving it.

[41] Ayres and Kneese, "Production, Consumption, and Externalities."

for accepting CO_2 might be waived (as being covered by the charge for oxygen) but there would be additional charges for using the atmosphere as a sink for other products of inefficient combustion. On the other hand, persons inadvertently receiving unwanted inputs from the atmosphere, such as smog or soot, would receive appropriate compensation.

The important point is that if all these services and disservices were exchanged on a market, there would be *finite* prices attached to them. While such a market cannot exist in actuality as long as the air is held in common as a public good, there may be means of simulating the relevant effects of such a market: namely, the exchanges of money and the adjustments in productive processes and technology which would inevitably follow. One such simulacrum is the proposed "effluent tax," which would require a residuals producer to pay the government (as a surrogate for the public) in proportion to the quantity of residuals dispersed in the environment.

Without belaboring the point unduly, an illustration may be worthwhile. At the present time, in the absence of either a market exchange mechanism or an effluent charge, an electric utility may produce any amount of soot it pleases.[42] Its products are: (1) electricity and (2) soot (disregarding other effluents for the moment). It buys fuel, sells electricity, and "gives away" its soot, and chooses the cheapest possible fuel. Suppose, however, that the utility is no longer allowed to give away its co-product, soot, but must pay its neighbors a price to accept it. Then it can do one of two things: it can continue to use the same fuel and the same combustion technology and simply charge more for the electricity, or it can shift to a cleaner fuel, use precipitators in the stacks, and reduce the output of soot. Since the demand for electricity will decrease if the price rises, profit considerations dictate that the electric utility will seek to keep the price of power low by finding cheap ways of eliminating the soot. Within a few years the "price" of eliminating soot will fall drastically, since many people will have a positive incentive to reduce it.

The *ad hoc* approach, which does not seek to preserve or improve the free competitive market, encompasses any number of variants, although the most common are the enforcement of arbitrary standards and subsidies. The first is a simple statement that emissions from such-and-such a process or engine shall not exceed a given amount, together with an appropriate amount of enforcement. Theoretically, this method might result in standards being set unrealistically low (or

---

[42] Except as limited by ad hoc smoke control laws.

even at "zero"), although in practice the proposed standards are invariably modified by considerations of what the affected industry
says is feasible. Unfortunately, the industry never really knows what
it could do, at what price, and neither does anybody else. Worse,
there is an historic tendency on the part of industry to grossly exag-
gerate the costs of any change whatever. The result is that standards
are almost invariably much too lenient.

The most popular approach, with industry, is government subsidy,
or—equivalently—tax credit. Unfortunately, by over-estimating the
cost, it is sometimes possible to make a sizable windfall profit.[43] On
the other hand, it is the case that certain industries would be severely
damaged by a strict application of an effluent tax or even by the imposition of a realistic standard of emissions. While it seems difficult to
justify making exceptions in favor of established interests, it is also
inequitable, in some pertinent sense, to hurt or eliminate an industry
by suddenly changing the rules of the game. This problem is not
hypothetical: for example, the leather industry, for one, can probably
not afford to clean up and remain competitive with synthetics.[44] In
time, other industries based on natural products (sugar refining, paper, etc.) may face the same problem. Thus a case could be made
for a public buy-out or a temporary subsidy to ease the period of
transition.

Passing from policy to technology, there are two basic approaches:
symptomatic treatment and process change. The first approach comprises the gamut of smoke precipitators, stack gas absorbers, filters
and washers, afterburners and catalytic mufflers for automobiles, etc.
These devices add complexity and cost to residuals-producing processes. Moreover, since the quantity of residuals is not actually decreased by add-on devices, the problem is very often merely shifted
from one medium to another. Thus sulfur dioxide can be removed
from stack gases by "washing"—but the sulfur-laden water still constitutes a disposal problem which may not be any less serious in magnitude. However, in some cases—as in the case of seaports—disposal
in this manner may be preferable to use of the air as a sink. Disposal as a solid, as with fly ash precipitated from stacks, would

---

[43] A typical method is to ascribe entirely or mostly to pollution control a large
capital investment which would have been made anyway. It takes a very alert and
knowledgeable bureaucrat to detect this sort of cheating.

[44] However, it must be remembered that if hides had no market, they would
be a disposal problem for meat packers; hence, the equilibrium market solution
would involve an appropriate payment from the meatpackers to the leather industry (in lieu of disposal costs), thus eliminating the need for a public subsidy,
but probably raising the price of meat.

virtually always be advantageous. (Indeed, this material has several potential markets, e.g., as insulation or filler). In the case of automobile exhausts, the main problem arises from inefficient combustion, rather than impurities in the fuel, and afterburners do perform a useful service if they simply reduce the amount of unburned or partially burned material which escapes.

The alternative basic approach is, in the long run, more promising, however. It is to decrease the amount of residuals produced by fundamental process changes. In the case of electric utilities, this may be done by shifting from high sulfur to low sulfur oil; or by using natural gas or gassified desulfurized coal. Conversion to electricity may also be carried out nearer the mine, thus reducing transportation costs as well as reducing residuals load (which includes heat as well as combustion waste products) on the urban airshed. A shift to nuclear power also will reduce the problem of combustion-by-products, although the thermal pollution problem will be worse and a new problem of radioactive waste disposal must still be faced. Ultimately, however, controlled thermonuclear reactions (fusion power) promises to eliminate most of the presently envisaged residuals problems, including the latter.

Combustion wastes from automotive vehicles can also be drastically reduced by changing the basic technology. The least disruptive change would involve a switch from the internal combustion engine (ICE) to an external combustion engine (ECE). It has been concluded elsewhere that a modern Rankine-cycle reciprocating ECE using steam or a synthetic working fluid with appropriate characteristics—such as one of the Freons—would provide very satisfactory service in all automotive applications with no sacrifice in power, weight, effective range, smoothness of operation or fuel consumption efficiency. Indeed, the evidence suggests that such an engine, mass-produced, would be simpler, cheaper to manufacture, longer-lived, and more economical to operate than the ICE.[45]

In the longer-term, electric propulsion for vehicles may be in the cards, since there is very rapid progress in battery and fuel cell technology, under the stimulus of military and space requirements. Extrapolating the recent rate-of-change in battery and fuel cell capabilities for another decade or two suggests that by 1985 or so, an electric car, using a fuel cell for primary power and batteries for peak power

[45] See R. Ayres, "Environmental Pollution." For a more thorough exposition, see R. Ayres, "Technology and Urban Transportation: Environmental Quality Considerations," to be published in *Resources for the Future* (Johns Hopkins University Press, 1969).

needs, will be economically and technologically competitive if marketed in such a way as to take advantage of its very low operating costs.[46]

Either an external combustion engine or the battery/fuel-cell option would reduce the emissions problem very drastically even from levels contemplated for 1985 by the large automobile manufacturers. To explore the circumstances under which a process-change of this magnitude might occur in an industry as massive and entrenched as the automotive industry is a major topic in itself and cannot be undertaken here.

However, there is good reason to believe that expenditures of government money may be most effective when, and to the extent that, they help to bring about process changes or large-scale technological substitutions such as the above. Thus, the technology of utility electricity generation has begun to reflect the massive federal government support of nuclear research. The government also can exert leverage by taxing a socially "undesirable" activity, or by explicitly creating a market for a desirable one through its own purchases. Indeed, the most likely way of encouraging the creation of a modern "steam-power" industry would be to specify that procurement for government agencies, the Post Office, police and so forth must utilize external combustion engines rather than internal combustion engines for propulsion. This strategy has not yet been tested, but it appears promising enough to warrant very serious consideration.

[46] This probably implies rental on a mileage basis in a manner analogous to the way Xerox copiers and electronic computers are rented currently. See R. Ayres, "Technology and Urban Transportation."

WHO'S GOING TO TAKE OUT THE GARBAGE?

Charles Einstein

The subject of this article is trash. That is said, I hope, not so much in self-criticism as to delineate at the outset a problem of near-staggering dimension. The accumulation, removal and disposal of what America wastes has reached, in more than one place, the point of no return.

Charles Einstein, "Who's Going To Take Out the Garbage?" WEST *Magazine* (LOS ANGELES TIMES), *March 2, 1969. Reprinted by permission.*

The situation locks itself in an impenetrable thicket of financial, logistical, even technological helplessness. It is the chief breeder of air and water pollution. It is sociological—no single piece of legislation has so defined the urban crisis as the rat bill that went before the congress during its last session. Inevitably, it is political—Mayor Sam Yorty of Los Angeles took to national television at one point to plead his trash-collecting woes, and at least one nationally-syndicated columnist has proclaimed that the New York City garbage strike was what kept Nelson Rockefeller from becoming President of the United States.

The thing even involves itself with love, not to mention pure sex. Not long ago, an article called *39 Ways to Be A Great Date* appeared in a national woman's magazine. Of the 39 steps, the three most important were, of course, saved for last: "Kiss him unexpectedly . . . Cook him a delicious meal 'just because' Never, no matter what, even if you're playing Camille's death scene, ask him to take out the garbage."

The only trouble is, if he doesn't, who will? And how? And where? And at what cost? At a recent conference on human ecology, a science which explores the interplay between man and his environment, already-nervous delegates were told that the United States—ever the leader in progress—now produces a ton of garbage per person per year. To get rid of it, according to a U.S. Public Health service estimate, runs up a bill of $3 billion. The annual cost to New York City alone is about $150 million.

Special extra problems abound. Some of them are quixotic. Today, experts are turning more and more to the recourse of burying garbage, as opposed to burning it, dumping it, processing it, or drowning it in the sea. Yet New York City, instead of burying it, excavates it: Thirty tons of trash a day are brought up from the subways. Similarly, paper was made to be burned, but not in Los Angeles, whose smog-wary laws forbid it. And consider, if you please, the question of what Hawaii is supposed to do with its worn-out automobiles. They simply accumulate. No car ever leaves the state under its own power: that first mile is a wet one.

One particularly distressing element in the overall situation has been the technological ability to provide short-range solutions and an accompanying sense of false comfort. These two things are proving, in combination, ever more deadly. The neo-classic example here was the decision of health authorities in North Borneo to eliminate malaria by spraying the villages with DDT. This did exactly what it was supposed to do: it killed the malaria-carrying mosquitoes. But more resistant cockroaches absorbed the DDT and survived. In turn, the roaches were eaten by larger creatures who in turn were eaten by cats. The DDT killed the cats. Without cats there were rats. "Unintentionally," reported the United Press International in a deadpan dispatch, "the health authorities had traded the threat of malaria for the threat of plague."

What is even worse in this connection is the fact that science, in its forward acceleration, outstrips itself. The DDT that killed 98 percent of the mosquitoes bred a new and even more virulent generation of DDT-resistant mosquitoes among the two percent that survived. Getting back to garbage, this can be related to the disposal equipment in the kitchen sink, without which no new home in today's real-estate market can be called complete. Here again appears the false sense of comfort. The more in-the-sink disposal units that are made, the more other products are made that the disposal unit doesn't know how to get rid of. The housewife of today will buy the can of frozen orange juice in preference to oranges themselves. But her kitchen disposal, which would have ground up the orange peels, can not grind up the can. In like vein, the same clothes-washing machine which sent soap in soluble form into the sewer system now discharges the scientific successor to soap—the detergent—in a clogging, insoluble mass.

The point has been reached, in truth, where it is totally likely that a routine housewife, doing a routine shopping, can arm herself in advance with the latest mechanisms for garbage disposal and yet come home equipped exclusively with products these latest mechanisms do not know how to get rid of. What used to be a large paper bag of potato chips became instead a large bag enclosing twelve "individual serving" bags. Result: 13 bags instead of one. To tempt the housewife even further, the food and packaging people brought out the "baker's dozen." Result: 14 bags instead of 13.

The whole industrial tendency of the container and packaging industries has been to create things the latest advances in waste-disposal can not keep pace with. An Associated Press survey showed recently that consumer waste products include, on an annual basis, four million tons of plastics, more than 30 million tons of paper, 48 billion cans, and 26 billion bottles and jars. To this, science has added aluminum foil, nonreturnable bottles, disposable diapers, and that ultimate contribution to our culture: the tray that comes with the TV dinner. Supermarket meat comes wrapped; what do you do with the wrapping? A half of a baked potato comes in a container; what do you do with the container? A new clothes dryer comes in a carton, and the problem of getting rid of the carton is about the same as it always was. But what do you do with the old dryer? The AP reports that DeKalb County in Georgia estimates it's disposing of 30 percent more junked appliances than a year ago. In Indianapolis, the report continues, seven new double-capacity garbage trucks have been put into service just in an effort to stay even with the overabundance of abandoned refrigerators, ranges and washing machines. "Everybody likes to eat, but nobody likes to do the dishes," one official has said. "Everybody likes to drive a car but nobody likes to provide it a decent burial." Indeed, the only decent burial publicly afforded to an automobile in recent times has been the job done on the new car by the automatic baler-compressor in the motion picture *Goldfinger*. This mighty machine turned the automobile into a solid cube. Unfortunately, there was a man inside it at the time.

The *Goldfinger* idea may yet take hold. Consider, for instance, the plight of John F. Ward, the purchasing agent for the city of Chicago, who a few weeks ago received an official request for 2,000 pounds of corrugated boxes, 1,000 pounds of newspapers, 600 pounds of heavy brown wrapping paper, 350 pounds of waxed milk cartons, 600 pounds of dry magazines, 250 pounds of junk office mail, 150 pounds of tissue paper, 1,100 pounds of tin cans, 400 pounds of aluminum cans, 150 pounds of plastic products and 200 pounds of chicken wire, as well as some "assorted household waste materials."

"Last year we had an average of a million dollars a day in requisitions," Ward said. "But nothing like this."

The request was a serious one. It came from James M. McDonough, acting commissioner of streets and sanitation, who wanted to test a new compression machine which would form the garbage into bales, for dumping into Lake Michigan as fill. Nevertheless, the notion that Chicago does not produce enough garbage, so that for this research purpose he had to go out and buy some, struck the purchasing agent as unusual.

"But you can't just take plain old garbage on the trucks for the tests and bale it," sanitation chief McDonough said, in defense of his requisitions. "You have to know, specifically, what is in there." Unfortunately, so long as the baling process depends to any real degree on a measured admixture of ingredients, it will be near impossible to apply on a large-scale basis.

The statistics on automobiles alone are, in their own way, the most frightening of all. At least, in *Goldfinger,* the car was consigned to a machine designed to handle it. But in real life in Philadelphia last year—and, perhaps sad to say, real life and Philadelphia are one and the same thing—20,000 cars were simply abandoned on the streets.

The Automobile Manufacturers Association says that nationwide in 1966, a total of 6,856,000 cars and trucks were junked.

Part of the false comfort mentioned earlier is the illusion that somehow science can come up, inevitably, with ways to make new uses of new garbage. Abandoned automobile bodies are regarded, for example, as ideal equipment in the infant industry of steam-mining, which taps the bowels of the earth for live steam: If a mine "blows" and goes wildcat, it can be capped and contained by throwing old cars into the hole. One of the problems here is that there are more old cars than there are wildcat mines. Another is that the mines can be one place while the cars are someplace else. Yet another is that when you do throw an old car into a mine, the pressure within the mine may throw it right back out at you.

At an earlier point in this article, several different ways were outlined for getting rid of garbage: disposal in water, disposal by burying, chemical processing, incineration, or the use of that oldest and most honored of customs: the city dump.

Actually, there is another process, known as landfill. In theory this is close to ideal, and in practice it has been employed time and again, such as in the San Fernando Valley. A tract builder digs a hole and quarries from it the ingredients with which he can stucco his houses. As people move into the houses, that artificial quarry becomes the place where they dump their garbage. When it fills up, it is covered. It becomes in turn a park or a site for several new homes, and the cycle goes on to be repeated elsewhere. This seems ideal, especially because the number of homes must exceed the number of holes. But the fact of life is that you wind up running out of holes anyway.

Instead, more and more of the major cities, like Chicago, Detroit and Philadelphia, are reaching the conclusion that their garbage must be buried—not nearby but somewhere far, far away. In this direction, San Francisco now has taken the lead. It has proposed—with preliminary okays from the boards of supervisors at both ends—to bury its trash in Lassen County, via the hauling facilities of the Western Pacific Railroad.

Some of the names proposed for the train that will do the job, in a christening contest recently held by the San Francisco *Chronicle,* were "The Excess Express," "Part of the City of San Francisco," and "The Twentieth Stenchery Limited." But, not to create another pun, some things were left up in the air. One was whether the prevailing Lassen breezes would blow the smell of San Francisco's garbage, if any, into neighboring Nevada. Another was whether the alkali wasteland that is Lassen County would be helped, hurt, or generally unaffected by having the soil soiled by the waste of urban civilization. Still another was that cities and towns along the way might elect—why not?—to start hooking their own carloads of garbage onto the end of the train.

The idea of rail haulage bloomed out of crisis: San Francisco's present system of garbage disposal, a landfill operation in nearby Brisbane, is doomed because within two years there will be more garbage than Brisbane. The first thought of the city fathers was to build a new incinerator, but no neighborhood would accept it.

"It will look beautiful where you live," the residents of the Hunter's Point area were told.

"If it's that beautiful, put it where you live," they replied.

The rail idea then began to be explored. Critics were quick to ask what would happen if there were a strike by railworkers. "Same thing that'll happen if there's a strike by the garbage collectors," they were told.

Financially, the arrangement seems sound enough. At an estimated added cost to the individual householder, who now gets one-can-a-week service, of not more than 25 cents per month, the railroad hopes to make a seven percent profit on a $3 million annual gross, and Lassen County will be paid an estimated $113,000 each year for providing the burial ground. If at first blush those figures seem flawed, the rectifying balance would lie in San Francisco companies getting rid of industrial wastes and householders who set out more than one can of refuse for the trash collectors.

"It's not really an experiment," one Western Pacific official said. "We've already invested more than $100,000 in investigating the specifics of the thing, and after all, garbage is freight, and we know how to haul different kinds of freight."

What nobody knows is what the garbage will do for Lassen County when it is deposited in the desolate high scrub desert—some 1,500 tons of it daily—after its scenic 375-mile journey from the Bay area. There are extremes among predictions. Some feel the garbage will serve as a compost, and the desert will become green; at the opposite pole, some claim it will breed rats underground. Then there are the moderates. "Might as well put it there," one long-time Susanville resident reasoned. "Land sure ain't good for anything else."

Such sentiments have been echoed by a 60-year-old gentleman named Cecil Duck, who will be stationmaster for the hitherto unscheduled stop on the Western Pacific. "When you come right down to it," Mr. Duck told reporter Michael Grieg, "the fact is I'm retiring anyway."

The Indians who inhabit the inhospitable Lassen area between Turtle Peak and Skedaddle Mountain—fewer than 200 of them, descended from the Paiutes—figure it's one more broken treaty and the hell with it. "The Indians didn't have any garbage," one of them told reporter Grieg. "They left the land clean. Everything was used—every part of the animal . . . bone, skin, all of it. And no beer cans. There was no waste until the white man came."

Inevitably, a "Keep Lassen County Beautiful Committee" was formed, opposing, possibly with a chance of ultimate success, the new edition of The Zephyr. One extra-interesting aspect, which intrigues this committee and should intrigue everyone, is that man has been without progress in the science of trash disposal. Without, that is, net progress. The technology has increased, but the garbage has increased faster. "In Colonial days," says Phil Thomas, the AP business writer, "New York City got rid of its garbage by letting pigs roam freely about the streets to eat it." Modern visionaries say if man knows how to get to the moon, he knows how to turn garbage into fertilizer and toys. The fact is that man does not know—feasibly, at least—how to do it.

He does know how to get to the moon. Indeed, the Apollo 8 astronauts, orbiting the cold moon on Christmas Eve, intimated it had great possibilities as a city dump. "My impression," radioed Capt. James Lovell, "is that it's a vast, forbidding expanse of nothing."

These words may have caused sanitation officials in our large cities to quiver for joy. But let them not exult unduly. First thing they'll run into, when they seek to send their garbage to the moon, will be a committee.

FOUR ENVIRONMENTAL CRISES

A characteristic of environmental issues is their tendency to abide at lower levels of the public consciousness; pollution is seldom invisible, but it is usually gradual, and people have a high capacity for accepting environmental deterioration as an inevitable accompaniment to progress. For these and other reasons, environmental issues seldom become officially "important" until they are very critical indeed.

The following four articles look at four different environmental situations which became critical—at least, to certain individuals. In each of these there is an active or potential conflict between groups representing various interests or points of view, and I recommend looking, in each case, for the underlying sources of political conflict.

The crisis concerning the Great Lakes is probably the largest in scope and complexity of the four: it is, in fact, one of the most spectacular examples of environmental pollution in existence. Former

Secretary of the Interior Stewart Udall, the author of the article about the Great Lakes, holds out the hope that a full-scale effort could restore the badly polluted Lake Erie in ten years—and also warns that if Lake Michigan becomes equally polluted, restoration may take from 100 to 1,000 years.

My article on the Salton Sea, a large inland lake in southern California, documents another aspect of environmental alteration—one that I find particularly interesting because the conflict has nothing to do with conservation, insofar as the word is taken to mean the preservation of conditions as they would exist without human intervention. The sea's very existence at the present time is due to human intervention, and the dispute over it is merely a conflict about which human purpose—agricultural or recreational—the sea should serve. There is, then, a certain purity about the issue which is usually less evident, although seldom entirely absent, from other environmental-political disputes: there is no argument at all for a "natural" resolution to the problem, because after fifty years and more of manipulation and alteration, nobody really remembers what the natural condition was.

Ross Macdonald, a mystery writer who lives in the Santa Barbara area, deals with another case of water pollution—but here again, the situation is vastly different, and a further illustration of the fact that water pollution cannot be looked at, much less solved, as a single problem.

The body of water of which Macdonald writes is the Pacific Ocean —more specifically, that part of it which occupies the space between California's Channel Islands and the long strand of beaches, yacht harbors, and costly homes which stretches southward from Santa Barbara. The pollutant is oil, escaping from a rupture caused by the Union Oil Company's offshore drilling under a federal oil lease. The political conflict resulting from the oil slick had as its main antagonists the oil industry on the one side and an alliance of Santa Barbara residents and businesses (particularly the tourism industry) and conservationists on the other. And it should be noted that an alliance between conservationists and promoters of tourism is never likely to be permanent; this one showed signs of strain only a few months after the incident, as conservationists continued to seek publicity in fighting for a major attack on offshore oil drilling and local businessmen began to argue that the continuing publicity would keep tourists away from Santa Barbara after the crisis had passed. It should be noted, also, that another kind of conflict had been going on behind the scenes long before the oil rupture occurred: that was the conflict between oil interests seeking leases and some public officials warned by conservationists about the dangers of offshore drilling. The fact that the federal leases had been granted for drilling in the Santa Barbara channel tells what the outcome of that conflict was; Stewart Udall, who was Secretary of the Interior at the time the leases were granted, later called the decision "a conservation Bay of Pigs."

The report on the Dugway incident was written by the editor of *Environment* magazine, in cooperation with a chemist and a geophysicist. In this case, prior to the development of the crisis, there was no conflict whatever: no one, not even some lonely handful of conservationists or residents of the areas near the proving ground, was mobilized in any way to *prevent* crisis. Had they been, they would undoubtedly have been generally regarded as cranks. Military secrecy, furthermore, created an enormous obstacle for anyone who might have been inclined to challenge the Army's assurance that all testing was done with adequate safeguards.

The Dugway incident, and criticism of the use of defoliant herbicides in Vietnam, increased public concern over the environmental aspects of military technology. That concern was reflected in the drive by some congressmen to make chemical and biological warfare political issues, and in the Nixon administration's decisions to renounce offensive biological warfare and to seek ratification of the 1925 Geneva Protocol prohibiting first use of chemical weapons in war. But the American chemical weaponry industry (like the pesticide industry to which it is closely related) continues to be one of the world's chief developers of techniques of destruction, and as such it will inevitably continue to be a focus of political-environmental controversy.

CAN WE SAVE OUR SICK GREAT LAKES?

Stewart L. Udall

Our Great Lakes, which make up the largest body of fresh water on earth, are under sentence of premature death. Born 20,000 years ago when the glaciers gouged out their huge basins, then retreated and

Stewart L. Udall, "Can We Save Our Sick Great Lakes?" TRUE, *August, 1969. Courtesy,* TRUE, *For Today's Man, Fawcett Publications, Inc. Copyright, 1969.*

filled them with the crystalline waters of melting ice, the Great Lakes are beginning to show signs of old age at a time when they are still geological youngsters. In Lake Erie great green skeins of algae have broken loose from rocky moorings and washed ashore to rot in long, malodorous, fly-infested windrows. At Green Bay, Wisconsin, people sun themselves on park benches that look out on Bay Beach—shut down by pollution in 1941, and now covered by marsh grass and weeds. In Chicago United States Steel Corporation's south works inflicts dark-purple bruises on Lake Michigan from its daily discharge of 440 million gallons of waste water. Just below Niagara Falls, the city of Niagara Falls, New York, pours sewage into the Niagara River after giving it what is euphemistically called "preliminary treatment": the raw sewage is merely passed through a screen. The oil-thick Buffalo River, a tributary to Lake Erie, necessarily, though perhaps unbelievably, has been declared a fire hazard by the Buffalo fire chief.

Since Samuel de Champlain first sailed into Lake Ontario in 1615 seeking a northwest passage to China but finding instead a waterway into the heart of a continent, the heavy hand of man has aged the Great Lakes at a rate exceeding geometric progression. It is quite likely that in the last 20 years more deterioration has occurred than in the previous 20,000, and that in the next 80, the remaining life expectancy of the lakes will be unconsciously and unconscionably compressed.

How did this happen? How could we have squandered this great treasury of fresh water to the point of bankruptcy? For years people had thought these inland seas capable of absorbing all the wastes of society. The attitude is summed up in the engineering profession's old bromide, "The solution to pollution is dilution." Rapid industrialization and a booming population left their mark, accompanied by a "robber baron" mentality that held economic progress—at any environmental or social cost—to be sacrosanct. All of a sudden, there were more than 25 million people congregated along the shores of the Great Lakes; industries were consuming more than 2,660 billion gallons of water a year; cities were drawing 1,400 billion gallons annually from the lakes and their tributaries to provide drinking water for over 15 million people.

As early as the turn of the century, events had forced the city of Chicago to act. Following a series of typhoid epidemics, engineers undertook to reverse the flow of the Chicago River. Instead of discharging into Lake Michigan, the river was caused to flow backward and now carries its enormous quantities of treated waste into the Illinois River system. This arrangement has provided protection for the Chicago area's freshwater supply and bathing beaches, but at the expense of other water users down the Illinois River system. Even so, Chicago's costs of treating its water supply have doubled in the last 20 years because of the contaminants from neighboring Indiana carried by lake currents into its water intakes.

The reversal of the river, however, has kept Lake Michigan from deteriorating with the rapidity that has marked Lake Erie's decline. In the summer one-fourth of Lake Erie's 9,930 square miles of water is "dead." The water at the bottom of the lake is completely without oxygen. And this suffocating phenomenon not only lasts for longer periods each summer but covers more area.

Yet scientists feel that Lake Erie's recovery could be spectacular—possibly within 10 years—if all sources of pollution were given adequate treatment, for Erie is flushed by the still relatively clean waters of Lake Huron. Lake Michigan, by contrast, is a cul-de-sac that receives no flushing action. If ever it slips to Lake Erie's degree of degradation, anywhere from 100 to 1,000 years would be required to restore its water quality. Indeed, despite all the technical skills that man might finally muster, some pessimists say that Lake Michigan might never recover from such pollution.

There is no single villain but we are all—individuals, even industries—victims. On the Cuyahoga River, which enters Lake Erie at Cleveland, a steel company must play a constant stream of water on the surface to keep floating logs, oil and debris away from its water intake.

The biggest single industrial polluter of the Great Lakes is the United States Steel Corporation. Its Gary, Indiana, plant alone discharges more than 330 million gallons of wastes a day into the Grand Calumet River, a tributary of Lake Michigan. This carries a load of pollutants equivalent to daily dropping 130,000 full-size automobiles into the lake.

The worst *municipal* polluter in the Great Lakes region is the City of Detroit, which discharges more wastes into Lake Erie than all other cities in the basin combined. Yet Detroit is one of the many cities that has agreed, in compliance with the Lake Erie Enforcement Conference, to install secondary treatment facilities by 1970. U.S. Steel's sheet and tin works at Gary has four new water-pollution control systems in operation; these are among the most modern in the country.

Lake Ontario, the easternmost and last link in the lake chain, receives its flow and, therefore, the pollution, from all of its sister lakes.
It is also doused with staggering amounts of pollution from cities and
industries discharging into the Niagara River, the connecting waterway
between Lakes Erie and Ontario. The river, which flows over Niagara
Falls, disgraces local communities along its banks, demeans the State
of New York and the nation, and does violence to an otherwise peaceful border. The Genesee, Oswego and Black Rivers also spill wastes
into the lake.

Lake Ontario resembles Lakes Erie and Michigan, with piles of
rotting algae and dead fish besmirching its shores. While all three lakes
have alewives, a tiny inedible "trash" fish, nothing in history rivals the
huge die-off of some 16 billion alewives in Lake Michigan in 1967.
No evidence has been found that poisons in the water caused their
deaths, but the huge numbers of fish washed ashore became a major
pollution problem with both odorous and economic consequences.
Moreover, an example of the interrelationships in our world cropped
up when a predatory fish, the coho salmon, was introduced to feed
on the alewives. The coho have now become so contaminated with
pesticides washed into the lake from farmlands that this spring the
Food and Drug Administration seized 22,500 pounds of commercially
landed coho, which contained up to 19 parts per million of DDT.
(The maximum safe limit for human consumption has been set by
the FDA at five parts per million.)

Another critical problem is caused by the combined sewer systems
used in most communities which have progressed beyond the privy
and septic tank. These sewers carry both sewage and rainwater, and
during heavy rains a sewage treatment plant often bypasses capacity
loads into lakes and streams. Thus, while the plant is not flooded,
there is a resultant discharge of raw sewage. Whiting, Indiana, whose
beach has been closed off and on for the past 10 years because of
bacterial pollution, bypasses to Lake Michigan. On a rainy day, one
can see a black puddle of pollution spreading out—much like an ink
stain on a blotter—near the deserted Whiting Beach, and similar scenes
can be observed on all the Great Lakes.

While old problems press in, new problems are appearing. The
large-scale planning of nuclear utilities on or near the Great Lakes is
an example. Near Minneapolis-St. Paul, Minnesota, residents have
protested the construction of a nuclear power plant at Monticello,
located on the Mississippi River north of the source of the Twin

Cities' drinking water. They complain that radioactive wastes contaminate the water supply and maintain that the standards approved by the Atomic Energy Commission are much more lenient than those adopted by the World Health Organization. Nuclear utilities also add substantial amounts of heat to the water—even moderate increases in temperature have killed fish or made them more susceptible to disease—and encourages the growth of new crops of algae. A committee formed at the Lake Michigan Conference has been meeting with AEC personnel to develop guidelines for the control of thermal and radioactive pollution.

A controversy also erupted in Ohio and Pennsylvania this past year over the potential pollution threat of offshore oil and gas drilling which, though a possible economic bonanza, could result in another nightmare.

Lakes Huron and Superior are being scarred for the first time by pockets of pollution. The Saginaw River system which drains approximately 6,000 square miles, carries a heavy burden of industrial and municipal pollution into Huron. The Superior, largest, deepest, coolest and cleanest of the Great Lakes, is developing pollutional sores from steel, sewage and paper-mill discharges pouring down the St. Louis and Montreal rivers and from Duluth Harbor; red TNT wastes from the E. I. du Pont de Nemours Company plant at Barksdale, Wisconsin, bloody Lake Superior's Chequamegon Bay.

Recently hearings have been held and a bitter argument has broken out over whether the Reserve Mining Company's taconite processing plant on Superior's Silver Bay is polluting the lake with its dull-gray outpouring of 59,000 tons a day of ore residues.

Thus, the next 10 to 15 years may require our spending as much as 15 billion dollars to save the Great Lakes. For we are not only dealing with a situation brought on by decades of neglect; we also face the prospect that industrial water use may triple with municipal consumption increasing at almost the same rate during the next 50 years.

In the Lake Erie Basin alone, construction costs just to provide adequate secondary treatment facilities for all municipalities will run to $1 billion. Equivalent industrial treatment facilities will add $285 million to the bill. By 1990 municipalities will have to spend another $1.4 billion to expand facilities. Secondary treatment, which is required by the 1965 Lake Erie Federal Enforcement Conference, achieves up to 90 percent removal of wastes. Advanced waste treatment, which has a 99 percent effectiveness, will ultimately be needed, along with techniques for removing phosphorus to curb excessive algae growth. These refinements will raise costs still higher, for the Great Lakes receive more than 75.5 million pounds of phosphates a year. A four-state Lake Michigan Enforcement Conference which I called in January, 1968, at the request of former Illinois Governor Otto Kerner will require all municipalities to achieve at least 80 percent reduction of phosphorus by December 1972.

To control agricultural runoff of pesticides into Lake Erie alone, we would have to invest approximately $400 million in a system of drains, dams, channel improvements and in grassing the slopes of waterways.

The cost of replacing combined sewers with separate systems for carrying storm water and sanitary wastes is also prodigious. In the Lake Erie basin, it would cost in the vicinity of $3 billion, and in Chicago, close to $2 billion. Yet such construction projects must one day be undertaken out of dire necessity. And certainly separate systems should now be installed in all urban reconstruction projects and new developments. The city of Chicago has received federal financial assistance to experiment with the retention of storm overflows in deep underground reservoirs. During rains the water would be stored in the reservoirs for future treatment, avoiding the bypassing of sewage to the lake or a tributary.

However, muscle as well as money is required. The Oil Pollution Act, which covers petroleum dumping into the lakes, is woefully inadequate. It requires proof that the pollution results from gross negligence or willfulness, a charge almost impossible to substantiate in a court of law against those ships which nonchalantly pump oil into the water when cleaning their bilges. And this act does not cover oil discharges from shore installations; that is the responsibility of the Army Corps of Engineers under the Rivers and Harbors Act of 1899. Legislation is now before the Congress to streamline and strengthen these laws, and a uniform law has also been proposed to regulate control of pollution from commercial and pleasure vessels. Needed legislation to control drainage from mines of acid and other pollutants also is pending.

Money and technical skills must also be applied to finding alternate sites and methods for the disposal of polluted dredgings. For years the Corps of Engineers dumped material dredged from harbors and channels into the open waters of the lakes. As Secretary of the Interior, I entered into a Memorandum of Understanding with the Secretary of the Army as a step toward solving this problem, and some progress has been made in finding other locations where polluted dredgings will not be harmful.

We must also enforce existing laws. We must hold industries and communities to the deadlines for cleaning up wastes that they agreed to meet at various enforcement conferences; and we must uphold the water quality standards established for interstate waters under the Water Quality Act of 1965. Under the law, these standards were made subject to the approval of the Secretary of the Interior, and while in office I approved in whole or in part the standards developed by all the Great Lakes states.

This is also an appropriate time for the United States and Canada to determine if more international efforts should be applied to lake pollution problems. While Canada, which borders four of the lakes on the north, needs to improve its treatment facilities and is acting to do so, the bulk of pollution comes from the United States.

In a number of Great Lakes states, the people now are being asked to decide on their future. Yet Illinois voters last fall rejected—I note with objective regret—an opportunity to pass a $1 billion bond issue for air and water conservation. What will other voters do in the critical years ahead when they have pollution control referendums in their own states?

UN Secretary General U Thant stated not long ago: "The truth, the central stupendous truth, about developed countries today is that they can have—in anything but the shortest run—the kind and scale of resources they decide to have. . . . It is no longer resources that limit decisions. It is the decision that makes the resources. This is the fundamental revolutionary change—perhaps the most revolutionary mankind has ever known."

If this were ever true anywhere on earth, it is true in America today. We do have the technology. Desalinization, for example, when coupled with power generation, is on the way to providing economical access to the greatest water resource of all—the seas. We do have the wealth: our gross national product is closing on the trillion-dollar mark. We have the resources and resiliency but we await the decision, the commitment.

Far too long we have viewed conservation as a peripheral endeavor to save a species, to clean a river or to restore a forest. Now, however, there is a growing awareness of a new dimension of conservation whose subject and substance is man himself. We are at last beginning to realize that all of life is a system, not unlike the Great Lakes, which is an intricate web of interdependent relationships. There is an ecological discipline that operates in nature to which man is subject. For every action there is a reaction; for every consequence, a cause. As man's power and prowess increase, so does his responsibility.

Instead of fragmented look at the pollution problem, we must examine the total system by which our industry, economy and society transform energy and materials from ground resources to finished products, to ultimate use and finally disposal. We must begin to examine the very goods and services we produce for their inevitable environmental impact *before* we produce them.

If, in the future, we are to make those decisions that will in fact create our resources, our wisdom must match our wealth. The present condition of our nation's waters is grim testimony to the fact that we have not done this. We have treated water as if we could make it when in reality we can neither make nor destroy—but only transform —it. We have used it and discarded it when it became overburdened with the chemicals and heat of our effluents.

It is a magnificent testimony to the indomitability of nature that the evolution of man's technical genius that at first threatened him with extinction has the potential now to save him.

But beyond any attempt to quantify our resources by their magnitude and to qualify them in terms of the manner of their use, is the overriding necessity to also view them in terms of the number of humans who must share them. The plentitude of resources on our planet is a constant; the only factor which bears on that constant is the variable of man's numbers. If we double our numbers, there will be only half as much water per person. The same is true of our foodstuffs, parklands, air, and physical space. Therefore, it is no longer possible to consider a program to extend, enlarge, and protect our resources of our environment without concomitantly considering what a rational population policy might be for our nation.

Adlai Stevenson in his last speech said: "We travel together, passengers on a little spaceship, dependent on its vulnerable supplies of air and soil . . . preserved from annihilation only by the care, the work, and I will say the love, we give our fragile craft."

Ever since Prometheus, of Greek mythology, stole fire from the gods to give to mankind, man has been trying to impose order on his environment: far too often he has created havoc. Of all the ransacked rooms in nature's house, none has been more abused—nor in so short a time—than the Great Lakes. Patchwork repair jobs will no longer do. We have not only exhausted our excuses for inaction and apathy; we have also run out of time. Quite simply, it is up to us. Man—if he wants—can be master of his fate. Indeed, he has no alternative.

STORM OVER THE SALTON SEA

Walt Anderson

The Salton Sea, spreading across its basin between sharp, bone-dry hills, is an incredibly peaceful body of water. When there is no breeze and you stand in the sunlight on the silent shore and look out across it, it seems impossible that there could be any life at all beneath its surface. Actually the waters are thick with fish, planted there years ago and coexisting in a thriving, if somewhat precarious, biological balance. And all around the shores churns human life, and it, too, is engaged in a struggle for survival.

That struggle has to do with the fact that the Sea is becoming continually more salty, and within 10 to 20 years, unless something is done, it will no longer be able to support life. If the fish die, so will the young economic boom that has been turning the Sea into a busy recreational area. Something can probably be done about the salinity, but that may affect the Sea's other function: drainage sump for all the irrigation water that flows from the Coachella and Imperial Valleys. With its artificial life chain, its warring economic factions and its uncertain future, the seemingly placid Sea is a gigantic example of how complicated things can get when men start manipulating nature.

The Salton Sea itself was created by men—accidentally—around 1905. The basin had been a part of the Gulf of California in prehistoric times, and then it became a dry seabed. There was a lake there about 700 years ago, and then that, too, dried up. Around the turn of the century the only sign of life thereabouts was a salt works in the basin and a railroad station named Salton. Then a group called the California Development Company began to build an irrigation system

Walt Anderson, "Neck Deep in a Sea of Troubles," WEST *Magazine* (LOS ANGELES TIMES), *Nov. 12, 1967. Reprinted by permission.*

in the Imperial Valley to the south, and they constructed a canal to bring in water from the Colorado River.

In December, 1904, a brief flood washed out some of the levees of the canal. Then, in April, 1905, the whole Colorado River came rushing through the breech toward the below-sea-level basin to the north, instead of south on its natural course to the Gulf of California. For nearly two years engineers, urged on by President Theodore Roosevelt's exhortations to "Stop that river," battled to get the Colorado back where it belonged as new floods repeatedly tore away the levees they built. By the time the engineers finally succeeded, the basin had been turned into a huge inland sea, over 35 miles long. As the water dissolved the old salt deposits, the new Salton Sea attained a salinity about equal to that of the Pacific Ocean.

After the flood, efforts to irrigate the valleys resumed—and eventually engineering projects such as the Hoover Dam made it possible to do so without danger of further floods. The farmers found a way to do away with the heavy salt content of the land that diminished its agricultural value: they laid porous tiles 4 to 10 feet below the surface of the ground, so that the irrigation water could soak down through the soil, carrying away the salts, and then flow along the tiles to the drainage system—which emptied into the nearest convenient body of water, the Salton Sea. The system transformed the Imperial Valley from a dry, salty plain into one of the world's richest agricultural areas.

Meanwhile the California Department of Fish and Game, noting that the inflow of irrigation water was keeping the Salton Sea from drying up, became interested in the idea of planting it with ocean fish. In the years from 1948 to 1956, over 35,000 fish, of 35 different species, were hauled in from the Gulf of California.

The species of fish that are now most prevalent in the Sea are mudsuckers, croakers, sargo and corvina. The mudsuckers run about 5 inches long, the croakers about 10, the sargo about 12, and the corvina, the favorite game fish, up to 42 inches long and 30 pounds in weight. The smaller fish feed on pileworms and the corvina feed on the smaller fish. It is a thin life chain compared to the ocean's, but it's an extremely rich one: the corvina population is now estimated to be over three million.

That's a lot of fish, and they're not hard to catch. The first day I visited the Salton Sea I walked out to the end of a pier on the east shore, where two men and a woman from Los Angeles were fishing with bait. They had a bucketful of croakers among them and a six-pound corvina hanging in the water from the side of the pier. "We caught a hundred and seven fish here last week," one of the men said.

Almost anywhere around the Sea, at almost any time of the day or any time of the year, you will see fishermen. They fish from the piers, from boats or from a barge called the *Lucky Strike,* which is anchored off the west shore. Some use a technique called "armpit fishing," which involves getting into a swimsuit and wading out into the water. Along the west shore I saw lots of armpit fishermen, some of them in the water up to their knees, a few up to their armpits and some in clear up to their necks, nothing visible but a head and a part of a pole.

With the growth in sport fishing there has also been a growth in the kind of business activity that naturally serves a recreational area. It's all part of the food chain, really: the fishermen feed on the fish, and the businessmen feed on the fishermen. In the last six years or so there has been a boom in the construction of marinas, stores, bars, motels and trailer camps. Residential areas are being developed as well, and the biggest community, Salton City, even has an 18-hole golf course.

But there is one very big flaw in this picture of happy fishermen and prospering business activity: the Salton Sea is continually getting saltier, as water evaporates and the salt-carrying irrigation runoff comes in to replace it. Everybody has known in a general way for a long time that this was happening, just as we all know we are getting older and will die sometime, but nobody knew how serious the problem really was. Then the State Water Quality Control Board hired a consulting firm—Pomeroy, Johnston and Bailey—to study the situation. The Pomeroy Report, which was completed in December of 1965, said that unless something is done to prevent it, "the Sea will become so salty that the fishery will be seriously damaged within a few years, probably some time between 1970 and 1980." As a further blow to the boosters who were beginning to talk of the Sea's future as a sort of inland Mediterranean, the report also pointed out that increasing salinity will not only kill the fish, but will make the water unpleasant for swimming, and—because of the corrosive effect—not much good for boating, either. The influx of salt, the report said, amounts to thousands of tons per day.

The report recommended that a system of dikes be constructed to keep the inflowing water from adding more salts to the Sea. But the Water Quality Control Board does not have the money to build such a system, nor is it the only government agency involved in the Salton Sea—not by a long way. When I visited the board's air-conditioned regional office in Indio, up in the date-growing Coachella Valley north of the Sea, its executive director, Art Swajian, had just finished a study of what agencies *are* interested. He showed me a list that looked like the table of contents of a Franz Kafka novel. On it were, to name a few, the California Department of Fish and Game, Department of Water Resources and Department of Parks and Recreation; the Federal Bureau of Reclamation, Bureau of Land Management and Department of Conservation; the Imperial Irrigation District; the Coachella Valley County Water District, and the Imperial and Riverside County Boards of Supervisors.

Also, the Bureau of Indian Affairs is involved because much of the land that was flooded in 1905 was and still is (even under water) Indian reservation. The Navy Department is concerned because there is a naval base on the Sea, and the Bureau of Sport Fisheries and Wildlife is interested because of the fish and also because there is a wildlife refuge on the south end of the Sea, where aquatic plants are grown to feed the thousands of migrating ducks and geese that pass through in the winter months. This is important to the farmers, because if the birds weren't fed they would eat the crops, and it has diplomatic importance because the migratory birds are protected by treaties with Canada and Mexico.

As this army of bureaucrats tries to mobilize itself, pressure is being exerted by the different private interests. Those seem to fall into two groups: the ones who are anxious to get some kind of a salinity control program going as soon as possible, and the ones who aren't so anxious. In the anxious class, and moving rapidly toward the frantic, are the various developers who are interested in exploiting the Sea's potential as a recreation area. Most invested money in the pre-Pomeroy Report period and are waiting to find out whether they stand to get rich or go broke.

"Hell, I'm over a barrel," said Hal Carlsen of Recreation Development Corporation. He pointed to a map of the Sea that showed his holdings on the north shore. "We've got four hundred acres here. We want to put in a big development—marina, trailer park, motel, everything. We can't get financing on it. The bank says sure, it's a fine program, but they want to wait and see what's going to happen. Everybody wants to wait and see what's going to happen."

Carlsen and some of the other businessmen in more or less similar positions have formed a group called Salton Sea Recreation Enthusiasts, described in its literature as "a group of people (non-political and non-technical), motivated by selfish interests as concerns the Salton Sea." What the Recreation Enthusiasts are mostly enthusiastic about is getting the government—any government—to do something to set the area back on the road to riches, on which everybody had assumed it to be.

All around the Sea is evidence that the boom has slowed down. Homes, businesses, marinas and trailer parks abound, as do people boating and fishing. But nothing more seems to be under construction. On one stretch along the east shore I saw a sign that said THIS LAND FOR SALE, standing in a field where tract markers were dimly visible in the sand. On the west shore, where most of the construction has gone on, there are large subdivisions with the streets laid out and a few lonely houses here and there among the empty lots. I went into a large real estate office decorated with elevations of homes and pictures of people sailing and fishing. The office was empty, except for one salesman and a few crickets that got in when I opened the door.

I asked the salesman if it was true that the water was becoming so salty the fish were going to die. He said that was just propaganda and he gave me a lot of publications about the area.

The Recreational Enthusiasts want to see the government come up with a plan that will insure the Sea's recreational future by controlling:

(a) The salinity.
(b) The level, which may drop eight feet or more in the near future if the Federal Government reduces the supply of irrigation water to the Imperial Valley.
(c) The ecology. At present, fish are not being harvested fast enough —in the summer they die in great numbers, causing anoxia at the bottom of the Sea that threatens the beginnings of the food chain and creates a bad smell that most of the natives blame on sewage from Mexico.

The Recreation Enthusiasts aren't sure how all these problems ought to be solved, but they think somebody ought to get going immediately, because it will undoubtedly take years for any major engineering project to be completed—during which the salinity will continue to rise. They are now in a hurry to see something get beyond the study stage. "We're sick and tired of studies," Carlsen said.

Several ideas have been suggested—including a plan to run pipelines and bring fresh sea water in from the Gulf of California—but all of them look expensive. This is one of the arguments of the other group, the Imperial Valley farmers. The Coachella Valley farmers, with generally smaller holdings and with Palm Springs in the neighborhood to make them conscious of the tourist business, tend to cooperate with the developers; the opposition comes from the Imperial Valley.

The developers and the Imperial Valley farmers not only have different ideas about what the Sea is best for—i.e., whether it is meant to be a booming recreational area or a nice, quiet irrigation sump—they also have different styles of operation. The businessmen go about things in the standard American zingo fashion, holding public meetings and issuing press releases. But the big farmers move in rather more mysterious ways. At one meeting, the representative of the Imperial Irrigation District voted for Coachella Valley Assemblyman Victor Veysey's proposal to appropriate state money for a new study. Shortly thereafter the farmers quietly torpedoed the bill by pressuring Sacramento.

But the Imperial Valley farmers do not for the most part go in for direct opposition. Usually their position is that the recreational use of the Sea is just fine, but nobody should be too hasty about moving ahead with any large-scale engineering project. This infuriates the developers, who are afraid the farmers may manage to drag their feet until it is too late to do anything.

Lom Thompson, an Imperial Valley farmer, truckline owner, and member of the Board of Directors of the Imperial Irrigation District, told me in a leisurely way that he thought the idea of protecting the Sea was just fine.

"Why," he said, "if we had some way we could keep it safe so the fish could survive, nothing would make us happier. But there's no way to control that salt. We're getting salty water from the Colorado, and that's getting saltier all the time, too. We've never opposed legitimate programs, but the ones I've seen have been ridiculous; it would be utterly impossible to finance them."

The farmers are, understandably, concerned about the likelihood that they might wind up paying part of the cost for a salinity control program, and they are also afraid that such a program might in some way affect the Sea's function as an irrigation runoff. The farms are part of a food chain, too—one that helps maintain life in Los Angeles —and the Imperial Valley would be useless without its irrigation system. And the farmers are correct in their claim that the irrigation water as they get it is becoming increasingly salty: there are more and more irrigation districts along the Colorado using water from the river and returning the drainage—with increased salt content—back to the river. I found it interesting that, although Thompson was skeptical about the practicality of the large-scale engineering projects that have been suggested for controlling the salinity of the Sea, he was most interested in the idea of a project to run fresh water down from the Snake and Columbia Rivers in the Pacific Northwest.

If some project to save the sports fishing in the Salton Sea is forthcoming, it probably will be federally backed. Riverside County does not have the money, Imperial County does not have the money or the inclination, the state government is on an economy kick and that leaves only the federal government. What *it* does will depend in part on what comes out of the studies *it* makes, and in part on who swings the most influence.

That is how things stand above the surface of the Salton Sea. Below the surface, life, at least for the time being, goes on: the microscopic life forms thrive on the rich silt and chemical nutrients, the pileworms and barnacles cluster along the bottom, and the thick schools of fish glide silently through water full of salt and fishhooks, in a world they never made.

LIFE WITH THE BLOB

Ross Macdonald

The blob five miles offshore had been growing for 24 hours before Santa Barbara, California, knew about it. Then, on Wednesday morning, an oil worker called the city editor of the *News-Press*. He said the new well being drilled on Union's Platform A had blown out the day before and was still blowing.

Tom Kleveland, a gray-haired columnist who acts as a local ombudsman, went out in a workboat to look at it. A thick surge of crude oil smothered the sea around the platform. Oil and large gas bubbles were coming up in at least five places, lifting the surface of the water two feet. "It looked like a big yellow boil bursting with pus," Tom told me later.

Our evening paper confirmed the disaster. Margaret and I went out on the patio and looked across the channel to the islands, 25 miles offshore. The soft blue scene seemed intact. But there was a difference in the light—or in our vision of it—now that we knew it was threatened and perishable.

Though we couldn't see the oil platforms through the narrow mouth of our canyon, we had been steadily aware of them. Their coming over the past year had brought a sense of impending change to Santa Barbara, to our beaches and our sea and our eggshell-fragile way of life.

Ross Macdonald, "Life with the Blob," SPORTS ILLUSTRATED, *April 21, 1969. Reprinted by permission of Harold Ober Associates Incorporated. Copyright © 1969 Time Inc.*

Offshore in the quiet evening the change was taking place, and there was nothing we could do about it.

"This could be another *Torrey Canyon,* couldn't it? How many seabirds did that kill?"

I turned my wife's questions aside. "A ruptured oil well isn't the same as a wrecked tanker. They may get it capped right away." I had just read in the paper that Union Oil's regional vice-president, John Fraser, had assured city officials that the spill should be under control or completely stopped within 24 hours.

The oil was still running uncontrolled on Saturday. Margaret and I went to a protest rally at East Beach, instigated by a group who called themselves GOO (Get Oil Out). One of their leaders, former State Senator Al Weingand, made a disturbing speech.

Several years before, he had flown over the channel and the islands with Secretary of the Interior Stewart L. Udall. Both men were interested in creating a Channel Islands National Park. Weingand had asked Udall for assurances against oil pollution. "No oil leases will be granted," the Secretary had promised, "except under conditions that will protect your environment."

But in spite of this assurance, the oil rigs had gathered offshore like a slow invasion fleet. The oil pumping had begun—and now it continued, even though the ocean floor had been hemorrhaging for four days. One mile of our beaches to the south had already been flooded with the black tarry stuff.

East Beach was still untouched. Sanderlings ran in close groups like shimmering gravel. Black cormorants flew low over the untainted white surf. But Margaret and I were living in suspense. Our region is a natural bird sanctuary surpassed by no more than four or five other places in the country. Scientists at the University of California's Santa Barbara campus were already predicting heavy losses. Biologist John Cushing was particularly concerned about the seabirds, which swallowed oil as they preened themselves and were often poisoned by it.

We didn't know how much oil was out there. Union Oil's estimates of the spillage were quite low: its initially quoted estimate (subsequently denied) of 5,000 barrels a day was later down to 500 barrels a day. But according to Alan A. Allen, a scientist with the General Research Corp. who regularly flew over the spill, at least 20,000 barrels of oil were floating just offshore.

On Sunday the wind rose. It blew seaward and kept the oil off our beaches, lulling all of us with foolish hope. The new Secretary of the Interior, Walter Hickel, came out from Washington on Sunday, and after a flight over the channel asked the oil companies to stop drilling voluntarily. But within 24 hours Hickel gave the companies permission to resume operation.

By 5 o'clock of that same afternoon the oil was coming in on our public beaches. It lay so thick on the water that the waves were unformed; they made a squishing sound. The next morning the harbor was full of oil. Fishermen and yachtsmen stood around, looking at the black water and the blackened hulls of their boats.

Toward evening I paid a visit to the shore nearest our home, Hope Ranch Beach. There I found something at the edge of the water that looked like a caricature of a western grebe modeled in tar. I tried to catch the poor black flopping thing. It struggled into the water and dived, or sank.

The smell of oil followed me up the canyon to our house, a mile from the sea. The smell, I thought, was beginning to flavor our lives. And we began to get some sense of the scope of our disaster. Ian McMillan, a noted wildlife expert, had come to town on behalf of The Defenders of Wildlife and made an aerial survey of the channel. Afterward, we had lunch together. Ian reported that the affected area was much greater than the Coast Guard's latest estimate, which was 200 square miles. But that was only the solid oil slick. Ian said more like 800 square miles were polluted, and he later increased his estimate to 1,200 square miles.

Though he is a world authority on the California condor, Ian more closely resembles an eagle. A screaming eagle note entered his voice when he began to explain the damage to marine life and birds. "Once the birds are oiled, there isn't much use trying to save them," he said. "They don't do well in captivity. Even if we manage to keep some alive for a time, it's difficult to release them back to the wild. The effects of the spill won't easily be undone, and I deplore"—his voice rose—"I deplore attempts to play it down. I talked to some State Fish and Game men at the harbor this morning. They said they had counted a total of 126 dead birds and rescued 108 live ones. This is just local and immediate damage, as they ought to know if they don't. But they're putting these figures out as official information. Meanwhile hundreds and probably thousands of birds are dying out at sea or being buried on the beaches."

That night an editor of *The New York Times,* who is a fellow birder, called from Washington and asked me what I would look for if I were there in his place. I said I would try to find out how the decision ever got made—under a conservationist Interior Secretary like

Udall—to sell oil-drilling leases in a geologically unstable channel between a projected national park and a coastline that was famous for its beauty. For further light on the question I referred my editor friend to ex-Senator Weingand.

Part of the answer came out in the Sunday *Times*. Udall had been reached in Phoenix and took responsibility for the decision. He added that there had been "no dissent" in the Interior Department, "because 12 years of experience in the Gulf of Mexico, off Louisiana and Texas, had not led to any big leaks, even during hurricanes."

This was strangely in conflict with the statements of an employee of Red Adair, the Houston expert on capping wild oil wells, whose team had been called in to control the Santa Barbara spill. He said that spills were so common off Louisiana that they seldom got into the newspapers. And a Santa Barbara teacher, Fred Eissler, revealed that Udall's account of the decision-making process needed further correction. As a national director of the Sierra Club, Eissler had corresponded with Udall during the battle against the oil rigs coming into our channel. He produced a memo written by Stanley A. Cain, an ecologist who was Udall's assistant secretary for fish, wildlife and parks. On Aug. 7, 1967, Dr. Cain came out in favor of making the Santa Barbara Channel a marine sanctuary. Several days later, under pressure from the Budget Bureau and after a talk with J. Cordell Moore, the assistant secretary in charge of mineral resources, Dr. Cain reversed himself.

As the pieces of the story gradually came together, they seemed to show that the decision was made in favor of oil in the channel, and $603 million of lease money in the U.S. Treasury, without any realistic concern for the local consequences. Dr. Cain wrote in his second memo, for instance, that the oil rigs would stand no closer than five miles to the shore, and that this "would certainly reduce platform visibility from land to negligibility." The fact is that, at the guaranteed distance, the 200-foot drilling structures loom up about as invisibly as aircraft carriers in the channel. I was told by a colleague of Dr. Cain's that the assistant secretary was originally a botanist who had done work on tropical vegetation.

Meanwhile, Secretary Hickel was under mounting pressure to stop the oil operations in the channel. The youngest and fieriest of Santa Barbara County's five supervisors, George Clyde, told Edmund Muskie's U.S. Senate Subcommittee on Air and Water Pollution that Secretary Hickel's 24-hour moratorium on oil drilling was "tokenism" that "smacks of cynicism and cold hypocrisy." Charles M. Teague, the conservative congressman from our district, asked Hickel to reconsider his rapid decision and later introduced a bill to stop the drilling permanently.

One of the voices raised in Washington in defense of drilling belonged to Fred L. Hartley, president of the Union Oil Co. He assured Senator Muskie and his subcommittee that his firm exercised "reasonable diligence" in its drilling. He talked like a man on whom the Santa Barbara Channel had played a dirty trick. His general explanation of the blowout—"Mother Nature, if you have had much contact with her, you will find is always teaching new things"— immediately made Mr. Hartley our favorite natural philosopher.

Within 48 hours we had an unexpected chance to meet him. Senator Muskie and Senator Alan Cranston of California flew out to Santa Barbara for an on-the-spot hearing. Several hundred local people went to the airport to greet them, carrying signs, including Margaret's own BAN THE BLOB. Just ahead of the senators' plane a blue-and-orange Union Oil jet landed. Out stepped Mr. Hartley, a heavyset man with a commanding eye. Many of us booed him, not so much for ruining our coast as for treating us like natives who could be quieted by the techniques of public relations.

Mr. Hartley, followed by several reporters, walked up to me and angrily demanded my name. I gave it to him and added for the benefit of the reporters that I was secretary of the Scenic Shoreline Preservation Conference. Mr. Hartley muttered, "That was quite a speech," and stalked away. I wondered why he had chosen me for his attentions. Margaret said that Mr. Hartley appeared to be accident prone.

Mr. Hartley's impatience carried over into the subcommittee hearing, which was held in the supervisors' meeting room before a packed house. He told Senator Muskie and us that our common disaster was not a disaster, on the grounds that no human beings had been killed. We groaned. Mr. Hartley did have one cheering thing to say. Now, in the 11th day of the spill, his company had assembled enough drilling mud and cement to stop the leaks in the ocean floor, it hoped. The headline in the next day's paper—LEAK PLUGGED, SAYS UNION OIL— made some of us let out a sigh of relief. Others, mostly geologists and oilmen, waited for the other shoe to drop.

Secretary Hickel, yielding finally to public or presidential pressure, had ordered the suspension of all federal oil operations in the Santa Barbara Channel. Because of the danger of further spills, most of us were determined to make the suspension permanent. Over the weekend hundreds of petition bearers spread out over the county. Margaret and I set up a table on Cabrillo Boulevard near the beach to catch the people from out of town.

Cabrillo Boulevard hadn't been so crowded with sightseers since the Fiesta in August. Most of the visitors at our Black Fiesta were glad to sign our Get Oil Out petition. A couple of embarrassed oil workers admitted to "mixed feelings." A few others, even some who signed, advised us gravely that we were wasting our time: the oil companies were too big to fight.

We didn't believe that, and neither did Supervisor George Clyde. He announced over the weekend that he would ask the other supervisors to join him in a resolution against all oil-drilling operations off county shores. On Monday it was passed unanimously before a standing-room-only crowd of citizens. As Supervisor Joe Callahan said, Santa Barbara hadn't been so united since the great earthquake of 1925—which just about wiped the town out.

In the middle of the week I spot-checked 20 miles of beaches to get an idea of the present damage, which was occurring in spite of the considerable efforts of Union Oil to keep the oil off shore and clean up the pollution. I saw no more than a dozen birds, and only three or four of them were shorebirds.

Carpinteria Beach was a black wasteland. Just back of it I found a bird rescue station that Union Oil had set up, and was guided through the two trailers that housed it by a pleasant young man in coveralls. The open plywood pens were full of diving birds, mostly western grebes and loons, sea ducks and cormorants. The hard-hatted oil engineers who looked after them had given each bird the same treatment: a pat of butter forced down its throat to clean it out, a bath of dispersant (Polycomplex A-11), a warm place to sit and pieces of fish to eat.

Of the 600 birds rescued in the 15 days since the well first blew, some 60 percent had survived. I didn't have the heart to tell the engineers that one month after the *Torrey Canyon* spill, of 7,849 birds rescued only 450 survived, and many of these died later, or that, according to English ornithologist James Fisher, for every bird washed ashore at least one was lost at sea.

I visited another bird rescue station, this one at the children's zoo in Santa Barbara. A pretty blonde girl wearing a smock told me in a soft Australian accent that her station had cared for more than 400 birds, of which more than half had died. She was able to show me one shorebird, a rather frazzled godwit standing under a heat lamp. I asked her if the shorebirds had gone inland. She didn't know. But on my way home I stopped at Shoreline Park, above the beach, and counted six oil-smudged sanderlings foraging in the grass.

When I walked into the house Margaret silently handed me the evening paper. The headline said: OIL IS FLOWING AGAIN FROM CHANNEL RUPTURE. We decided to have a look, and reserved a plane for the next day. Then we lined up several expert observers, including a naturalist-photographer, Dick Smith; a writer, Robert Easton; and Waldo Abbott, the ornithologist of the Santa Barbara Museum of Natural History.

The pilot, Margaret Mead of Powderpuff Derby fame, flew us directly out over Platform A and circled the blue skyscraper several times. Oil was welling up in at least three places, coming to the surface on an east-west front of about 1,000 feet. I later found out from a geologist what this meant. "It's leaking along the line of the fault," he said, "which is bad. These multiple leaks are awfully hard to plug."

We flew due south to the mountainous island of Santa Cruz. Much of its shoreline had been blackened, and there was oil on the water far out to sea beyond it. Anacapa, a cliff-surrounded island that is small enough to be seen from the air all at once, was encircled by oil on the beaches and on the water. Anacapa is a national monument.

The last time I visited the island, the beaches had had a primeval quality. Surfbirds and black and ruddy turnstones had crouched on the wet rocks. A few black oyster catchers had poked at shellfish with their surreal red beaks. Now the only visible birds were the gulls speckling a sandbar. We sat in silence as our pilot turned back toward the mainland. The oil lay everywhere on the water in globs and windrows and iridescent slicks.

Flying from Port Hueneme westward to Santa Barbara, we surveyed 45 miles of polluted beaches. The tide line was a broad black band that looked from the air like something marked on a map with a black crayon. Or, when we flew lower, a spattering black brush.

The simile was Waldo Abbott's. "The tide works like a paintbrush on the intertidal zone," he was saying. "It puts on a new coat of oil every time it comes in and recedes. It's hard on the smaller plants and animals—the things that the birds and the larger fishes live on." And then his mind moved in a swoop from the tiny world to the large one: "This is just a little sample of what could happen." He meant the next major earthquake that some seismologists said was overdue, the earthquake that could give us the ultimate oil bath.

The present one was enough. Over the weekend a southeaster rose, driving the floating oil in from the channel, dislodging it from the kelp beds and blowing it to the shore. Suddenly the Biltmore beach, which had already been cleaned by state prisoners and Union Oil men, now looked worse than it ever had, with oil flung 10 feet high along its seawall. Close offshore the sea was a brown emulsion plowed by one forlorn grebe.

Dr. Joseph H. Connell and other university scientists were studying the effects of this oil on life—both animal and human. So far the larger fishes seemed undamaged, though professionals had detected no significant schools of fish in the channel since the spill began. Some of the intertidal life, mussels and anemones, could live with the oil. But some other small species were not so durable. The damage to their populations might cause changes in the food chain, the consequences of which could not yet be measured.

I was particularly interested in the findings of two young environmental scientists, Dr. Norman K. Sanders and Dr. Robert R. Curry. For Sanders the disaster was mainly a human one. The danger, as he saw it, was that the degradation of the environment could ruin Santa Barbara's pride and turn it into just another technological slum. Dr. Curry considered an even more frightening danger: "We had more than 60 moderate earthquakes here last summer and they all originated in the channel. What happens when a major earthquake or a seismic wave comes along? Sooner or later one will. It could knock the whole thing over, shear off the wells if they're still there. The oil could run for years."

Curry is a young man of striking appearance and temperament, with black curly hair and flashing brown eyes. He is also widely qualified in geophysics, geology, hydrology and ecology. About 10 days after our conversation he testified as an expert witness before the Senate. Pointing out the dangers of further drilling in the channel, Curry concluded that "federal leases . . . should be revoked and the offshore fields declared petroleum reserves to be used only in the event of a national emergency." Failing that, the oil operations should be shut down "while the technology caught up to the need for safety." The senators were so impressed that they hired Curry as an adviser.

It seemed to a layman that the senators—and the government—were in need of some new experts. Donald W. Solanas of the Interior Department, whose job it was to supervise our offshore oil operations, defended both the government's widely criticized drilling regulations and the activities of Union Oil. The company complied with the rules, he said, but "Mother Earth broke down on us." Mr. Solanas sounded as if he'd been studying natural philosophy with Mr. Hartley. But his former boss, Secretary Udall, now recognized the seismic dangers in the channel and confessed that he and other Interior Department officials had been "overconfident" in permitting oil drilling there.

Fred Eissler argued that the oil spill could have been averted if the government had listened to the objections of local people. (A high Interior Department official, Eugene W. Standley, had advised against a public hearing on the oil issue because it would "stir up the natives.") Now, Eissler told the subcommittee, the channel should be made into a marine sanctuary under legislation similar to the Wilderness Act.

Toward the end of the day, walking with Bob Easton in the foothills, I told him what had been said at the hearing. He had worked with Fred Eissler for years to get the San Rafael Wilderness established in Santa Barbara's backcountry. Now his imagination was touched by the idea of an ocean wilderness complementing our mountain wilderness and completed by a Channel Islands National Park.

We paused on Mountain Drive and looked out over the platform-studded sea. "It isn't enough just to get rid of them," Bob said. "We've got to convert this horror to positive good. Perhaps we can use it as a pivot to turn the country around before we completely wreck our living space."

On an afternoon near the end of the first month of the era of the Blob, Dr. Sanders brought his wife over to meet mine. By a nice coincidence, Gillian Sanders turned out to be the blonde Australian girl who cared for rescued birds at the children's zoo.

Norman Sanders belongs to a new academic breed. He is a tall, young outdoorsman who once flew the Alaska salmon patrol for the Fish and Wildlife Service and once attempted, with his wife, to sail his 20-foot boat eastward from Tasmania to California.

Now he talked about the necessity of saving our coast. "Some scientists are saying that before long we may not be able to live anywhere else—the interior will be completely polluted."

"Do you believe that could happen?"

"It could, unless we learn to use the planet without destroying it. Our society has failed miserably in letting this spill occur. What if Bob Curry's nightmare came true? What if southern California lost all its sea life and its beaches? What would the people do?"

"Riot, maybe."

"I wouldn't be surprised. Degraded living conditions are a major source of unrest." Sanders paused in a listening attitude, as if he could hear distant rumblings. "There's just one positive thing about this oil mess. Until quite recently, it wouldn't have created such a national uproar. People are finally catching on to how much we have to lose, and how fast we're losing it."

As we talked, our wives moved in from an adjoining room. Margaret was telling Gillian that Hope Ranch Beach had been less severely damaged than some others. The shorebirds were returning, and in spite of the ever-present blob, even a few western grebes could be seen offshore. So our own beach had been lucky. But dead and dying birds were still being picked up along 200 miles of shoreline.

I asked Gillian how her rescued birds at the zoo were doing. She answered with downcast eyes: "They're dying."

She took it hard. As her husband had said, the main disaster is ours. If the oil spillage is ever completely controlled, most of the birds and the other wildlife will eventually renew themselves. But the human damage is irreparable. Our ease and confidence in our environment has cracked, slightly but permanently, like an egg.

THE WIND FROM DUGWAY

Virginia Brodine, Peter P. Gaspar, and Albert J. Pallmann

Security is tight around the Army's Dugway Proving Ground. Restrictions are designed to keep out unauthorized persons and keep in the chemical and biological weapons tested at Dugway. But that security was breached one day in the spring of 1968 when a chemical agent got out of bounds. It carried sickness and death to the flocks of sheep grazing in nearby valleys. It told the world that something was wrong with the safety procedures that should protect living things outside the Proving Ground.

The Army is sufficiently confident of its knowledge of these weapons to manufacture and stockpile them, but it turned out that there were some things it didn't know about the movement of one of the chemical agents through the air and about its biological effects.

Dugway is in thinly populated Tooele County, Utah. The Great Salt Lake Desert covers the western half of the county, and in the

Virginia Brodine, Peter P. Gaspar, Albert J. Pallmann, "The Wind From Dugway," © ENVIRONMENT, *Jan.-Feb. 1969. Reprinted by permission.*

eastern half is a series of small mountain ranges—Cedar, Stansbury-Onaqui and Oquirrh. The Proving Ground is at the edge of the desert, near the southern end of the Cedar Mountains and about eighty miles southwest of Salt Lake City. There are a few ranch houses in the valleys, and the little town of Dugway, with a population of three thousand, is at the southern tip of the Cedar Mountains. The nearest substantial settlement is at Tooele, a town of nine thousand on the eastern side of Rush Valley. Highway 40 crosses the desert some thirty miles to the north of Dugway, and approaches Salt Lake City between the northern ends of the mountain ranges and the southern tip of Salt Lake.

Utah is still cold in the early spring, and a traveler on that route on the cloudy late afternoon of March 13 might have seen patches of snow at the side of the road. The Cedar Mountains, rising two to three thousand feet above the desert on the west and Skull Valley on the east, were snowcapped. No snow fell that day, but occasional rain showers began in the early afternoon.

At five that afternoon, work at Dugway was not yet over. Two tanks of VX had been loaded onto a plane, and the field test with this material was yet to be carried out. The V agents are less volatile substances of the same type as the "G" gases—the nerve gases—developed during World War II by Germany and later by the United States. That is, although they are sometimes referred to as "gases," the V agents, at normal temperatures, are liquids. Like the insecticides parathion, malathion, Azodrin and others, they are organophosphates. If a drop of a V agent falls on an exposed part of the body, it can penetrate the skin. Tiny drops suspended in air can be breathed in; clinging to food or forage, they can be taken in by mouth.

Once in the body, these chemicals intervene rapidly in the processes of the central nervous system. They block the action of a natural chemical, cholinesterase, at the junction of nerves and muscles. When cholinesterase is blocked, there is a dangerous buildup of another chemical in the blood, acetylcholine. Acetylcholine normally conveys nerve signals to the muscles and viscera and then is inactivated by cholinesterase. When cholinesterase cannot do its work, nerve signals are not cut off as they should be and the muscles and viscera no longer function in a normal way. By disrupting the nervous system in this way, the V agent indirectly affects all the body's functions. Symptoms progress from respiratory troubles and loss of muscular coordination to excessive salivation, perspiration and involuntary elimination and finally to convulsions and death. If a victim is given the antidote atropine and artificial respiration immediately, he may recover. The lethal dose for humans has not been reported in the United States, but is known to be very small.

Mixed with VX in the Dugway tanks was a red dye to permit observers to see the otherwise colorless material and to photograph it. A third ingredient was a diluent which gave the final preparation a consistency similar to motor oil.

All those working on the test were doubtless wearing masks and protective clothing and were probably sheltered upwind of the target area. There have been some accidents at Dugway leading to exposures of the field crew and subsequently to tighter safety requirements.

There was apparently nothing particularly new or unusual about this test. Brigadier General William W. Stone, of the office of the Director of Research and Laboratories of the Army Materiel Command later told the Utah congressional delegation that this chemical weapon had been tested literally hundreds of times since 1953, with more than a hundred of these tests being spray trials. The March 13 test was the third of a series of three in an "operational test and evaluation program for an aircraft chemical spray system."

According to the Army Materiel Command, the plane took off, climbing only to 150 feet (about the height of a fifteen story building). The pilot made two practice runs over the target grid, then, heading northwest, turned on the nozzles attached to the tanks and sprayed the target with 320 gallons of the chemical mixture. Five seconds later he ejected the tanks over a drop area. However, a story by Philip Boffey in the News and Comment Section of the December 21, 1968, issue of *Science* reports that there was a malfunction of the ejection equipment. One or both tanks failed to drop. The pilot had no way of halting the flow of the chemical and whatever remained in the tanks was therefore released at a higher altitude—according to Boffey—at about 1500 feet. The *Science* account was read to Dr. G. D. Carlyle Thompson, Utah State Director of Health. He agreed that it was substantially correct.

Field test number three in the operational test and evaluation program was completed, and Dugway officers and men went to bed apparently without knowing that enough VX to cause trouble had slipped past the outer limits of the installation, had crossed the Cedar Mountains into all-too-appropriately named Skull Valley, and some had gone further still, across the Stansbury-Onaqui Mountains into Rush Valley.

Up and down these valleys, and on the lower slopes of the mountains, scattered flocks of sheep were grazing. As night fell, there were more showers, and the temperature, which had dropped suddenly in mid-afternoon, remained low.

On Wednesday, March 14, shepherds from the Hatch Ranch in Skull Valley noticed that some of the sheep near White Rock, on the eastern slope of the Cedar Mountains, were acting in a most peculiar fashion—dazed, staggering, jerking their necks spasmodically to the side, and finally dropping to the ground, apparently exhausted and unable to rise. During the day there were snow flurries, and the sheep continued to graze and lick the snow. More and more of them in two separate flocks showed the strange symptoms and by night some had died. On Thursday, the ranch foreman called the veterinarians who usually cared for the ranch's sheep, Dr. Marr Fawcet and Dr. Richard Winward. The veterinarians had never observed symptoms like this before and were unable to diagnose the illness or to help the sick animals. They called in Dr. Lynn James and Dr. Kent van Kampen, a U.S. Department of Agriculture veterinary pathologist, who arrived on the scene Sunday. Their diagnosis was that a chemical intoxicant was affecting the nervous systems of the sheep, they advised contacting Dugway for information about recent tests. Monday scientists from Dugway appeared, but they had no suggestions to make for the diagnosis of the illness or for therapy.

Several days later, sheep grazing farther from the test site began to sicken and die. A week after the test at Dugway a flock on the west side of the Onaqui Mountains began to show the now familiar, but still puzzling, symptoms.

The first story of what was described as a "mysterious epidemic" appeared in the *Deseret News,* a Salt Lake City paper, on March 19. By this time, men from the U.S. Department of Agriculture's Agricultural Research Service, from the Utah State Department of Health, from the University of Utah and from Dugway had examined the sheep and inspected the area. Dr. J. E. Rasmussen, veterinarian in charge of the Department of Agriculture's Animal Health Division, told the *Salt Lake Tribune* on March 20 that the sheep did not have a contagious disease, but were experiencing the effects of "some sort of poison." An insecticide or a poison plant were suggested as possible causes. As for a chemical weapon from Dugway, the same news story quoted a Dugway information officer: "When we first found out about it, we checked and found we hadn't been running any tests that could cause this." A United Press International story which appeared the next day reported that Dugway officials assured the State Agricultural Commissioner's office "no tests which could be harmful to animals" had been conducted recently at Dugway.

Senator Frank Moss of Utah expressed concern and obtained from the Army Testing Command in Washington the first information about the spray test of a persistent chemical agent at Dugway on March 13. He released this information on March 21.

Meanwhile, toxic plants, pesticides and viruses were eliminated one by one as possible causes. Laboratory tests were made on the tissues and blood of the sheep. Samples of the sheep's food, that had been eaten but not completely digested, were taken from the rumen and stomachs of dead sheep and also tested in the laboratory. The people who live in Skull Valley and those who had been working with the sheep were given blood cholinesterase tests; results were all within normal limits. Normal blood cholinesterase is within a range from 7.5 to 16.2; 40 people tested by the Utah Department of Health showed levels between 9.2 and 14.1. Lowered blood cholinesterase was found in sheep, however, and to a lesser extent in cattle and horses. Several days after the illness first appeared sheep were treated with atropine, an antidote for organophosphate poisoning. The sheep failed to respond, except to massive doses, and even then the recovery was only temporary. Atropine was tried again, also unsuccessfully, in succeeding days.

Five sheep were taken into the test area on March 19. After grazing there, all five showed the same symptoms as the Skull Valley sheep, but all survived and recovered. Healthy sheep were placed in the Skull Valley pasture in early April. These, too, developed symptoms of central nervous system damage. Some sheep not seriously sick were sent to the U.S. Department of Agriculture's Research Station at Logan, Utah, for continued investigation. Among these were pregnant ewes, so that effects on the lambs could be observed.

Dugway personnel began to feed VX to healthy sheep on an experimental basis. Some of these sheep were then given atropine with better response than when these drugs were given to the range sheep after a time lag of a week or more.

General Stone explained at a hearing in the office of Senator Wallace F. Bennett of Utah on March 25 that prior to this experiment with feeding the V agent, there had been "meager information concerning its effects on sheep." In response to a later question, Joseph W. Penton, Public Information Officer for the Army Materiel Command,

stated on May 6 that previous tests of the agent had been on laboratory animals. Direct information about its effect on sheep was apparently not only meager, but non-existent.

There were now nine agencies participating in the investigation:
Dugway Proving Ground and Edgewood Arsenal from the U.S. Army,
the Department of Health and the Department of Agriculture from
the State of Utah, the National Animal Disease Laboratory and the
Poisonous Plant Laboratory from the U.S. Department of Agriculture,
the Department of Ecology and Epizoology from the University of
Utah, the Department of Animal Science from the University of California at Davis, and the National Communicable Disease Center of
the U.S. Public Health Service.

Only by testing the forage, the snow, and the blood and stomach
samples from the affected sheep for the presence of a chemical and
comparing the results with the same tests of VX could it be determined
whether VX was the cause of the disaster. But until three weeks after
the incident only Dugway and Edgewood Arsenal, of the nine investi-
gative agencies, had samples of the chemical weapon.

On April 4 a sample of the chemical weapon tested on March 13
was supplied to the National Communicable Disease Center (NCDC)
in Atlanta, Georgia. NCDC was also given a sample of another chemical which, because of its similarity to VX, was sometimes used in
Dugway tests. The sample provided by Dugway was small and dilute.
The first laboratory tests were inconclusive. The NCDC chemists persisted, however, and on April 12 sent a telegram to Dr. G. D. Carlyle
Thompson, Director of the Division of Health of the Utah Department
of Health and Welfare, which was released to the press. It said in part:

Chemists of NCDC have isolated an identical compound from snow water
and grass from White Rock area and from liver, blood and stomach contents of dead sheep from same area. . . . Compound has been shown
identical to test agent supplied by Dr. K. M. Brauner, Dugway April 4,
1968.[1]

To chemists who were not involved in the investigation, one of the
most puzzling aspects of the whole affair was the month-long lag between the dispersion of the agent on March 13 and its identification
in animal and environmental samples on April 12.

[1] And material that follows on NCDC testing from *Investigation of Sheep
Deaths—Skull Valley, Utah,* Department of Health, Education, and Welfare,
Health Services and Mental Health Administration, DP, National Communi-
cable Disease Center, Atlanta, Georgia, April 29, 1968.

Techniques for detecting minute amounts of chemical compounds are well known, and sensitive equipment is in use in many laboratories. The Dugway laboratory, in particular, where the composition of the test agent was known, where samples of it were available, and where sheep tissue samples were also available only a few days after the exposure, should have been the first to detect the similarities later found by the NCDC laboratory. Yet on March 29, two weeks after the first sheep deaths, a release from Senator Moss's office reported that General Stone, who was then heading the investigation in Utah, "said . . . that none of the nerve agent which was released from the airplane on March 13 has been discovered in the soil, water, or forage of the area where the sheep died."

The need for techniques which would detect minute amounts of organic substances became acute some years ago, with the introduction of organophosphate pesticides. These chemicals are very efficient contact poisons with physiological properties similar to nerve gases. They are, however, much less persistent than pesticides like DDT. They are changed by contact with air, water and sunlight, and therefore lose their toxicity rapidly once they are out in the environment.

Fortunately, our ability to isolate and detect infinitesimal amounts of such chemicals has improved vastly in the last dozen years. The detection of one chemical present in a mixture was often difficult in 1955 if it made up only one part in a hundred. Since the introduction of a new technique called gas chromatography, limits of detectability have rapidly decreased, first to one part in a thousand, then to one part in a hundred thousand. In the last ten years it has become possible to detect as little as one part in a million or even, for certain mixtures, one part in a hundred million.

Gas chromatography is a process by which mixtures of gases, liquids or solids in the form of vapors are separated. The mixture is swept through a tube in a carrier gas stream. The walls of the tube are coated with a stationary liquid, or the tube is packed with an inert substance with the consistency of sand which is coated with the stationary liquid. The components of the gaseous mixture are retarded in the tube differently, depending on their individual tendencies to be absorbed in the stationary liquid. A difference of seconds in the time each component is retained in the tube separates it from the rest of the components in the mixture and each component is swept out of the tube by the carrier gas individually. The time required for passage through the tube varies for different substances and is a *distinctive characteristic of the substance*. Although occasionally two substances may be retained for the same time, there are additional laboratory tests which can further differentiate them. Sensitivity depends on how little of a given substance can be detected in the carrier gas stream as it emerges from the tube.

Gas chromatography has replaced distillation as an analytical tool and has thereby revolutionized chemistry. Where distillation requires about one-thousandth of a liter and can separate substances with boiling points several degrees apart, gas chromatography can separate one ten-millionth of a liter of a mixture of substances with *identical* boiling points.

The identification of pesticide residues has become an important application of gas chromatography since it is necessary to determine whether the parts per million of pesticides which could be injurious if ingested by humans are present in fruits, vegetables, grains or products manufactured therefrom.

An example of rapid analysis for traces of a pesticide occurred in the Tijuana bread tragedy of 1967, when hundreds of people were stricken and many died from eating foodstuffs contaminated with parathion, an organophosphate pesticide. Many more people would have died had not gas chromatography analysis in the California Department of Agriculture Pesticide Residue Laboratories rapidly identified the culprit, allowing doctors to halt the death toll by administration of atropine. Within 2 hours of the receipt of samples, and within 31 hours of the first death, chemists detected 8 parts per million of parathion in a sample of contaminated bread and 19.5, 16.6 and 31.2 parts per million of parathion in the stomach contents of three victims.

The prompt identification of parathion as the poison responsible for the Tijuana tragedy contrasts sharply with the time required for the identification of VX as the poison which felled the sheep in Skull Valley. As early as March 24, an anonymous rancher told the *Salt Lake Tribune* that he had a laboratory report "confirming the presence of organic phosphate," while a Department of Defense press release on April 18 stated that the agent tested was an organophosphate compound. Furthermore, the Dugway test agent was apparently similar in structure and ease of analysis to parathion. This was suggested by a report in *Chemical Week* on April 6 that para-nitrophenol, which is also derived from the decomposition of parathion, had been isolated from the sheep and environmental samples.

All the nine agencies participating in the investigation presumably possess the chromatography equipment to do trace pesticide analysis. Why then was positive identification of the test agent in snow samples, grass, and sheep's blood and stomach contents delayed until early April when the NCDC obtained identical response from the Skull

Valley samples, the test agent and degradation products of the test agent?

Samples from the sheep and from the environment did not reach the NCDC until March 2, although the test agent was known to be chemically unstable and early information from the Army was that it would have a lifetime in the field of only six or seven days. By the time the samples were taken the concentration of the agent was low.

No comparison between the Skull Valley samples and the authentic test agent was possible until April 4, when an apparently minute amount of test agent was supplied. Without virtually simultaneous comparison between suspected and authentic materials, positive identification by gas chromatography is very difficult. Once authentic material was available, identification by NCDC was quite rapid. It should be added that NCDC worked under the double handicap of no prior standardization of the analytical equipment for the test agent and a very small amount of test agent with which to work. The rapid identification of parathion in the Tijuana bread tragedy was possible only because the analytical instruments were constantly being checked and corrected for parathion identification. Constant recalibration of the instruments is important because the characteristic time required for the passage of a substance through the gas chromatograph varies with daily fluctuations in instrumental conditions.

VX is far more toxic than parathion, one of the most poisonous agricultural chemicals. A lethal dose for sheep is twenty milligrams of parathion per kilogram of body weight taken orally. After the experimental work with the sheep had been done at Dugway, the lethal dose of VX was determined: it took only a tiny fraction of a milligram of the nerve gas to kill the sheep exposed. Therefore, instruments of maximum sensitivity, designed specifically for phosphorus compounds, were required to detect the tiny, but lethal, amount present in the animals pastured in Skull Valley and in their environment.

The California Department of Agriculture laboratory in the Tijuana episode was using instruments which would easily detect one-tenth part of parathion per million parts of the sample. The NCDC laboratory in the sheepkill episode had instruments which could probably detect one-hundredth part per million of parathion or materials similar to it such as the test agent. The Utah State Department of Health, according to its director, Dr. G. D. Carlyle Thompson, could have detected the agent in amounts only down to ten parts per million. It had no phosphorus attachment for its detector at that time. The amount of the test agent reported by NCDC to be present in the Skull Valley samples was too little for the Utah State Health laboratory to detect. Even for its more sensitive equipment, the NCDC concentrated its samples before analysis so that the agent was less dilute and easier to identify.

It is not clear why the Dugway Proving Ground itself and the Edgewood Arsenal (the chemical warfare depot of the Army) lagged behind the NCDC in a relatively straightforward, albeit specialized analysis. It would be surprising if Dugway and Edgewood were not equipped to do the most up-to-date analyses for trace amounts of nerve agents. (Some of the other agencies whose laboratories may have had the capability to do so were not supplied with pure samples of the test agent.) A more important question is whether Dugway and nearby civilian health authorities are *now* equipped to do rapid analyses for any and all nerve agents which might be loosed in their midst, and whether they will be supplied with samples of materials being tested at the Proving Ground.

In order to effectively protect the populations for which they are responsible, health agencies must not only possess the sensitive analytical equipment, but they must also have access to the various agents which they might be called upon to detect. Further, monitoring for these agents must be continuous, *or* warning must be given when tests are to take place.

We were informed by Dr. Thompson that the Utah State Health Department *now* has the capability to detect one-tenth part per million of the test agent responsible for the sheep death.

There is a final puzzling aspect to the difficulties encountered in determining whether the test agent had indeed escaped from Dugway.

The mixture sprayed from the airplane at Dugway was mixed with a red dye. The extract of snow water from Dugway prepared at NCDC was found to have a red color. What this means is that the ratio of dye to nerve gas was sufficiently great that a crude test could have been done: shaking melted snow with a small amount of ether or some other organic solvent. The ether would extract the dye, thus concentrating it and making it easier to see. This would have given instant, albeit circumstantial evidence of the presence of the test agent. This crude test could have been done immediately after the observation of the first symptoms in the sheep. It could have been done in the field with no more equipment than a large jar and a campfire or ranch house stove. Furthermore, since the dye is persistent, its presence could have been sought by this method even after the nerve gas itself had begun to decompose. True, dye had also been mixed with a simulated agent which had been sprayed at Dugway, but this crude test would have indicated the presence of either VX, or the simulant or both, and this knowledge would have brought the investigation much closer to its goal.

Following the NCDC report on April 12, Dugway supplied the NCDC laboratory with additional samples of VX as well as samples of GB, another nerve gas. Further tests confirmed that the former was identical to material in the samples from sheep and from the Skull Valley environment.

The cause of the sheepkill had now been found to the satisfaction of everyone but the Army, which continued to call the findings "inconclusive." But the answer to one question raised another: how could the spray from the test find its way across a mountain range— in fact, across two mountain ranges? The answer to this question is not to be found in the laboratory, but in the weather reports. Although there is a weather tower at the Proving Ground, detailed weather data obtained there on March 13 were not released. In answer to a question about meteorological conditions, a Dugway spokesman gave this summary:

There was a wind from the south-southwest at the time of the 13 March 1968 test. The wind shifted about two hours later and blew from the west. There were scattered cumulus clouds in the general area at the time of the test and scattered rain showers developed during the early evening.

An analysis of the large scale movements of the atmosphere based on data from other weather stations, especially from the nearby municipal airport at Salt Lake City reinforces what is suggested in the brief paragraph from Dugway. *Weather conditions on March 13 were unfavorable for the atmospheric testing of a chemical weapon.*

This is not simply hindsight. Weather indications on the preceding days and in the morning and early afternoon of the day of the test pointed to a distinct possibility that spray released at the Proving Ground might be drawn up into the clouds and released east of the mountains. Army statements have emphasized the wind shift which occurred two hours after the test, implying that it may have been an unexpected shift of wind that was responsible for the escape of the deadly chemical. However, any wind shift as long as two hours after the test may have been irrelevant. Droplets of the chemical had probably already been deposited in Skull Valley pastures by that time.

When droplets of a liquid are discharged from an airplane, they will disperse in a cone-shaped plume and gradually fall to the ground. How far the plume will extend, and how long it will take the droplets to fall depends upon the height at which they are discharged, the size of the drops and the speed of the wind. The smaller the drops, the more slowly they fall to the ground; the greater the wind speed, the faster and farther the drops will be carried. Although a uniform size of droplets may be desired, complete uniformity is impossible—and therefore exact prediction of size is difficult—because of the air turbulence around the spray nozzles in the wake of the airplane and the wind shear off the plane's wings.

Sprayed from a plane at a height of 150 feet, in a windy atmosphere as in the chemical weapons test of March 13, droplets down to a size of about 200 microns in diameter—that is, so small there would be 127 of them in an inch—would fall out within a few miles downwind from the spot at which they were discharged. They would reach the ground in less than three minutes. Even droplets of half that size would not be carried much farther before reaching the ground. However very tiny droplets of ten microns or so could be carried many miles.

But if there is turbulent air movement to carry the drops upward, the picture changes. Forest insecticide spray programs in mountainous areas often run into trouble with vertical eddy motions that interfere with the fallout of the drops and operate to pick them up and carry them a considerable distance from the point of discharge. As much as 25 percent of the amount sprayed has sometimes been lost in this way. If the ground has been warmed by the sun, there may be updrafts which pick up the droplets and carry them over even rather high ridges. Or, a cloud may draw the droplets up, hold them as it travels with the wind, and deposit them some distance away in a shower of rain. It was probably this mechanism which operated at Dugway on March 13. Even some of the spray released as low as 150 feet could have been drawn up into the clouds, while the probable accidental release as high as 1500 feet makes this mechanism appear still more likely.

For several days prior to the test on the thirteenth, an intense low pressure system was approaching the North American continent from the west over the Pacific. By March 12, evidence was mounting that it would influence Utah weather in subsequent days. Cloudiness pertinent to the cold front of the system appeared over Nevada and northwestern Utah. On the thirteenth, this maritime cold front passed through Utah. As is well known, a front passage is often accompanied by wind shift, gustiness, increased cloudiness, temperature changes and precipitation, and all these occurred and were observed at the U.S. Weather Bureau station in Salt Lake City. A cold front passage disrupts the stratification of the atmosphere and vertical air movements develop, with small parcels of air moving upward and downward almost independently of each other. Cumulus clouds with flat bases and rounded outlines may be formed, and sometimes (as in this case) there is a cumulonimbus formation—a mountainous cumulus cloud extending to great heights and topped with a veil of ice crystals.

At the U.S. Weather Bureau station at the municipal airport in Salt Lake City, an apparent front passage was noted just before one o'clock in the afternoon of March 13, with the wind shifting from the south-southwest (190°) to the west (270°) and changing from 14 to 15 miles per hour with gusts up to 23. At 3:15 there was a seven degree drop in temperature to 42° F. The cloud ceiling lowered from 5500 to 1900 feet, and there were rain showers in the area. The surface winds continued to shift in the late afternoon from north-northeast to west and back to northwest, but higher up, where the clouds were, *the wind was steadily from the southwest* at a speed of 29 miles per hour and more. Occasional rain showers were observed southwest of the station just before five and again two hours later, with scattered cumulus clouds throughout the day and evening. There were heavy cumulus clouds in all directions between five and six o'clock, including the southwest, the direction of Dugway.

In the jet stream high above the earth, a core of high-speed wind was measured over northern California and Oregon on March 12, shifting southeastward toward Utah. At five o'clock on the thirteenth, the maximum wind speed of this core was measured near Salt Lake City. Wind was recorded from the southwest (235°) at a height of 33,000 feet and a speed of 115 miles per hour. It appears, therefore, that this wind passed over Dugway earlier in the afternoon. The consequence of such a passage of high speed jet wind is an intense interference with the dynamics of the weather layers below.

From the combined effects of the cold front and the jet stream wind, increased vertical mixing of the atmosphere below could be expected, favoring the development of precipitating cumulus clouds. Such a cloud could suck particulates such as the oily droplets sprayed at Dugway into its updraft. If their size was less than 250 microns, they could be drawn into the interior of the cloud at a velocity of one meter (39.37 inches) per second. In exceptional cases, eddies of turbulence near the earth's surface produce vertical speeds of two meters per second. When this occurs, particulates up to 500 microns can be carried into the cloud. The cloud would hold these particles until it started to precipitate.

A surface wind from the northwest would have moved the spray particles southeast as they were being drawn up into the cloud. The cloud would then have been blown northeast by the wind in the upper weather layers. This is consistent with the position of the affected flocks.

It is not unlikely that such a cloud would travel a distance of about 30 miles before precipitation began. A shower would then deposit much of the chemical agent in the cloud along with the rain. However, the smaller spray droplets might well be kept in the upper part of the cloud even after the first precipitation. Such a remainder could be forced to precipitate later, when the cloud traveled over another mountain ridge, where the upslope motion from below would stimulate coalescence among the cloud elements which would fall as rain on the other side of the mountain. This could readily explain the spotty deposition of the chemical in Skull Valley and beyond the next ridge in Rush Valley. It also suggests that the town of Dugway, which is in the sector probably traversed by the clouds, may have had a narrow escape.

Cumulus cloud formation, with southwest or west winds, falling temperature, and precipitation, could have been expected from the large-scale weather developments and strongly indicated against dissemination of a persistent lethal agent on that day.

Still another question relates to the monitoring of the spray plume. Recently, the U.S. Forest Service, in cooperation with the Stanford Research Institute, has employed an improved technique for monitoring plumes from insecticide spraying. Taking advantage of developments in laser technology, *lidar rays* have overcome many of the difficulties in tracking spray plumes. The lidar gun shoots a beam of light into the plume. The reflected beam is measured on an instrument that registers variations of light in electric current and records them photographically. The lidars used by the Forest Service are able to track tiny droplets for as long as twenty minutes after they are released. Lidar is certainly available to Dugway, and if used during the March 13 test would have revealed the escape of the spray northeast toward Skull Valley. Lidar can be used even after dark. But even if some other photographic monitoring process had been used rather than lidar, there should have been ample light to follow the spray, since the sun did not set till 6:30.

We asked R. L. McNamara, the chief of Dugway's Information Office, what technique the Army used to monitor the amount of materials reaching the ground and how long the monitoring was continued. The reply was that this is "defense information not releasable to the public."

In 1968, when the sheepkill was in the news, concern for improved safety measures around Dugway was repeatedly expressed by Senators Moss and Bennett of Utah, by other public figures and by people in the area. A federal Interagency Advisory Committee was formed to review "the procedures, talents, monitoring equipment facilities and safety regulations" at Dugway. The Committee's report, released on December 20, made sweeping recommendations for changes in safety procedures.[2] In doing so, they revealed quite clearly the deficiencies that had existed. Indeed, given the state of safety precautions revealed by the report, it can only be concluded that the people of Utah, and perhaps of neighboring states as well, were fortunate that the accident was no worse, and involved only sheep, not people.

The Committee's first recommendation was that persistent lethal agents should not be tested in amounts exceeding one artillery round, rocket or mine without modifications of safety procedure. Two tanks —320 gallons—of VX is far more than this, and it may be that even greater amounts were dispersed in other Dugway tests.

The Committee felt that past procedures were adequate for continued testing of agents and munitions for riot control, for those that are incapacitating rather than lethal, and for those that are lethal but non-persistent. A fourth category, "new and/or more toxic agents and munitions" was not discussed. The changes in safety procedures required for the resumption of tests of *persistent lethal* agents and munitions (such as VX) took up most of the Advisory Committee's attention in its report.

No release, the report advises, should be made at heights greater than 300 feet; no significant fraction of the agent cloud should be composed of particles smaller than 100 microns in size; and positive control of agent dissemination should be maintained by automatic flow devices. Also, when high performance aircraft are used for dispensing toxic chemical agents having properties equivalent to those of the nerve agent VX, control by radar and radio, by the establishment of limitations on total quantity of agent dispersed and by other available means, is recommended.

On March 13, part of the release was probably as high as 1500 feet. Smaller particles, as stated earlier, fall to the ground more slowly and are more easily picked up by vertical drafts of air; it was probably

---

[2] *Report of the Interagency Ad Hoc Advisory Committee for Review of Testing Safety at Dugway Proving Ground,* Department of the Army, Washington, D.C., Nov. 1968.

these smaller particles which travelled across the mountains. Positive control of agent dissemination means that the pilot should be able to shut off the dissemination promptly if anything goes wrong. This was apparently not possible on March 13.

The advisory report's discussion of weather conditions states that heretofore the presence of turbulent winds, which would mix and dilute any of the agent not falling rapidly to the ground, was considered a desirable weather condition for a test. The other problems of turbulent winds, namely, changing wind directions, updrafts into clouds, and rapid transport of these clouds beyond the Proving Ground, were apparently given little, if any weight. Moreover, *concern with wind and weather was restricted to a few miles from the release.*

These changes in procedure having to do with meteorological conditions were recommended: winds should be from the south-southeast, blowing toward the salt flats where little vegetation, no domestic animals and no people would be exposed until Highway 40 is reached. The wind at the surface should be no more than fifteen miles per hour, and the agent cloud should not cross Highway 40 for at least three hours. Confidence in the weather forecast should be high; there must be past experience demonstrating the reliability of predictions from similar weather situations. Concern must now be extended to several tens of miles. No thunderstorms should be present within one hundred miles of the test site at release time nor predicted to occur within one hundred miles of the cloud trajectory for at least eight hours from actual release time.

The discussion of weather earlier in this article makes the need for most of these recommendations quite clear, but a few words should be added about the danger from thunderstorms. When thunderstorms are imminent, updrafts into the clouds are very strong. Quite large particles can be drawn up from low altitudes and carried tens of miles before being dumped in a thundershower. Moreover, thunderclouds may grow to towering heights and travel at great speeds; smaller particles could be held in the upper portions of the thunderclouds and carried still farther. A test of VX, or some other persistent lethal chemical, was apparently quite possible in such weather under the old procedures. With or without a malfunction of the tanks and a high release of the agent, a deadly load might have been picked up and carried the eighty miles to Salt Lake City.

The surface winds referred to in the Advisory Committee report are those that can be measured with an anomometer—a device attached to a pole which measures wind direction and speed from ten to thirty feet from the ground. This seems to imply that radiosonde soundings from balloons are not taken prior to tests—that perhaps, indeed, the weather station at Dugway was not even equipped to make these soundings, which can give wind direction and speed up to great heights. The Committee recommends "improved meteorological capability" but does not spell this out in detail. This capability should certainly include radiosonde soundings at the Proving Ground or close coordination with the Salt Lake City weather station, which takes these soundings on a regular basis.

Better understanding of what can happen to drops of VX and like materials under various weather conditions is also recommended, but not spelled out in detail. One way this can be achieved is by spraying a harmless material in the same diluent used for chemical agents in a variety of winds and weathers and monitoring the spray closely; planes could be sent aloft to see if any of the material could be picked up at various heights, as is done with fallout from nuclear weapons tests. Planes with continuously recording photospectrometers are used for air pollution monitoring in California.

The Committee also points out that the death of the sheep suggested the possibility that scavenging of the air by rain or snow may be a crucial contributor to hazard from the dispersal of chemical agents in the atmosphere, and advised testing only when confident predictions can be made that there will be no precipitation for eight hours after the test.

A very much more extensive and intensive research program is recommended, beginning with determination (or estimation) of the toxicity to animals and humans of both sexes and all ages and to pregnant females of any compound released into the environment. This should be studied by single and repeated doses, and by low-dose chronic administration. The Committee stated that on June 14, 1968, the values for the LD_{50}, that is, the amount of the agent that would kill half those exposed, was available for the mouse, rat, guinea pig, rabbit, cat, dog, monkey and chimpanzee among laboratory and pet animals and for the pig, goat and horse among domestic animals. No information was available on the sheep, the most important domestic animal in the vicinity, nor on the cow, nor on any of the wild species living in that area.

Research was recommended on the fate of the agents in the environment, in the soil, plants, water supplies, snow and indigenous plants at the test site and up to several tens of miles away. The kind of study needed is outlined in some detail. The report then remarks that "the greater the risk of the agent reaching off-post locations [inhabited by man, domestic animals and wildlife] the greater the need and the degree of understanding of the behavior and fate of the agent in the environment." While this is true, it leaves a somewhat disquieting loophole in the research recommendations. In March, Dugway officials stated unequivocally that there was *no* risk of the agent reaching *any* off-post location. If the need for environmental research is to be determined by Dugway estimates of the likelihood of off-post exposures, the sheepkill incident can give the people in the surrounding area little confidence that this research program will be pursued with vigor.

The sheepkill incident showed that on-post monitoring of chemical agents was inadequate and off-post monitoring was non-existent. There was no alarm system, and no medical countermeasures for man or animals were prepared. The Committee gave some pages of its report to the "need to develop and implement a monitoring program designed to detect the immediate presence and/or verify the absence of chemical agents in areas outside the Dugway Proving Ground grid areas, including the off-post areas contiguous to the Proving Ground."

The Committee recommended ten permanent monitoring sites of about five acres each, three of them west of the Cedar Mountains, five east of the Cedar Mountains in Skull Valley, and two east of the Stansbury Mountains in Rush Valley. It would seem that in addition, and especially if the Committee's recommendation to test only when the wind is from the south-southeast is followed, there should be at least one station between Dugway and Highway 40. The Committee proposed that the monitoring system be developed in coordination with the Utah State Department of Health and other appropriate state and federal agencies.

Monitoring as outlined by the Committee would have three aspects: regular sampling schedule (at least monthly) to determine the presence or absence of the agent chemicals in soil, water, snow and plants; a "sentinel" system using sheep, since they have proved to be susceptible to at least one of the chemical agents tested at Dugway, or, when the sensitivity of indigenous wild animals has been determined, using one of these species; and an alarm system based on an air sampler which automatically tests for the chemical agents. However, the Committee warns, the lack of sensitivity of the air sampler may limit its usefulness.

Three types of monitoring not mentioned by the Committee could well be added: the use of treated cards which are sensitive either to the agent itself or to the oily carrier, as used with good results to monitor forest spraying programs; use of dye, with a specific color being limited to a specific agent, and environmental sampling for the presence of the dye immediately after every test; and the addition of fluorescent particles to the oil carrier. When fluorescent particles are used, vegetation can be quickly checked by placing it in a dark box equipped with an ultraviolet light. This equipment is easily portable and can be carried on a small truck. The U.S. Forest Service has used this method for detecting drops as small as 26 microns.

The Committee found Dugway's routine safety measures on the post adequate, but recommended coordination with the off-post medical community, state and federal health authorities, and agricultural agencies concerned with animal health. Also recommended were preparations for that "accidental event which might occur only one time every 25 years," which might expose "groups of personnel not involved with testing who live on Dugway Proving Ground or in areas surrounding the test installations." These recommended preparations include: a mass casualty plan with specific care and evacuation procedures for patients exposed to chemical agents, liaison and coordination with outside medical resources to insure a feasible medical evacuation, and at least annual exercises to test mass casualty and medical evacuation procedures.

In order that the surrounding community may have confidence that testing is being done safely, and so that in the event of an emergency, animals and people may have some protection, the Committee stated that general knowledge of Dugway activities, of the characteristics of the agents being tested, and of the safety precautions on and off the post must be communicated to certain responsible state officials. In addition, some officials must have specific technical knowledge. A review by the Department of the Army of the present public information policy was also recommended "for possible provision of information before, during and after testing concerning the general nature of the tests and the comprehensive safety program associated with the tests."

Finally, the report concluded with a recommendation for a permanent chemical safety committee to provide at least annual review and advise the commanding general at Dugway, and a suggestion that possibly the Army should manage additional land adjacent to the Proving Ground.

The Army has announced that all the recommendations of the Committee have been adopted.

Improved safety precautions may insure that the same disaster is not repeated, but a larger problem was illuminated when the sheep died. Chemical and biological weapons cannot be used in war without extensive testing under various meteorological and field conditions; without such testing the military will not know the capabilities of the weapons and there is also danger of backfire on the users. Yet field testing, which releases these agents into the environment, where to some extent they may escape from control, is itself hazardous.

One simple mistake in chemical or biological testing can have far-reaching consequences. Dugway officials will now be alert to prevent a recurrence of the particular accident of March 1968, but a test plane may crash someday, some chemical agent other than VX whose environmental or biological behavior is not fully understood, some other imperfectly assessed meteorological conditions, some malfunction in a dispersion system or trial of an untried system, some other human error may cause some other accident. Next time, the consequences may not be limited to sheep.

THE URBAN ENVIRONMENT

Public concern about the quality of the urban environment is increasing rapidly in America: one reason for this is that the country itself is becoming increasingly urbanized, as rural residents move into cities and as cities, their populations swelling, spread ever-farther into once-rural areas; another reason is that the problems of cities tend to be visible and immediate and explosive. Few Americans have had the opportunity to see and to experience at first hand the gradual destruction of a wild river, but most of us have in our lifetimes experienced the deterioration of a neighborhood. It takes some study to appreciate and fear the effects of thermal pollution or DDT, but no special competence is required to fear crime in the streets or rebellion in a ghetto.

This last subject, the struggle of racial minorities to survive in the urban environment, is raised first in this section. Irving Kristol, who is a vice-president of Basic Books, Inc., and co-editor of the magazine *The Public Interest,* looks at it from a historical perspective and, while conceding the seriousness of the conditions which affect blacks in American cities, criticizes many of the prevailing liberal assumptions about the problem. But, while Kristol's point of view is wider than most, it also has its aspects of narrowness: one is the expectation, common to analyses which approach problems historically, that the people actually involved in a situation can *experience* it historically— that it can be any consolation at all for a black man to learn that he is doing better than the Irish did as newcomers to the city, when he is quite obviously worse off than the Irish are today. Another narrowness is contained in the references to the Cadillac as a goal of economic achievement. It is reasonable enough for the author to accept the Cadillac as a kind of symbol of the value system which possesses white and black alike, but in doing so he fails to raise the question of how long we can continue to live in cities full of Cadillacs.

Lewis Mumford, a uniquely American philosopher who was writing of relevant American problems—machines and cities, buildings and the need for a human scale in human surroundings—long before relevance became a catch-phrase, does raise the question. In doing so he picks up where Kristol—and a whole set of values connected with transportation, urban life, and the role of the citizen as consumer—leaves off.

The wisdom of Mumford's warning about one-dimensional transportation has been borne out in many ways since the article was written in 1958: transportation was an important factor, for example, in the riots of the Watts section of Los Angeles. Studies have revealed that one of the sources of frustration in the ghetto was the extreme difficulty of getting a job outside the ghetto unless one owned a car. In the city of the automobile, not owning a car was a special kind of deprivation, and still is: it is not uncommon for people in Watts to spend three hours a day riding to and from work, and other political forces have made it likely that no sudden change will be forthcoming. In 1968, voters in Los Angeles turned down a proposal to build a rapid transit system; automobile and highway interests, including the Southern California Automobile Club, contributed to the campaign against rapid transit. Transportation is one of the keys to both urban and rural environmental conditions, and it is an area of decision-making dominated by powerful interest groups: airlines, construction firms, trucking businesses, and the automobile industry are some of them.

Lyle C. Fitch is president of the Institute of Public Administration in New York City and a writer on social and urban problems; in his essay "Eight Goals for an Urbanizing America," he attempts to put forth a set of general objectives which might be agreed upon by those who will live in, work in, alter or help to plan American cities.

This, of course, means most Americans: in an urbanizing nation, the environmental problems that are immediately important to the greatest number of citizens are urban problems. The quality of the urban environment is a national issue of the highest priority; as we come to realize this, we must realize also that we cannot look at problems in a piecemeal way—suddenly becoming concerned about law and order, or education, or air pollution—but must also begin to talk more about the whole question of how human beings can exercise their rights to life, liberty and the pursuit of happiness in modern cities. That kind of political dialogue will require, as Fitch says, visions of efficiency, beauty, and social justice.

THE NEGRO TODAY IS LIKE THE IMMIGRANT YESTERDAY

Irving Kristol

Let us suppose that, a century ago, Harvard had been host to a conference on "the crisis in our cities." Let us suppose further that there were sociologists in those times (sociologists such as we know them today, I mean) and city planners and professors of social work and directors of institutes of mental health and foundation executives— and that these assembled scholars were asked to compose a description of the urban conditions in the United States. They would have been at no loss for words, and their description would have gone something like this:

"Our cities are suffering a twofold crisis. First, there is the critical problem arising from the sheer pressure of numbers upon the amenities of civilized life. Our air becomes ever more foul from the activities —both at work and at play—of this large number; our water is shockingly polluted; our schools are overcrowded; our recreational facilities vandalized; transportation itself, within the city, requires ever more heroic efforts.

Irving Kristol, "The Negro Today Is Like the Immigrant Yesterday," THE NEW YORK TIMES MAGAZINE, *Sept. 11, 1966. © 1966 by the New York Times Company. Reprinted by permission.*

"As if this were not enough, there is this second phenomenon to observe: our cities are being inundated *by people who are themselves problems.* These are immigrants—Irish, mainly—who are more often than not illiterate and who are peculiarly unable to cope with the complexities of urban life. Their family life is disorderly; alcoholism is rampant among them; they have a fearfully high rate of crime and delinquency; not only do they live in slums, but they create slums wherever they live; they are bankrupting the resources of both public and private charities; they are converting our cities into vast cesspools of shame, horror and despair; they are———" And so on and so forth.

Any American of the nineteen-sixties could complete this bleak catalogue without overly exerting himself: it is the identical catalogue that any such conference today would come up with.

Now, it is important to realize that the scholars of a hundred years ago would have been telling the truth. Because we surmounted the particular crisis they endured, we would be inclined to think their concern bordered on hysteria, and that they unduly exaggerated the evils around them. They did nothing of the sort—I say "did" because, while this conference is hypothetical, the urban crisis was real enough at that time. We sneer gently at the agitation of years ago as representing a lack of imagination on the part of "The Brahmins"—the "old Americans"—and as testifying to a fear of historical change combined with an overrefined distaste for plebeian realities. We think of Henry James lamenting his "sense of dispossession"; and we do not think too flatteringly of him for doing so. But the question might be asked: are we not all Brahmins now?

I am not saying that the problems of American cities today are identical with, or even perfectly parallel with, those of yesteryear. Such identities do not exist in history; and all historical parallels are, in the nature of things, less than perfect. But I do think it important that we keep American urban history always in mind, lest we be carried away by a hysteria all our own.

Just how close we are to such a hysteria may be discovered by directing to ourselves the question: *how much of a disaster would it be if some of our major cities were to become preponderantly Negro?* I rather doubt we would answer this question candidly, but I am sure we would find the prospect disturbing—just as disturbing, probably, as the 19th-century "proper" Bostonian found the fact of his city becoming preponderantly Irish. *His* disaster happened to him; our disaster is still only imminent. I do believe that there is a sense in which we can properly speak of such transformations as "disasters"; but I also believe that it takes an impoverished historical imagination to see them *only* as disasters.

No one acquainted with the historical record can fairly doubt that American cities such as Boston and New York were much nicer places to live in before the immigrant mobs from Western Europe descended upon them in the eighteen-thirties and forties. Our conventional history textbooks—sensitive to the feelings (and to the political power) of yesterday's immigrants, who are by now very important people—tend to pass over this point in silence. They concentrate, instead, on the sufferings and privations of the immigrants, the ways in which they were discriminated against by older settlers, the fortitude they displayed in adverse circumstances, and the heroism of so many of them in coping with this adversity.

That is all true enough, and fair enough. Still, though it may not be advisable for our textbooks to make the point, it would be helpful to all of us if we could somehow do justice to the feelings of the older urban settlers. While chauvinism and xenophobia and gross self-interest certainly affected their attitudes, it is also true that their complaints and indignation had a quite objective basis. The fact is that American cities in the early decades of the 19th century seemed to have relatively few of those "urban problems" which were a traditional feature of the older cities of Europe, and which we now tend to regard as inherent in the urban experience itself.

There is no difficulty in explaining why this should have been the case. It had to do with no peculiar American virtues or unique American "genius." The reason there was no "urban crisis" is that the kinds of people who create an urban crisis simply didn't live in those cities. There was no urban "proletariat" to speak of—the comparatively high standard of living, the existence of free land, the constant creation of "new towns" out West, the general shortage of labor, the traditional mobility of the average American, and the religion of "self-reliance" that most Americans subscribed to: all this made it impossible for the condition of the urban working classes in New York or Boston or Philadelphia to resemble that of the working classes of London or Manchester or Glasgow.

Even more important: there was no dispossessed *rural* proletariat whom the cities had to absorb—the rise of commerce and industry in this country, as contrasted with their rise in Europe, was not connected with the displacement of masses of people from country to city. American cities, in those early decades of the 19th century, grew larger, wealthier, and more populous; *but on the whole they performed no assimilatory role*—unlike the older cities of Europe, or the American cities subsequently.

All this changed, of course, with the arrival of European immigrants —heterogeneous in religion, language and customs, with few skills and no money who settled in the larger seaboard cities. Instead of assimilating individually to American life, they challenged the city to assimilate them en masse. Despite the "melting pot" myth that later developed, it was a challenge that the American city did not meet with either grace or efficiency. The main reactions were resentment and anxiety and anger. Public order, public health, public education and public life were all thrown into disarray—and who can blame the older citizens for disliking these consequences? The transformation of the American city was a very real and very personal disaster for most of them. It destroyed their accustomed amenities, disrupted their neighborhoods, and quite ruthlessly interrupted their pursuit of happiness. Many of them began to move into what was then suburbia.

Well, that urban crisis was overcome, if ever so slowly. Not many people now think this would be a better country had those immigrants never come: their contributions to American life have been too notable, their indispensability for our American civilization is too obvious. And today it is the children and grandchildren of those immigrants who, faced with the mass movement of a rural Negro proletariat into "their" cities, echo all the old American laments and complaints.

They, too, have good reason—their discomfort and distress are not at all imaginary, despite what many liberal sociologists seem to think. (It is one thing to say abstractly that the great American city is, and has been for more than a century now, a social mechanism for the assimilation of "foreign" elements into American society. It is quite another thing for a concrete individual to try to live out a decent life in this "social mechanism.") But it does help to see this discomfort and this distress in historical perspective. And in such a perspective, the key question—often implicitly answered, less often explicitly asked —is: will we be able, decades from now, to look back upon our present "urban crisis" as but another, perhaps the final, stage in the "assimilation" of a new "immigrant" group, or is this crisis an unprecedented event that requires unprecedented and drastic social action?

That the American Negro is different from previous "immigrant" groups is clear enough. (I use quotation marks because there is patently something ironical in referring to Negroes as immigrants, when most of them are technically very old Americans indeed. Nevertheless, I think it is accurate enough, if one has in mind movement, not to America, but to the city; and I shall henceforth refer to them as immigrants, simply.) The color of his skin provokes all sorts of ancient racial fears and prejudices; and he lacks a point of "national origin" that could provide him with an authentic subculture of his own—one on which he could rely for psychological and economic assistance in face of the adversary posture of American civilization toward him.

The very special problems of the American Negro have been the subject of a literature so copious and so insistent that it is surely unnecessary to do more than refer to it. What I should like to empha-size, instead, is the danger we are in of *reducing* the Negro to his problematic qualities.

Underlying practically all of the controversies about the American city today there lies the question: can the Negro be expected to follow the path of previous immigrant groups or is his a special, "patho-logical" case? This word "pathological" turns up with such surprising frequency in sociological literature today—on slums, on poverty, on education—that one might suspect a racist slur, were it not for the fact that those who use it most freely clearly intend to incite the authorities to corrective action by presenting the Negro's condition in the most dramatic terms.

Indeed, there has developed an entire rhetoric of liberal and melioristic slander that makes rational discussion of "the Negro prob-lem" exceedingly difficult. Anyone who dares to suggest that the Negro population of the United States is not in an extreme psychiatric and sociological condition must be prepared for accusations of im-perceptiveness, hardheartedness, and even soullessness. And when it is a Negro who occasionally demurs from this description, he runs the risk of being contemptuously dismissed as an "Uncle Tom."

From my own experience as a book publisher, I think I can say confidently that if a Negro writer today submits a manuscript in which dope addiction, brutality and bestiality feature prominently, he has an excellent chance of seeing it published, and of having it respectfully reviewed as a "candid" account of the way Negroes live now; whereas, if a Negro writer were to describe with compassion the trials and anxieties of a *middle-class* Negro family, no one would be interested in the slightest—middle-class families are all alike, and no one wants to read about Negroes who could just as well be white.

It is worth lingering on this last point for a moment—precisely be-cause this unrelieved emphasis on the hellishness of the Negro condi-tion reminds us, paradoxically, of the literature of previous immigrant groups. No one can doubt that, of all immigrants, it is the Jews who have been most successful in exploiting the possibilities that America offered them. Yet if one examines the literature that American Jews created about themselves, in the years 1880-1930, one discovers that it was a literature of heartbreak and misery. All during this period, we now know, the Jews were improving their condition and equipping themselves for full participation in American life.

There is not much trace of this process in the Jewish novels and stories of the period. This is not to be taken as a deficiency of the literature: it is never literature's job to tell the whole sociological truth —the literary imagination is "creative" exactly because it transcends mere social description and analysis. But it does serve to remind us that such a book as Claude Brown's *Manchild in the Promised Land,* powerful and affecting as it is, cannot be taken to represent a definitive statement of the facts of Negro life in America—any more than one could take Michael Gold's *Jews Without Money,* written in 1929, as a definitive statement of the facts of Jewish life in America.

Every year, tens of thousands of Negroes are moving out of poverty, and thousands more are moving into the middle class, both in terms of income and status of employment. Moreover, the rate of such movement is noticeably accelerating every year. More than half of Negro families in the North have incomes greater than $5,000 a year; and, over the nation, the proportion of Negroes living in dilapidated housing has been cut in half during the past decade.

These people exist and their numbers are increasing—just as the number of poor is decreasing: approximately one-half million Negroes per year are moving above the poverty line. It is similarly worth noting that there are now something like a half-million Negroes in *each* of the following occupational categories: (a) professional and technical, (b) clerical, and (c) skilled workers and foremen. The total is about equal to that of Negro blue-collar factory operatives, and will soon be substantially larger.

But all this receives little attention from our writers and sociologists, both of whom are concerned with the more dramatic, and less innocently bourgeois, phenomena of Negro life. This is to be expected of the writers; it is less expected of sociologists, and the antibourgeois inclination of so much of current American sociology would itself seem to be an appropriate subject for sociological exploration.

The fact, incidentally, that so much of our indignant attention is centered on the northern urban Negro—who is, by any statistical yardstick, far better off than his Southern rural or small-town counterpart

—is in itself reassuring, since it follows a familiar historical pattern. In England and France, in the 19th century, the movement of the rural proletariat to the cities was accompanied by an increase in their standard of living, and a vast literature devoted to their urban miseries. These miseries were genuine enough—and it might even be conjectured that there is something qualitatively worse about urban poverty than about rural poverty, even where the latter is quantitatively greater.

But, in the absence of a corresponding literature about the life of the rural poor, one can too easily see, in this process of urbanization, nothing but mass degradation, instead of a movement toward individual improvement—which, in retrospect, one can perceive it was. Obviously, it is absurd to expect the average Negro immigrant to the American city to have such a historical perspective on himself—he would have to cease being human and become some kind of sociological monster to contemplate his situation in this detached and impersonal way. But one does wish that those who are professionally concerned with our Negro urban problem, while not losing their capacity for indignation or their passion for reform, could avail themselves of such a longer view. After all, that presumably is what their professional training was for.

One could also wish that these same scholars were less convinced a priori of the uniqueness of the Negro's problem and more willing to think in terms of American precedents. A casual survey of the experiences of the first two generations of Irish immigration can be instructive in this respect. There is hardly a single item in the catalogue of Negro "disorganization," personal and social, that was not first applied—and that was not first applicable—to the Irish. *The Dangerous Classes of New York* was the title of a book published in 1872; it referred primarily to the Irish. Ten years later, Theodore Roosevelt confided to his diary that the average Irishman was "a low, venal, corrupt and unintelligent brute."

Alcoholism wreaked far greater havoc among the immigrant Irish than all drugs and stimulants do today among the Negroes. The "matrifocal family"—with the male head intermittently or permanently absent—was not at all uncommon among the Irish. Most of the Irish slums were far filthier than they need have been—and, if we are to believe contemporary reports, were not less filthy than the worst Negro slum today—because the inhabitants were unfamiliar with, and indifferent to, that individual and communal self-discipline which is indispensable to the preservation of civilized amenities in an urban setting. (We easily forget that our extensive public services rely, to a degree not usually recognized, upon rather sophisticated individual cooperation: for garbage to be collected efficiently, it must first be neatly deposited in garbage cans.)

It is one of the ironies of this matter that some of the very improvements in the life of the urban Negro are taken to represent the more problematic aspects of his condition. Everyone, for instance, is terribly concerned about the spread of Negro slums, both in the central city and, for some time now, in our suburbs. Why? The answer has been provided by Raymond Vernon in his excellent little book *The Myth and Reality of Our Urban Problems.*

"As long as the slum was contained in a small congested mass within the old center of the city, most of the middle-income and upper-income inhabitants of the urban area could live out their lives without being acutely aware of its existence. As the slum dweller has taken to less dense living, however, the manifestations of his existence have not been quite so easy to suppress."

It will doubtless come as a surprise to most people that the density of habitation in the urban Negro slum today is less than it used to be —and is *considerably* less than it was for the Irish, Italian and Jewish immigrants when *they* lived in slums. Nevertheless, this is indisputably the case. (There is one slum area, on the Lower East Side of New York, where the Negro population is *one-third* of what the population was when this same area was a white slum 50 years ago.)

The population of the slum ghettos in our central cities is steadily decreasing, as the Negroes use their improved incomes to acquire more dwelling space per capita. To be sure, this means that poor Negroes now spread out more, that their slums and poor neighborhoods are more extensive, that they impinge far more powerfully upon the white neighborhoods than used to be the case. The whites, in turn, become highly agitated, as they discover that the problems of the slums and its inhabitants are now becoming their problems too, and can no longer be blandly ignored. Things *look* worse, and are *felt to be* worse, precisely because they have been getting better. This is one of the most banal of all sociological phenomena—but even sociology itself is being constantly caught off guard when confronted by it.

Another such ironic instance is the by-now famous "cycle of dependency." This ghost now insistently haunts all discussions of Negro poverty, and is invoked by all the authorities of the land, from the highest to the lowest. We are constantly being told, and are provided with figures to prove it, that not only do poor Negroes tend to beget poor Negroes—this tendency is true for whites as well, and does not astonish—but that poor Negroes on public welfare tend to beget poor Negroes who also end up as recipients of public welfare. Public policy, we are told, must—at whatever cost—aim at breaking this "vicious cycle" of dependency, if the Negro is ever to be truly integrated into American society and American life.

What we are *not* told, and what few seem to realize, is that this "vicious cycle" is itself largely created by public policy—and that, indeed, so far from this being a vicious cycle, it is a function of humanitarianism. The point is really quite simple and, once made, exceedingly obvious: *the more money we spend on public welfare, and the easier we make it for people to qualify for public welfare, the more people we can expect to find on welfare.* Moreover, since—as we have noted—the children of poor people are always and everywhere more likely to end up as poor than the children of rich people (not *as* poor as their parents, of course, but poor by new and more elevated standards of poverty), it follows that dependency on welfare may easily flow from one generation to the next.

I have discovered, to my cost, that one must be very cautious in making this point, and I should therefore like to emphasize that I am *not* calling for a reduction in welfare expenditures, or for more restrictive qualifications for welfare. On the contrary, I believe that in most parts of the country such expenditures are niggardly and the qualifications idiotically rigid. I also believe that, everywhere in our affluent society, the poor and the distressed get too little money with too much fuss. We can afford to be more generous and—as a matter of both equity and morality—should be more generous. But what I do *not* think makes any sense is for us simultaneously to give more money to more poor people—and then to get terribly excited when they take it!

Does the "cycle of dependency" come down to much more than this? I doubt it. If anything like our present welfare system had been in existence 50 years ago, or 100 years ago, this same "cycle of dependency" would have been a striking feature of the Italian and Irish immigrant communities. In those days, however, the ideology of "self-reliance" was far more powerful than the ideology of "social welfare." In effect, American society coerced poor people into working at any kind of jobs that were available, at any rate of pay, in whatever disagreeable conditions. American society did this in easy conscience because Americans then thought it was "good" for poor people to experience the discipline of work, no matter how nasty.

We have changed our views on this matter, and I should say for the better. But if we hadn't changed our views, we would not be witnessing, or worrying about, the "cycle of dependency." All of those women who now, as heads of households, get welfare and Aid-to-Dependent Children grants, would be forced to go into domestic labor —of which there is a great and growing shortage—or to take in washing and mending at home, as they used to. Our more humane welfare policies have liberated them from this necessity. It is this liberation that is the true meaning of the "cycle of dependency."

It is, to be sure, a frightening thought that generation after generation of a whole segment of society will be cut off from the mainstream of American life, by virtue of their status as welfare clients. But just how valid is such a projection? Robert Hunter, in his book, *Poverty,* written in 1904, was already concerned about the "procreative" power of poverty, over the generations. His concern turned out to be baseless —will ours be less so?

After all, the basic premise of our welfare ideology is that people's moral fiber, their yearning for self-improvement and economic advancement, is not sapped by a more generous system of social welfare. We assume that most of those who receive welfare would prefer not to, and that once they are qualified to join the labor force, and once the labor force is ready to receive them, they will happily remove themselves from the welfare rolls. If this assumption is false the very essence of the welfare state will be called into question. I happen to believe that the assumption is not false. And that is why I regard the vision of self-perpetuating and self-generating dependency as spectral rather than sociological.

To say that the problems of Negro migration into our large cities have relevant precedents in American history is not to assert that these immigrants do not face unique and peculiar dilemmas of their own. The fact that their "ethnicity" is racial rather than cultural, and the corollary fact that racial prejudice seems more deeply rooted than cultural prejudice, are certainly not to be minimized. It is not likely, for instance, that an increase in social acceptance—holding out the prospect of a substantial degree of intermarriage—will keep pace with an improvement in the Negro's social and economic status.

Even here, however, one cannot be sure: the whole world gets a little less bemused by skin color every day, as the new nations of Asia and Africa shed the colonial stigma; and many young people are militantly color-blind. In any case, unless one really believes in inherent and significant race differences, which I do not, then this question of social acceptance does not appear to be so terribly important for the visible future.

What is important is that, if anti-Negro prejudice is more powerful than, say, anti-Irish prejudice ever was, it is also true that public policy today is far, far more powerfully anti-discriminatory than it ever was. The Negro migrants to the city start under a more onerous handicap than their predecessors—but they are receiving much more assistance than their predecessors. It is impossible to strike any kind of precise equation out of these opposed elements; but my own feeling is that they are not too far from balancing each other.

Another problem, one which is receiving a considerable amount of controversial attention, is that of the Negro family: specifically, the fact that the Negro father so often—at least relative to the white population—refuses to assume a permanent position as head of household, while the Negro mother so often (again relative to the white population) will have a large number of children by different and transient "husbands." The Moynihan Report dramatically focused on this issue. Anyone who has taken the trouble to read Daniel Moynihan's study of the United States Negro family cannot fail to be impressed by the truth of his claim that this unstable family situation makes it particularly difficult for the urban Negro both to cope with the disadvantages of his condition and to exploit the possibilities for advancement that do exist. Nevertheless, this problem, too, must be kept in perspective. Without going too deeply into a subject whose ramifications are endless—involving, as they do, the entire sociology of family life and the whole history of the Negro race—the following points can be made:

(1) We tend to compare the Negro urban family today with the white suburban family of today, rather than with the white urban family of yesteryear. Family life among the raw urban proletariat of 19th-century America, as in 19th-century Britain, showed many of the "pathological" features we now associate with the Negro family. Statistics on broken homes and illegitimacy are impossible to come by for the earlier times. But anyone familiar with the urban literature of that period cannot but be impressed by the commonplace phenomenon of Mrs. Jones or Mrs. O'Hara raising her brood while Mr. Jones and Mr. O'Hara have vanished from the scene.

(2) Having said this, one must also say that it does seem to be the case that the Negro family—not only in the United States, but in Canada, the West Indies and Latin America as well—is a less stable and less permanent unit than the "bourgeois" white family, as the latter has developed over the past four centuries. But it is not at all certain that this instability will persist indefinitely: there is no more passionately "bourgeois" a group than the middle-class Negro family in the United States today. And even if it should persist, to one degree or another, there is no reason I can see why American society cannot quite easily cope with it. Working mothers are not exactly a rare occurrence these days; and a comprehensive network of

crèches and nursery schools should be able to provide the children with a decent home-away-from-home during the working hours.

(3) The evidence clearly suggests that the major problem of the Negro family is, quite simply, that there are too many children. Three-quarters of the poor children in the United States today are in families of five or more children. If the average Negro family size were no larger than the white's, Negro per capita income would soar, a large section of the Negro proletariat would automatically move above the poverty line, and the question of the fatherless Negro family would become less significant.

A mother who has one or even two young dependents can manage, given a decent program of social assistance; the larger the family, the closer her situation approaches the impossible. The availability of birth-control information and growing familiarity with birth-control techniques should eventually work their effects. ("Eventually" is the operative word here: our experience with poor and highly reproductive people all over the world demonstrates that the deliberate control of family size is not something that can be achieved in a single generation.) In the more immediate future, a program of family allowances could certainly be helpful.

But all this is, if not beside the point, then all around the point. We can legitimately worry about the Negro's capacity to achieve full inclusion in American society only after our society has seriously tried to include him. And we have consistently shirked this task. The real tragedy of the American Negro today is not that he is poor, or black, but that he is a late-comer—he confronts a settled and highly organized society whose assimilatory powers have markedly declined over the past decades. The fact that the urban Negro is poor is less important than the fact that he is poor in an affluent society. This has both subjective and objective consequences.

Subjectively, it means that the poor urban Negro feels himself at odds with the entire society, in a way that was not true 50 years ago. He was then much worse off than he is today—but he was then also surrounded by lots of poor whites who were obviously not much better off. Misery loves company, as we know; and when misery has its company, it is far more tolerable. The lonely misery of the poor Negro in our society today takes a tremendous psychological toll, and it can so exacerbate his sensibilities as to hinder him from taking advantage of the modest opportunities to improve his status that do present themselves.

When Bayard Rustin writes—and I am quoting literally—that "to want a Cadillac is not un-American; to push a cart in the garment center is," he is writing absolute nonsense. Pushing a cart in the garment center is the traditional point of departure for pushing one's way into the garment industry—and, at the very least, it has always been thought to offer advantages over hanging around a street corner and perhaps "pushing" less innocent items than ladies' wear. But one can easily understand how, in view of the isolation of the Negro and his poverty, such nonsense can be persuasively demoralizing to those Negroes who listen.

But I myself suspect that fewer Negroes listen to "their" spokesmen (or should it be their "spokesmen"?) than is commonly assumed. We have convincing opinion-poll data to the effect that the overwhelming majority of American Negroes look to the future with confidence and hope, and that they feel they have been making real progress since the end of World War II. Even on specific, highly controversial issues there is a marked divergence between what Negro leaders say and what the average Negro thinks.

School integration, for instance, is one such issue. Despite the fact that this matter has been so urgently pressed by the civil-rights movements, all public-opinion polls show that a clear majority of Negroes— in the city's ghettos and out—think the quality of education in their neighborhood schools is a more important issue than the racial integration of these schools.

One could presumably infer from this that the mass of the Negroes are lagging in their "social consciousness." I think the more accurate inference is that the mass of Negroes are more rational in their thinking, and less affected by demagogic slogans, than their spokesmen. After all, it is a fact—and one which becomes more certain with every passing year—that, simply as a consequence of demographic forces now at work, the great majority of school children in our central cities are going to be Negro, and that there just aren't going to be enough white school children around to integrate. To be sure, one could bus white children in from the suburbs, or Negro children out to the suburbs. But this is political fantasy; and, interestingly enough, the majority of Negro parents who have been polled on this question are indifferent to or opposed to both kinds of busing.

In short, then, while the lonely poverty of the Negro in our affluent society renders his situation more difficult, it does not place him beyond the reach of intelligent social policy. There may be—there doubtless are—some unhappy few who, not seeing a Cadillac in their future, will decide this future is beyond redeeming. One cannot help but sympathize with their resentment and their resignation—it is unquestionably better to have a Cadillac than not to have one. But one is also glad they constitute, as they clearly do, a tiny minority. And even if and when they picket, or riot, they are still a tiny minority.

But will social policy achieve its potentialities? Here we run up against an "objective" consequence of the affluent society that is infinitely depressing. For this society is constantly in the process of so organizing itself as to exclude those who, like the Negroes, are poor, uneducated, and without previous ownership of a monopoly in any craft or trade. I am not referring to the process of "automation" which —as the report of the President's commission on this subject pointed out—has not yet had any observable effect on the labor market. I do mean the process of "pseudo-professionalization," which has received very little critical attention but whose consequences are notably pernicious.

We are all familiar with the way in which, over these past years, plumbers have become "sanitary engineers" and elevator operators have become "transportation specialists." One does not begrudge these men their fancy titles—we are all allowed our harmless vanities. Only it's not really so harmless as it seems. For this change in nomenclature is the superficial expression of a basic restrictionist attitude that is remorselessly permeating the whole society. The majority of the population that has secured its position in this society seems determined to make it ever more difficult for others to gain new entry.

A superb example is provided by the New York City civil service, which now establishes formal educational requirements for jobs—firemen, maintenance men, mechanics' helpers, etc.—where none were required 10 years ago. The jobs themselves have not changed; even the official descriptions of tasks, duties, and skills have not been revised; but the barriers have gone up.

This sort of thing is happening all over, with the enthusiastic cooperation of unions and management. There is no economic sense to it, or economic justification. Sociologically, of course, it is easy to understand—it is a reflection of that protectionist-guild state of mind that comes with a society's advancing years: everyone and everything seeks to "establish" itself. One would be content to go along with this trend, for the peace of mind it seems to provide—were it not for the fact that, in present circumstances, it threatens to *dis*establish, more or less permanently, a not insignificant proportion of America's Negroes.

Our social policy is *not* to provide suitable jobs for the Negroes; it is to provide suitable Negroes for the jobs. We have undertaken to reeducate, rehabilitate, retrain, readjust, recompense and re-just-about-everything-else the American Negro. Faced with the choice between modifying our occupational structure and transforming the people who seek a place in it, we have chosen the latter.

A nice instance of this choice can be found in the present activities of the U.S. Post Office. It is generally agreed that our postal service is in a sorry state, with only one mail delivery a day to noncommercial residences. To revert to a twice-daily delivery in our cities—one doesn't have to be even middle-aged to remember when this was the practice —would demand something like 60,000 new employes. These, in turn, would require little else than a minimum of literacy to be able to do the job—and if even this minimum were found to be an obstacle, a brief apprenticeship could be used to teach them what they needed to know.

This proposal had a short life in Washington. It was rejected in favor of (a) spending money trying to automate the postal system, and (b) spending money on the Job Corps, on elaborate programs of vocational training, and so on. Meanwhile, over the last three years the nonwhite proportion of postal workers has declined by a couple of percentage points.

This episode evoked no comment or protest from Negro spokesmen, civil rights leaders or warriors against poverty. They, too, seem more interested in ultimate Cadillacs than in actual mailbags. If asked about the matter, they would have doubtless dismissed it—as one did to me—with a few clipped words about the pointlessness of placing people in "dead-end" jobs. To which one can only reply that most people, even in our affluent society, end up in "dead-end" jobs of one kind or another; and that, for most *poor* people, "social mobility" is something that happens to their children, not to themselves. It goes without saying that it is preferable to have the unemployed or underemployed become engineers instead of postmen. But to try to enforce such a preference, as a matter of social policy, is utopian to the point of silliness.

Behind all this is a more fundamental choice: to put the emphasis on the elimination of relative *inequality* between Negro and white, rather than on the mere improvement, in absolute terms, of the Negro's condition. That the elimination of such relative inequality is a worthwhile goal, needs no saying; and all of those programs directed toward this end are highly meritorious. But the goal is a distant one, depending as it so largely does on equality of educational experience. And progress toward this goal is not likely to be at a steady and uniform pace; it will proceed through sharp and intermittent spurts, separated by long periods during which nothing seems to be happening. (The experience of the Japanese-Americans is illustrative of this point.)

In contrast, *poverty* can be abolished within the next decade—if we concentrate on the task. Right now, one of every four Negroes in their early twenties has not gone beyond the eighth grade; over half have not completed high school. These people exist; the formative years of their lives are passed beyond recall; it is cruel and demagogic to offer them an impossible "second chance"—while blithely refusing to offer them a realistic first chance.

We go around in a circle which, while one can hardly call it vicious, is nevertheless decidedly odd. We begin by prissily categorizing the Negroes as "pathological," we end by proclaiming vast and dubious programs for their instant conversion to middle-class values and upper-middle class status. Within this circle, the majority of our urban and suburban Negroes—these latter, incidentally, rapidly growing in numbers—are making substantial progress in their own way, at their own tempo, and largely by virtue of their own efforts.

In comparison with previous waves of immigration to the great cities, they are "making out" not badly at all. They need, and are entitled to, assistance from the white society that has made them—almost our oldest settlers—into new immigrants. But the first step toward effective help would seem to be a change in white attitudes. Until now, we have spent an enormous amount of energy and money trying to assimilate Negroes into "our" cities. Is it not time we tried helping them to assimilate into "their" cities?

THE HIGHWAY AND THE CITY

Lewis Mumford

When the American people, through their Congress, voted a little while ago (1957) for a twenty-six-billion-dollar highway program, the most charitable thing to assume about this action is that they hadn't the faintest notion of what they were doing. Within the next fifteen years they will doubtless find out; but by that time it will be too late to correct all the damage to our cities and our countryside, not least to the efficient organization of industry and transportation, that this ill-conceived and proposterously unbalanced program will have wrought.

Yet if someone had foretold these consequences before this vast sum of money was pushed through Congress, under the specious, indeed flagrantly dishonest, guise of a national defense measure, it is doubtful whether our countrymen would have listened long enough to understand; or would even have been able to change their minds if they did understand. For the current American way of life is founded not just on motor transportation but on the religion of the motorcar, and the sacrifices that people are prepared to make for this religion stand outside the realm of rational criticism. Perhaps the only thing that could bring Americans to their senses would be a clear demonstration of the fact that their highway program will, eventually, wipe out the very area of freedom that the private motorcar promised to retain for them.

As long as motorcars were few in number, he who had one was a king: he could go where he pleased and halt where he pleased; and this machine itself appeared as a compensatory device for enlarging an ego which had been shrunken by our very success in mechanization. That sense of freedom and power remains a fact today only in low-density areas, in the open country; the popularity of this method of escape has ruined the promise it once held forth. In using the car to flee from the metropolis the motorist finds that he has merely transferred congestion to the highway and thereby doubled it. When he reaches his destination, in a distant suburb, he finds that the countryside he sought has disappeared: beyond him, thanks to the motorway, lies only another suburb, just as dull as his own. To have a minimum amount of communication and sociability in this spread-out life, his wife becomes a taxi-driver by daily occupation, and the sum of money it costs to keep this whole system running leaves him with shamefully overtaxed schools, inadequate police, poorly staffed hospitals, overcrowded recreation areas, ill-supported libraries.

In short, the American has sacrificed his life as a whole to the motorcar, like someone who, demented with passion, wrecks his home in order to lavish his income on a capricious mistress who promises delights he can only occasionally enjoy.

For most Americans, progress means accepting what is new because it is new, and discarding what is old because it is old. This may be good for a rapid turnover in business, but it is bad for continuity and stability in life. Progress, in an organic sense, should be cumulative, and though a certain amount of rubbish-clearing is always necessary, we lose part of the gain offered by a new invention if we automatically discard all the still valuable inventions that preceded it.

In transportation, unfortunately, the old-fashioned linear notion of progress prevails. Now that motorcars are becoming universal, many people take for granted that pedestrian movement will disappear and that the railroad system will in time be abandoned; in fact, many of the proponents of highway building talk as if that day were already here, or if not, they have every intention of making it dawn quickly. The result is that we have actually crippled the motorcar, by placing on this single means of transportation the burden for every kind of travel. Neither our cars nor our highways can take such a load. This over-concentration, moreover, is rapidly destroying our cities, without leaving anything half as good in their place.

What's transportation for? This is a question that highway engineers apparently never ask themselves: probably because they take for granted the belief that transportation exists for the purpose of providing suitable outlets for the motorcar industry. To increase the number of cars, to enable motorists to go longer distances, to more places, at higher speeds, has become an end in itself. Does this over-employment of the motorcar not consume ever larger quantities of gas, oil, concrete, rubber, and steel, and so provide the very groundwork for an expanding economy? Certainly, but none of these make up the essential purpose of transportation. The purpose of transportation is to bring people or goods to places where they are needed, and to concentrate the greatest variety of goods and people within a limited area, in order to widen the possibility of choice without making it necessary to travel. A good transportation system minimizes unnecessary transportation; and in any event, it offers a change of speed and mode to fit a diversity of human purposes.

Diffusion and concentration are the two poles of transportation: the first demands a closely articulated network of roads—ranging from a footpath to a six-lane expressway and a transcontinental railroad system. The second demands a city. Our major highway systems are conceived, in the interests of speed, as linear organizations, that is to say as arteries. That conception would be a sound one, provided the major arteries were not overdeveloped to the exclusion of all the minor elements of transportation. Highway planners have yet to realize that these arteries must not be thrust into the delicate tissue of our cities;

the blood they circulate must rather enter through an elaborate network of minor blood vessels and capillaries. As early as 1929 Benton MacKaye worked out the rationale of sound highway development, in his conception of the Townless Highway; and this had as its corollary the Highwayless Town. In the quarter century since, all the elements of MacKaye's conception have been carried out, except the last—certainly not the least.

In many ways, our highways are not merely masterpieces of engineering, but consummate works of art: a few of them, like the Taconic State Parkway in New York, stand on a par with our highest creations in other fields. Not every highway, it is true, runs through country that offers such superb opportunities to an imaginative highway builder as this does; but then not every engineer rises to his opportunities as the planners of this highway did, routing the well-separated roads along the ridgeways, following the contours, and thus, by this single stratagem, both avoiding towns and villages and opening up great views across country, enhanced by a lavish planting of flowering bushes along the borders. If this standard of comeliness and beauty were kept generally in view, highway engineers would not so often lapse into the brutal assaults against the landscape and against urban order that they actually give way to when they aim solely at speed and volume of traffic, and bulldoze and blast their way across country to shorten their route by a few miles without making the total journey any less depressing.

Perhaps our age will be known to the future historian as the age of the bulldozer and the exterminator; and in many parts of the country the building of a highway has about the same result upon vegetation and human structures as the passage of a tornado or the blast of an atom bomb. Nowhere is this bulldozing habit of mind so disastrous as in the approach to the city. Since the engineer regards his own work as more important than the other human functions it serves, he does not hesitate to lay waste to woods, streams, parks, and human neighborhoods in order to carry his roads straight to their supposed destination.

The fatal mistake we have been making is to sacrifice every other form of transportation to the private motorcar—and to offer, as the only long-distance alternative, the airplane. But the fact is that each type of transportation has its special use; and a good transportation policy must seek to improve each type and make the most of it. This cannot be achieved by aiming at high speed or continuous flow alone. If you wish casual opportunities for meeting your neighbors, and for profiting by chance contacts with acquaintances and colleagues, a stroll at two miles an hour in a concentrated area, free from needless vehicles, will alone meet your need. But if you wish to rush a surgeon to a patient a thousand miles away, the fastest motorway is too slow. And again, if you wish to be sure to keep a lecture engagement in winter, railroad transportation offers surer speed and better insurance against being held up than the airplane. There is no one ideal mode or speed: human purpose should govern the choice of the means of transportation. That is why we need a better transportation *system,* not just more highways. The projectors of our national highway program plainly had little interest in transportation. In their fanatical zeal to expand our highways, the very allocation of funds indicates that they are ready to liquidate all other forms of land and water transportation. The result is a crudely over-simplified and inefficient method of mono-transportation: a regression from the complex many-sided transportation system we once boasted.

In order to overcome the fatal stagnation of traffic in and around our cities, our highway engineers have come up with a remedy that actually expands the evil it is meant to overcome. They create new expressways to serve cities that are already overcrowded within, thus tempting people who had been using public transportation to reach the urban centers to use these new private facilities. Almost before the first day's tolls on these expressways have been counted, the new roads themselves are overcrowded. So a clamor arises to create other similar arteries and to provide more parking garages in the center of our metropolises; and the generous provision of these facilities expands the cycle of congestion, without any promise of relief until that terminal point when all the business and industry that originally gave rise to the congestion move out of the city, to escape strangulation, leaving a waste of expressways and garages behind them. This is pyramid building with a vengeance; a tomb of concrete roads and ramps covering the dead corpse of a city.

But before our cities reach this terminal point, they will suffer, as they now do, from a continued erosion of their social facilities: an erosion that might have been avoided if engineers had understood MacKaye's point that a motorway, properly planned, is another form of railroad for private use. Unfortunately, highway engineers, if one is to judge by their usual performance, lack both historic insight and social memory: accordingly, they have been repeating, with the audacity of confident ignorance, all the mistakes in urban planning committed by their predecessors who designed our railroads. The wide swathes of land devoted to cloverleaves, and even more complicated multi-level interchanges, to expressways, parking lots, and parking garages, in the very heart of the city, butcher up precious urban space in exactly the same way that freight yards and marshalling yards did when the railroads dumped their passengers and freight inside the city. These new arteries choke off the natural routes of circulation and limit the use of abutting properties, while at the points where they disgorge their traffic they create inevitable clots of congestion, which effectively cancel out such speed as they achieve in approaching these bottlenecks.

Today the highway engineers have no excuse for invading the city with their regional and transcontinental trunk systems: the change from the major artery to the local artery can now be achieved without breaking the bulk of goods or replacing the vehicle; that is precisely the advantage of the motorcar. Arterial roads, ideally speaking, should engirdle the metropolitan area and define where its greenbelt begins; and since American cities are still too impoverished and too improvident to acquire greenbelts, they should be planned to go through the zone where relatively high-density building gives way to low-density building. On this perimeter, through traffic will by-pass the city, while cars that are headed for the center will drop off at the point closest to their destination.

Since I don't know a city whose highways have been planned on this basis, let me give as an exact parallel the new semicircular railroad line, with its suburban stations, that by-passes Amsterdam. That is good railroad planning, and it would be good highway planning, too, as the Dutch architect H. Th. Wijdeveld long ago pointed out. It is on relatively cheap land, on the edge of the city, that we should be building parking areas and garages: with free parking privileges to tempt the commuter to leave his car and finish his daily journey on the public transportation system. The public officials who have been planning our highway system on just the opposite principle are likewise planning to make the central areas of our cities unworkable and uninhabitable. Route 128 in Boston might seem a belated effort to provide such a circular feeder highway; but actually it is a classic example of how the specialized highway engineer, with his own concerns solely in mind, can defeat sound urban design.

Now it happens that the theory of the insulated, high-speed motorway, detached from local street and road systems, immune to the clutter of roadside "developments" was first worked out, not by highway engineers, but by Benton MacKaye, the regional planner who conceived the Appalachian Trail. He not merely put together its essential features, but identified its principal characteristic: the fact that to achieve speed it must by-pass towns. He called it in fact the Townless Highway.[1] Long before the highway engineers came through with Route 128, MacKaye pointed out the necessity for a motor by-pass around the ring of suburbs that encircle Boston, in order to make every part of the metropolitan area accessible, and yet to provide a swift by-pass route for through traffic.

MacKaye, not being a one-eyed specialist, visualized this circuit in all its potential dimensions and developments: he conceived accordingly a metropolitan recreation belt with a northbound motor road forming an arc on the inner flank and a southbound road on the outer flank—the two roads separated by a wide band of usable parkland, with footpaths and bicycle paths for recreation. In reducing MacKaye's conception to Route 128, without the greenbelt and without public control of the areas adjacent to the highway, the "experts" reduced the multi-purpose Bay Circuit to the typical "successful" expressway: so successful in attracting industry and business from the center of the city that it already ceases to perform even its own limited functions of fast transportation, except during hours of the day when ordinary highways would serve almost as well. This, in contrast to MacKaye's scheme, is a classic example of how not to do it.

Just as highway engineers know too little about city planning to correct the mistakes made in introducing the early railroad systems into our cities, so, too, they have curiously forgotten our experience with the elevated railroad—and unfortunately most municipal authorities have been equally forgetful. In the middle of the nineteenth century the elevated seemed the most facile and up-to-date method of introducing a new kind of rapid transportation system into the city; and in America, New York led the way in creating four such lines on Manhattan Island alone. The noise of the trains and the overshadowing of the structure lowered the value of the abutting properties even for commercial purposes; and the supporting columns constituted a dangerous obstacle to surface transportation. So unsatisfactory was elevated transportation even in cities like Berlin, where the structures were, in contrast to New York, Philadelphia, and Chicago, rather handsome works of engineering, that by popular consent subway building replaced elevated railroad building in all big cities, even

[1] See *The New Republic*, Mar. 30, 1930.

though no one could pretend that riding in a tunnel was nearly as pleasant to the rider as was travel in the open air. The destruction of the old elevated railroads in New York was, ironically, hailed as a triumph of progress precisely at the moment that a new series of elevated highways was being built, to repeat on a more colossal scale the same errors.

Like the railroad, again, the motorway has repeatedly taken possession of the most valuable recreation space the city possesses, not merely by thieving land once dedicated to park uses, but by cutting off easy access to the waterfront parks, and lowering their value for refreshment and repose by introducing the roar of traffic and the bad odor of exhausts, though both noise and carbon monoxide are inimical to health. Witness the shocking spoilage of the Charles River basin parks in Boston, the arterial blocking off of the lake front in Chicago (after the removal of the original usurpers, the railroads), the barbarous sacrifice of large areas of Fairmount Park in Philadelphia, the partial defacement of the San Francisco waterfront, even in Paris the ruin of the Left Bank of the Seine.

One may match all these social crimes with a hundred other examples of barefaced highway robbery in every other metropolitan area. Even when the people who submit to these annexations and spoliations are dimly aware of what they are losing, they submit without more than a murmur of protest. What they do not understand is that they are trading a permanent good for a very temporary advantage, since until we subordinate highway expansion to the more permanent requirements of regional planning, the flood of motor traffic will clog new channels. What they further fail to realize is that the vast sums of money that go into such enterprises drain necessary public monies from other functions of the city, and make it socially if not financially bankrupt.

Neither the highway engineer nor the urban planner can, beyond a certain point, plan his facilities to accommodate an expanding population. On the overall problem of population pressure, regional and national policies must be developed for throwing open, within our country, new regions of settlement, if this pressure, which appeared so suddenly, does not in fact abate just as unexpectedly and just as suddenly. But there can be no sound planning anywhere until we understand the necessity for erecting norms, or ideal limits, for density of population. Most of our congested metropolises need a lower density of population, with more parks and open spaces, if they are to be attractive enough physically to retain even a portion of their population for day-and-night living; but most of our suburban and exurban communities must replan large areas at perhaps double their present densities in order to have the social, educational, recreational, and industrial facilities they need closer at hand. Both suburb and metropolis need a regional form of government, working in private organizations as well as public forms, to reapportion their resources and facilities, so as to benefit the whole area.

To say this is to say that both metropolitan congestion and suburban scattering are obsolete. This means that good planning must work to produce a radically new pattern for urban growth. On this matter, public policy in the United States is both contradictory and self-defeating. Instead of lowering central area densities, most urban renewal schemes, not least those aimed at housing the groups that must be subsidized, either maintain old levels of congestion, or create higher levels than existed in the slums they replaced. But the home loan agencies, federal and private, on the other hand, have been subsidizing the wasteful, ill-planned, single-family house, on cheap land, ever remoter from the center of our cities; a policy that has done as much to promote the suburban drift as the ubiquitous motorcar.

In order to cement these errors in the most solid way possible, our highway policy maximizes congestion at the center and expands the area of suburban dispersion—what one might call the metropolitan "fall-out." The three public agencies concerned have no official connections with each other: but the total result of their efforts proves, once again, that chaos does not have to be planned.

Motorcar manufacturers look forward confidently to the time when every family will have two, if not three, cars. I would not deny them that hope, though I remember that it was first voiced in 1929, just before the fatal crash of our economic system, too enamored of high profits even to save itself by temporarily lowering prices. But if they don't want the motorcar to paralyze urban life, they must abandon their fantastic commitment to the indecently tumescent organs they have been putting on the market. For long-distance travel, a roomy car, if not artfully elongated, of course has many advantages; but for town use, let us insist upon a car that fits the city's needs; it is absurd to make over the city to fit the swollen imaginations of Detroit. The Isetta and the Gogomobil have already pointed the way; but what we need is an even smaller vehicle, powered by electricity, delivered by a powerful storage cell, yet to be invented: the exact opposite of our insolent chariots.

Maneuverability and parkability are the prime urban virtues in cars; and the simplest way to achieve this is by designing smaller cars. These virtues are lacking in all but one of our current American models. But why should our cities be destroyed just so that Detroit's infantile fantasies should remain unchallenged and unchanged?

If we want to make the most of our new highway program, we must keep most of the proposed expressways in abeyance until we have done two other things. We must replan the inner city for pedestrian circulation, and we must rebuild and extend our public forms of mass transportation. In our entrancement with the motorcar, we have forgotten how much more efficient and how much more flexible the footwalker is. Before there was any public transportation in London, something like fifty thousand people an hour used to pass over London Bridge on their way to work: a single artery. Railroad transportation can bring from forty to sixty thousand people per hour, along a single route, whereas our best expressways, using far more space, cannot move more than four to six thousand cars: even if the average occupancy were more than one-and-a-half passengers, as at present, this is obviously the most costly and inefficient means of handling the peak hours of traffic. As for the pedestrian, one could move a hundred thousand people, by the existing streets, from, say, downtown Boston to the Common, in something like half an hour, and find plenty of room for them to stand. But how many weary hours would it take to move them in cars over these same streets? And what would one do with the cars after they had reached the Common? Or where, for that matter, could one assemble these cars in the first place? For open spaces, long distances, and low population densities, the car is now essential; for urban space, short distances, and high densities, the pedestrian.

Every urban transportation plan should, accordingly, put the pedestrian at the center of all its proposals, if only to facilitate wheeled traffic. But to bring the pedestrian back into the picture, one must treat him with the respect and honor we now accord only to the automobile: we should provide him with pleasant walks, insulated from traffic, to take him to his destination, once he enters a business precinct or residential quarter. Every city should heed the example of Rotterdam in creating the Lijnbaan, or of Coventry in creating its new shopping area. It is nonsense to say that this cannot be done in America, because no one wants to walk.

Where walking is exciting and visually stimulating, whether it is in a Detroit shopping center or along Fifth Avenue, Americans are perfectly ready to walk. The legs will come into their own again, as the ideal means of neighborhood transportation, once some provision is made for their exercise, as Philadelphia is now doing, both in its

Independence Hall area, and in Penn Center. But if we are to make walking attractive, we must not only provide trees and wide pavements and benches, beds of flowers and outdoor cafés, as they do in Rotterdam: we must also scrap the monotonous uniformities of American zoning practice, which turns vast areas, too spread out for pedestrian movement, into single-district zones, for commerce, industry, or residential purposes. (As a result, only the mixed zones are architecturally interesting today despite their disorder.)

Why should anyone have to take a car and drive a couple of miles to get a package of cigarettes or a loaf of bread, as one must often do in a suburb? Why, on the other hand, should a growing minority of people not be able again to walk to work, by living in the interior of the city, or, for that matter, be able to walk home from the theatre or the concert hall? Where urban facilities are compact, walking still delights the American: does he not travel many thousands of miles just to enjoy this privilege in the historic urban cores of Europe? And do not people now travel for miles, of an evening, from the outskirts of Pittsburgh, just for the pleasure of a stroll in Mellon Square? Nothing would do more to give life back to our blighted urban cores than to reinstate the pedestrian, in malls and pleasances designed to make circulation a delight. And what an opportunity for architecture!

While federal funds and subsidies pour without stint into highway improvements, the two most important modes of transportation for cities—the railroad for long distances and mass transportation, and the subway for shorter journeys, are permitted to languish and even to disappear. This is very much like what has happened to our postal system. While the time needed to deliver a letter across the continent has been reduced, the time needed for local delivery has been multiplied. What used to take two hours now sometimes takes two days. As a whole our postal system has been degraded to a level that would have been regarded as intolerable even thirty years ago. In both cases, an efficient system has been sacrificed to an overfavored new industry, motorcars, telephones, airplanes; whereas, if the integrity of the system itself had been respected, each of these new inventions could have added enormously to the efficiency of the existing network.

If we could overcome the irrational drives that are now at work, promoting shortsighted decisions, the rational case for rebuilding the mass transportation system in our cities would be overwhelming. The current objection to mass transportation comes chiefly from the fact that it has been allowed to decay: this lapse itself reflects the general blight of the central areas. In order to maintain profits, or in many cases to reduce deficits, rates have been raised, services have decreased, and equipment has become obsolete, without being replaced and improved. Yet mass transportation, with far less acreage in roadbeds and rights of way, can deliver at least ten times more people per hour than the private motorcar. This means that if such means were allowed to lapse in our metropolitan centers—as the interurban electric trolley system, that complete and efficient network, was allowed to disappear in the nineteen-twenties—we should require probably five to ten times the existing number of arterial highways to bring the present number of commuters into the city, and at least ten times the existing parking space to accommodate them. In that tangled mass of highways, interchanges, and parking lots, the city would be nowhere: a mechanized nonentity ground under an endless procession of wheels.

That plain fact reduces a one-dimensional transportation system, by motorcar alone, to a calamitous absurdity, as far as urban development goes, even if the number of vehicles and the population count were not increasing year by year. Now it happens that the population of the core of our big cities has remained stable in recent years: in many cases, the decline which set is as early as 1910 in New York seems to have ceased. This means that it is now possible to set an upper limit for the daily inflow of workers, and to work out a permanent mass transportation system that will get them in and out again as pleasantly and efficiently as possible.

In time, if urban renewal projects become sufficient in number to permit the design of a system of minor urban throughways, at ground level, that will by-pass the neighborhood, even circulation by motorcar may play a valuable part in the total scheme—provided, of course, that minuscule-size town cars take the place of the long-tailed dinosaurs that now lumber about our metropolitan swamps. But the notion that the private motorcar can be substituted for mass transportation should be put forward only by those who desire to see the city itself disappear, and with it the complex, many-sided civilization that the city makes possible.

There is no purely local engineering solution to the problems of transportation in our age: nothing like a stable solution is possible without giving due weight to all the necessary elements in transportation—private motorcars, railroads, airplanes, and helicopters, mass transportation services by trolley and bus, even ferryboats, and finally, not least, the pedestrian. To achieve the necessary overall pattern, not merely must there be effective city and regional planning, before new routes or services are planned; we also need eventually—and the sooner the better—an adequate system of federated urban government on a regional scale.

Until these necessary tools of control have been created, most of our planning will be empirical and blundering; and the more we do, on our present premises, the more disastrous will be the results. In short we cannot have an efficient form for our transportation system until we can envisage a better permanent structure for our cities. And the first lesson we have to learn is that a city exists, not for the constant passage of motorcars, but for the care and culture of men.

EIGHT GOALS FOR AN URBANIZING AMERICA

Lyle C. Fitch

Whatever happens here or in the rest of the world in the final third of the twentieth century, American life will profoundly change. U. S. population will grow by 75 to 125 million, with the increase locating in urban areas. Between 150 and 250 new cities of half a million each will be the measure of minimum expansion, both physical and social, that must be accomplished in little more than thirty years. Growth of knowledge and technological potential deriving from knowledge will continue, probably at an increasing rate. The flaring discontent of Negro and other minority groups will also continue until they approach full economic and political equality.

Nothing short of catastrophic war will avert these forces or the changes which they imply. The great challenge before Americans concerns whether the forces can and will be directed toward improving the urban order.

Present trends of urban development hold out both promise and threat for the future. On the one hand, despite the glaring deficiencies in such areas as housing, transportation, crime prevention, health, education, and the quality of public services, urban life has improved enormously in this century. We have come a good way from the

Lyle C. Fitch, "Eight Goals for an Urbanizing America," DAEDALUS, *Fall 1968. Reprinted by permission from* DAEDALUS, *Journal of the American Academy of Arts and Sciences, Boston, Massachusetts, Volume 97 Number 4.*

times when urban conditions were synonymous with periodic ravage by fire and epidemics, with muddy streets, corrupt and compliant courts and police, and large sections having no pretense to law and order. Measured by material well-being, life for the majority of American families has improved more or less steadily since the depths of the Depression. Per-family real incomes after taxes has risen by 50 percent in the past two decades. Educational levels have zoomed. In 1967, the proportion of young people completing college was as great as that which completed high school in the early 1920s.

On the other hand, experience thus far gives us no basis for hoping that the present largely unplanned processes will produce efficient, secure, and beautiful cities. Smog, pollution, and congestion, frustration, delinquency, violence, and other manifestations of social pathology are all on the rise, along with affluence. The highest rate of population increase is occurring among groups most hopelessly caught in the poverty trap.

Obsolescent commercial and industrial buildings, bad taste in design, careless destruction of open space, and residential slums manifest a failure to recognize the needs of the human spirit for variety, vistas, openness, and grandeur. Nor can we flatter ourselves that in the twentieth century we have gained the functional city or the efficient products in the private sector is by formulating, debating, and getting

It is quite possible in the last third of the century to achieve greater variety and less dullness, more beauty and less ugliness, clean streets, pure air and water, and fast, comfortable transportation. These potentialities will not be realized, however, by way of the aspirations commonly ascribed to the middle class: a secure job, a house in the suburbs, an agreeable wife, and three lovely children. There is nothing wrong with such aspirations, but they will hardly suffice to bring forth the good urban life. Progress requires visions of what we would like to become, visions of efficiency, beauty, and social justice.

Over the objections of proponents of "disjointed incrementalism,"[2] I argue that the social-action analogue for developing and marketing products in the private sector is by formulating, debating, and getting consensus on goals that express the community's aspirations for itself.

---

[1] It is said that splendid and beautiful cities are not a realistic goal in a democratic society based on a mass culture, and that the grand cities of the past (notably medieval and renaissance cities) were products of autocracy. But we should not forget that the splendor of ancient Athens was a product of the world's first great democratic society.

[2] See D. Braybrooke and C. E. Lindblom, *A Strategy Of Decision: Policy Evaluation as a Social Process* (New York: 1963).

Goals provide the sense of direction essential in a purposeful, dynamic society.

We have not suffered for want of goals statements in recent years, to be sure, but these efforts have concentrated on special problems or subjects such as housing and renewal, poverty and conservation.[3] I share with many others a concern that, in overreacting to these most compelling, immediate problems, we will neglect other things equally important over a longer time-span. Thus, it is said that today's urban problem is that of the Negro; I submit that if we concentrate on the Negro "problem" alone, we will neither be solving that particular "problem" nor creating the urban society and environment we should like to see in the long run.

The eight goals listed here represent my own sense of what is most important and reasonably comprehensive. They are not presented as objectives to be realized overnight, but as suggestions of the directions in which we should be going. Moreover, in a society dominated by rapidly evolving knowledge, technology, and culture, these goals, or any other set of goals, will need to be revised and replaced as new needs and possibilities present themselves.

GOAL I

An urban society with values, environment, and service systems that respond fully to the needs and wants of families and individuals; a society drawn to the "human scale." This society should be open, with freedom of choice, freedom to move up occupational and social ladders, and opportunity to participate fully in economic and political life. It should be a pluralistic society in that it honors cultural differences which particular groups may wish to maintain. It should offer a variety of ways of life and opportunity to choose among them.

I mean by "human scale" the qualities of a city that provide people with comfort, satisfaction, spiritual uplift, a sense of identification with the city and their fellow men, a care for those whose needs tend to be neglected in the hustle of the market place, a regard for graciousness in relationships, a care for beauty and grace in urban design. The city

[3] For example, the Rockefeller panel reports in *Prospect For America* (1960); the report of the President's Commission on National Goals in *Goals for America* (1960); "Urban Revival: Goals and Standards," *The Annals* (Mar. 1964); and numerous publications and symposia such as W. Z. Hirsch, *Urban Life and Form* (New York: 1963); L. Rodwin, ed., *The Future Metropolis* (New York: 1961); the report of the NASA Conference on Space, Science, and Urban Life; and L. Lecht's study *Goals, Priorities and Dollars* (New York: 1966), for the National Planning Association.

falls far short of such ideals. It is hostile to women and young children; it fails to provide a social environment for courtship, neglects recreation for adolescents, lacks trees and parks, unthinkingly destroys neighborhoods and with them neighborhood values and traditions. Relations between public servants and the public are commonly uncivil and not uncommonly brutal.

"Human scale" is implicit in the traditional American commitment to freedom; freedom has been associated, in part, with that enlargement of choice made possible by the advance of technology, output, and income on education, careers, dwellings, recreation, styles of life. But today freedom of choice is suppressed in numerous ways. The city's many people who are impoverished as to education and income are correspondingly impoverished as to choice, forever strangers to many sorts of opportunity. Those who would prefer to live and rear their children in a heterogeneous cosmopolitan environment are frustrated by the predominance of homogeneous communities ranging from the racial ghetto to the high-income suburb. We need neighborhoods for the villager and the cosmopolite, for young people, for the aged, and for mixed age groups; we need communities of low density and high density, of single, multiple, and mixed dwellings, neighborhoods which are homogeneous and neighborhoods which are mixed as to income, racial, and ethnic characteristics; we need stable and changing, historic and contemporary communities.

Along with the traditional American ideal of freedom goes its necessary complement, a pluralistic society. But it is essential that cultural differences, where they are maintained, reflect pride in race, origin, and group accomplishment—not a sense of inferiority, exploitation, and alienation.

Such adaptation to the human scale—making the city more responsive to individual need and fostering individual freedom of choice of life style—will not result from uncoordinated market decisions nor from the actions of a myriad of governments separately providing routine services. It requires of business, labor, and other private sectors as well as public leadership a commitment to the values served by a city of "human scale."

GOAL II

A national commitment to the work of developing the urban frontier, as pervasive and compelling as the national commitment to developing the western frontier in the nineteenth century. Such a commitment must draw on federal, state, and local governments, business and labor, and educational, religious, and other organizations. It must be based on a heightened sense of common interest among all urban dwellers, with increased communication and mutual understanding across class lines, and a general concern for the well-being of each community.

Although the "cultural gap" between rapid accumulation of scientific knowledge and its technological application, on one hand, and the evolution of social and political institutions capable of coping with the new technological age, on the other, cannot be measured quantitatively, it seems to widen mainly because of the unprecedented scale and speed of technological change. From electricity to nuclear power, from the first adding machine to the computer, has been only a few decades, but the difference in corresponding beliefs, customs, and institutional requirements is epochal.

Technology has made possible the great population increases, and the high-density concentrations, of today's megalopolitan and metropolitan areas. These emerging concentrations of people, wealth, talent, influence, and prestige represent a new phenomenon of power and its distribution. But we are still trying to manage them with political forms devised for cities in the nineteenth century.

To attain goals as ambitious as those listed here requires effective local government, responsive to citizens' needs and wishes. But most local governments are anachronisms, characterized by excessive numbers of units, lack of public interest, and inadequate machinery for planning, policy-making, and administration.[4]

Clearly, if states are to maintain their historic role in the federal system, state governments *must* respond more adequately to urban needs. But with a few important exceptions, most state governments have lagged in meeting responsibilities imposed by the urban revolution, refusing to come to grips with the problems created by immigration and poverty. They have deemed cities unworthy to exercise powers of home rule and have dragged their feet on needed political and governmental reorganization. State governments can assist in modernizing tax and fiscal systems and providing financial support to meet urban development needs. They must promote the organizational changes in local government necessary to meet the needs of expanding metropolitan areas. They must move into areas which, as a group, they have thus far scarcely touched: economic growth, civil rights, education of the culturally deprived, eradication of poverty, ugliness, pollution of air and water, traffic congestion, metropolitan planning, modernization of zoning and building codes, eradication of

[4] For suggested improvements, see Committee for Economic Development, *Modernizing Local Government* (1966).

restrictions on technological progress, and assistance in raising the quality of local government personnel.

The federal government will continue to be called upon for direct and indirect assistance in obtaining funds for urban development and renewal simply because, as things now stand, the federal government alone has access to the resources necessary for underwriting the vast task of redoing the present physical environment, and bringing up to par the nation's underdeveloped human capital. And only the federal government can take into account interstate spillovers of the benefits from and costs of public services: for example, costs imposed on northern cities by the grossly inadequate education of migrants from the South.

The Congress, historically dominated by rural and conservative interests, has also lagged in responding to the transition from western to urban frontier, despite the proliferation of federal assistance programs initiated since World War II, which have created the new profession of grantsmanship. In the first seven years of the 1960s, the federal government spent on net balance about $1.6 billion for housing and community development to improve the urban environment in which 70 percent of Americans now live. Agriculture and space each got $27-$28 billion; defense and war, $384 billion.

Federal and state governments can facilitate and assist in defining what an urban community wants to do and in mobilizing resources to get it done, but they cannot provide the leadership. Such leadership must come from the community itself—out of livelier participation in public affairs. In particular, the business sector has now been challenged by social imperatives and invited by the Administration to play a leading role.

Even the most active business and political leadership will come to nought without the interest and active involvement of the citizens. The metropolitan community as a whole will fall short of its potential and may deteriorate beyond repair if its citizens accept only its amenities and evade its problems.

To the majority of Americans the personal experience of urban living is one of more or less continuous improvement. Middle- and higher-income people are highly mobile; their roots tend to be in professional, cultural, and other interests rather than in the geographic neighborhoods where they happen to be living at the moment. Manifestations of trouble tend to be concentrated in central cities; the middle class can, and frequently does, escape by moving to the suburbs where its members spend much of their civic energies building fortifications against incursions by the poor.

Interest in urban goals at the lower end of the income-culture scale has been lacking until recently; the poor have tended to look to the great welfare bureaucracies, rather than to political organization, for assistance in meeting pressing needs. In both the central cities and the suburbs, political control has tended to be dominated more by the middle class, which demands less from government, than by the lower class, which demands more. Various circumstances—one being perennial financial stringency and another unimaginative leadership—tend to magnify the negative or veto powers of groups at the urban government level. In the urban political game, the defense has dominated the offense.

But new political winds are blowing in the forms of both violent protest and more extensive political involvement. The needs of those on the lowest economic plane are being forcefully articulated by people who want employment opportunities, better housing, more adequate education facilities, and a better social environment beginning with neighborhoods free from violence, dope pushers, and vagrants. None of these things is revolutionary; all reflect existing middle-class values and middle-class opportunities. People caught in the poverty trap want mainly what the majority of Americans already have.

GOAL III

Eradication of poverty and increase of productivity by:

(a) providing job opportunities for all who wish to work and opportunities for able older people to continue contributing to society;

(b) raising the levels and extending the coverage of social insurance and public assistance programs to promote incentives and stable family life, and to be more responsive to need.

In 1966, about 6 million families comprising 25 million persons, and another 5 million unrelated individuals were in poverty.[5] The proportion of nonwhite households (families and single individuals) in poverty was 30 percent, 2.5 times that of the white (12 percent). The poverty roster in 1966 included 3.8 million one- and two-person

[5] The definition of poverty is that of the Social Security Administration: the poverty line there varies according to size of family, number of children, and farm-nonfarm status. It is equivalent to an annual income of about $3,300 for a nonfarm family of four. This amounts to about $2.25 per day per person, of which one third is allocated for food. Poverty statistics are occasionally attacked by apologists for poverty who point out (a) that some households with incomes below the poverty line can draw on previously accumulated assets, and (b) that some families on the poverty rolls at any given time are there only temporarily. But the conclusion does not follow that the statistics necessarily overstate poverty. In other special cases even an income above the arbitrarily defined poverty line may not be adequate for an above-poverty level of living.

households with head age sixty-five or over (more than 5 million persons), and 1.5 million women heading fatherless families with 4 million children under age eighteen. About 3 million families in poverty were headed by men under sixty-five, most of whom were employed full or part time during the year. Their poverty was due to low wages, intermittent employment, and large families (a principal cause of poverty).

Like the rest of America's population, the poor have been drawn into urban areas. Once there, they are confined by poverty and discrimination to large cities and to older core areas. Another large segment of the poor lives in urban communities outside metropolitan areas.

The proportion of poor people living in large cities is still increasing as middle-income residents flee to the suburbs and poor immigrants take their places. Thus between 1960 and 1966, 1.2 million whites left the nation's twenty largest central cities, and 3.2 million non-whites moved in. Skyrocketing welfare costs are one result: 7–10 thousand people were added monthly to the AFDC program in New York City alone during 1967.

Poverty is a relative not an absolute condition—people measure their well-being by comparison with the population at large, not by how far they are from starvation. If we use a relative poverty line, such as 50 percent of median family income, we find that poverty has not decreased in the last two decades; if anything, it has increased.

The extent of persistent and rising unemployment in large-city slums is indicated by a Bureau of Labor Statistics survey of ten slum areas in eight cities in November 1966, which found an under-employment rate of 34 percent.[6] Lack of employment opportunities, or the conviction that they will be lacking, appears to be the greatest deterrent to both aspiration and persistence.

One of the principal demands from the slum-ghetto is for jobs, and one of the principal causes of rioting is lack of economic opportunity. The notion is still widespread that those who remain unemployed in times of high prosperity lack initiative or are simply

[6] The underemployed include:
  (a) the unemployed (those currently seeking work);
  (b) part-time workers seeking full-time jobs;
  (c) heads of households under sixty-five earning less than $60 a week in full-time employment;
  (d) non-heads of households under sixty-five earning less than $56 a week in full-time employment.
  (e) 50 percent of the nonparticipants in the male age group twenty to sixty-four.

unwilling to accept work-discipline or are content to subsist on welfare. In fact, the problem is far more complicated; it reflects in part the failure of the educational process, in part lack of organization of the job market, in part timidity of individuals, in part separation of jobs from housing and deficient transportation facilities, and only in some residual part ingrained laziness or irresponsibility. Although blue-collar and less skilled jobs have moved to suburban locations, suburban communities fiercely resist efforts by Negroes to follow.

To conclude that joblessness is due in part to automation, and that income must be distributed on some basis other than productive effort, is premature in my judgment. The job of maintaining the growth rate, building new cities and rebuilding old ones, and doing other necessary things will for some time require more human energy than we shall probably be able to supply.

There is no simplistic solution to the job problem. One main approach is making more employment more accessible to ghetto residents. A second is providing improved information on the labor market. A third is specific job training and other measures to equip and rehabilitate workers for available jobs. We also have to face the fact that low-pay menial jobs with no career opportunities are not going to attract, much less inspire, young people from any income or social class, even the lowest. The need is for more career opportunities which hold forth the prospect of climbing as high as one's talents permit.

Finally, the negative philosophy that attempts to shove older people out of the labor force as soon as possible to make room for younger workers should be discarded. To cite Margaret Mead:

We have been living through a period in which the old have been recklessly discarded and disallowed. . . . Given an opportunity to participate meaningfully in new knowledge, new skills, and new styles of life, the elderly can embody the changing world in such a way that their grandchildren—and all children of the youngest generation—are given a mandate to be part of the new and yet maintain human ties with the past which, however phrased, is part of our humanity.[7]

Over time we have built up a bewildering profusion of devices for keeping individuals and families from complete destitution. The welfare system, however, militates against incentives to work, against stable family life, against effective education. It also fails to rescue from the direst poverty people unable to work—the very young, the very old, mothers of small children, the disabled. Average monthly

[7] M. Mead, "Establishing the Shared Culture," *Daedalus* (Winter 1965).

payments for old-age assistance range, among the states, from $124 in the high state to $41 in the low state. For the Aid to Families with Dependent Children program, the range is from $51 to $8 per person. In 1966 about a third of the poor received social security benefits, but even with these they remained below the poverty line.

Clearly the whole income-maintenance system must be strengthened.[8] In June 1966, the Advisory Council on Public Welfare in a report to the Secretary of the Department of Health, Education, and Welfare recommended that public assistance be extended to "all people whose income is below the national minimum standard of health and decency, with 'need' the only criterion of eligibility." It should be possible to design a system that would create incentives rather than destroy them—a system more effective and coherent than the present hodgepodge of welfare unemployment compensation, housing subsidies, and other income-maintenance devices. A foundation income for all households would not solve all problems, but it would be a start.[9] It does contravene long-standing notions about work incentives which are difficult to refute or to support with available statistical data. A great fear is that a foundation income would reduce the supply of labor. This concern springs from simplistic and questionable assumptions about the nature of work and why men work. First is the assumption that work is something to be avoided. Yet in the American culture, holding a job is part of the male role (from which follows the observation that denial of the opportunity to work is a form of social emasculation), and more and more women feel the same social pressures. Second, as machines take over both the ditch-digging and the dull routine, more and more of the nation's work is of the sort that

[8] The Ninetieth Congress moved in this direction in 1967 by amendments to increase gradually the scale of payments. At the same time, however, Congress took a backward step by limiting the number eligible for AFDC payments.

[9] Under the simplest form of foundation income, every family receives a basic allowance (which may depend on size of family) to which all earned and other income can be added, income tax being based on total income including the foundation payment. Admittedly we are a long way from that goal now, both psychologically and economically. To bring families now below the "poverty line" only up to the line would cost in the neighborhood of $11 billion a year. A foundation income averaging $4,000 per family would cost approximately $200 billion a year gross, through the net cost would be very much less since from the gross there would be deducted income taxes on marginal income, public assistance, at least part of the social security payments which otherwise would be necessary, housing, food, and other subsidies. The remainder would presumably be financed by adjusting income tax rates so as to bring about some redistribution of income.

gratifies the human urge to be of service and to be creative. Some imagination and conscious effort would accelerate this transformation.

The existing welfare system is one of the most effective devices yet invented for stifling incentive. For those families living in poverty who supplement earnings with public assistance and unemployment insurance, a dollar's increase in earnings has meant a dollar's cut in their welfare allotment. The 1967 amendments to the Social Security Act somewhat mitigated this harshness in the case of AFDC recipients by allowing them to keep the first $30 of earnings and 30 percent of the excess. Even so, the marginal tax rate—70 percent—equals the rate in the top tax bracket on income gained by other means. If a recipient is allowed to keep as much as 50 percent of his earnings, the effective tax rate is 50 percent.[10] (Similar problems arise under the negative income tax plan.) A foundation income to which earnings could be added would provide incentive for effort.

In addition to their other bad features, present income-maintenance systems based on detailed supervision and demeaning investigation are directly at odds with the American belief that government paternalism and coercion should be minimized. Of course, some control over such matters as insuring education and adequate health services for children is indispensable, and in some areas the need may be for more rather than less paternalism. Subject to these exceptions, a society stressing freedom and responsibility should not deny these values to the unfortunate; rather it should take the risk that those who are treated as responsible citizens will turn out to be so.

We have come a long way from the degradation of the poorhouse. We accept the principle that society owes all of its members the chance of a reasonable start in life. We have not yet, however, related either the problems of an automated society or the possibilities of an enormously affluent one to the basic needs of all our citizens.

Some states, like New York, have already achieved a minimal income system in the sense that no needy person is left out. Pending a radical overhauling of the present system of social security, public assistance and other benefits in the nation at large could be strengthened greatly by raising social security payments to above-poverty levels, by reducing the discrepancies among states in levels of public

---

[10] Under the federal income tax on ordinary income, the 50 percent rate does not apply until taxable income (after deductions and exemptions) has reached $44,000 (for joint returns). For the affluent this high rate is ordinarily held to damage incentive.

assistance benefits, and by moving to eliminate the present disincentives embedded in public assistance programs.

GOAL IV

Extending new meaning to the traditional American ideal of equality of opportunity by making available to all citizens:

(a) lifelong educational opportunities, through a system designed to give each person incentives and facilities to develop fully his own capacities and to contribute to society;

(b) decent and adequate housing;

(c) health and medical services adequate to allow each person to achieve his full potential productivity and sense of physical well-being;

(d) a variety of recreational and cultural outlets.

America's high and rising productivity unquestionably rests on its broad-based educational system and rising educational levels. Education is no longer solely for the young—what with the pace of knowledge accumulation and the obsolescence of knowledge already acquired, people will spend more of their lives being educated and will go back to school at intervals for retraining and updating. And there is a growing demand for study for self-fulfillment, for developing creativity and talents.

The most difficult and complicated task of American education is raising the levels at the bottom of the scale. It is a matter not only of providing better educational opportunities, but also of persuading the children of ignorance and poverty to want to be educated. Aspirations and incentives are even more important than the educational apparatus.

The environment in which disadvantaged children are educated, however, must be far different from that of most of today's slum schools.[11]

Supplementary and remedial programs must be made available to every person, young or old, who needs help. Present innovational programs, such as Head Start, are a step in the right direction, but so far they have reached only a small fraction of the educationally deprived.

Educational efforts cannot stop with the schools; they must reach into the home and the community. Indoctrination of parents and the

---

[11] See T. Kozol, *Death at an Early Age: The Destruction of the Hearts and Minds of Negro Children in the Boston Public Schools* (Boston: 1967).

cultivation of community attitudes are part of the educational process, as is employment which supplies motivation.

In the context of educational and cultural development, housing is not a consumer good, but an essential ingredient of stable family life and effective rearing of children. At least a sixth of the present housing stock is substandard. These buildings are vermin-ridden and inadequately heated, lighted, or ventilated, or lack other minimum essentials for decent family life. The number of dwelling units started in 1966, however, was the lowest of any year in the 1960s. If the goal of twenty-six million new units over the next ten years announced in the president's 1968 urban message to Congress is to be reached, the annual rate of production must more than double. Nonetheless, replacing present slums with housing and other neighborhood amenities of below-average quality is an almost certain road to new cycles of slum and blight. Low quality may be a necessary concession to political expediency in the short run, but it is likely to be very costly in the long run.

It is paradoxical that in the world's wealthiest country health standards for a considerable part of the population are in some respects below those of other advanced countries. One manifestation is in the proportion of selective service draftees rejected for medical reasons—in most years, more than 20 percent. The importance of this datum lies less in what it implies for military recruitment than in its implications for the national economy and living standards. Poverty, with its correlatives of ignorance, bad habits, and lack of medical care, is an underlying cause of poor health, and poor health is a cause of poverty in that it reduces productivity and working time.

Health services are notoriously deficient in urban ghettos and slums, and even more deficient in rural areas. Such services as exist tend to be provided by many different programs which are frequently located in different places; people are often denied service because they go to the wrong institution, to the wrong government jurisdiction, or because they cannot pay even minimum fees. Some deficiencies are attributable to the growing shortage of hospitals and professional personnel, but they also reflect bad organization, lack of attention to education, failure to train and use paraprofessional personnel, and other factors technically manageable.

As for recreation, there are already great deficiencies resulting from lack of access to outdoor recreation and open space, inhibition of water recreation by pollution and private enclosure of beaches. Slum and ghetto residents are deprived of facilities of all kinds. Possibly

because of Puritan inhibitions about the use of public funds for fun
and games, public recreation tends to be poorly represented in the
competition for resources, even though American life and the American economy are more and more dominated by recreational pursuits
and by the recreational industries. Ubiquitous television (a type of
recreation), featuring the more exotic recreation habits of the affluent,
constantly fans the flames of discontent by reminding people at the
bottom of the extent of their deprivation.

GOAL V

Extending the meaning of individual freedom to include:

(a) freedom from personal aggression, security of person and property in public
and private places;

(b) freedom from the physical and psychological damage caused by environmental aggression, including obtrusive noise, polluted air, overcrowding.

(c) freedom from the threat of uncompensated losses by public action for the
benefit of others, whether in the name of public welfare or "progress";

(d) freedom from discrimination under the law: assurance of opportunity for
defense against prosecution, protection against loss of rights owing to poverty or other personal circumstances, and protection against exploitation of
poverty and ignorance.

Freedom from personal aggression, obviously a first essential of
the good society, is increasingly endangered in city and suburb as
crime and delinquency rates rise. Although all classes suffer, the
incidence of crime is highest in the ghetto and slum. Moreover, the
poor suffer most. Even though ghetto and slum residents complain of
police brutality, they also deplore their lack of security. [12]

Eradication of slums and poverty, along with other achievements of
the good society, should substantially reduce the incidence of crime.
The immediate need in most cities, however, is for wholesale change
in the role of the policeman, in police technology, and in parole and
penal systems. The kinds of change now being proposed are implicit
in the suggestions that the designation "policeman" be changed to
"human relations officer," and that the rubric "law enforcement" be
changed to something like "public protection."

The concept of law enforcement and which laws are to be enforced
should take into account, as it now ordinarily does not, the mores of

---

[12] A public opinion survey conducted by John F. Kraft, Inc., in Harlem in
1966 found that in a list of complaints about neighborhood conditions the three
highest were prevalence of narcotics addiction, bad housing, and crime rates
(closely related to narcotics addiction).

the community. It is well known that the police are highly selective in the laws they enforce. Conventional police practices arouse the animosity of the community either by imposing locally unacceptable standards of law enforcement or by conniving in violations while mulcting the violators (as by levying on numbers and bookmaking operations).

It is no more than ordinary common sense to recruit the police serving minority group neighborhoods from minority groups. But added to the difficulty of finding and preparing minority group recruits who meet acceptable standards is their reluctance to go into police work.

The consciousness of environmental aggression also rises as changing technology imposes new nuisances and as knowledge grows of the physical and psychological damage to the human machine from noise pollution, overcrowding, and other impositions. Environmental noise frequently reaches levels which not only frazzle nerves, but damage hearing. The statement that a day of breathing New York City air is equivalent to smoking two packs of cigarettes is more than fantasy. And the economic cost, beginning with mundane cleaning bills, of stench, airborne dirt, and chemical pollution in the nation's largest cities is already reckoned in billions of dollars annually.

Congestion and overcrowding — vehicle congestion in roadways, people congestion in transit cars and buses, schools, recreation centers, and other public places — impose other economic costs and personal discomforts. It is well established by now that with most animal species overcrowding leads to neurosis and regressive behavior. Implications for *homo urbanus* have not yet been fully explored, but it is clear that environmental crowding may cause both psychological and physiological damage. [13]

The traditional principle that people should not be unduly damaged for the benefit of others and that unavoidable damage should be reasonably compensated takes on new dimensions as more and more people find themselves standing in the way of "progress." A case in point is the sonic boom: imposing the boom on populated areas for the benefit of the relative few who would be using supersonic aircraft can hardly be labeled "progress"; for the majority it would be quite the opposite.

In theory, government can regulate much of the damage caused by private interests, or it can require private interests to pay for the social

---

[13] See R. J. Dubos, "Man Adapting: His Limitations and Potentialities," *Environment for Man,* ed. William R. Ewald (Urbana, Ill.: 1967).

costs they impose. In practice, however, government agencies themselves are often the offenders in pre-empting private property, dispossessing people without adequate compensation, and imposing other social damages on the grounds that the "public interest" justifies such damage. Thus it is estimated that between 1964 and 1972 the Federal Urban Renewal and Interstate Highway Programs alone will uproot 625,000 families and individuals and 136,000 businesses and non-profit organizations. There are serious questions about the equity and adequacy of many compensation provisions; in many instances, there is no relocation assistance at all. Most seriously affected are old or poor individuals and small businesses. [14]

If it is not possible to compensate within reason those who are damaged by "progress," there is good justification for not undertaking the project unless the public benefits clearly and preponderantly outweigh the aggregate damages. If some people are to be unduly penalized for the benefit of others in the name of "public interest" or "progress," the resultant controversies are likely to damage both the public interest and the cause of progress.

Not much disputed but often frustrated are the high principles of Western political philosophy and Anglo-Saxon common law that the law and its officers should not discriminate among individuals except in the interest of reasonable and constitutional objectives and that all charged with violating the law should receive equal treatment and protection. The sophisticated and affluent can protect themselves. The poor and ignorant, by and large, are without legal recourse against unscrupulous landlords, merchants, loan sharks, and other would-be exploiters; the law is usually on the side of the exploiters. Ordinarily the poor are unable to protect themselves against arbitrary treatment by the government bureaucracies on which they must so heavily depend. When they get into trouble with the law, their chances of obtaining adequate counsel, reasonable bail, expeditious hearing and trial, and other protection are far less than those of the more sophisticated and affluent. Recent court decisions respecting right to counsel improve this situation, but it is still far from satisfactory. Minimizing the extent to which exploiters can bend the law and take advantage of the poor, and providing recourse against arbitrary action by

[14] U.S., Congress, House, Committee on Public Works, *Study Of Compensation and Assistance for Persons Affected by Real Property Acquisition in Federal And Federally Assisted Programs,* 88th Cong., 2d Sess., 1963 (U.S. Government Printing Office: 1964), p. 258; and *Metropolitan America: Challenge to Federalism, a Study Submitted to the Advisory Commission on Intergovernmental Relations,* 89th Cong. (U.S. Government Printing Office: 1966), chap. 4.

government agencies which deal with the poor are more than just additional welfare measures. It is rather a matter of maintaining traditional American principles of liberty and justice.

GOAL VI

Application of modern technology to the improvement of amenity, efficiency, and beauty of the urban environment, and development of new concepts and techniques for guiding metropolitan growth.

With the exception of television and air conditioning, there has been little hardware innovation for two generations which has bettered in any basic way the day-to-day life in cities. (The betterment that has occurred is attributable mainly to rising real incomes and marginal improvements in already existing household gadgetry. And there have been many worsements which are also attributable to technology.)

If one compares the vision, the daring, the mobilization of technical performance, the fruitful cooperation between government and private enterprise that characterize the program for outer space, it is hard to believe that the same community should deal so timidly and tardily with its inner space. The space program, uncluttered with existing institutions and vested interests, could set new aims and move forward expeditiously. But the methodology of setting objectives and organizing technology and science to meet them, assisted by new public and private instruments of collaboration, should be applicable to the urban sector.

One of the most fruitful applications might lie in joining public and private financial and technological resources to create new towns and entire new cities. The initial purpose should be primarily that of testing and demonstrating new technologies of urban life uninhibited by already existing institutions, traditions, development patterns, transportation and utility systems, and land-holding patterns, all of which have effectively frustrated innovation in and around established central cities in metropolitan areas.

GOAL VII

Maintenance of central cities as vital, healthy centers of knowledge and culture, of management and commerce, and of residence for city-lovers.[15]

[15] This and the following goal (concerned with urbanism outside central cities) should be considered together. The metropolis is an organism of closely interacting parts and of policies pursued either in center or in periphery which interact at every point and vitally affect each other's success or failure.

The role of central cities is rapidly changing in today's world of giant metropolitan areas and emerging megalopolises. One of the things that Melvin Webber and others seem to imply is that the concept of the central city is obsolete, and that modern transportation and communication will continue their decentralizing forces to produce more and more dispersal of activities and services. This view is confirmed in part by growth patterns in Los Angeles and other new southwestern urban centers, but does not yet apply, I think, to urban areas of central cities with established patterns and traditions, institutions, monuments, and cultural centers. Moreover, the growth patterns of New York, Chicago, Atlanta, the Twin Cities, and other national and regional management and financial centers indicate a preponderant tendency for office and related industries to cluster. And there are many people who continue to value the central city for aesthetic as well as economic reasons. It offers excitement and drama in life, a sense of great activity, monuments, vistas, and cultural opportunities that can be found nowhere else.

Central cities do face many dilemmas. For the most part, they have developed to meet the needs of industry and commerce, rather than for living; they are not built to the human scale. There is also the outmovement of middle-income groups, mainly white, and their replacement by the poor, mainly nonwhite. For the latter, the city appears to be losing its effectiveness in its traditional roles of acculturating agency and melting pot. The latest waves of migrants to the central city, instead of climing up the ladder to join other metropolitan residents, see widening gaps in social and cultural status, economic productivity, and stage of development. The job of revitalizing central cities is one of reclaiming people even more than of physical rebuilding.

There is also the cumulative obsolescence of buildings which cannot be economically replaced under present institutions because of the high costs of assembling land parcels suitable for new buildings and of demolishing old ones. Congestion of people and vehicles jumbled together frustrates the central city's prime economic function of reducing transportation friction.

The first and most important element of rejuvenation has to do with offering a greater variety of choices of residence and ways of life to people of all racial and income groups, in and out of the central city. This is the most effective answer for the person trapped in the ghetto and for the middle-class city-lover who flees to the suburbs to find amenities which the city should offer, but does not.

Separation of vehicular and pedestrian traffic, arcaded sidewalks, outdoor play and recreation facilities on rooftops or open floors, and pedestrian shopping and recreational areas are all devices for bringing beauty, style, convenience, interest, and other values of environmental design to the city. New York's Rockefeller Center, Chicago's lakefront, Philadelphia's Penn Center, and Montreal's Place Ville Marie indicate some of the potentialities.

Social and physical rebuilding will not be achieved with dabs of urban renewal here, a housing project there, and an adult education or Head Start program somewhere else. Physical and social renewal and development programs must be concentrated in specific limited areas. Billions of dollars must be invested to build new towns in town. [16] The principle of the coordinated approach is recognized in the Model Cities Program, but the program thus far provides little either in the way of integrating machinery or financing. Compared to need and to the country's resources, the funds provided thus far are no more than a token.

The immediate danger is that the cost of providing special services for, or alternatively repressing, the poor who are concentrating in central cities, to the extent that it must be financed by the cities themselves, will become one more force driving business firms and middle- and upper-income residents out of town. Fiscal reform to relieve cities of public assistance and other special social service costs must have high priority. But this is after all a matter of recognizing that it is a bizarre order of priorities which provides so little for restoring cities and so lavishly for destroying them.

GOAL VIII

Metropolitan development planning for efficiency and aesthetic appeal, and for conservation of urban natural resources and regional ecology.

The specter of endlessly sprawling urban development, heedless of of any human values save the immediate need for a room and four walls, unconcerned with monotony and lack of coherence: this is the prospect for most metropolitan areas in America, even today. Existing institutions and market forces do not provide for coherent relationships or strategies for mutual benefit between central city and surrounding region, or for efficient spatial relationships between residential, employment, and other activity centers. There are no mechanisms for assembling the vast amounts of capital and talent required for large-scale innovations in design, technology, or organization.

[16] See H. S. Perloff, "New Towns Intown," *Journal of the American Institute of Planners* (May 1966).

Any alternative to unplanned sprawl requires an orderly expansion of existing centers and new-town-building. Catherine Bauer Wurster states one philosophy of metropolitan design:

Instead of scattering houses, factories, shops, offices and services all over the landscape, we should pull them together into compact cities with adjacent open space saved for recreation, agriculture, and general amenity. . . . Suitable housing for a cross-section population should be provided, with more emphasis on row houses and garden apartments. A variety of employment opportunities should be encouraged, as well as bona fide urban centers. The cities would be readily accessible to each other and to the central city.[17]

The United States alone among advanced nations has no public policy for new-town-building. For the most part, the few new towns in this country have been privately planned and financed and are necessarily small and partial. By the end of the century, however, the United States will have to build the equivalent of between 150 and 250 cities, each of 500,000 population. They will require a total investment in the magnitude of $3.5 to $5 trillion. It would be only simple prudence to undertake with public and private resources a half dozen or so "demonstration cities" in the next decade, using all the resources of modern physical and social science, for guidance in building the remainder.

We also need new concepts of urban resources—open space, air, and water. Fields, hills and valleys, streams and wetlands purify the air, provide climatic and hydrological control, conserve wildlife, serve as spawning grounds for marine life, and affect urban man and urban environment in dozens of drastic and subtle ways. Such ecological considerations, along with the multiplying needs for public park and recreation areas, impose a new dimension on urban planning.

ECONOMIC POTENTIAL FOR GOAL REALIZATION

The economic potential is encouraging. The value of the Gross National Product in 1967 was $785 billion. The average annual GNP growth rate during the 1960's has been about 4.7 percent in constant value dollars though the rate dipped to 2.4 percent in 1967. If an average growth rate of 3 percent is maintained for the last third of the century, the cumulative GNP would amount to some $44 trillion in 1967 prices. A 4 percent growth rate, which many analysts consider not out of the question, would yield $54 trillion.[18]

---

[17] C. B. Wurster, "Form and Structure of the Future Urban Complex," *Cities and Space,* ed. Lowden Wingo (Baltimore: 1963).

[18] The average growth rate in real GNP between 1929 and 1966 was 3.2 percent. This period included the Great Depression and World War II, when private capital formation for peacetime production was held back.

With a 4 percent growth rate, assuming a population increase of eighty million, we would accomplish the following by the last third of the century:

(1) Double average consumption per household. The increase might be more evenly distributed by developing a higher quality in education and training for the labor force and by moving toward more generous income-maintenance programs for those not in the labor force.

(2) Provide new dwellings for all new households, replace approximately three fourths of present dwelling units, and provide second units for approximately 25 percent of all households.

(3) Double, by 1975, education expenditures per pupil; eliminate elementary and secondary school dropout; increase college enrollments by 50 percent.

(4) Triple average annual expenditure over the period on public facilities, including transportation, water, and sewer lines, recreational facilities, health centers and hospitals, and so forth.

(5) Increase federal, state, and local government nondefense expenditures on services by an average of 4 percent per year.[19]

(6) Allocate 1 percent of GNP (about two and a half times the present level of effort) for expediting development of less-developed nations.

I have made some rough estimates of the amounts of Gross National Product required to meet such objectives in the last third of the century (*see* Table, below):

	Trillions of dollars
Consumption	27.2
Housing	1.6
Education	4.4
Urban public facilities (infrastructure)	2.0
Business investment (plant and equipment)	7.7
Federal government	
Defense	2.2
Other	1.2
State and local government (excluding education and public facilities)	3.1
Foreign balance and unallocated	2.1
	$51.5

[19] With a 3 percent growth rate, there would be about $10 trillion less available, equivalent to about thirteen years' annual production at 1967 rates. Even this amount (a total of $44 trillion) would be a vast pool of resources compared with anything we have known in the past. The total gross production of the American nation thus far is in the magnitude of $18-20 trillion, but the amount of the potential difference does indicate the crucial importance of maintaining a high growth rate.

A 4 percent growth rate would supply the demands as projected; a 3 percent rate would fall some $7.5 trillion short; with a rate substantially under 4 percent, demands on GNP would have to be reduced accordingly.

Many things might deplete the potential resource pool. The most serious danger now apparent is the continued escalation of expenditure on defense and military adventures. A second would be a growing indifference of organized labor toward productivity or long-continued periods of wage-price inflation. A third is the possibility that as more employment shifts to service industries, the margin for productivity increases will diminish (although production of many services can be mechanized).

In my perhaps overly optimistic judgment, these factors will not preclude rising productivity and affluence. Whether or not rising productivity is used to achieve the kinds of goals suggested here[20] depends on whether such goals can win public consensus and whether present prejudices, habits, and institutions can be bent sufficiently to implement them if they are widely accepted.

Already there is at least a half-formed consensus on all of the goals; on most of them, the nation is already committed to some measure of implementation. Policy-makers and legislatures have addressed themselves to employment, housing, urban renewal, welfare, education, recreation, and law enforcement. The difficulty rests with lack not so much of programs or program objectives, but of knowhow. Moreover, the scale of effort thus far would not in another hundred years solve the problems which we now consider urgent.

Whether we will be mentally and socially nimble enough to adapt prejudices, habits, and institutions to the needs of the fast-moving age is another question. Here, too, I am optimistic. I recall what John Maynard Keynes said in the early 1930s with reference to the Great Depression:

If we lacked material things and the resources to produce them, we could not expect to find the means to prosperity except in hard work, abstinence and invention. In fact, our predicament is notoriously of another kind. It comes from some failure in the immaterial devices of the mind. . . .

[20] To a considerable extent, rising productivity will depend in turn on goal achievement. Thus skimping on such items as education and training, or planning for greater efficiency of urban areas will dampen productivity. The 1966 annual report of the Council of Economic Advisers stated that if nonwhite employment and productivity were equal to the white, Gross National Product would be an estimated $27 billion higher.

Nothing is required and nothing will avail except a little, a very little, clear thinking.

With Keynes's assistance we did produce enough clear thinking to establish the means for eliminating the scourge of great depressions. The challenge now before us is to come forth with a comparable response to the multifaceted needs of the urban frontier.

● THE RURAL ENVIRONMENT

An urbanizing nation with an increasing population and an aggressive technology places enormous demands upon its rural resources. Unfortunately, the same process of urbanization and population growth which increases the demands upon the land diminishes the land itself. Spreading cities and highway systems eat up open country; farm areas become new suburbs and sometimes entire new towns; once-remote wilderness regions are developed as resorts and opened up to crowds of vacationers. In the United States, about 340,000,000 acres of land have been used up by urbanization, highway construction, and erosion; and only about seven percent of the original forests remain.

This section deals with three of the basic kinds of consumption of the resources of the rural environment: the consumption of recreational space, the consumption of wildlife, and the consumption of agricultural produce. In each case technological change and population growth have resulted in spectacular increases in consumption to the point of creating serious threats to the natural ecology, and in each case existing political institutions are attempting to deal with some kind of environmental crisis.

The report "Man and Nature in the National Parks" was prepared by F. Fraser Darling, an ecologist, and Noel D. Eichhorn, a geographer, under the auspices of The Conservation Foundation. The following condensation of their report points out, first, that the United States has pioneered among nations of the world in developing a policy of setting apart areas to be preserved for recreational use; and, secondly, that the administration of the national parks has become a governmental task of great complexity, as agencies interact and as differing sets of recreational demands are made.

Sometimes a difference of opinion about the best use of a recreational area can become an intense political issue: this happened in California when advocates of the preservation of a wilderness area opposed promoters of a skiing development in the Mineral King area of Sequoia National Forest. The Mineral King dispute is the main subject of the article by Wesley Marx, a California reporter, but Marx goes beyond that specific issue to make a general argument against what he calls "The Disney Imperative" and in favor of restraint in redesigning the rural environment. With five percent of the world's population, the United States consumes about 50 percent of the world's natural resources. This statistic is fairly well known, and generally understood to apply to minerals, lumber, and so forth—but Americans also consume a gigantic portion of the world's wildlife. The article by William Conway, general director of the New York Zoological Society, tells what animals are consumed, what forms the consumption takes, and what are some of the problems wildlife consumption presents to regulatory agencies.

Throughout the history of civilization, the urban environment has functioned as the supplier of food; as human population grows, one of the most critical problems it faces is how long the food supply will keep pace. Actually, the problem is rather more serious than a matter of keeping pace: world food supply is inadequate at the present time, and large portions of the world's population live out their lives without proper nourishment. For conditions to remain at a merely status quo level, food supplies will have to double within the coming 35 years. This problem is made even more serious by the fact that increasing population, with attendant increases in urban area, reduces the amount of land available for farming. Many authorities—such as the Paddocks (see p. 34)—consider the problem insoluble, but others—among them

Lester R. Brown, senior research fellow of the Overseas Development Council, and sociologist Gail W. Finsterbusch—believe that new developments in agricultural technology will provide an adequate food supply for our growing world population. The authors hope that a technological victory over food shortage will increase the confidence of leaders of underdeveloped nations in the ability of technology to solve other problems; the situation, however, might be stated another way: if technology postpones the threat of the death rate solution without also lowering the birth rate, then the further increases in population will create problems of such magnitude that more technological innovations will *have to* be accepted.

MAN AND NATURE IN THE NATIONAL PARKS

F. Fraser Darling and Noel D. Eichhorn

We start from the point of view that the national park idea is a major and unique contribution to world culture by the United States. The idea has now been in practice for nearly a century from the time when 3,400 square miles of high country in Wyoming were designated as Yellowstone National Park. Its origins lie within the Romantic Movement and it is a later manifestation of the spirit of equality and brotherhood of the American and French Revolutions. The reawakening of the awareness of nature so evident in the writings of Rousseau and in the poems of Wordsworth and Coleridge was expressed for Americans by Emerson, Thoreau and Bryant with a typical desire to weave it into the stuff of life in a country of opportunity.

The carrying of the national park idea into fruition in the United States has continued to be an inspiration to the rest of the world. The idea has also borne fruit in other parts, particularly in Africa, but the parentage is never forgotten, and the National Park System and the National Park Service of the United States are looked up to in a very special way. The sanctity of the parks, the careful blending of architecture, the ways of doing things to give animals and plants and scenery their foremost places: all this is appreciated abroad as well as at home.

The early history of the national park movement was one of idealism

F. Fraser Darling and Noel D. Eichhorn, "Man and Nature in the National Parks," 1967. Abridged and reprinted with permission of THE CONSERVATION FOUNDATION.

and solid propaganda effort. Roads were begged as a means of getting people into the areas to gain support for the idea. Certain animals were protected even to the extent of reducing the numbers of natural predators. Large hotels in pleasant rustic style were built near the major scenic attractions. In addition to appreciation of nature, healthful outdoor exercise was encouraged.

Since that earlier time both parks and country have changed. The impacts of the internal combustion engine and the increase of leisure were not clearly foreseen and the National Park System is now suffering physically from the success of public interest expressed as numbers of visitors. As population and productivity have increased, wild country outside the parks has diminished, and the fishing and camping which were once found close to home in abundance are increasingly looked for in the national parks which no longer seem remote.

The initial unselfish and generous gesture of sanctuary and inviolability for animals, coming from an era when wildlife management had not been studied, has later raised problems of conservation of vegetation. The larger numbers of visitors with more modern standards of comfort and more sophisticated ways of amusing themselves have raised other sorts of conservation problems. The pressures of these human and animal populations in the parks have demonstrated the necessity for continuing ecological research and land management evaluation if the areas are to be sustained for posterity. The dangers to the parks from within must be met as surely as attempts by exploiters to log or mine the areas.

The inquiry which this report represents was envisaged in the spring of 1961, at a time when ecological conditions in many national parks were causing concern to those individuals within the National Park Service sensitive enough to be aware. Members of the Service who talked with The Conservation Foundation made it plain to us that research in depth of a socio-ecological kind was necessary and that guidelines to such research were far from clear.

In some measure the urgencies of 1961 have been relieved by the reorganization which has taken place within the National Park Service and by the reports of two official committees appointed after our work began.

The Leopold Committee[1] reported early in 1963 with admirable plainness and brevity. The report was reprinted by several outdoor

---

[1] U.S. Department of the Interior Advisory Board on Wildlife Management, A. S. Leopold, chairman. Its report, *Wildlife Management in the National Parks,* was submitted in 1963 and published by the Interior Department in mimeographed form.

magazines and many thousands of copies were distributed. Its influence on National Park Service policy has been considerable.

The Robbins Committee,[2] on which one of us had the honor of serving, spent more time and made more detailed inquiry. Its report was disturbing in that it showed the low status of research in the National Park Service despite the obvious need for such work to solve existing problems. The report was critical and widely quoted, but the influence on National Park Service policy seems less marked than that of the Leopold Committee, which also commented on the paucity of research. Many of the Robbins Committee's specific recommendations have been acted upon, however, and a new position of Chief Scientist has been established.

Our survey has been of a more informal kind than is possible for a formal committee and we have cast our net very widely. A national park exists in an intricate complex of political, social, legal, intellectual and sentimental factors. The terrain of a national park cannot be treated as a museum piece to be preserved behind glass. Some things are possible and some are not; compromise is necessary and inevitable, but it would be wise not to follow a policy of expediency. However biological our initial approach may have wished to be, as ecologist and geographer we have faced the larger field, knowing our limitations, and aware that our report must be concerned with policy-making more than with biological detail.

We are grateful to the Department of the Interior and Secretary Udall for constant encouragement and kindness to us in the course of this study; the National Park Service, in the field and in Washington, has been most generously helpful in discussion, making documents available and giving us the time of its representatives in the parks, often at busy periods. Our thanks to the Director and to the members of the Service can never be adequately expressed. If they will take it that way, our plain criticism of certain items in policy and administration is the highest compliment we can pay to what is a *corps elite* in the service of the United States.

THE NATURE OF A NATIONAL PARK

Our first question is both provocative and pragmatic: "What is a national park for?" We have consistently asked this artless question in the course of our travels and have received widely different replies.

[2] National Academy of Sciences-National Research Council Advisory Committee to the National Park Service on Research, W. J. Robbins, chairman, 1963.

The question has been put to many members of the National Park Service in Washington and in the field, with equally divergent replies.

We can forgive the fluffiness of the description in the Yellowstone Act of 1872, for the draftsmen were treading where angels have burned their toes, but it says, "a public park or pleasuring-ground for the benefit and enjoyment of the people," and also that "the natural curiosities or wonders" were to be retained "in their natural condition."

What is a pleasuring-ground? This phrase is truly archaic, at least 18th century, and given to such London gardens as Vauxhall. Presumably the 19th century Congress passing the act did not see the wilderness of the Yellowstone quite like that, but as the national parks have developed through nearly a century of increasing population, wealth, leisure and mobility, there are certain people who would like to see some parts of the parks much like a Vauxhall, with the equipment for entertainment and enlargement of concessionaire interests.

We can surely take it as an overall expression of informed and serious opinion in the nation, that people do wish the national parks to be unspoiled by development, and that they do wish the heritage to be preserved "unimpaired," as the acts and official proclamations have it, for posterity. Nevertheless, we must emphasize the difference of types of country involved in the system, the difference in reasons for designation, and the difference of ways of acquisition of the terrain.

Yellowstone was the first and the place which Congress called "pleasuring-ground." It remains as nearly typical as any one park can be of the large, virgin, western national parks. It is unlikely that many people thought the Yellowstone Act was intended to preserve what is now called wilderness; the area of the park was far better explored than most of the mountainous west and, therefore, less wild. The pleasures of the park were first: curiosities of nature, geysers and hot springs; second: spectacular scenery, the canyon and the falls; and third (perhaps): the abundant wild game and the setting of grasslands, lakes and forests. For most people the order of these remains unchanged, although the "perhaps" has been removed from the third as less and less of wild nature remains outside the parks, and there are some parks, like Isle Royale, which are nearly pure wilderness.

Yellowstone was public domain, not fully explored, and the start of a national park was from scratch: but what of Acadia, Cape Cod and the Virgin Islands? New attitudes of what is a national park are necessary, and to bring the present-day Yellowstone notion or the undisturbed wilderness notion to bear on these three properties would be merely silly. Even Yellowstone is hardly undisturbed wilderness.

Acadia began with a gift of 6,000 acres by local landowners and since has been much increased in size by the munificence of the Rocke-feller family. The island was already much changed from any primitive condition. The area had had permanent settlement for 200 years and sporadically by the French long before. Now, in addition to local ways of earning a living from the sea, it is a popular holiday resort with summer homes and yachting anchorages.

Why have people come to Acadia in the past? For a wild coast, woods coming down to the sea, good anchorages and a way of life slower than in the rest of the country. National park intention here, surely, is to restrain development but not stop it; rather to guide it in traditional fashion and prevent unsightly advertising. There is nothing disturbing in essence because the boundaries of such a national park are intricate and rather odd, and private landholdings either in or adjacent to the park should have no fears of their quiet style being upset. A national park of the Acadia type requires a careful planning or zoning scheme which can be enforced and which can give continuity.

Cape Cod is another example of a long settled area receiving wel-come protection in the national park system. The architecture of the traditional houses is part of the delight and the long-established golf course is a green, well-tended, man-made landscape which is an asset in the total environment of Cape Cod. The work of the National Park Service as a body with power in rehabilitating the sand dunes is beyond praise. If drivers of sand-buggies object to their amusement being curtailed they must remember that the sport of setting light to haystacks has also been curtailed. Here again, the National Park Serv-ice intent is care in managing a pleasing man-made landscape and continuing living place, by means of overall planning.

St. John in the Virgin Islands is an entirely changed landscape from the primitive, but it is still a pleasing one. The Caribbean is becoming a vast holiday ground with soaring real estate prices, a premium on beaches, and all the possibilities of unsightly development. Indeed, spoliation has already gone far with building on tiny lots. The national park will have considerable biological value in allowing recording of the rehabilitative powers of nature, and on the occasion of our visit we were glad to see botanical research in active progress. The park will preserve some beaches from commercial exploitation and prevent the littoral fauna from being impoverished. The Virgin Islands Na-tional Park will for many years be primarily an adjunct to a popular holiday area, but this in no way belittles the high educational and natural history value this reservation of land can have. The climate will cooperate with the National Park Service in recreating a Caribbean wilderness through time.

These three newer national park areas are near to being "pleasuring-grounds" in a style of decorum and sense of preserving for future generations. But "unimpaired" is not the word to be used in managing them. There will be development and change within the range of what these parks represent. Portions of Acadia and Virgin Islands will certainly be restored to nearly as close an approximation of the pristine state as can be found in Yellowstone, but to lose the existing integration with the neighboring human communities in accomplishing this would be tragic.

Our feeling in discussing the problems of these areas with people inside and outside the National Park Service is that opinion has scarcely become flexible enough as yet to accept them as pointers of change in national park conception. To treat them in the arduously learned discipline of the wilder parks would lead to frustration and possible disaster.

We shall deal later with the misfortune the national park system suffers from having no adequate planning or zoning legislation governing the type of development of areas adjacent to the parks. Sometimes, the United States Forest Service marches with a national park and the result is as near perfection as could be hoped, but there are Gatlinburgs, Cherokees, Estes Parks and White's Cities, which show that some people visiting national parks desire some of the amusements reminiscent of Coney Island; and others, not expecting these, will nevertheless use them on a wet day. Enjoyment of a pleasuring-ground can be interpreted anywhere between the extremes of walking alone in deep wilderness and rubbing shoulders with others on a beach. Is national park enjoyment to compass this span entirely? We have had uncritical and philanthropically-intended answers that it should, although most answers have piously included the proviso that the provision for enjoyment should be such that the national parks are "maintained in absolutely unimpaired form for the use of future generations."

We can neglect that small, uncritical, overgenerous section of opinion, that would include Jones Beaches, but would point quite plainly to the fact that we have found no uniformity of interpretation of what a national park can be within the administration of the National Park Service itself. Whatever the pattern a fabric must have a warp fiber.

We have heard so often the remarks, "Parks are for people" and "It is no good having beautiful areas if the public cannot get into them

and see them." Uncritical acceptance of the implications of these remarks would push aside the welfare of the biological communities
represented in the parks, reduce scenery to the bare physiography and
its interplay with the climate, and deny continuing existence of truly
remote places. Further, in a time when the population is expected to
increase considerably along with leisure time and technical ability in
moving over remote country, we are bound to ask whether the parks
are to be considered as expendable assets, and what kind of enjoyment of national parks will be available for posterity. It is our belief
that many people "enjoy" the parks although they do not visit them.
The very fact that such preserved areas exist is a matter of immense
satisfaction to people who take the view that nature exists in her own
right and that it is the duty of reflective man, with his dominance over
the planet, to conserve the areas represented by national parks for the
reasons they were chosen for that dignity.

Our own definition of legitimate enjoyment of national parks would
be that it should be of that order which places first the ecological well-
being of those areas in relation to their perpetuation as natural biological communities and expanses of natural scenery. The question
should be asked: "What is *this* national park for?" This does not preclude development but it limits it to that which is appropriate and calls
for individual consideration of every situation where development is
contemplated.

THE NATIONAL PARK RESOURCE

There is, in the histories of communities in relation to their resource
base, a period of learning how to reach the resource and use it, followed by a period of rich enjoyment which seems endless in that happy
time; then there comes a choice of working out the resource and losing
it, or learning the art and science of conservation that the resource
may be perpetuated by wise use. The forest estate of the United States
passed through the stages of being a menace to be pushed back, a
resource to be used without thought, and finally an estate to be cared
for under a body so eminent and able as the United States Forest Service. It is fully realized that there is some blessed, happy moment when
the population and the resource are in some momentary balance of
usefulness, enjoyment and ecological repose. Unfortunately, the moment of our human enlightenment comes later than the moment of
optimum and in the whole story of conservation we are stopping gaps
and trying to repair the damage we have allowed to occur. In mention-
ing the forest estate we have used an example where the resource is

finite at any one time, the measure being board-feet and the variables being climate, water supply and fire. These variables are studied intensively to build up a corpus of knowledge of forest management.

The national park estate is finite in acreage, but the resource of national pride, enjoyment and usefulness in the life of the people cannot be set down as board-feet. It is in large measure intangible and we find that most inconsiderable plants, animals and ecological relationships are important parts of the resource both for enjoyment and for maintenance of the biome. The fact that few people understand the scientific detail of the ecology makes no difference to the assumption that a landscape in ecological repose is generally one that gives pleasure.

We return to the question, "What is a national park for?" which, if satisfactorily answered, should help to define what a national park should be, irrespective of the several differing reasons why areas are designated as such. Everglades was designated primarily because of the wonders of the wildlife, plant and animal, in the unique set of circumstances. A new research plan for this park indicates a re-emphasis of the primary obligation and the need to implement it. Certain developments and trends in other national parks in the last 15 years cause us to doubt whether, even if now feasible, there will ever be a real return to a purer conception of the national park. We are well aware that there must be evolution in conceptions and trends but we find ourselves unable to get away from the uncomfortable impression that policy is philosophically unsure and that this is contributing to the general deterioration apparent in several properties.

Further uncertainty is exhibited by the multiplicity of decisions and different policies resulting from excessive decentralization. The early conception of the National Park Service was for close overall control of properties by the central agency. Despite the obvious necessity for some proliferation and for more flexibility of action within each park, the need remains for the service to act as one being, firmly convinced in its policy.

The story of the growing pains of the national park heritage has been admirably told by John Ise in his critical history, *Our National Park Policy*. Part Two of this great book describes the several administrations under different directors since the establishment of the National Park Service in 1916 with Steven Mather in charge. This date is memorable for it unified administration and made codification possible. Mather was an example of a rich man giving the rest of his life and a large part of his fortune to achieving what he thought a national park system and a National Park Service should be. Through the vigor and charm of his personality elan was high and the panache incomparable. Not only has the force and excellence of his administration persisted far beyond his short directorship of 12 years, but the spread of the national park idea about the world has been attended with the same ideals as to standards even if these are not always reached.

Ise quotes the now famous letter of May 13th, 1918, of Secretary Lane to Steven Mather outlining administrative policy, (but) throughout (the letter) one finds no mention of wildlife or wildlife policy and no ecological notions whatever; we can see that from such a wise and statesmanlike manifesto following nearly half a century of almost failure, it would be difficult to graft on the biological philosophy which is now generally held by critics of the policy of the National Park Service. Our thinking is almost entirely in line with the Leopold and Robbins Committees whose attitude in short is that unless a biologically informed policy is fully accepted and initiated immediately, the status of the national park heritage is going to deteriorate in all those qualities which inspired its designation.

One thing is certain: there can be no absolute set of standards and statement of policy, and any manual of national park management must emphasize the need for flexibility and impress the fact that every park or monument is such by virtue of individual claims to beauty, history or scientific interest and uniqueness. Flexibility should be always in the realm of procedure enlightened by knowledge and not in principles driven by expedience.

It is necessary to examine certain democratic convictions critically in relation to national parks: because they are out of doors, is the visiting capacity to be limitless? A national park has linear boundaries and a vast amount of empty air but its capacity is a matter of subtle and expert assessment. If the stage of "standing room only" is reached, the natural pageant which the people have come to see is largely obscured. The fact must be faced up to that in our era of growing population, more leisure and increased mobility, a national park has need to post a "house full" sign at the gates long before "standing room only" is reached.

We have been under the impression throughout our survey that visitor statistics showing high rates of increase year by year are welcomed as valuable weapons in getting larger appropriations for the National Park Service. Development takes place which will encourage more visits rather than conserve the unique habitats which the parks represent. The supreme example of what appears to us as wholly mistaken policy at this time is the erection of a large building at Petrified

Forest on Highway 66, specially designed to entice the public from the highway and to advertise the national parks and monuments. This large building deriving from the pueblo style is so much larger than any pueblo and so lacks the varied surface texture of genuine pueblos that the effect is saddening. An intimate style carried to the megalithic is self-destroying. The building itself violates pristine national park thinking, but its function seems to us out of phase because the present urgent problem is how to cope with 120 million visitors each year to the parks; there is no call for advertising the attractions.

Thinking independently as individuals we have both felt uneasy about the conception of Mission 66. It has seemed to us that this operation over 10 years has been to increase visitation, making it easier to get into the national parks and that the visitors should be more comfortable in various ways once they are there. Mission 66 has done comparatively little for the plants and animals.

The enormous increase in drive-in campsites is an example of very expensive facilities which do nothing at all for the ecological maintenance of a park. Some superintendents have resisted proposals to increase drive-in campsites because they restrict ranger activity and impose a burden beyond the capacity of the existing staff. Part of a ranger's responsibility is to get around his beat of the park and to know what is happening in fields other than the human; in fact, at the busiest time when he should be everywhere he tends to become a camp-ground supervisor. We would go farther and say that in an age of better roads and automobiles no more campsites should be made in national parks, and when the present ones need repair, in most cases they should be abandoned and helped to return to the biome by natural succession. Demand for camping space might be controlled to some extent, while at the same time reducing the considerable uncertainty attending a hopeful camper's finding an empty spot at a busy weekend, by requiring advanced bookings for the most popular camp grounds.

Since national parks, too, have limited capacities, it does not seem unreasonable to require those persons wishing to remain overnight also to make reservations in advance. Indeed, it would not be inappropriate to extend the idea to include even day use of such over-popular national park attractions as the Yosemite Valley and Cliff Palace at Mesa Verde. Another possible control on camp ground and park use might be a higher entrance or user fee. Rates could be adjusted to make the most popular spots the most expensive. Curiously, the new Land and Water Conservation Fund entrance permit, called the "Golden Passport," reduces season rates at most national parks by more than half. Where an increased charge for entrance to a national park would seem sensible in a time of overuse, here is an inducement to entry.

One officer in one of the parks we visited gave us a phrase which we think cannot be bettered. He thought that if the parks were to be preserved in face of steeply rising numbers of visitors which are politically difficult to control, advantage should be taken of what he called "built-in frictions" to apply the brake. The 30 miles of dusty road into Chaco Canyon was precisely such a built-in friction; failing immediate power to implement a well-planned policy of how to deal with the increased use which the automobile is bringing, it was folly to improve the existing road. Thinking in these terms we would emphasize again that each park presents a particular ecological situation and the only absolute administrative principle can be to consider first the ecological health of a park so that it shall endure for posterity.

We have implied that thought on policy must be flexible and have regard to history and change. How far is present policy an unthinking continuation or adherence to that of the pioneer stages of the national park idea? Yellowstone covers 3,200 square miles of high, rough and remote country. At least it was remote in 1872 and until, possibly, 1920. If it was to be visited, it was obvious that lodges such as those at Mammoth and Old Faithful should be constructed. The journey from Gardner to Old Faithful which once took two days now takes two hours. It is our opinion that the conditions of travel which necessitated accommodation centers within the parks have served also as a mental block to provision of all such facilities outside the parks, where they should be in an age of swift travel and heavy use.

If the national parks are to continue to be a retreat from urban civilization for increasing numbers of people, much of what was permissible in the less crowded past will need to be more carefully controlled or eliminated. The Park Service has begun to move hotels and camp grounds away from the most spectacular scenery, but not very far away; the parks are still dotted with little islands of civilization. Current expensive development, designed to meet present demands, too often does not envisage long range values.

The Yosemite Valley is the heart of that lovely national park and its most wonderful feature. The Independence Day visitation in 1966 was 54,700. There are nine grocery and general stores in the valley, seven service stations, a laundry, a barbershop, three swimming pools, a stock stable, and 4,500 hotel accommodations. Camp grounds are heavily crowded and even the crime rate is increasing.

Our statement that the only absolute administrative principle in the National Park Service is to make ecological health or repose of an area the first consideration is but one way of expressing an idea which has been independently put already by the Leopold Committee on Wildlife Management in the Parks. Their report says, "The major policy change which we would recommend to the National Park Service is that it recognize the enormous complexity of ecological communities and the diversity of management procedures required to preserve them." The Leopold Committee was considering wildlife management; our field is larger in that it includes the traumatic action and metabolic activities of that dynamic seasonal immigrant animal, Man. We have had the uncomfortable feeling in the course of our work that such members of the National Park Service as have a high ecological awareness are not taking a significant part in formulation of policy. They should be brought to the ultimate council table.

DEVELOPMENT

The National Park Service tells us, we think much too frequently, that "Parks are for People." Our earlier dismissal of the phrase as inappropriate huckstering does not mean that we are unaware that the parks are indeed for people. In fact, "people," "park visitors," whatever they are called, are responsible for most of the change and development which takes place in and around the national parks. In a sense, even the wilderness portions of the parks are developed since there are trails even in the most remote places. In speaking of development, however, we are referring primarily to those constructions which prepare the park for the ordinary, nearly carbound, tourist.

We learn that 5 percent of the Yellowstone National Park is taken up by development, a proportion which seems to us inordinately high, for the traumatic influence of this 5 percent will be over a much larger area. However, our point is that much of the recent development need not have been within the park at all. For example, the new employee housing area at Mammoth Hot Springs is plain poor planning (especially when remembering that Yosemite is taking ranger housing outside the park, but here we have two administrative regional headquarters pursuing opposite policies). Gardner, five miles to the north and outside Yellowstone National Park, 1,000 feet lower and far more accessible in the winter, would have been a better location for many reasons of cost, landscape and access to schools and stores. The good sense of this is admitted by the National Park Service but a policy of hesitation has won the day and the new Mammoth is a new eyesore. Canyon Village is another seasonal community which covers large acreage and is difficult to justify in its present position. It could just as well have been outside the park and would have played a larger part in the economy of the state of Wyoming. Some would justify the existence of Canyon Village because of its proximity to points of high scenic value in the park. We would take the view that this is a prime reason why Canyon Village should not be there. The same objections apply to trailer camps and automobile camps. They could be outside the park.

We have referred earlier to what appears to be timidity in allowing further building to take place where it is admitted existing buildings would be better removed. Big Bend National Park has as its heart a magnificent basin surrounded by the steep and spectacular Chisos Mountains. The park headquarters has been built 10 miles away outside the basin and it might have been hoped that further development would not have been in the basin. There had been some building of modest accommodations before the property was given to the nation by the state of Texas, when a CCC camp was established in the 30s. These hutments had later been run as a hotel operation and further service buildings had been erected. National Park Concessions, Inc., put up some more and better accommodations and there is now a good deal of sporadic unplanned development to be seen from the ground above the basin. In our opinion the basin is getting too full. More building is to be done by the concessioner but the new facilities will replace Dallas huts and there will be no increase in the number of beds. The National Park Service has tried unsuccessfully to reduce the campsites, realizing how easily the basin could be spoiled.

A bolder policy of bringing back the basin to something approaching its pristine state would result in a major scenic asset being able to make its full impact. We realize, of course, that we are suggesting a counsel of perfection, but it would be deplorable if the basin became a little Yosemite Valley by small stages for lack of a forthright initial policy. The camp ground at least could go or be redesigned, but the concessioner's new and existing buildings must be accepted for the coming 25 to 30 years till they need renewal.

In many respects the period 1935-1940 could be thought of as an optimum in the management of the national park resource of the United States. The standard of national park architecture was very high indeed, achieving a fitness with the environment which had obviously needed sensitivity in the design office. A well-illustrated book on park structures was issued by the National Park Service in 1935, compiled by Conrad Wirth 16 years before he became director of the service. The architectural principles and ideals set forth are impeccable and are supported by photographs of existing entrances, signs, restaurants, accommodations and so on.

When we were in Santa Fe we visited the regional headquarters office of the National Park Service and found the building and interior furnishing a most pleasurable experience. The Hispano-Pueblo type of construction is entirely satisfying here.

With these standards so much in mind we have been less happy about more recent buildings, especially if the office of design is far removed from the site. We have remarked on the new staff housing at Mammoth in Yellowstone, which could scarcely be more out of keeping, and though there is nothing wrong with the individual houses of the new ranger village at El Portal outside Yosemite National Park, the layout of the site with a grid of streets is unimaginative and depressing. Not the National Park Service but Congress must be blamed for the parsimony which left the whole site in a raw unfinished state to be landscaped by the rangers themselves.

Another distressing departure from the standards of 1935 is apparent in Camp Eielson Visitor Center far into McKinley National Park, Alaska. The building itself is an appallingly ugly structure set ostentatiously on a knoll in a sublime valley, looking across to the massif of Mount McKinley. The building bears no relation of any kind to the landscape and is obtrusive to say the least. Earlier standards made a point of the buildings not being so.

Lest we be thought to be architecturally reactionary, may we record our delight in the controversial building in Dinosaur National Monument which exhibits the actual face of the quarry in which the skeletons of dinosaurs were set by nature. The glass roof follows the line of the hill which would appear had not the quarry been excavated. This visitor center-*cum*-museum is brilliantly conceived and we cannot imagine the spirit not being lightened by seeing and entering this building. Further into this 205,000-acre property the natural sandstone architecture of canyons and gorges is superb and uplifting. We were desolated, then, gazing from an overlook to see camp grounds below. Their siting here was quite unnecessary.

It would seem that the presence of a resident landscape architect in a national park is a considerable insurance against bad siting and bad design. Presumably he becomes identified with his terrain and feels for it. First thoughts are given a second time round and revised or even drastically altered or abandoned. It needs time for the unconscious to work and throw up significant points to the conscious mind. One of the reasons for the change from architectural styles of 1935 may well be that the buildings produced from such designs today would be far too expensive. We should accept the point and say how doubly careful one must be in siting them and modifying them to fit a particular landscape.

Camp grounds are extremely expensive of space and it is always difficult to make them esthetically pleasing when in use, for the automobile and trailer together are no architectural addition to our culture. The camp ground seems to us rather a fetish: it is supposed to recreate for the public the joy of living in the open air, smelling wood smoke and seeing the stars, as so many pioneers were able to do. Putting aside false sentiment, the main attraction of the camp ground is that it costs so little to the user. It is a principal anxiety to the ranger staff.

The psychology of the camp ground is something else and to some of us a quite baffling phenomenon. Mr. Lon Garrison told us of his study in Yosemite in the '30s during which he found that many people apparently liked being crowded in camp grounds. At least, when the density of occupation of camp grounds decreased after Labor Day, there was a general movement from the outliers to the center, where the density consequently remained high.

We would repeat that throughout the national parks and monuments the whole principle and policy of camp grounds should be reexamined and clarified and not be obscured by romantic notions which are not quite true. Obviously, a family must be able to accommodate itself cheaply on a tour of many of the parks and monuments, and camp grounds are popular, but as the significant camping population moves in automobiles, these facilities should not continue in the choice areas of national parks. In most cases there is plenty of room for them outside the parks.

An incidental facet of the whole motor camping movement is the change in the character of the motel. These were once called "tourist cabins" and were very modest accommodations, cheap but decent, but such are now hard to find. The modern motel is more ambitious, with wall-to-wall carpeting and television, and far more expensive. Perhaps the National Park Service could subsidize plain accommodations outside the parks rather than make costly and unsightly camp grounds inside the boundaries.

If buildings and camp grounds are important as objects of early research preparation, they are no less so than roads and their location. Roads draw traffic, quite apart from relieving it elsewhere. Also roads have a habit of acquiring power in their own right. Throughout our history, roads, rights of way and easements concerning them have been major items of legal argument. Roads in and near national parks are tongues of penetration calling for highly concentrated thought and expertise in their planning, yet in the eyes of many people, not least the local politicians and business communities, roads are of essence good and rewarding. This philosophy is constantly pressing on the National Park Service and is even accepted by some individuals in the service.

Allied to the notion of roads is that of footpaths to points of particular interest in national parks, and such magnificent walks as the Appalachian Trail. Nobody likes black-topped paths on nature trails in what is hopefully thought to be near wilderness, but the human foot in large numbers of pairs is extremely wearing on terrain. Nature has remarkable powers of recovery; indeed, the ecology of natural rehabilitation could be the subject of a valuable textbook, because the vast interplay of plant and animal species and climatic and geological factors is quite inadequately understood.

The Appalachian Trail itself, so grand in conception and achievement, is taking heavy punishment. We allowed ourselves to follow a self-guided nature trail of three-quarters of a mile in the higher ground in the spirit of uninformed interest, using our eyes and being helped by the excellent printed guide (which Uncle Sam offered at 5 cents, but if we felt we could not afford this sum, we were at liberty to take the folder and would we please replace it in the box on our return. This is a good gesture and we learned later that nickels were plentiful in the collection box). The feet of nature lovers had worn through the moss-covered, spongy forest path to expose the roots of the spruces and balsam firs. The Appalachian Trail crosses this nature trail twice and here we found a trench 12-18 inches deep in the forest floor. Even the purest of nature lovers has physical weight and boots on his feet. Regrettably, we endorse the view that in the absence of any restriction in numbers, portions of the Appalachian Trail will have to be black-topped.

We would now touch upon a very large problem on which nothing we are likely to say will have much influence, but the problem can scarcely be set down too often, namely, the conduct of areas immediately adjoining national parks and monuments. The magnificent heritage of natural wealth represented by the parks is being endangered by the lack of planning control outside. We had this impressed on us forcibly early in our investigation travelling through Shenandoah

along the Skyline Drive and along the Blue Ridge Parkway towards
Great Smokies. Shenandoah and the Blue Ridge Parkway are inspiring
examples of public endeavor towards beauty in development. Admittedly, we thought the craze for views was perpetuating too much of
the sick upland farming, because land in the possession of the National
Park Service is actually being leased back to farmers to keep it grazed.
There were several bad stretches of erosion. Nature cries out that
this ill-used land should go back to trees. Even on the glorious Shenandoah Skyline Drive there are those who complain it is becoming an
alley in the trees. This is mere carping, for in fact, numerous viewpoints are kept clear and allow sudden surprises of superb quality.

The pleasure we experienced is emphasized to put our horror in
proper perspective when we approached Great Smokies National Park
through Maggie Valley. We were really upset by the billboards and
signs, the decrepitude of subsistence farming and what it had done to
intrinsically beautiful country, and the banal quality of resorts and
souvenir trash. Cherokee was shattering, our cup of unhappiness being
filled by seeing an Indian feathered from crown to heel sweeping up
cigarette ends outside a souvenir shop. To pitchfork a facet of Plains
Indian culture into Cherokee is affronting, but for the trappings of
chieftainship to be worn by a sweeper-up of cigarette ends was revolt-
ing. Soon we were in the park and grateful.

Land prices rocket as soon as a national park is designated and
there is little or no control of development on the land adjoining the
national park. It may be said, indeed, that designation of a park pre-
cipitates unsightly development outside. Cherokee and Gatlinburg,
Estes Park at Rocky Mountain and White's City at Carlsbad Caverns—
these, surely, are misfortunes which the majority of American citizens
would wish to prevent. Such communities have so much to offer in the
way of service and that not unprofitably, that space trips at 75 cents,
waxworks and the bawl of billboards could be dropped. The opposite
extreme was apparent in that area of the Blue Ridge Parkway adjoining the Pisgah National Forest. Worn out farms had become summer
homes and the proximity of forest and parkway would make a prospective purchaser confident that he would not be swallowed up in piecemeal development. Proper zoning control of areas adjoining national
parks may come in due course, but it is probably a long way ahead.
The National Park Service is alive to the handicap it suffers in controlling the situation and, in the example of Great Smoky Mountains,
is setting a pattern which may well give an excellent temporary solution, but certainly not a radical cure.

The large problem of development in national parks is inevitable; whatever is done and whoever does it is going to be criticized, probably unfairly. We are very conscious that as outsiders investigating wear and tear and maintenance of pristine landscape and natural communities of plants and animals, it would be so easy to descend into the ranks of unfair critics without any wish or intention to do so. We wish to emphasize once more our immense pride in the achievement of the National Park Service, spiritually and physically. The qualities which brought the achievement to fruition are still there and will continue; it must be remembered, however, that the Service is greatly expanded from earlier days, the national park system is expanded, and above all, the nation's use of the parks has expanded at a greater rate than has either the Service or the area concerned. The course of visitation since 1945 has been of the order of a flash flood, the simile breaking down in the fact that the visitation is no flash after which the terrain will be much as it was before, but a permanent inundation. Government, National Park Service and nation will have to adapt to a new way of life. But this does not mean necessarily that the ideals which brought the national parks into being and the Service to its achievement will have to be relinquished.

MANAGEMENT OF PLANTS AND ANIMALS

We have indicated in the previous chapter that the human animal is, in a sense, an intruder in the national parks which must be protected from him by careful planning and regulation of use. But what of the animals which live in the parks, and the plants; what are the datum lines that might guide policy in making decisions on preservation of natural communities?

The first uncritical reply might be that it is fundamental in national park thinking that natural communities of plants and animals should be conserved. Of course it is: does not every ranger and naturalist, every museum, every admonishing and educational signboard draw our attention to the need for care? Indeed yes, but through park after park it is inevitable that certain species and groups of species are not quite getting full opportunity to survive. Only two national parks consistently hold wolves, namely, McKinley in Alaska and Isle Royale in Lake Superior. We know that it was not easy to get sanctuary for the wolf in McKinley, but the studies of Adolph Murie published in 1941 had early effect for the benefit of the animal. The wolves in Isle Royale came across the ice one winter and stayed. Their prey is the moose population and Durward Allen has directed a most enlightening protracted study of the relationship of the two species. Six hundred moose and 20 wolves appear to live in balance and we can say that by these two populations being together, the vegetational habitat is conserved. This in itself must mean the conservation of insect communities and other invertebrate relationships. In short, the National Park Service as managers are being saved a lot of trouble, work and thinking.

How different is the great pseudo-wilderness of Yellowstone where the wolf has no place because of down-country filtration into Montana and Wyoming. The result is an elk problem which was analyzed and pointed out in the '30s but which had to wait until the '50s and '60s before action was taken to reduce the elk population to 5,000. One of us had the opportunity to travel in the Yellowstone in 1950 at the time when the aspen groves were wrecks, and the general appearance of these areas was shocking. Our visit in the course of this study was in 1963 when the senior member was impressed by the generally improved look of the park but *the aspen groves had disappeared*: they had been replaced by grasslands which looked neat and tidy. This is how we might have seen it had not one of us had the longer memory. In truth, allowing the elk in the northern herd to remain at a population of over 12,000 had removed an important species from the ecosystem and Yellowstone was less wilderness than before.

It has been suggested[3] that the national parks should present a "vignette of primitive America" and that "the biotic associations within each park be maintained, or where necessary recreated, as nearly as possible in the condition that prevailed when the area was first visited by the white man." There is a danger that these phrases might be misinterpreted as meaning that the change and progression which are basic to natural conditions must be checked and the parks maintained as static museum exhibits. We should prefer to say that the wilderness character of the parks should be preserved by permitting natural processes to continue (except that no catastrophe could be permitted to lay waste an entire park). In some cases recreation of an earlier, more primitive scene may be desirable, but the opportunity for new landscapes and habitats to develop should not be proscribed. The larger parks have room for many differing successional stages, but no area is sufficiently large or sufficiently remote to remain entirely unaltered by the activities of man. In some parks the effect is very slight and little corrective action is needed.

[3] In the report of the Interior Board on Wildlife Management, op. cit.

For others a semblance of wilderness is possibly only with careful and intensive management.

At Yellowstone the National Park Service is saddled with the unpleasant task of killing a large number of elk each year when the animals are on winter range and more or less useless as food. Further, the reduced population will have a better calving rate and the numbers to be killed will remain high. The waste is dreadful but the alternative is not good. We talked with a member of the Wyoming Outfitters' Association who did not go as far as many of his associates who wished hunting to be allowed. He would like to see elk on the summer range moved eastward by helicopter or by good scouts, into the shooting country of Wyoming, and out of their Yellowstone sanctuary. His thesis is that the Yellowstone herd is being incremented annually by Wyoming elk because of the sanctuary the park provides. Also, he was dead against shooting in January and February and wished all reduction to be by live trapping and the animals to be let loose elsewhere in Wyoming. However, we learned from other sources that Wyoming already has elk problems and that live-trapped elk from Yellowstone are being more or less set down in feed lots until places can be found for them.

We talked with Dr. John Craighead, who has done so much work on the grizzly bears in Yellowstone. He would like to see more elk shot and left in the high ground as carrion for bears and any other carnivores and scavengers, but he admits this might create a build-up of grizzlies which would cause further trouble in due course. Our own comment on this would be to say that if there were to be a build-up of the grizzly bear population, they would begin to prey on the elk calves and this might be the best way of keeping the elk population stable.

The question of hunting in national parks has been debated with heat through the years wherever there is an animal population which might grow beyond the safe grazing capacity. So far hunting has been resisted except in Grand Teton where there has been controlled activity of this kind. In fact, public hunting is an extremely inefficient method of thinning a population of, say, deer or elk; sport hunters in general do not like walking very far and still less carrying a carcass out of remote country. Many studies of amateur hunting pressures show this "roadside" quality of the Nimrods. The chief naturalist of Yellowstone, answering demands for public hunting to reduce the elk herd, said, "If their ability was equal to that of the 1,002 hunters in Grand Teton, nearly 18,000 hunters would have killed the 5,000 elk, plus 196 illegal moose, 410 illegal elk and 17 men, along with an undetermined number of bears, coyotes, bighorn sheep, antelope, bison, mule deer and horses." The idea is laughable when reduced to this kind of logic, but more detail is needed to make the situation clear.

We were alarmed to find the old established privilege of fishing in the national parks being given an odd twist by biologists of the Bureau of Sport Fisheries and Wildlife working on Yellowstone Lake: they alluded to the valuable fishery of the lake as if it were a commercial asset and we heard questioned the fact that the white pelicans probably extract a catch equal to that extracted by the public. Could the pelicans continue to be allowed so much in view of the sharply rising number of sports fishermen?

Imagine our surprise on learning that the N. P. S. actually did control (a nice euphemism) the Yellowstone pelicans between 1924 and 1931, when the fish hatchery at the lake was in operation. Fortunately such activity has not been resumed and policy, stated first in the early 1930s and adhered to since, has protected the rights of native predators "to share normally in the benefits of fish culture."

We would put the point of view at this juncture that the privilege of fishing in the national parks is one that needs radical reconsideration. The privilege was given without question at the beginning of national park history: the right to fish with a rod is the almost inalienable right of every American; but again we are up against what was once a perfectly sensible decision being carried forward into a period and circumstances entirely different. This right in our day is of the nature of vestigial remains in evolution. Earlier in national park history a certain amount of living off the country was considered a legitimate part of the park experience. To a limited extent fishing continues in this category today with some campers catching and cooking their suppers. The National Park Service promotion called "Fishing for Fun" emphasizes the fact that angling as a sport is completely unrelated to any feeling of man's dependence on nature. This idea seems so foreign to the ethics of the National Park Service as we have known it, that we wonder how it came to be used even while admitting that the intention is to protect fish populations by reducing the kill.

In the past the National Park Service was so philanthropic and unthinking as to follow a policy of stocking remote lakes in fragile country where no sport fish existed formerly. The use of live bait introduced undesirable species, a most unecological procedure in conserving the parks unimpaired. Fortunately, the service outlawed live bait in the parks many decades ago, but stocking once begun is difficult to stop. Fishermen "collect" remote lakes as status symbols and talking points; they will make great efforts to fish these remote lakes, involving much wear of trails and detrimental treading round lake edges.

Fishing, surely, is one of those outworn privileges in a national park of the later 20th century, the more so as so many impoundments of water have been made in many parts of the United States and where fishing is properly encouraged.

Shooting of wild game has long been prohibited in the national parks and the idea is so firmly implanted in the public mind that the proper control of animal populations by the National Park Service has been uncritically resisted until disaster point has been reached. The killing of fish is still something quite different in the public mind; yet if scientists, moralists and aesthetes were to sit down together to talk round the subject, they would find it difficult to state logical reasons for treating these various park vertebrates by such different criteria.

Our opinion is that giving sanctuary to the indigenous fish as well as to many other forms of life in the national parks would be a logical development which would have an immediate beneficial effect on the ecological pressures of various kinds we have mentioned. A beginning has been made in a few national parks where some waters formerly open to fishing are now closed because fishing and an overabundance of fishermen were clearly detrimental to scenery, wildlife and vegetation. All lake shores and river basin systems should be protected and the avian fauna depending on the lakes and streams for its food should have its first right respected. There is the further significant point that many human visitors to the national parks find immense pleasure in the bird life to be seen. Any restriction of it, such as of the white pelicans which appear to be direct competitors with the sport fishermen, would be abhorrent if the restriction were to allow a greater take by the fishermen in a national park.

At this point we should like to comment on the general problem of exotics without suggesting that we presume to offer solutions. There is a general belief that the presence of exotics in a national park is to be deplored and that is probably sound enough. All the same, the ecology of exotics is quite complex and it is difficult to subscribe to the purist attitude we have heard so often both inside and outside the National Park Service. How many areas are free from exotics? What is and what is not an exotic by this time? Why is an exotic present? What is an exotic doing—good or harm, or both?

Of course, man is the great conveyor of exotics, purposely or accidentally, and everybody knows about rats and mongooses and garden weeds. Remarkably few people know that exotics have difficulty in breaking into a stable climax community, or that in the course of natural succession an exotic appearing, say as an annual weed, at an early stage is unlikely to persist into later and more complex stages of succession. The question of the status of exotics should not cause hysterical reactions until each example is thought through.

Our opinion is that even if one would prefer to be without these exotics, there is no point in wasting time and money getting rid of them. The appearance and spread of any exotic plant almost axiomatically should cause us to say, "What have we done to this ecosystem that allows this plant to take hold?" It is often a matter of the mote and the beam.

But what of the goat, that Mephistophelean disastrous exotic which is established almost ineradicably over half the world? It is hurtful to have such hard feelings as we must have for this lovable, humorous, intelligent and persistent creature, but the species is a major problem, not least in national parks. But even here we have had disturbing doubts: our month in the islands of the Hawaiian group was most enlightening to our general education, including contemplation of the goat and its works. We sat along the Hilina Pali trail looking down from about 2,250 feet over the inhospitable lava slopes to a coastal plain west of Halape. Behind us were forests of *ohia* which all of us wish to conserve; the coastal strip was green with grass, the miles between were a-a lava. As we gazed through binoculars, about 1,000 goats were grazing and resting on the few hundred acres of grass. We grew reflective.

The Hawaiian group of islands is purely volcanic and, being so far from any other islands or continents, acquired naturally relatively few plants and animals. The natural communities were simple because Hawaii was hard to reach by floating seeds, spores and so on. Polynesian man colonizing Hawaii possibly 1,200 years ago found very little to sustain him in the forests of tree fern. It would seem that in his wisdom gained by occupancy of so many islands, the Polynesian brought the breadfruit, the taro, and the yam with him and possibly a score more plants. Hawaii, then, gained some exotics and many others followed, plant and animal. The European discovery of Hawaii in the 1770s was not of a pristine plant and animal community. Introductions of new species were almost the order of the new experimental age. Some grasses had certainly arrived in Hawaii by then, but many new ones came with the Europeans and the weeds of arable land. Captain Cook presented the goats and was doubtless convinced of the benefits of this step.

So here were 1,000 descendants of those exotic goats comfortably ensconced on these few hundred acres of exotic grass. One does not have to be immoderately pure to declare war on the goats which sometimes come up the slopes and attack the fringes of the *koa* forest, but to be a logical purist on the matter of exotics, the grass should be pulled up and got rid of as well. Is that likely, or even possible? We think not.

But what of the grass? In the absence of goats to eat it, the grass will grow long and wither and become a fire hazard to the forest above. Possibly, lacking any better animal (and God forbid the rabbit!) there is an optimum population of goats which would subsist by keeping down the grass without having to go up to the fringes of the forest. If an ecological study supported such a view, the goat in severely pruned numbers in this particular situation would not be an altogether harmful exotic.

Let us now move over to the island of Maui where the great caldera of Haleakala lies at around 7,000 feet altitude between peaks of 9,000 and 10,000 feet. It is a superb property of the National Park Service, managed with impeccable restraint for the benefit of the natural communities of plants and animals in the crater. The goat is the enemy and nothing whatever can be said in extenuation of its presence. The leguminous *mamane* tree is indigenous and is being bitten back to extinction by the goats which are partial to it. The particular type of *ohia* is also being attacked. That unique and spectacular plant, the silversword, is a favorite food of the goats; only the fact that most of the remaining plants are in a part of the crater which leaves the goats without any retreat into cliffs, has saved them so far.

There could be no driving of goats here in the crater in a habitat of cliffs; it must be steady picking off by shooting. But that would be useless unless infiltration could be stopped and that means a goat-proof fence along the 26 miles of the perimeter. The National Park Service has undertaken this $75,000 task since our visit and every United States citizen should be grateful. This was a task undertaken solely for the benefit of the silent community of plants, and in the finest tradition of the national parks.

We have already noted our admiration for the National Park Service and system as they were during the 1930s. A particularly promising development of that period was the acceptance by the service of the recommendations of Messrs. Wright, Dixon and Thompson as published in *National Park Fauna Series Numbers 1 and 2*. The authors of these reports were absorbed into the service as a new Wildlife Division

and a corps of biologists was established. For a few years park development plans had to be approved by the biologists as well as the engineers
and landscape architects.

In most essentials the Leopold and Robbins Committees have only
restated, 30 years later, the conclusions of Wright, Dixon and Thompson. It seems incredible that such a promising line of management
should have been abandoned, particularly since ecological deterioration in many parks has now progressed so far that it is noticed by even
the casual park visitor. We have spoken of what appears to be inde-
cision in many areas of national park management. In the matters of
ecological awareness and responsibility there seems to be positive
resistance to new ideas, or reacceptance of old.

THE CONCEPT OF WILDERNESS IN NATIONAL PARKS

Wilderness is another of those words which have suffered some
erosion or derogatory change of connotation through the years. The
Oxford English Dictionary derives the word from Old English, possibly wild-deer-ness, but the plain definition is wild, uncultivated land,
uninhabited by human beings but occupied by many wild animals.
Webster says "a tract of land or a region (as a forest or wide barren
plain) uncultivated and uninhabited by human beings ... an empty or
pathless area ... a part of a garden devoted to wild growth." Through
history the tendency has been to think of a cultivated place as being
better or more acceptable than a wild one; then an untended garden
became a wilderness in common parlance; and finally the politicians
gathered the word into their fevered vocabulary to signify the state of
being out of power. Webster, at least, has lifted the word from an utter
abyss by speaking of a part of a garden *devoted* to wild growth.

The word has also kept its nobility for the few and in this day of
human crisis we know there is nothing derogatory or outmoded in
the notion of wilderness. The dedication of wilderness was a large
part of the early national park idea, although but a few could have
foreseen a time when little wilderness would remain. The Wilderness
Act of September 3, 1964 was hard fought before it became law and is
a true sign of our predicament.

The definition here is practical, a basis from which a Wilderness
System can be identified and designated:

"A Wilderness, in contrast with those areas where man and his own works
dominate the landscape, is hereby recognized as an area where the earth
and its community of life are untrammeled by man, where man himself is
a visitor who does not remain. An area of wilderness is further defined to

mean in this act an area of undeveloped federal land retaining its primeval character and influence, without permanent improvements or human habitation, which is protected and managed so as to preserve its natural conditions and which (1) generally appears to have been affected primarily by the forces of nature, with the imprint of man's work substantially unnoticeable; (2) has outstanding opportunities for solitude or a primitive and unconfined type of recreation; (3) has at least 5,000 acres of land or is of sufficient size as to make practicable its preservation and use in an unimpaired condition; and (4) may also contain ecological, geological, or other features of scientific, educational, scenic, or historical value."

The wilderness we seek to protect in the national parks and forests carries much more than the necessarily bare description of the act. True wilderness has no voice except that drawn forth from the few human beings who have spent their 40 days there and have returned with that which they are unable to tell. Even so, we believe the wild areas we seek to protect have meaning also for the many who will never know them in their physical aspects. There is a wilderness of mind and spirit which those who are called have the courage to enter, dwell there a space and return again; yet our minds and language are so full of simile and metaphor that this intellectual and spiritual wilderness is set about with forests, ocean, desert, and mountain; with storm, maelstrom, sunlit glades and far distance. To deprive the globe of physical wilderness would be to give a deep wound to our own kind.

We would say the national park idea in its highest expression is an aspect of true religion, and to have it beset by expediency in our time of need is grievous. All now realize that the national parks cannot be wholly a wilderness system in a modern world, but the national parks of the roads, the museums, visitor centers, campsites and scenic outlooks are in effect a staging point to the wilderness. When we are tempted to turn away, sickened at misuse and apparent non-participation by some types of visitors, let us remember the responsibility of our deep convictions of the true significance of national parks as part of our faith. If we become faint of heart this noble idea is lost.

Many, even most, national parks contain wilderness areas, but at this moment in time they need proclamation and the firm decision to hold them as such. When the Yellowstone was made a national park most of the country around was equally wild. This is so no longer and within the park we see that the true wilderness areas are not at the center but towards the boundaries, and we cannot but fear, though these areas are something special in our conception of the Yellowstone, not just wild country to walk in but the fiber of the national park itself. The parks are where they are because of these unique wonders which can be sustained only if the general wild quality of the park is respected.

The act instructs the National Park Service and other federal agencies over a period of years to identify parcels of land larger than 5,000 acres which might qualify as wilderness and to evaluate them for inclusion in a wilderness system. No minimum area is specified if it is worthwhile, even so little as 500 acres. Restriction of use of the parcels of wilderness will be mainly by controlling means of transportation. There will be no roads made into the land and no engines will be allowed, such as tote goats or inboard motors for boats. There will be no flying in. Pack horses are to be allowed, and rather surprisingly there does not seem to be a definite limit put on the size of the trains. No permanent structures will be erected.

The act does not allow itself to be bogged down by any scientific criterion of wilderness, and wisely. In general a wilderness area will appear in essentials to be unaltered by man, but the act recognizes that secondary forest or grassland may still attain to wilderness quality. Happily, elimination of mining is envisaged. Management, so far as it is necessary, will be permitted, but there will be no rules of management. All of this seems to us wise and far-seeing.

Procedure in terms of the instruction of the act seems fairly simple for the Forest Service, but the National Park Service will be in greater difficulty because of its innate philanthropic ethos which, perhaps, the service does not quite realize is one of its potential weaknesses. Tentative wilderness zoning plans are already in circulation and we wonder whether some of these have been drawn on the basis of wilderness now, or of thinking in terms of zoning for development of visitor facilities in the future.

A decision not to build roads into a wilderness area surely should not mean that when wilderness (in terms of ecosystems) lies athwart an existing road, the boundaries of such a wilderness must go back in half a mile or more. Such a decision would leave wide corridors along roads as areas of potential development not managed as wilderness. Restriction on parking, picnicking or camping along such stretches of existing road would be all that would be required to maintain the roadside corridors as essential wilderness. The National Park Service has given itself another arbitrary limitation, that wilderness should exclude those areas which might be in sight or sound of civilization. All of us might prefer it that way but it could be too harsh a criterion. An island in Florida Bay serving as a nesting site for roseate spoonbills and other water birds could be excluded for such a reason, whereas, as long as the public does not go ashore, such an island is essentially wilderness.

The criterion of roads in evaluation for wilderness will much affect Great Smoky Mountains National Park. We see from the tentative plan that whereas three-quarters of the park could be wilderness, imposition of arbitrary corridors either side of existing and proposed roads will reduce wilderness to only half of the park. This appears to us an unnecessary penalty to be placed on this magnificent area of natural forest.

We must realize here, of course, that there are two main calls for wilderness: first, the opportunities for ecosystems of plants and animals to survive; and second, the need of wilderness for the human soul, for shriving, purification and recreation. The difference between a strict wildlife reserve and wilderness in its mystical aspect may not be easy to set down on paper but the notions should be separate enough in the mind not to let one or other conception exclude an area from being designated and respected as wilderness. It is a primary duty of management of any national park that as much of its area as possible should be wilderness or near wilderness if management is to fulfill the intent of the 1916 act setting up the service.

We have been impressed by the documents emanating recently from the National Parks Association on the subject of delineation of wilderness. In the principles set forth in the association's plan for Sequoia-Kings Canyon National Parks appears this statement which could scarcely be more terse and less equivocal: "Wilderness starts at the road and any buffer to remove the sights or sounds of man should be internal to the boundary of wilderness. Otherwise, new incursions will result in a steadily retreating wilderness."

The president of the association, Anthony Wayne Smith, has repeatedly emphasized in recent years how wilderness-consuming activities could be removed to the outside of national parks, and how planned deployment of recreational activities in existing publicly-owned lands adjacent or close to the national parks would go far to conserve those unique qualities for which the national park itself was dedicated and of which wilderness is of never-lessening significance. We ourselves have often had the uncomfortable feeling that the philanthropic ethos of the National Park Service has overshadowed the primary necessity to conserve the habitat. Implementation of the Wilderness Act by the service should strengthen the ecological resistance of the parks to the pressures which beset them, but a misguided leaning towards dichotomy of values in assessments of national park terrain could well hasten decline of habitat rather than prevent it. Such a trend would be an ironical negation of what the Wilderness Act is designed to achieve.

Finally, we would emphasize that the National Park Service Act of 1916 contained all that was necessary to preserve the wilderness quality of the national parks. The interpretation of the act by the National Park Service achieved this end fairly successfully until the end of World War II, but the inundation of the parks by visitors in the post-war years was not grasped by the authorities for the destructive phenomenon it was. We feel that the eclipse of Park Service Director Newton Drury was a function of this failure in understanding what was happening. The service as it later reacted to pressures was over-generous with a perishable and shrinking resource and did not act quickly enough in coordinating with other agencies to spread the load and to divert fun-seeking recreation to other areas than the national parks. The U.S. Forest Service was, in our opinion, much more politically aware of the trend of the times, as the National Park Service was naive. Mission 66, instead of being a far-sighted planning operation to conserve these choice areas, seems to have been conceived to allow more complete infiltration and uncritical use. We remain somewhat puzzled by—as it seems to us—the unfair political pressures which have been brought to bear on the National Park Service to dilute wilderness quality, e.g., the extravagant utterances concerning motor-boating on Jenny Lake in Grand Teton National Park, and the relative peace with which the Forest Service has been able to conduct its wilderness-preserving and recreational policy.

The national park policies of the '20s and '30s were not adequate in the '50s and '60s, and the National Park Service has not adapted quickly enough to the new situation. Indeed, Mission 66 was in some measure in reverse trend. In singling out wilderness for special protection the 1964 act has certainly forced the National Park Service to reconsider some portions of its management policy, but a restatement of general national park principles in terms of the situation in the 1960s might have been more productive of safeguards for the parks. The present desire of the National Park Service to designate as wilderness only areas of some subjective and probably hypothetical purity is another sample of high-toned fluffy thinking. Nearly all the parks were wilderness in reality or intention at their inception and should be so considered, without drawing imaginary lines of purity within the parks, caused by our intellectual differentiations of wilderness qualities. And effort must be concerted to moving outside the parks those so-called facilities which at present encumber them. Canyon Village in the one-time wilderness of the Yellowstone remains for us the type specimen of misconceived pandering to the less appreciative and more uncritical section of public taste. Surely the responsibility and part function of the National Park Service is to educate for taste and lead it.

In conclusion, we foresee a time of greater realization that in an area of large, mobile, leisured populations, it is a privilege rather than an unheeded right to visit the superb national properties maintained as well as they are by the devoted labor of the National Park Service in the field. Certain forms of decorous behavior should be accepted and not questioned. The National Gallery of Art and the great museums expect and get such behavior within their precincts. The national parks of the United States present the glorious creations of nature and no expediency or misconception of their beauty must endanger the world heritage of which they are so shining a part. Art is but an emanation from the matrix of nature to which we must return always for refreshment and new inspiration.

THE DISNEY IMPERATIVE

Wesley Marx

Recently, a newspaper headline proclaimed that a "game preserve" would be set aside near my home in Southern California. My heart jumped. For many months, I have belonged to a citizens' group that seeks to protect Southern California's last remaining natural bay, Upper Newport Bay, from being compressed into a boat storage area for luxury waterfront residences. This life-giving estuary lies near my home; I dared to envision a bay sanctuary for blue herons, scallops, young halibut and red-berried California toyon trees. However, the game preserve turned out to be a commercial zoo spectacle called Lion Country Safari. It is being sponsored by the same developer who, with the sympathy of public authorities, makes a paying proposition of the bay. If my faith in land developers is justified, a game preserve

Wesley Marx, "The Disney Imperative," THE NATION, *July 28, 1969. Reprinted by permission.*

called Grizzly Bear Rodeo is rising in a jungle clearing somewhere in South Africa.

This curious expression of conservation confirms my suspicions about the increasing persuasiveness of a trend I call the Disney Imperative. It is the compulsion to create artificial environments in place of natural environments. Fantasy thus becomes reality, i.e., Lion Country Safari in Orange County, Calif., and residential marinas atop life-giving estuaries. It is a trend particularly attractive to developers on the make as well as to impetuous architects, and it promises to play more hell with the cause of conservation and environmental quality than the fixations of dam builders and lumber harvesters.

I don't want to hold the late Walt Disney responsible for all the aberrations of the Disney Imperative. However, Disney was instrumental in setting a pretty high standard to inspire disciples for many years to come. I don't have Disneyland in mind. That Magic Kingdom in Anaheim was a dress rehearsal, an entertainment if you will, for the precedent-setting application of the Disney Imperative at a place called Mineral King. If you haven't heard of Mineral King, that's to be expected, because, in terms of the Disney Imperative, Mineral King doesn't yet exist—it is still natural. Mineral King is a glacial valley set in California sequoia country. It contains twenty lakes, numerous cascades, incense cedar and bold rock outcroppings. It lies in the Sequoia National Forest, right next door to Sequoia National Park, which gives you some idea of just how unreal it is.

In Disney's later years, Walt Disney Productions submitted a master plan for Mineral King to the Forest Service. "Disney stressed that his master plan is based on the need to preserve Mineral King's natural beauty," declared a Disney press release. That certainly is a laudable objective. This alpine valley is rather rare, being part of the last remaining 2 percent of land in the United States in the "wild" category. Ostensibly, the spirit of Smokey the Bear, not Donald Duck, would reign. Yet the means of preservation seem odd, to say the least. Forested hills are to be stripped to make way for ski slopes serviced by fourteen lifts. Mountain peaks will be topped with restaurants. The valley floor will provide space for a conference center, two hotels, a cafeteria, a skating rink, a chapel, convenience shops and a heliport. For some reason, this sounds more like a plush ski resort than natural beauty preserved. Just where does preservation come in? In response, the press release declares that Walt Disney Productions "would preserve the area's natural character by camouflaging ski lifts, situating the village so that it will not be seen from the valley entrance, and putting service areas in a 60,000-square-foot underground facility beneath the village." Remember the alpine trees and the bold rock outcroppings? "Stout columns of timber and concrete set with stones brought up from a nearby quarry will establish the American-Alpine style," declares Disney Productions.

"Preservation" thus becomes an outdoor type of interior decoration to provide a contrived environment. The bulldozers become sculptors' chisels, the road graders become paint brushes, and the chain saws on the tree slopes become magic wands. Nothing cheap like colored snow or litter baskets in the shape of tree stumps. Wilderness is not being desecrated; it is just being out-charmed. The result is a Swiss ski resort 55 miles from Visalia, Calif., a Disneyland with guts. "When I first saw Mineral King more than five years ago," Disney recalled for reporters, "I thought it was one of the most beautiful places in the world, and we want to keep it that way. It is going to be a pleasure to make it even more attractive and accessible so that more people will enjoy its beauty."

There may well be room for such real estate creativity, particularly in the urban environment, but why Mineral King? It is here that one begins to realize that there is more to the Disney Imperative than artistic indulgence. Old-fashioned wilderness preserves don't lend themselves to high-density, high-revenue outdoor activities. While lumber people, mining people and amusement park operators grouse about such public land lying "idle," their buzz saw and pickax enterprise hardly conveys a sense of public service and responsibility. The artificial environment approach, on the other hand, oozes with public service. Skiing interests have been eyeing Mineral King for some time, but their straightforward plans were a bit too brutal even for the Forest Service. About a decade ago, Walt Disney Productions purchased a small amount of private land in Mineral King Valley. After that, came the Disney master plan to make Mineral King "even more attractive and accessible."

And if a suit brought by the Sierra Club, and now before the courts, does not prevail, that is exactly what they will do. The Forest Service is so excited that it has given Disney Productions a thirty-year lease to indulge in its style of wilderness improvements. Walt Disney Productions expects 2.5 million paying visitors by 1976. The National Park Service, albeit reluctantly, will permit 8 million cubic yards of Sequoia National Park land to be pushed about for a high-speed access highway into Mineral King. The highway, which will undoubtedly become a linear butcher block for mule deer and other unwary pedestrians, will be named the Walt Disney Memorial Highway, if the promoters have their way. While this may be a fitting monument, I wouldn't wish this designation on anybody.

This transformation of wilderness into an artistic profit-making venture doesn't miss any bets. During the summer, the fourteen ski lifts will be available for "hikers, campers and wildlife students." While Walt Disney Productions makes no promises to the effect, I have a hunch that chairborne hikers and wildlife students may find themselves gazing down upon Son of Lion Country Safari.

The Forest Service's willingness to succumb to the Disney Imperative at Mineral King will not be lost on the creators of Six Flags Over Texas, Marineland, Frontierland and other mass-rec promoters. Ski and marina promoters are undoubtedly scanning Forest Service maps and latching onto architects itchy to outdo nature. The ability of the National Park Service to be suckered into this frenzy for packaged fantasy is probably not being overlooked either.

Another semi-natural domain in public hands promises to become an even greater victim of the Disney Imperative. I read recently an advertisement in which a landscaping firm was expanding into "underwater landscaping." I wondered if the market for plastic sharks in Bel Air swimming pools was really that large; then I read on. "Specialists in preserving, restoring and creating special effects in the undersea environment utilizing the natural beauty and ecology of the region," explained the advertisement. "We travel anywhere . . . No job too small."

Disney sea is already in the making. The Santa Monica shore consists of a long, spacious beach that abuts the metropolitan Los Angeles area. The present use—public beach—is natural enough, in fact too natural. One agency noted for its inventive verve proposes the creation of a giant marina. A 6-mile-long earth-filled breakwater would protect the boats and be the basis for an artificial, i.e., real, offshore beach. Let's see if you can apply the Disney Imperative by filling in the blank. The breakwater will be topped by ———. The answer is not barnacles but freeway. This perhaps suggests the identity of the fantasy maker: it is the California Division of Highways. The Division would set aside generous shoulders on the proposed Santa Monica Causeway to accommodate marinas, high-rise apartments and other institutions eager to leapfrog public beach frontage and acquire high-revenue footholds on the "idle" nearshore. A sure sign of the Disney Imperative at work is the developer's willingness to defy natural laws. The curtaining off of the nearshore into a still lagoon permits the laying of underwater air hoses to keep the pollution circulating. Curiously enough, the Los

Angeles City Council has been reluctant to endorse the Santa Monica Causeway project. The highway people have demonstrated that they don't have closed minds about this thing. They have offered to move the freeway off the causeway and onto the present existing beach. To "replace" this beach, underwater artificial reefs would be installed to nurture an artificial offshore beach. The fact that the "perched beach" concept is untested suggests how well the planners are remaining true to the Disney Imperative. Dr. Kenneth Inman, of the Scripps Institute of Oceanography, a beach erosion expert, suggests two possible accidents: the shunting of the sand into deep water beyond recovery and the stimulation of potentially destructive waves. However, a consultant on the project, James Dunham of Moffat-Nichol Engineers, sees the "greatest single problem of the entire project" as being a supply of enough earth fill. Mr. Dunham then goes on to suggest a suitable "borrow pit"; a coastal hill range. And once Mr. Dunham gets going, there is no stopping him. Why not, he asks, borrow from the hills in such manner as to transform them into the site for another freeway and for terraced homes?

Other noted fantasy makers have their own master schemes to improve on the nearshore. Airport planners now realize that the solution to airplane noise is not quieter airplanes but the extension of runways out to sea. These runways, seductively tipped with marinas and beaches, are packaged as complete environments, ostensibly soundproofed. At last count, some twenty coastal cities were considering such seaward intrusions. At this rate, the United States itself may become a borrow pit to accommodate the air age. Once installed, the runways have a way of continually growing outward. Kennedy International Airport, outside New York, is even now proposing to push a super runway out into Jamaica Bay, used from time immemorial as a resting and feeding site for migratory water birds. It is feared that this intrusion might put an end to the entire Atlantic flyway by forcing the birds to make too long a jump. Some people feel that San Francisco Airport and Oakland Airport will finally bisect San Francisco Bay, to form the world's first supersonic runway.

There is no end of ways to reclaim the ocean. I heard one planner talk about the "Real Estate Potentials of Offshore Island Development." His inspiration did not come from traditional islands. He suggests that offshore oil drill platforms can double as real estate if mounted on earth fill. He proposes that these oil-inspired islands be connected to the mainland by causeways, there being no sense in having islands entirely surrounded by water.

Natural islands can also be upgraded by recourse to the Disney Imperative. The owner of one pastoral island off Southern California, Santa Cruz Island (being considered for national park status), plans to dredge out part of the scenic shore to accommodate a marina. But he doesn't call it a marina; he calls it an "artificial fjord." Part of the shore already boasts a vacation camp, Polynesian style. Progressive developers in Tahiti may see the light and erect igloo motels.

The craze to redesign the nearshore, particularly as a luxury boat storage area, suggests that we may soon be able to claim that there are more boats than fish in the offshore waters. The hectic transformation of estuaries into high-revenue environments already promises to sterilize the offshore and the skies above. Some two-thirds of our marine catch, as well as our shore birds, are estuary dependent. Yet the fantasy makers even have a way of capitalizing on this purge: box-office aquariums, featuring seals who can balance rubber balls on their noses.

The most disconcerting fact about the spread of the Disney Imperative is its misdirection. There is a place for well-designed, man-made environments that provide underground services and transportation facilities, achieve thematic architecture, diversify recreational opportunities and create an illusion of beauty and excitement. But this place should be the urban environment, not the prime wilderness. Perhaps the greatest service our conservation agencies can perform in the future will be to tell the devotees of the Disney Imperative to get the hell out of the Mineral Kings and go back to Chicago, New York and Newark. The concepts of compact beauty and illusion that Disney employed in Disneyland deserve much larger application, but not in the role of improving nature.

THE CONSUMPTION OF WILDLIFE BY MAN

William G. Conway

I once knew a lady who owned a cheetah. The big cat was graceful, slender, and stately. The lady said she loved the cheetah, though she

William G. Conway, "The Consumption of Wildlife by Man," ANIMAL KINGDOM, *June 1968. Reprinted by permission.*

knew little about the big cat or its habits; certainly she lavished affection on it whenever there was someone about. But I never could tell much about the cheetah's feelings and it died after a few months.

Although all this happened many years ago, the practice of keeping exotic animals as pets has recently increased and, like many zoo men, I have become greatly concerned with the effects of the pet trade on delicate rare animals. More than 28 million live wild animals were imported by American pet businesses, laboratories, and zoos last year. More than 22 million pounds of wild animal skins were imported by American furriers and leather goods concerns. United States hunters killed over 60 million birds and mammals at the same time. Man's rising consumption of diminishing wild animal populations shows little sign of abatement and his efforts to manage the wildlife resources on a sustained yield basis are disgracefully inadequate.

When Texas tortoises, South American goldenheaded quetzals, and even hummingbirds and saki monkeys began to appear in New York pet shops, my concern changed to indignation, a feeling enhanced by the apathetic remark of one pet dealer who, in response to my questioning of his need to sell endangered Texas tortoises, replied, "Are turtles really worth saving?"

The work of unqualified importers of unsuitably rare and delicate creatures results in unnecessary animal suffering, certainly. At the same time, it is important to evaluate the problem coolly and to see the exotic pet trade in relation to additional drains on wild animal populations: food and sport hunting; poaching; pesticide poisoning; hide, feather, or skin trade; and habitat destruction. All this raises questions of critical importance to conservation: of what relative importance is each of the drains on wild animal populations and what are the special characteristics of each?

Naturally, I have been especially interested in problems stemming from the live animal trade. After all, zoos buy live animals too and sometimes from the same dealers that supply pet shops and laboratories. For this reason, I first looked into the trade in living wildlife.

It did not take long to find out that some truly unusual wild creatures were being more or less regularly offered to the unsuspecting pet buyer by even the smallest New York City pet shops. Monkeys are common imports, usually woolly, spider, or squirrel monkeys. "Squirrel monkeys—$13.50, tame, affectionate—the perfect house pet" said the advertisements. Spider and woolly monkeys are more expensive but still common and even guenons can be found. But I have never seen one of these primates adequately housed or cared for in a pet shop. In fact, so many are kept in such woefully inadequate quarters under such filthy conditions that I wonder if the sympathy thus engendered in the viewer is a sales device. Pet shop sales personnel with whom I have talked have been uniformly uninformed about the biology or the needs of their charges. Several were apparently temporary employees. They knew enough to assure prospective buyers what "wonderful pets" monkeys would make, but little else. Almost all monkeys make exceptionally delicate, difficult, and occasionally dangerous pets but these common imports are only a small part of the picture.

During the past year, golden-headed quetzals, South American cock-of-the-rocks, equatorial barbets, Indonesian fairy bluebirds, South American hummingbirds, saki monkeys, and Malayan flying lizards have been offered in New York pet shops. And pet shops are not the only vendors of these exceptionally delicate creatures: even department stores and dime stores have found the exotic pet trade profitable. Emaciated iguanas and anoles clambering over the bodies of their already dead and dying fellows now vie for the shopper's attention with pencils and plastic flowers. It is remarkable that such relatively rare and expensive creatures as Central American parrots and such precariously delicate ones as tamanduas (arboreal anteaters) and three-toed sloths can be offered in an unregulated way to the public at large. Moreover, all these animals and many more may be ordered by mail from numerous animal supply houses by anyone almost anywhere. Even a child for instance, can order a dangerous animal.

Undoubtedly, there are good pet shops and suppliers with informed personnel who know their imports and choose them wisely. This is clearly the case with a number of New York businesses which specialize in the sale of tropical fish, and do so most admirably; but they are very few. There are good reasons for importing some species of wild creatures for pets and I, for one, am strongly in favor of wild animal pets. But importation ought to be done carefully and humanely.

After all, the values of a well-chosen, wild animal pet are impossible to duplicate. Wild animal keeping is a historically ingrained activity; it was probably the origin of the development of domestic animals. The pet owner has the pleasure of bringing a living element of far-off wilds into his own home. The beauty or the strangeness of a wild creature which may be examined and observed regularly can provide stimulating intellectual insight and excitement and create a concern with wildlife—and with far-off places. Wild pets properly chosen and cared for can provide recreation and education in the best sense. Surely many a zoologist, amateur and professional, can trace his abiding interest to just such pets. But much of the trade is not being conducted humanely and the animals are not being wisely chosen.

Almost all of the creatures I have named require highly specialized care, constant attention, complex diets, and special conditions of warmth or humidity, shelter and space. Their wild population cannot, in most cases, be very large, and many will be found to be infected with diseases which require specialized treatment. Some are so sensitive that they must have seclusion while others require company—of their own kind. Many will die within weeks if not days of capture. And I am afraid that many of those that live longer will do so despite the care they receive rather than because of it.

Although the exotic pet trade has tangible and intangible values it must be regulated. Many wild animal populations can withstand well-managed collecting but many rare forms cannot. Moreover, exceptionally delicate or highly specialized animals must not be sold as personal pets whether they are rare or common. The problem is one of cruelty as much as conservation. A few days ago, as I wandered through the pet department of a local five-and-ten-cent store, I happened upon a terrarium filled with "common" horned lizards.

The trade in horned lizards has been going on for decades. Thirty years ago, these creatures sold for 25 cents each; the price is $1.50 now. The unforgivably immoral nature of this piece of commercialization is that horned lizards almost invariably starve to death after a few weeks in captivity. This tells us something about the character of the exotic pet trade for it is well known that horned lizards have highly specialized and poorly understood food and temperature requirements, which few pet buyers could hope to meet.

If pet dealers are properly informed about the animals they sell and solicitous of their well-being, they must know that not even zoos have been successful with three-toed sloths and flying lizards. (The latter have been offered for sale through an advertisement in *Natural History* magazine.) Dealers must know how specialized and delicate such animals as sakis and quetzals are, how rare or delicate cock-of-the-rocks and fairy bluebirds and Texas tortoises are and they must know that these animals are completely unsuitable as pets—and that it is inhumane to sell them as such. They must also know that most of these "pets" will be dead within weeks if not days. Even the endangered Galapagos tortoise and the orang-utan have been sold as pets in this country.

It seems inconceivable that a people whose care of dogs, cats, and horses is watched over by innumerable regulations and protective societies should be allowed to starve, mistreat, and buy and sell rare and delicate wild creatures.

Unhappily, the tale begins to unfold overseas. The live animal business depends mostly upon exports from developing nations and the animals are usually captured by untrained local people. Naturally, many delicate animals perish in the process of collecting, before they ever reach the compound of the exporter. Once there, the delicacy of the species or incompetent care may result in further deaths. Although the captive may be sold in its native land most are shipped abroad.

The urge to cut costs often leads the shipper to pack his wild cargo inadequately. Animals die in their shipping boxes of thirst, heat, cold, starvation, overcrowding, and fighting. When it has been my task to identify birds in a shipment destined for the pet trade for federal officials who wished to be sure that the allotment did not include any obscure prohibited (potential pest or quarantinable) species, I have occasionally happened upon shipments of small birds where 75 percent of the birds in the shipment were dead upon arrival at the John F. Kennedy International Airport. I am told it is not uncommon for hundreds of birds to be lost in a single shipment. Of course, some species are remarkably hardy during shipment and today most shippers do a thoughtful job in providing for their cargos but, with the truly delicate species, no one can say how many individuals must die in order to insure that some unsuspecting pet buyer will receive one unsuitable, already doomed pet.

But the pet trade is not the only element in the live animal business. Medical research and pharmaceutical laboratory needs contribute significantly to the drain on wild animal populations. The demand for some species of monkeys is so extensive that it is actually beginning to threaten their future and, consequently, the future of important biomedical research. In 1967, 62,526 wild primates, mostly for laboratory research, were imported into the United States. Although this figure may surprise many, the figures from several past years are far more remarkable. Primate importations for 1958 were 223,000; for 1959, 190,000 and for 1960, 221,000.

Importations in the late 1950's and in 1960 probably reflect the peak years of polio vaccine production. Today, the increasing success of organ transplantation from animals to man poses a new threat to the future of the great apes. For example, each year 30,000 people die from kidney deterioration in the United States alone. If organ transplants become more successful, it is well to remember that the total population of the most abundant large great ape, the chimpanzee, is surely less than 250,000.

The recent expansion of the animal business has been made possible by the airplane. Ninety-two percent of all wildlife imported into the United States comes by air. Today, it is practical to penetrate almost every wild frontier. An animal far too delicate to intrust to the long sea voyage of former years may now be whisked aboard an airplane and transported to his pet shop destiny before his frail constitutional reserves fail. While this is wonderful for zoos and laboratories prepared to deal with specialized creatures and most advantageous for the animals consigned to them, it simply prolongs the suffering of those species which can go days without food but require specialized diets and care if they are ever to eat again.

An idea of the drain upon the wildlife of an important animal export nation can be formed from the following figures provided by Ian Grimwood for 1964 from Peru. In that year, 39,522 live animals were exported and of these, 26,226 were squirrel monkeys; 6,325 were other small monkeys. Few African nations keep track of their exports but a recent United Nations Food and Agricultural Organization report quoted admittedly incomplete 1962 figures for nine months of live export from Ethiopia as 40,000 birds and 5,283 monkeys. Argentina by contrast reports the export of only 28,243 live animals, mostly birds, in ten years from 1951 through 1960.

Large as all these figures are they pale beside the import figures for one nation, the United States. In 1967, United States imports included 74,304 mammals, 203,189 birds—excluding all psittachines and canaries—405,134 reptiles, 137,697 amphibians, and 27,759,332 fish. This, reported the United States Fish and Wildlife Service, is the first time that virtually complete records have been obtained at ports of entry.

As a zoo professional, I have looked especially hard at the zoo part of wildlife importation but found that zoos contribute remarkably little to the trade. For example, during the nine years from 1958 through 1966 the total number of ungulates (giraffes, deer, antelope, wild cattle, goats, and sheep) imported by U. S. zoos was only 1,231. As a matter of fact, the world's more than 500 zoos contain a total of only about 500,000 vertebrates. Zoos do not usually conduct terminal experiments and they breed increasing numbers of animals. Several species have been dependent upon zoological collections for their very existence. For instance, the Pere David deer, the European wisent, the Swinhoe pheasant, and the Przjewalski horse are all extinct or nearly so in the wild and dependent upon captive collections for survival.

On the negative side is the fact that zoo demands have contributed importantly to the decimation of the orang-utan. Fortunately, the zoo orang trade has now been reduced by self-imposed zoo boycotts (but orang collecting continues and mothers are still being shot to obtain their babies for the pet trade in their native land).

The total trade in living wild creatures is frighteningly large in the suffering it causes as well as the numbers it devastates no matter who imports what and the next question is: how does it compare with other drains on wildlife population? What about the traffic in hides, skins, and furs?

Among the most precious and beautiful exhibits at the Bronx Zoo are the snow leopards. Finally, after years of effort, the zoo had just bred snow leopards when I read the following advertisement:

UNTAMED . . . The Snow Leopard. Provocatively dangerous. Uninhibited. A Mankiller. Born free in the wild whiteness of the high Himalayas only to be snared as part of the captivating new fur collection by . . . Styled and shaped in a one-of-a-kindness to bring out the animal instinct in you. Call Mr. . . . for your private showing.

Published with a photo of a model draped with two or three snow leopard skins, this ad occupied a full page in *The New York Times Magazine* on August 28, 1966.

The idea of a supposedly sensitive, educated woman supporting the slaughter of three to six of these exquisite creatures so that she might show off a coat a dozen times a year, or until the next fashion change, is unacceptably callous. And other ads are easy to find. Neiman-Marcus advertised in a recent *New Yorker,* "Puss and boots . . . prize catch in natural tiger, edged and buttoned in black leather. From our collection of famous fur trophies." It is highly unlikely that there are more than 4,000 Bengal tigers left in all the world! The latest IUCN world population estimates for other tiger populations which are or have been targets for the fur hunter include: The Caspian tiger, 50-80; Amur or Siberian tiger, 250; Javan tiger, less than 25; Bali tiger, 3 or 4; Sumatran tiger, unknown.

And witness another ad affecting threatened creatures:

A dozen or so terribly spoiled ladies in New York will get this gift for Christmas . . . Last year's little surprise was a pale blue Rolls to match her eyes. How to top it this year? The "Ultima" II "1200," our twelve hundred dollar travel case of finest African baby alligator [there is no such thing; they mean crocodile] . . .

Until I began looking for fashion advertisements, I never realized how many wild creatures were being senselessly killed to adorn the girl who needs nothing.

What possible justification is there for the fashion-fad slaughter of a wild creature? With what right and what conscience can a civilized woman adorn herself with the mummified reliquiae of diminishing wild creatures? How can she help but see an ugly death in a far-off land, the loss of one more portion of the international resource in beautiful wild creatures, each time she dons her "fun fur"? But, moralizing aside, the conservation question requiring investigation is: how does the hide and skin trade compare to other wildlife uses?

Unhappily, the number of animal lives claimed by the hide, skin, and animal products businesses dwarf the "take" of the live animal business. Often, but not always, different species are involved and where the species is subject to both drains the skin trade is almost always much larger. For example, Peru exported 11,244 ocelot skins in 1964 but only 174 live ocelots. Total skins and hides exported were 247,956 or more than six times the number of live animals; one animal killed for its skin every two minutes, year-round! Again, African figures are difficult to obtain but we do know that more than 26,000 Colobus monkey skins were exported from one Ethiopian port alone in 1961. The total number of animal lives represented by Argentina's official export figures are hard to even imagine. In the decade from 1951 through 1960, the skins and hides of 7,669,758 native animals were apparently exported. It surprised me to find that 104,238 rheas and more than five million iguanas were represented in these figures. Here again, the trade in live animals, 28,243, seems relatively insignificant for the same period. Naturally, I began to wonder what part of this importation the United States trade was sponsoring.

Unfortunately, United States customs reports for hides and skins are not usually zoologically specific. They may report hide and fur importation in terms of dollar value and pounds of skins rather than in terms of species and numbers. However, several interesting figures are available. The total 1967 sea shipping weight of imported undressed fur skins was 7,869,000 pounds; the recorded air shipping weight was 2,160,000 pounds. Undressed raw hides and skins other than fur aggregated a weight of a further 11 million pounds for a grand total of nearly 22 million pounds. This does not include the huge trade in finished fur and hide products and leather goods representing wildlife usage by the American market.

Perhaps it is more instructive to examine the tallies for a few more specific groups.

All told, 115,458 ocelot skins, whole, raw, or undressed, were passed by United States Customs last year. They came from seven Latin American countries, the majority from Brazil, Bolivia, and Colombia in that order. A total of 35,748 otters of various species were represented in skins from 11 Latin American countries. Deer and antelope skins imported from Peru, Brazil, Somali, and the Republic of South Africa totaled 970,809. These are evidently all skins of wild animals. And let us not forget that they represent only the consumption of our own country. Who knows what the world totals in wild animal products consumption might be? The point is that the deaths of very large numbers of animals are annually necessary to support the animal products industry and who is to say that the degree of animal suffering in this toll is less than that in the living animal trade? Indeed, *The New York Times* snow leopard article unabashedly uses the word "snared" to account for the capture of the snow leopards, and I doubt that a "quick kill" snare has ever been invented.

Unfortunately the fur and skin and animal products trade is demonstrably endangering a number of species from leopards to blue whales and from tigers to alligators. There is no question that far, far larger numbers of animals are annually destroyed to satisfy this trade than to fill pet stores; there is a very real question whether, in the case of those fashion furs dependent upon wild animal populations, this part of the industry has any redeeming features. This does not mean, on the other hand, that reasonable people can or should quarrel with the reasonable exploitation of wild animals. After all, science uses dead animals too and museum zoologists have amassed large collections. A 1962 estimate of the number of mammal skins in some 307 public and private collections was 1,586,000. The American Museum of Natural History alone has nearly a million bird skins in its permanent collection. But these collections are permanent and basic to our understanding of wildlife.

Today, a very high percentage of all commercial furs sold come from ranch raised mink and fox, animals bred for the purpose. It is not such well managed farming of wild species or, for that matter, the beef and poultry industries that trouble me but the unmanaged unregulated slaughter of diminishing wild animals in the world's few remaining wild areas. The carefully supervised utilization of the fur seal herd in Alaska's Pribilof Islands can scarcely attract criticism. Here, after unregulated slaughter reduced the herd to an unproductive

130,000 animals, careful management and regulated annual cropping has restored the herd to an estimated four million seals.

In contrast, the unregulated shooting of tigers, leopards, and jaguars and the failure of whaling nations to abide by whale protection recommendations has resulted in a nihilistic industry which knows full well that there will be no tomorrow and does not care. In a time of almost universal preoccupation with economic values and potentials, it seems incredible that nations and businessmen are allowing the immense renewable resources in wildlife to be mined to a point of no return.

What part does sport and food hunting play in the picture of annual animal use? Thorough studies of hunting patterns and annual kill are characteristic of the American approach to hunting which is, despite its failings, far better managed than hunting almost anyplace else. The results are figures depicting an enormous annual harvest of wildlife, a managed cropping of a renewable resource that, if sensibly provided for, can be repeated year after year. Nevertheless it is animal killing pure and simple and no better in its humane aspects than the other drains discussed so far. It differs in one especially important way, however; it happens entirely at home.

We can see and act to regulate the depletion of our own wildlife but our commercial sponsorship of the destruction of the wildlife of others passes unnoticed and unchallenged. The few American hunters that pursue their sport overseas cannot, except in rare cases, have a significant effect upon foreign wildlife. However, the sport kill figures from the United States are so immense that they are important in our effort to pull the picture of wildlife use into perspective for they emphasize the enormous human utilization and potentials of some wildlife populations and enable us to guess at the sport toll abroad. The figures for bird kills are especially instructive.

In the 1965-66 hunting season, the United States Fish and Wildlife Service reports that 1,523,600 waterfowl hunters shot 11,986,800 ducks, coots and geese (over ten million were ducks). During the 1965 season, 900,000 woodcock were also killed, and the estimate for rails and gallinules was 110,000 and for snipe, 387,000. The estimated mourning dove kill, amazingly, was 41.9 million birds. The federal government does not, in general, exercise control over non-migratory wildlife; thus the national figures for mammal kills are less consistent. However, the national kill of white-tail, black-tail, and mule deer in 1966 was 2,020,885. The black bear kill was 23,424.

The lesson here is that some wildlife populations are enormously productive. As a matter of fact, wildlife farming could produce many more pounds of protein from most kinds of land than could ever be realized from herds of the usual domestic animals. In the Transvaal alone, for instance, over five million pounds of meat were produced from wild animals taken under permit on farms in 1959.

Food hunting is not so important as formerly in the United States except for fish, although an enormous number of small animals from frogs and squirrels to raccoons and rattlesnakes must annually be taken for this purpose, especially in the South and West. Naturally, no accurate estimates are available. We must remember that it was food hunting, not sport hunting, that pushed the United States passenger pigeon and Eskimo curlew into the abyss of extinction (and near extinction) and that these events occurred when a larger proportion of the country's population included wild game in its diet than now—significantly, when conditions in the United States approximated those in many developing nations today.

In Africa, Asia, and Latin America, wildlife is an indispensable part of the pot, but an endangered and diminishing part among peoples already referred to as protein starved. FAO reports that over 50 percent of all fresh meat consumed in the Congo comes from game, more than 80 percent in Ghana. Those of us who have spent time afield realize that all animals, be it a Colobus monkey in Africa or a cock-of-the-rock in South America, are fair game for local menus. There is no doubt that hunting, especially food hunting, accounts for a larger annual take in numbers of animal lives than the trade in live wildlife and the business of furs and skins together, but the first two uses are more necessary than the fur trade.

Although organized, regulated sport hunting does not seem to be a major factor in the permanent destruction of wild species, food hunting is. And, although it may not be fashionable, people have to eat.

The most regrettable part of the food hunting situation takes place on a governmental level where politicians and officials fail to initiate adequate wildlife management and habitat protection measures and simply sit back to watch their burgeoning populations hunt themselves out of house and home.

But there is another, most important, factor in the regular decimation of wildlife: the destruction of habitat.

To a wild creature, habitat means home—a specific kind of area in which to live, to find food, to dig a burrow or build a nest. It is a place with the right temperature, the right amount and kind of water, and the right kind of plants and other animals. When a wild animal is shot, snared for the fur trade, or collected for the pet business, there is always the hope that there are others of its kind in the wilds from which it came, other creatures which will reproduce.

Wild animals are self-replacing, as long as they have a proper place to live and are not so disturbed or so reduced in numbers that they cannot effectively reproduce. But the key is "a proper place to live." It is not necessary for us to shoot, snare, or collect a single tiger, a quetzal, or an alligator to completely annihilate the species. We need only destroy its forests, drain its swamps, introduce strange animals or diseases with which it cannot compete or survive. We need only alter the chemical balances in its environment or destroy the plants and animals upon which it depends and which in turn depend upon it.

In the United States, 50 million of our original 127 million acres of wetlands have been "improved." With each new concrete expressway, we blanket an average of 50 acres of countryside per mile. In our country alone nearly a million acres of green plants are paved over each year. Indeed we could examine figure after figure from around the world oh-ing and ah-ing over the destruction of rain forests in one part of the earth and deserts in another, the loss of prairies and the destruction of savannas, the despoliation of beaches and the draining of marshes, but the evidence is all around us and this scarcely seems necessary. It may be worthwhile to remember that the insidious increase of pesticides in our environment has now proceeded to such a point that not even seals and penguins in Antarctica are free from contamination.

Change in habitat is inevitable and a basis of biology. We cannot stop change; we can only alter its direction, hasten or slow its pace. But it must be our concern to see that a sufficiently rich and varied habitat is retained to provide the scope and opportunity for long term biological change as well as for man's commercial requirements of the moment. Every effort must be bent to prevent the loss of a species. When it becomes necessary to destroy a species or a habitat, as it may, the reasons must be very good ones transcending immediate needs and the act must be performed in the realization that it increases man's mortgage upon its future.

The point is a simple one. Habitat destruction is going on at a fearful pace, a direct result, for the most part, of human population increase. We have only to look at the deserts of the Middle East to see the effects of unregulated human exploitation. Most habitat destruction is, for all intents and purposes, irreversible and the loss of a discontinuous area of wild land is a final one for wild creatures. They cannot continue to reproduce; they cannot continue to find food. The destruction of the forests, jungles, savannas, and swamps is a far crueler business than that we have described in any of man's other activities in wild animal slaughter. At one and the same time, it imposes disease, starvation, fear, and sure death. It is remarkable that these simple facts are so little understood. So many generous persons interested in humane treatment of wild creatures have made large gifts to those generally misguided efforts to move animals into surrounding forests when rising waters threaten them as new dams are created.

What has been lost of first importance is the habitat covered by the waters of the new dam. The suitable surrounding forest will almost always be already filled to capacity with populations of the species threatened by the rising waters. If a census were taken in such an adjoining area before a doomed forest had been flooded and then a year or so later after it had been deluged by escaped and rescued animals, it will almost surely be found to have the same population as previously. The destruction of habitat almost inevitably means the proportional destruction of the animals in it.

Thus fortified with this simplified view, perhaps we can appreciate the factors in man's destruction of animal life anew. Clearly, different species are affected by different trades. Quetzals and monkey-eating eagles and Colobus monkeys are affected directly by the skin trade, by habitat destruction, and to a lesser extent by the live trade. Alligators are affected by the skin trade and by habitat destruction; most hoofed animals by food hunting, habitat destruction, and the skin trade; leopards by the skin trade and habitat destruction. And so it goes. It is clear that the trade in living animals has grown immensely and in such an unregulated way as to be a source of unnecessary suffering if not endangerment to many species of animals. Yet the trade in hides, skins, and furs affecting some but not all of the same species is a much larger source of wild animal destruction and one that is threatening increasing numbers of species. Hunting for sport takes a tremendous number of animal lives but now usually tends to affect species which can withstand this annual "harvesting" better, perhaps, than many of the delicate species in the pet trade and rare species in the skin trade. The total slaughter of wildlife for food obviously takes not millions but hundreds of millions of animals each year. Although we have no overall figures, I think we may safely assume that this wildlife use far surpasses all other direct utilization by man combined. But, in its lasting effect, in the finality of its impoverishment, habitat destruction dwarfs all other threats to the existence of wild creatures and ultimately of man. It proceeds in direct proportion to the number of its prime consumer, a large mammal increasing at the rate of about 180,000 every 24 hours. Today, man's reproductive explosion is the most inexorable and unanswerable menace to the preservation of all life. Considering the cause and the irreversibility of the damage, I see no reason to resist paraphrasing that irritating pet shop manager's question, Is man worth saving?

MAN'S QUEST FOR FOOD: ITS ECOLOGICAL IMPLICATIONS

Lester R. Brown and Gail W. Finsterbusch

Millions of species had come and gone before man entered that thin film of life which covers the earth. He may have appeared as early as two million years ago which is very recent in geologic time.

For hundreds of thousands of years he hunted, fished and gathered wild food, living as a predatory animal. He lived in small groups and eventually spread into every part of the earth where plants and animals in nature were sufficient to sustain him. During pre-agricultural history, when man depended entirely on hunting and gathering, his numbers probably never exceeded ten million—the estimated human population that the earth could support under these conditions.

Then, somehow, perhaps as recently as ten thousand years ago, man learned to domesticate animals and plants and began the transition from hunting to tilling, the great step forward.

Although the origin of agriculture is a mystery still being solved, scholars agree that its earliest beginnings occurred in southwestern Asia, in the hills and grassy northern plains surrounding the Fertile Crescent. Wheat and barley grew wild there as did sheep, goats, pigs, cattle, horses and deer. To this day wild barley and two kinds of wild wheat (emmer and eikorn) flourish in the region.

In time knowledge of farming spread. It moved westward across Asia, southward into the Tigris-Euphrates Valley and along the Nile into Africa, northwestward into Europe through the Danube Valley, and along the Mediterranean coast. Agriculture apparently

Revision of paper presented at the Symposium on Problems of Overpopulation sponsored by the Memorial Student Union Organization, University of New Hampshire, September 25-26, 1969. Reprinted by permission.

had independent origins in the Americas and perhaps even in the Far East as well. But these developments came later than the Neolithic achievements in Southwestern Asia.

The great Neolithic achievements in agriculture and husbandry gave man a more abundant and secure food supply, allowing him to increase his numbers and establish a base for civilization. Grain fields fed growing urban populations. But the problem of obtaining enough food remained; it has plagued man since his beginnings.

As man multiplied he added to the food supply by expanding the land area under cultivation. When there was no more land that could readily be brought under the plow some populations—like the British and other western Europeans recently and the Greeks and Romans earlier—resorted to importing food. The only alternative to increasing imports or decreasing food consumption is raising the productivity of existing land area. Confronted with this, some countries were able to achieve a breakthrough in agricultural productivity: they generated a yield per acre takeoff.

RAISING LAND PRODUCTIVITY

The yield takeoff—a transition from the condition of near static yields to rapid and continuing increases in yields—is a twentieth century phenomenon. It is difficult to say which country was the first to coax significantly higher crop yields from an acre of land. Japan and some of the small northwest European countries like Denmark and the Netherlands engendered yield takeoffs around the turn of the century, but Japan was probably the first. A group of industrial countries including the United Kingdom, the United States, and Australia, achieved yield takeoffs around 1940. And just recently, in the late 1960s, several of the poor countries have experienced dramatic breakthroughs in yields.

Japan's yield takeoff was not dramatic, but year to year crop yields have increased consistently for the past several decades, except during war. Toward the close of the nineteenth century, densely populated, Japan was forced to turn to the oceans for protein and to use her limited land for producing starchy staples, principally rice, to meet food energy needs. Rather than grow more dependent on food imports at the early stages of industrialization Japan chose to intensify farming efforts for greater crop yields. As it turned out, income per capita and per acre yields began their climb almost simultaneously, and by 1900 it was clear that a takeoff had occurred.

Generating a yield takeoff is difficult for any country and requires an abrupt departure from traditional ways of farming. A continuing flow of new practices and inputs of capital and labor is required. In Japan the effort to modernize agriculture was supported by government at national, provincial, and local levels from the time of the Meiji restoration of 1868. Japanese officials visited England, Germany, the United States, and other advanced agricultural nations, learning of new scientific technologies. To raise yields, the Japanese improved irrigation, drainage, and water storage, used fertilizers more abundantly and skillfully, and developed price supports that would make the use of these new technologies possible.

The United Kingdom achieved a takeoff in yields around World War II. England had practiced agriculture since the first bands of farmers arrived on her southern shores between 2000 and 1500 B.C., and had cradled the technological revolution that for the last two hundred years has been spreading over the globe, affecting agriculture and industry on all continents. But England placed priorities on developing industry, exporting manufactured goods in exchange for foodstuffs and industrial raw materials. Improvements in agriculture were designed primarily to save labor, not to raise the productivity of land. It took the U-boat threat of World War II and the severing of her food supply lines to spur the United Kingdom to a yield takeoff.

The United States tried for two and a half decades after the closing of the frontier before finally reaching a yield takeoff around 1940. No one factor accounts for the transition. Hybrid varieties of corn and sorghum, the growing use of chemical fertilizers, government price incentives, and in general the massive application of science to agriculture all contributed. Once the yield takeoff was underway, American agriculture began to modernize at an unprecedented rate.

The mid-twentieth century proved to be a global turning point in the man-land-food relationship. For the first time in history increases in productivity came more from the rising productivity of land than from expansion of the land under cultivation.

GROWING FOOD DEFICITS IN POOR COUNTRIES

It was clear, however, that intensive modern agriculture was confined mainly to the rich industrial countries and to plantation or export crops in the poor countries. This was unfortunate, because in the decades following World War II Malthusian forces were vigorously at work in the poor countries, which, with the exception of Taiwan and Mexico, had failed to achieve a yield takeoff. Population growth rates soared to runaway proportions with the spread of modern medicine and sanitation in Asia, Africa, and Latin America. New land that could easily be brought under cultivation was being used up. And food production was lagging.

The less-developed world was losing the capacity to feed itself—to either produce or to buy the food it needed. Through the mid-1960s the poor countries were becoming year by year more dependent on food imported from the United States under the $1.5 billion yearly food aid program. The crisis deepened with the failure of the 1965 and 1966 monsoons in the Indian subcontinent. Six hundred shiploads of U.S. wheat were required to stave off famine in India in 1966. Some sixty million Indians living virtually ship-to-mouth subsisted on U.S. wheat.

Many great Asian cities turned more toward their harbors for food than toward their own countrysides. Needless to say, the situation was alarming. In 1966 the USDA produced a chart indicating that by 1985 the United States would no longer have the capacity to produce exportable surpluses sufficient to cover the developing world's expected food deficits. In 1967 the president's Science Advisory Commission report pointed out that during the first half of the 1960s population in the developing world was increasing at 2.5 percent a year, whereas food production was growing at only 1.6 percent. In short, food and population trends were on a collision course.

BREAKTHROUGH AGAINST HUNGER

Just in the past few years—in the late 1960s—a breakthrough in food production in the hungry countries has occurred so abruptly that it has taken many by surprise. Unprecedented increases in cereal harvests are being reported in more and more of the developing countries. Takeoffs in wheat yields in India and Pakistan make the earlier corn yield takeoff in the United States or the rice yield takeoff in Japan seem pedestrian in comparison. The main impetus for the current agricultural breakthrough springs from the creation and rapid diffusion of new, high-yielding varieties of wheat and rice.

To date the new, high-yielding varieties are being adopted most rapidly in Asia, where the countryside is alive with change and ferment, from Turkey across to the Philippines. And the new seeds are beginning to affect several countries in Africa and Latin America.

Both India and Pakistan have increased their wheat crops more than fifty percent in the past four years—a most remarkable upward leap. Pakistan, the number two recipient of U.S. food aid through 1968, was on the brink of self-sufficiency in 1969. India has halved its food imports from the peak levels of 1967. Kenya has an exportable surplus of corn. The Philippines ended half a century of dependence on imported rice in 1968; it is now exporting rice. Mexico has surpluses of wheat, rice and corn. Turkey is expected to reach self-sufficiency soon. Iran exported wheat in 1969 for the second year.

THE NEW SEEDS

The new varieties—dwarf wheats developed in Mexico by the Rockefeller foundation and new dwarf rices bred in the Philippines at the International Rice Research Institute—are the most exciting agricultural technology ever to enter the poor countries. They are not just marginally better than traditional or indigenous varieties. They actually double yields with proper management.

As a result of their high-yield capacity, the new seeds have spread like prairie fire in the poor countries where ecological conditions are suited to their use. So dramatic are the harvests that they easily convince tradition-bound farmers to adopt the new seeds and the necessary modern farming practices. In the 1964-65 crop year, only two hundred acres in Asia were planted to the new varieties; then there were 37,000 acres, then five million, then twenty million, and in 1968-69 the total reached 34 million acres. This is close to one-tenth the grain land of Asia. The acreage of Mexican wheat in Asia today is seven times that in Mexico.

The key to the productivity of the new varieties is a remarkable feat of biological engineering which greatly enhances their responsiveness to fertilizer. Plant breeders redesigned the wheat and rice plants, producing plants with short, stiff straw that stands up under the weight of heavier yields. With the old thin-strawed varieties, yields began to decline when the application of nitrogen reached forty pounds per acre. The grain would become too heavy and lodge or fall down. Much grain was lost, particularly with rice. Yields from the new varieties increase until nitrogen application reaches 120 pounds per acre.

The new varieties not only respond to much larger quantities of fertilizer, they also use fertilizer more efficiently. One pound of nitrogen used with the old varieties would produce, on the average, ten pounds more grain. A pound applied to the new varieties usually results in fifteen to twenty pounds of additional grain. Thus, a given level of production can be reached using far less fertilizer with the new seeds.

The other important characteristic of the new varieties is that they are adaptable to a wide range of geographical locations. Their great adaptability stems from the fact that they are aseasonal, that is, not very sensitive to variations in day length (photoperiod). The old varieties are very sensitive to day length and must be planted when the monsoon begins; through centuries of selection they have become accustomed to that particular seasonal cycle of day length. Germ plasm from widely scattered parts of the world was used in breeding the new varieties and helped to lower their photosensitivity. The new wheats now flourish throughout a wide latitudinal range stretching from Turkey in the north to Argentina in the south.

Many of the new varieties mature early. IR-8, the new "miracle rice," is ready for harvest in four months; the old varieties take five or six. The early maturing and aseasonal qualities of the new varieties offer many new possibilities for multiple cropping.

The extraordinary new varieties, with their cosmopolitan parentage, represent the telescoping into one package of several decades of technological advance in plant breeding. The new Mexican wheats are the offspring of American, Colombian, Australian, and Japanese wheats. The important dwarf gene is inherited from Norin 10, a Japanese variety. IR-8, the most productive of the new rices, is a cross between Dee-geo-woo-gen, a short, stiff-strawed rice from Taiwan, and Peta, a rather tall, high-yielding, and disease resistant tropical rice plant from Indonesia.

ENGINES OF CHANGE

The word "revolution" is used frequently these days, and is greatly abused, but no other word adequately describes the effects of the new seeds on the poor countries. Agricultural scientists have achieved a technological breakthrough that foreshadows widespread changes throughout the developing world. And the effects will not be limited to the poor countries. Already the new varieties are altering long-standing patterns of global agricultural production and trade.

These new varieties may be to the agricultural revolution in the poor countries what the steam engine was to the Industrial Revolution in Europe. Once farmers have broken with the past in agriculture, they are more susceptible to new ideas in other areas such as education and family planning. Now many governments in the hungry world are

shifting priorities to the agricultural sector as the source for modernization, after being biased toward industry for years.

SECOND GENERATION PROBLEMS

Of course, major advances like the ones alluded to are not lived
through without problems and strain. There are many second generation problems associated with the current food breakthrough. For one
thing, not all farmers benefit from the new technology equally. In
Turkey the farmers along the well-watered and fertile coastal plain,
where ecological conditions are ideal for the new wheats, are benefiting much more than are farmers situated on the arid Anatolian
plateau. West Pakistan's success with the new varieties is far greater
than East Pakistan's, where ecological factors are not suited to the new
seeds. Political strains associated with this situation contributed to
President Ayub's demise. In any country farmers who have plentiful,
well-controlled water supplies have the advantage. In addition to these
ecological and political problems, countries are experiencing difficulty
in marketing and distributing the larger harvests.

THE IRISH FAMINE BACKDROP

Whenever exogenous varieties are introduced on a large scale as
with the new wheats and rices, farmers must be constantly alert to the
threat of plant disease. A classic example is the Irish Potato Famine
of the late 1840s. Ireland had become dependent for its food supply
on the lowly potato introduced from the New World, but the potato
proved susceptible to blight. As the result of devastating crop losses,
a million and a half Irishmen died of starvation. There was more
emigration to the United States in ensuing decades. Famine and
emigration, together with the delayed marriages and low birth rates
over the century and a quarter since the famine, have reduced Ireland's
population to four million, just half of what it was when the potato
blight hit.

The potato does not readily contract blight. The temperature and
humidity, among other factors, have to be exactly right—or, rather,
wrong. But when these very specific conditions occur the crop failure
can be total. The same is true of wheat rust and some other diseases
attacking cereals. Since a major share of the 34 million acres of high-
yielding cereals in Asia is planted to exogenous varieties, the disease
threat is particularly acute. The new wheats were developed in Mexico;
these are rather resistant to the wheat rusts currently prevalent in

Mexico, but not necessarily to those found on the far side of the globe.

Rice seems to be more plagued by disease than is wheat. In part this is because it is almost always grown in a warmer, moister environment, more conducive to the spread of diseases. To achieve optimum yields with the new varieties, the density of the plant population is invariably increased. Combined with much heavier fertilization which brings with it lush vegetative growth, the "crowding" creates ideal conditions for plant epidemics and infestation of pests, quite like similar crowding does in human societies. The dominant disease of rice in Asia is rice blast, a disease which occurs most frequently as the use of nitrogen fertilizer and the density of the vegetation increases.

While the threat of rice disease is a real one, there is much more preventive technology in the research bank than when the potato blight struck in Ireland. As the exogenous varieties are crossed with local ones, the risk of an outbreak of disease on that scale is reduced. At the same time a greater number of new varieties are being used, and sources of germ plasm are becoming more diverse.

DISTORTIONS IN WORLD AGRICULTURE

Introduction of the new seeds into the tropical-subtropical regions, with their greater abundance of solar energy and year round growing temperatures, is strengthening the competitive position of the poor countries. But just when many of the tropical and subtropical countries are beginning to produce exportable surpluses of cereals, many of the rich industrial countries like those in the European Economic Community and Japan are pursuing protectionist policies. These trends are leading to a confrontation between rich and poor countries. If the poor countries cannot gain access to the markets of the rich countries, their overall development will be thwarted.

An even greater distortion exists in world sugar production than in cereals. At present much of the world's sugar comes from sugar beets, but if economics alone prevailed there would be little if any beet sugar produced in the world; sugar would come from cane, and virtually all of it from the tropical and subtropical countries. The production of sugar is one commodity in which the poor man living in the tropics has a pronounced advantage over his counterpart in the temperate regions. Beet sugar costs between six and nine cents a pound to produce, while cane sugar costs only two to three cents.

Virtually all the industrialized countries in North America and Europe, both East and West, are guilty of protecting inefficient beet sugar production. If the gap between rich and poor is ever to be narrowed, the barriers to sugar imports in the rich countries must be lowered. The failure to do so will not only frustrate the poor countries but deprive them of one of the few competitive advantages nature has given them.

However exciting and encouraging in the short run, the current wave of yield takeoffs in the poor countries should not reduce concern over the population problem. The new breakthrough is not a solution to the population problem. It is, however, a means of buying time with which to achieve a breakthrough in contraceptive technology comparable to that in plant breeding.

REDEFINING THE POPULATION PROBLEM

The food breakthrough forces us to redefine the population problem. By lifting the spectre of famine in the immediate future, expanded food supplies make it possible to focus concern on other dimensions of population pressure that loom large.

During the 1960s the world population problem was equated with the food-population problem. But in looking ahead we can see that the nature of the population problem is going to change. By 1975 we will in all likelihood be equating the population problem, in its most immediate sense, with the employment-population problem.

If the dramatic gains in cereal production continue in the developing countries, the problem of feeding the world during the next two decades promises to be more manageable than was earlier thought. This does not mean that the food problem will be solved completely over the next few years. But it does mean that producing enough food for people is going to be much easier than creating enough jobs. The more serious dimension of the population problem will be that of creating enough jobs to accommodate the first of the large age groups now beginning to move into the labor market.

When the population explosion began in most poor countries nearly two decades ago, it had a rather immediate, albeit modest, effect on the demand for food. As soon as babies enter the world they begin demanding food. They do not begin to demand jobs until fifteen or twenty years later. There is thus a grace period for employment that does not exist for food.

For most developing countries the grace period will end in the early seventies when the first wave of the expanded age group enters the job market. And the tide will swell. The number of people moving into the job market in the developing countries is going to be very large during the next five to fifteen years. If millions of young people entering the labor market are not able to find jobs, the labor force explosion of the seventies could pose an even greater threat to peace and stability than the threat of famine in the sixties.

The employment crisis of the 1970s may come to dominate policy making and economic planning in much the same fashion as the food crisis did in the 1960s. The principal criterion influencing formulation of economic policies and allocation of resources will increasingly be the impact of these actions on employment.

The employment question looms large not only in and of itself, but because it bears directly on some of the most pressing social and economic issues the poor countries face. It is closely associated with the distribution of wealth within societies and with the movement of rural people into urban areas, particularly when this move is not paralleled by industrialization. When unemployment is transferred from rural to urban areas the social costs become much higher and the possibilities for political disruption even greater. If the threat of famine is indeed lifted during the seventies it is essential that we redefine the population problem, making it clear that famine is not the only threat posed by overpopulation.

The ecological implications of man's growing numbers and unceasing quest for food are only beginning to be understood. Over time man, the tiller, has been altering his environment at an accelerating pace. His efforts to produce more food as his numbers increase are resulting in both the physical destruction and the pollution of the environment.

OVERPOPULATION AND SOIL EROSION

Man has been changing his environment through his agricultural practices ever since Neolithic times. As population grows, an ever expanding area of land to be used for cultivation is cleared of natural cover. Man has slashed and burned, harvested a crop, and moved on to new land to do the same again. Vast herds of goats, sheep, and cattle have been allowed to multiply and overgraze the land.

Fuel needs of growing populations, both for heat and cooking, cause the cutting of forests far in excess of natural replenishment, gradually reducing the earth's forest cover in densely populated areas. Some such areas include the Indian subcontinent, where much of the population is now reduced to using dung for fuel. Livestock populations tend to increase with the human population, but forage needs for cattle now far exceed the rate of replenishment in many poor countries, and again the countryside is being denuded of grass cover.

As population pressure builds, not only is more land brought under the plow, but the additional land is less suited to cultivation. Once the valleys are filled, farmers begin moving up the sides of the valleys, creating serious soil erosion problems. As natural cover that retards runoff is reduced and as soil structure deteriorates, both floods and droughts become more severe.

The denudation of the countryside and resulting erosion of soil are widespread throughout much of the developing world. The relationship between man and the land from which he derives his subsistence has become very unstable in large portions of India, particularly in the north and west, and in parts of Pakistan, the Middle East, North Africa, and Central America. Millions of acres of cropland are becoming so severely eroded that they are being abandoned—many of the displaced farmers and their families are moving to urban areas, swelling the slums of nearby cities.

In addition to destroying soils, severe soil erosion can impair and eventually destroy irrigation systems as well. The overcutting of forests in Java, an island of seventy million people, is silting the irrigation canals, steadily reducing the capacity of existing irrigation systems. And each year the damage from floods, droughts, and erosion becomes more severe.

West Pakistan provides an unfortunate example of the cost of denudation of the countryside. Recently completed Mangla Reservoir, situated in the foothills of the Himalayas and part of the Indus River system, cost 600 million dollars to construct. Its current life expectancy is estimated at less than fifty years, far less than indicated in the feasibility study which justified its construction. The Mangla watershed is eroding rapidly as Pakistan's rapidly expanding human and livestock populations bare the countryside. Gullies, cut through the fertile countryside within a half hour's drive of Rawalpindi, are so deep that they have become minor tourist attractions.

If man presses nature too hard, the results can be disastrous. The "dust bowl" years of the mid-thirties offer an example very close to home. Only after some 20 million acres of cropland were set aside for fallow each year, after soil cover was improved, and after thousands of miles of windbreaks were planted was a reasonably stable situation reestablished in the southern Great Plains. The United States had the resources to correct the mistakes man had made, particularly the ability to withdraw large areas of land from cultivation each year. These options are not readily available to the poor countries where man is pressing nature so hard today.

MORE FOOD—AT WHAT COST

The pressure of population not only causes man to move onto marginal land, it also forces him to intensify agricultural production. This in turn forces the use of fertilizer and pesticides, both of which pollute the environment. Among the pesticides the chlorinated hydrocarbons, including DDT and dieldrin, pose a serious threat in that they are both quite toxic and break down slowly, or in a relevant time span, not at all. Thus the amount in the environment keeps building, reaching damaging concentrations in some situations.

DDT tends to concentrate in the more predatory forms of land and sea life, including man. It adversely affects reproductive capacities of certain birds, such as eagles and hawks, and some types of fish at existing levels. Exactly what effect it has on human life at current levels of concentration in the environment is not known. A congressman recently pointed out that the DDT levels in mother's milk were far above the established tolerance levels for interstate trade.

Biologists and medical men are worried about the potentially harmful effects of DDT on man and other forms of life. Several countries either have banned its use or are considering doing so. Among these are the United States, Sweden, and Denmark.

Meanwhile, USDA researchers are hard at work attempting to develop biological controls. The release of sterile (through radiation) insect males to eradicate insect pests has been eminently successful in some situations. Breeding plants for disease resistance has eliminated the need for chemical pest controls in many others.

The fertilizer problem is caused by the runoff of nitrates into lakes, streams, and rivers. This stimulates excessive growth of certain kinds of plant life, often causing the body of water to literally suffocate and die. Perhaps the most striking and tragic example of this is the death of Lake Erie, once one of the world's finest inland lakes.

A MATTER OF PRIORITY

The question man now faces is not so much whether he can produce enough food to meet the needs of projected increases in his numbers, but whether he can cope with the environmental consequences of doing so. At present national priorities within the United States seem very much askew; the allocation of resources to deal with the environmental dimensions of the quality of life occupies a low position on the totem pole of priorities. Unless a more rational set of priorities can be developed, the prospects of dealing effectively with environmental consequences of attempts to increase food production are not bright.

FORMULATING
ENVIRONMENTAL POLICY

Although most Americans are only beginning to become concerned about environmental problems, and political candidates are only beginning to discover any campaign value in environmental issues, governments have been formulating and executing environmental policies—often with massive and far-reaching consequences—for many years. One agency which has had great freedom in formulating environmental policy in the United States, with little public awareness of its actions, is the Army Corps of Engineers. But recently the Corps has become less obscure, and is often uncomfortably the center of attention; the indictment by Supreme Court Justice William O. Douglas, who calls the Corps "public enemy number one," is a good example of the kind of criticism of past environmental policy which is becoming fairly common. In his article Justice Douglas shows some of the underlying political forces which have permitted the Corps to move so freely for so long.

The history of the Corps of Engineers justifies raising some questions about the liberal, pluralistic idea of government which dominates American political thinking—the essentially complacent notion that there is competition among interest groups which protects the interests of society as a whole. The evident weakness in that view is that there have not been any interest groups with enough size or power to protect against deterioration of the environment.

Conservationist organizations, which might be expected to fill this need, have generally been rather mild-mannered groups without much political power. The Sierra Club, which began as a small and exclusive group of people interested in hiking and camping in western mountain areas, developed into a conservationist organization and then into the largest, most militant, and most effective such organization in America. But, as the article by San Francisco reporter Robert A. Jones shows, the transition has been anything but peaceful. Since the article was written, David Brower was fired from the presidency of the Sierra Club and has since launched a new conservationist organization called Friends of the Earth (FOE). Other new and apparently militant groups are springing up everywhere, but a really powerful national conservationist force or alliance has not yet emerged.

One of the difficulties in the way of adapting American political institutions toward more effective management of environmental resources is the rigid value system which controls decision-making; natural resources are considered to have economic value, and economics is a science of measurable things—dollars and cents, goods and services—which falters when it is called upon to deal with such intangibles as human emotions. This split, characteristic of contemporary western thinking, has had great effect upon governmental decisions about the environment. Fortunately for conservationists, many kinds of pollution have tangible, economically measurable and hence "real," detrimental consequences; if they did not, arguments for better environmental policies would probably be even less interesting to public officials than they are. Nathaniel Wollman, professor of economics at the University of New Mexico, presents the case for a "new economics of resources" which would take a wider view of the value to human beings of environmental quality.

Harvey Wheeler, co-author of *Fail Safe* and fellow of the Center for the Study of Democratic Institutions, deals with a difficulty which is at least as serious as that of finding a place in the language of economics for human intangibles of environmental experience— namely, the difficulty of reconciling our assumptions about how decisions are made in a democracy with the awesome capabilities of modern technology. The beginning of the atomic age, says Wheeler, was also the beginning of a new political era: "Legislatures might continue to operate in their accustomed fashion, politicians might continue to campaign for office as of old, but those who were really determining the outlines of the future belonged to a scientific, rather than the political, establishment." Wheeler proposes some entirely new kinds of national constitutional organizations to formulate and administer scientific policy; readers should note, by the way, that one of the agencies which Wheeler offers as a model—the Tennessee Valley Authority—was cited by Justice Douglas as a contender for the "public enemy number one" title.

Wheeler also points out the need for international or trans-national forms of environmental policy-making; and this is the theme of political scientist Dennis Livingston's article on international problems of pollution control in such areas as water and air pollution. Many, if not most, environmental problems have international implications: while our state and national agencies struggle with the issue of DDT use, for example, they must consider the evidence of the ability of pesticides used in one area to turn up in the tissues of animals in distant regions. The task of formulating solutions to international environmental problems will be a difficult one; there is not much cause for optimism about the potential of world leaders and international institutions to become aware of the truth that, however fragmented the world may be politically, it is a single ecological whole.

THE CORPS OF ENGINEERS: THE PUBLIC BE DAMNED

Justice William O. Douglas

"The Army Corps of Engineers is public enemy number one." I spoke those words at the annual meeting of the Great Lakes Chapter of the Sierra Club, early in 1968; and that summary supplied an exclamation point to a long discussion of the manner in which various federal agencies despoil the public domain.

Justice William O. Douglas, "The Public Be Damned," originally appeared in PLAYBOY *magazine, July 1969. Copyright 1969 by HMH Publishing Co.,Inc. Reprinted by permission of William Morris Agency, Inc.*

It is not easy to pick out public enemy number one from among our federal agencies, for many of them are notorious despoilers and the competition is great for that position. The Tennessee Valley Authority, for example, like the Corps of Engineers, has an obsession for building dams, whether needed or not. Its present plan to wipe out the Little T River and its fertile valley is rampant vandalism. TVA is also probably the biggest strip miner in the country, using much coal for its stand-by steam plants. The sulphuric acid that pours out of strip mines, ruining downstream water, is TVA acid.

The Bureau of Mines sits on its hands in Washington, D.C., pretty much a captive agency of the coal-mine owners, and does precious little about strip mining.

The Public Roads Administration has few conservation standards; it goes mostly by engineering estimates of what is feasible and of cost. In the Pacific Northwest, it has ruined 50 trout streams through highway design. Everywhere—East and West—the Administration aims at the heart of parklands, because they need not be condemned, and plays fast and loose with parts of the public domain that were reserved for wildlife and outdoor recreation.

The list is long; and when the names of federal agencies are all in, the balloting for public enemy number one will not be unanimous. But my choice of the Army Engineers has a powerful case to support it.

The Corps is one of our oldest federal agencies. It is small and elite, highly political and very effective. It is honest and, with exceptions I will note, quite efficient. It is also largely autonomous and inconsiderate of the requirements of conservation and ecology.

There has been a recurring effort to get rid of it. The Hoover Commission Task Force on Water Resources and Power recommended in 1949 that the functions of the Corps and the Bureau of Reclamation be transferred to the secretary of a proposed Department of Natural Resources and consolidated there in an agency to be known as the Water Development Service. The training provided "in peacetime for the 215 Army engineers at present utilized on this civilian program can surely be secured in some far less costly fashion."

In 1966, Senators Joseph S. Clark, Lee Metcalf and Frank E. Moss sponsored a bill that would have turned the Department of the Interior into a Department of Natural Resources and transferred the Corps to that new department. But the power of the Corps is so strong that that bill died in committee. Indeed, senators and congressman who are so bold as to urge that the Army Engineers be abolished find themselves wholly out of favor when it comes to projects for their states.

At the time of the Hoover Report, the budget of the Corps was about $440,000,000 a year. It is now 1.3 billion dollars and is expected to reach three billion dollars in the 1980s. So the Corps shows no sign of diminishing political influence.

Its specialty is in pork-barrel legislation on the Hill. It commonly outmaneuvers the president and has its way, irrespective of his wishes. The Corps gave F. D. R. one of his soundest political thrashings. The Corps also has few public critics; it has become one of the sacred cows of Washington.

The Corps farms out many of its research and development projects. There is hardly a federal agency in Washington that is not offered a piece of it in amounts from $200,000 to $400,000 or more a year. Federal bureaucrats love that kind of money, for they do not have to depend on Congress for it. There is a rule of thumb in Washington that 15 percent of an amount obtained in an appropriation is used for permanent overhead. That means that if agency A receives $500,000 for research on siltation, water purification, or what not, it uses $75,000 to add to its permanent personnel and the rest for the current annual project. But agency A, like the other agency donees who receive funds from the Corps, is anxious to have a similar amount, year after year. Therefore, never do they raise their voices against ill-conceived projects; never, when the Corps is throwing its weight around and the public is protesting, do these federal agencies align themselves with the people.

In the late fifties, I was a member of a group of conservationists fighting the Corps on the huge River Bend Dam on the Potomac River. The dam was virtually useless as a power project and of no value for flood control. Its justification was the creation of a head of water that could be used to flush the polluted Potomac of sewage. Some of the huge federal agencies were silently opposed; but none would speak up, for fear of losing the Corps' good will and its research and development funds. We ended by getting an independent engineering study that actually riddled the project. That dam—which would have flooded 80 miles of river and shown a drawdown of 35 vertical feet—would have been known in time as the nation's greatest folly. It would have despoiled a historic river; and the 35-foot vertical drawdown would have resulted in several hundred yards of stinking mud flats exposed to public view. Yet the Corps had the nerve to get a public-relations outfit to make an estimate as to the millions of tourists who would be drawn to this ugly mudhole from all over the East.

The Engineers gave up on River Bend and offered an alternative of an upstream dam at Seneca for water supply. Public hearings exposed its destructive qualities. It, too, would ruin a beautiful free-flowing river. Moreover, there was a growing awareness that dams for municipal water are unnecessary along the Potomac; for the estuary in front of Washington, which is 20 miles long and moved by the tides, contains billions of gallons of potable water, which is all the water the metropolitan area will ever need.

At the peak of its promotional activities along the Potomac, the Corps had plans for 16 big dams and 418 small ones. How many were actually discarded? I do not know. But their active promotion of Potomac River dams has shrunk from 434 to 6. Those six are for water for metropolitan use—a needless expenditure, because of the ample supply of estuary water.

The estuary water is polluted, but so is the entire Potomac. Why not expend our energies and fortunes in building sewage-disposal plants, not dams that put fertile bottom lands under muddy waters from now to eternity and drive thousands from their homes?

As I said, the Corps sometimes turns out to be mightier than the commander in chief, the president of the United States.

Franklin D. Roosevelt tried to draw the lines of authority governing the Corps quite sharply: if a project was primarily concerned with navigation or flood control, then the Army Corps of Engineers had jurisdiction; if, however, irrigation and power were the dominant features of the project, then the Bureau of Reclamation would be in charge. The matter came to a head in 1944, when the Kings River project and the Kern River project—both part of a development program for California's Great Central Valley—were before Congress. Roosevelt was firmly on record as having said, "I want the Kings and Kern River projects to be built by the Bureau of Reclamation and not by the Army Engineers."

But the Corps had its way before both the House and the Senate. Roosevelt countered by directing the secretary of war to make no allocation of funds nor submit any estimate of appropriations without clearing the matter with the Bureau of the Budget. F. D R. provided funds in his new budget only for the Bureau of Reclamation respecting these projects. But before the budget cleared the House, the Army Engineers got included in the budget funds for initial work on the projects.

F. D. R. signed the bill reluctantly, saying he would ask Congress to transfer jurisdiction over all these Central Valley projects to the Department of the Interior. Then he died and Truman took over the problem. The maneuvering against Truman was long and involved. In time, the Corps had pretty much its own way (a) by taking the stump against the White House in California to elicit the support of greedy landowners who wanted the benefit of irrigation without paying the costs as provided by law, and (b) by lobbying in Congress.

Every president has known something of the freewheeling nature of the Corps and its tendency to undercut the White House and curry favor with its friends on the Hill. Early in 1968, it was busy dodging the Bureau of the Budget on six Potomac dams and making its own recommendations to Congress. L. B. J., probably the dearest friend the Corps has had, tried to keep the Engineers in line. But the Corps is incorrigible, violating the fundamental principle that while an administrative agency is the creation of Congress, it must report through the chief executive, in order for a centralized, coordinated plan of administration to be successful. Even though the president advises that a Corps project is not in accord with White House policy, the Corps transmits its report to Congress anyway, sometimes, though not invariably, including in the transmittal a statement of the president's position. In this sense, the Corps is *imperium in imperio,* enjoying a status no other administrative agency has.

The Corps goes way back in our history, the present one dating from March 16, 1802. It is a small, elite group of officers, not many over 200 in number. But it supervises over 40,000 full-time civilian employees.

The permanent staff of civilian employees obtains its pay *only* when there is some public-works program to which the salary can be charged. That is why every civilian member is eager to suggest, initiate or create a role for the Corps that will keep everyone employed. In time of war, the Corps has military assignments, but its essential work over the years is concerned with civil functions. The chief of engineers is responsible to the secretary of defense regarding his civil duties and does not report to the chief of staff nor to any general. Actually, the Corps in operation is largely independent of the secretary.

The committees of the House and Senate through which it operates are the Public Works committees. The inception of a Corps project starts with the congressman or senator representing the district where the project will be located. What member of Congress does not want $10,000,000 or, preferably, $100,000,000 coming into his district? He therefore tries to get the item included in an omnibus bill authorizing a preliminary examination. Once that is done, the preliminary examination may or may not be made. The appropriation is in a lump sum and there is usually not enough to make all the investigation authorized. So the Corps, at its own discretion, decides which has priority.

The Corps finally obtained by an act of Congress special permission to spend up to $10,000,000 on any project without approval by Congress, provided the project has been approved by resolutions adopted by the Senate and House committees. This is an advantage shared by no other federal agency; and it is a measure of the rapport between Congress and the Army Engineers. Moreover, it gives the Corps a tremendous momentum. Once $5,000,000 or $10,000,000 is spent on a project, the pressure to get on with it and finish it is tremendous.

A member of Congress who is in good with the Corps will receive favors; those who may have been critical of it will be kept waiting. The game is boondoggling played for high stakes by clever, cunning men.

There are few members of Congress who do not early learn the lesson that an obsequious attitude pays off when it comes to pumping millions of dollars into a district that may save an election for a deserving Democrat or Republican but destroy a lovely free-flowing river.

The Corps operates in part through NRHC, the National Rivers and Harbors Congress. All members of Congress are ex-officio members of NRHC. Five of the 21 directors are members of Congress. Ten are national vice-presidents. The all-important operative committees are, with one exception, chaired by members of Congress. At its annual meeting, the National Rivers and Harbors Congress decides which rivers and harbors projects it should present to Congress; and then the Congressional members change hats and go to work lobbying one another.

One who is in a campaign opposed to the Corps has very few important allies. I remember the Buffalo River in Arkansas and the Saline River in the same state—both destined by the Army Engineers to be destroyed as free-flowing rivers. The Buffalo I knew well, as I had run it in canoes and fished for bass in shaded pools under its limestone cliffs. Much of the land bordering the Buffalo is marginal woodlot acreage. Those who own that land were anxious to sell it for a song to Uncle Sam. Chambers of commerce blew their horns for "development" of the Buffalo. Bright pictures were drawn of motels built on the new reservoirs where fishing would abound and water-skiing would attract tourists.

The Corps had introduced Arkansas to at least 14 such river projects that buried free-flowing streams forever under muddy waters. The fishing is good for a few years. Then the silt covers the gravel bars where bass spawn and the gizzard shad—a notorious trash fish—takes over.

The people are left with the dead, muddy reservoirs. There is electric power, to be sure; but Arkansas already has many times the power that it can use. So why destroy the Buffalo? Why destroy the Saline?

What rivers are there left where man can float in solitude, fish, camp on sandspits and rid himself of the tensions of this age? These are questions people are beginning to ask. And these questions eventually won over enough of the Arkansas delegation to save the Buffalo—at least temporarily—but the Saline is still in jeopardy.

Down in Kentucky last year, my wife and I led a protest hike against the plans of the Corps to build a dam that would flood the Red River Gorge. This gorge, which is on the north fork of Red River, is a unique form of wilderness that took wind and water some 60,000,000 years to carve out.

This is Daniel Boone country possessed by bear, deer and wild turkey. It has enough water for canoeing a few months out of the year. It is a wild, narrow, tortuous gorge that youngsters 100 years from now should have a chance to explore.

The gorge is only about 600 feet deep; but the drop in altitude in the narrow gulch produces a unique botanical garden. From March to November, a different wild flower blooms every day along the trails and across the cliffs.

This is wonderland to preserve, not to destroy.

Why should it be destroyed?

Flood control has been brought into the story; but it is a makeshift, for flood control could be achieved with a dam farther downstream that would preserve the gorge. The same can be said for water supply. The real reason: recreation. The Corps and promoters of the dam say that the reservoir will attract tourists who will spend their money in motels, lodges and boat docks. That's the way the dam was sold to the local people, who naïvely expect to get rich by the influx of tourists.

And so Red River Gorge was doomed for extinction until 1969, when Senator John Sherman Cooper of Kentucky and Governor Louie B. Nunn proposed an alternative plan to save the gorge by putting the dam farther downstream. The Corps, minding its politics, accepted the proposal; and the names Cooper and Nunn have become revered by the Sierra Club and all other conservationists for that move.

(Army Engineers now have plans for the big south fork of the Cumberland in Kentucky. It is one of the very best white-water canoe rivers we have left. It is a wild, unspoiled waterway running through uninhabited lands; and those who know and love it are now mustering their forces for another great contest.)

The Corps is an effective publicist. After my wife and I led the protest march against the Red River Gorge project, we flew back to Washington, D.C. that night. The next day was Sunday; and that morning, every paper I saw had a wire-service story saying that we had been driven out of Kentucky by 200 armed men who did not want "a senile judge" telling them how to run their affairs. It was not until two days later that the conservationists had their statement ready for the press.

The most alarming thing is the very number of dams proposed by the Corps. One of our wild, wild rivers is the Middle Fork of the Salmon in Idaho—a 100-mile sanctuary that should be preserved inviolate like the Liberty Bell. White sandpits make excellent campsites. The waters so abound with trout that barbless hooks should be used. Mountain sheep look down on the river from high embankments. Deer and elk frequent the open slopes. When I ran that scenic river and returned to Washington, I discovered that the Engineers had 19 dams planned for the Middle Fork. . . .

The problem with dams is that they silt in: mud, carried to the dam by its source waters, settles in the reservoir and accumulates steadily. In time, the silt completely replaces the water. The Corps faces this prospect everywhere. Some dams in Texas lose eight percent of their capacity annually due to silting. Numerous ones lose two percent a year and at least six lose three percent or more. Most of those I examined were not Corps dams; but its Texas dams suffer the same fate. Once a dam is silted in, there is no known way to remove the silt and make the dam useful again.

The Waco Dam in Texas is a classic failure of the Engineers. Inadequate testing of the foundation shales below the embankment was the cause of the disaster. Parts of the embankment slid 700 feet from the dam axis. Correcting the failure amounted to about four percent of the original estimated cost of the dam.

The Corps has been embarrassed by hush-hush dams that are so leaky that the waters run under—not over—the dams. This failure is due to gypsum beds that underlie the reservoirs, a mineral that seems to baffle the dam builders and causes them to fall into all kinds of traps.

One conservationist, in speaking of a dam that carried water under, not over it, said rather whimsically, "This may be the perfect solution. The Corps and the congressmen get the facility constructed, the money pours into the district, yet the river valley is saved. We should encourage gypsum bases for all Corps dams."

But the two dams where the water ran under—rather than over—have now been fixed. So the hope to make them monuments to the folly of the Engineers has vanished.

The trend is ominous. The Corps expects by 1980 to flood new areas about the size of Maryland (6,769,280 acres).

I mentioned how the Engineers planned to build a dam on the Potomac to flush the river of sewage. That is by no means the sole example. The Oakley Reservoir on the Sangamon River in Illinois has been proposed to create a huge reservoir that will wash the river of sewage from Decatur on downstream. The trouble is that a reservoir large enough will inundate Allerton Park, a unique bottom land owned by the University of Illinois where valued research in biology and ecology goes forward.

The Corps has curiously become one of our greatest polluters. It is dedicated to the task of dredging channels in rivers and in the mouth of harbors so that vessels can get in and out. These days, the bottoms of channels are not mud but sludge formed from sewage and industrial wastes. The Corps takes these dredgings and dumps them into Lake Michigan. In fact, the lake is used as a dumping ground for 64 separate dredging operations. There was a public uproar in 1967 and 1968 and hearings were held. Lake Michigan is going the way of Lake Erie, which has become a big bathtub full of stinking waste material. Lake Erie is dead; and it is feared that Lake Michigan is on its way.

The dredging of estuaries has had a similarly shocking effect. A third of San Francisco Bay—or 257 square miles—has been filled in or diked off and is now occupied by homes, shopping centers and the like. Oyster production is ended; so is clam production; only a minimal amount of shrimp production remains. There are 32 garbage-disposal sites around the shores of the Bay. Eighty sewage outfalls service the Bay. Daily, over 60 tons of oil and grease enter the estuary, the cradle of the sea. The Army Engineers are not responsible for the pollution; but they are responsible for the dredging. The National Sand and Gravel Association has the estuaries marked for billions of tons of sand and gravel for the next 30 years. The Corps issues dredging permits; and ten years of dredging, according to the experts, makes an estuary a biological desert.

But the Corps has no conservation, no ecological standards. It operates as an engineer—digging, filling, damming the waterways. And when it finishes, America the beautiful is doomed.

The ecologists say that estuaries are 20 times as productive of food as the open sea. An estuary has been called a "nutrient trap." Being shallow, it is exposed to the energy of sunlight. Rooted plants of the land and drifting plants of the sea commingle. Thick beds of grasses, sea lavender, bulrushes and cattails, provide hiding areas, as well as food, for minute forms such as diatoms and for young fish, clams, mussels and oysters as well. Indeed, it is estimated that two thirds of our ocean catch has been estuary dependent for part of its life. The reality is that by the year 2000, California will not have a single running river to the ocean. What will be left, for example, of San Francisco Bay will be dead saltwater sewage.

The Corps seems destined to destroy our estuaries. The estuarine areas of our coast line have distinctive features. South of Boston are salt marshes where flounders spawn and grow to a size that permits their exit to the ocean. Down in Florida, the estuaries attract many species of commercial and sport fish and the valuable pink shrimp as well. The shrimp breed there and the young stay in the estuary until they are large enough to risk the Gulf. And so it goes from estuary to estuary. The estuaries have one thing in common—a balance between fresh water and salt water. Once the fresh water dries up and salinity increases, the estuary is avoided entirely by some species and used by the remaining species for a lesser time.

The results are revolutionary. The birds that are dependent on these sloughs for their feed must leave. The wood ibis, for example, which nests in the mangroves of Florida and feeds on the teeming estuarine life, flourishes when the annual flow of fresh water is 315,000 acre feet or more and does not nest successfully when the flow is less than that amount. Some dominant waterfowl foods—notably chara and naiad—tolerate only mild salinity. They have all but disappeared in Coot Bay in the Everglades, as a result of a Corps canal. With the elimination of those foods, the number of waterfowl in Coot Bay has declined more than nine-tenths.

The Cape Fear River development is now booming along in North Carolina. In 1934, the Corps reported that flood control was not justified in the lower Cape Fear basin. In 1947, after a disastrous flood, it again reported that no dam was justified. In the 1960s, the Engineers have been saying that Cape Fear flood control is essential. They add that if flood control is not needed, a dam or a series of dams will make great recreational areas. The principal rivers feeding the main reservoir are the Haw and the New Hope, both heavily polluted. The estimated cost will be $72,000,000 plus. Residents of the valleys where 35,000 acres of choice lands will be taken are much opposed. Those are farm units, handed down from generation to generation and greatly loved. It is tragic to hear them talk about the conversion of those gorgeous acres into a gigantic cesspool for raw sewage on which enthusiastic tourists are destined, it is said, to shout with joy.

Since 1936, federal investment in flood protection, largely through Corps activities, has amounted to more than seven billion dollars. Despite this massive investment, flood damages (according to the President's Task Force that reported in 1966) have been as much as ten times what they were in 1936. The Corps approach is purely an engineering approach. What is needed are conservation standards that regulate land use and reduce the risk that land will be so used as to accentuate runoffs and actually imperil property and lives because of man's grotesque ways of despoiling the earth. But these are no concern of the Corps. It exists to turn rivers into sluiceways and to raise the height of levees, so that man's misuse of the land may be borne by all the taxpayers. The report of the President's Task Force is a severe indictment of the Corps' mentality and techniques in dealing with water.

The disease of pouring money into a district to do something about water is a pernicious one. The Army Engineers can dredge channels, build levees and erect dams. Getting a man off heroin is easy compared with getting Congress off the kind of pork barrel the Corps administers. On July 30, 1968, Congress approved a one-and-a-quarter-billion-dollar appropriation for the civil activities of the Army Engineers. Forty-seven states were included. Texas, as might be expected, was granted 24 projects for construction during fiscal year 1969 that amounted to almost $40,000,000. Everybody is taken care of; under the cloak of flood benefits and the like, great vandalism is committed. Beautiful river basins are wiped out forever and one of our most pressing problems—water pollution and sewage—goes begging.

The Everglades National Park in Florida is a unique national treasure. It lies in a shallow limestone bowl not higher than 12 feet above sea level. Its lifeblood is the gentle, persistent flow of fresh water from the northern part of Florida, mostly the overflow from Lake Okeechobee. The biological and botanical life of the Everglades is intricate and amazing. The lowly gambusia fish and the alligators are the key, the gambusia feeding on mosquito larvae and starting the food chain for 150 species of fish that, in turn, nourish the alligator. The alligator wallows and forms the mudholes where this chain of aquatic life is maintained. Moreover, within the Everglades are 95 percent of all of our remaining crocodiles.

The birds come to nest and to feed on fish—white-crowned pigeons, white ibis, herons, roseate spoonbills, wood ibis, swallow-tailed kites, great white pelicans, millets, black-necked stilts, boat-tailed grackle, the anhinga, and others almost too numerous to mention. The most vulnerable of all fish is the bass that is dependent on the oxygen in the water. So when there is a drought, bass die by the hundreds. Since the garfish and the bowfin surface to get oxygen, they survive droughts somewhat better. But severe droughts kill everything; and the Corps, with no conservation standards, is the greatest killer of them all.

The park has 47 species of amphibians, all dependent on standing water for reproduction. The reptiles are dependent almost entirely on aquatic food. Of the 200 species of birds in the park, 89 are almost totally dependent on aquatic food. Five thousand pairs of wood storks, for example, require more than 1,000,000 pounds of small live fish to raise 10,000 young. Of the 12 different mammals in the park, most are amphibious or partly so. The 150 species of fish in the park are mostly dependent on estuaries for their existence. The invertebrates are also estuarine. The vegetation of the park is dominantly aquatic.

The Corps decided with the connivance of real-estate developers and prospective tomato farmers to divert all the overflow of Lake Okeechobee to the Atlantic or the Gulf. It sponsored and promoted various canals, which directly or indirectly served that end. Over the years, the Corps juggled costs and benefits—it lowered construction costs though they had risen some 36 percent; it found "land enhancement" values theretofore overlooked; but, naturally, it failed to deduct the destruction of the Everglades, a unique bit of Americana, and beautiful free-flowing streams such as the Oklawaha River, which it would destroy.

Over the past ten years, the toll on the Everglades has been enormous. The park's alligator population dropped drastically between 1961 and 1966. Thousands of birds and tens of thousands of fish died. Watery expanses of saw grass became stinking mud flats where nothing could live. There were no fish even to feed the young in the rookeries. The rains in 1966 saved the Everglades; but over the years, it cannot survive on rain alone. It needs the oozing fresh water from the north.

The Corps, greatly criticized for bringing the Everglades close to complete destruction, has come up with a plan to provide the park with fresh water—a plan that has just been presented to Congress. The plan is to raise the levees around Lake Okeechobee to provide for additional water storage; it would recover some fresh water by back-pumping through canals on Florida's east coast; it would improve the canal system leading south toward the park to provide additional capacity for conveying water into the park.

But the plan, though noble on its face, utterly lacks schedules showing the guaranteed deliveries of acre feet, come the dry season or drought weather. A contest is on between fresh water for real-estate developers and farmers and the park; and the Army Engineers are strangely allied with economic interests. The concept of the public welfare that those special interests have is how well lined their pockets are with public money.

One of the worst things the Corps is doing is the methodical destruction of our riverways. Some of its plans call for a conversion of river beds into sluiceways that eliminate gravel beds for spawning of fish and islands where birds nest. In the state of Washington, the Corps is bent on destroying the last piece of the native Columbia River.

From Bonneville Dam to Grand Coulee, there are now 11 dams on the Columbia, the only natural part of the river left being a 50-mile stretch from Richland to Priest Rapids. The plans of the Corps to install Benjamin Franklin Dam will destroy that piece of the river, making all of it a big lake or reservoir.

The reason advanced is commercial. It is pointed out that with the locks of Benjamin Franklin, the apple growers of Wenatchee will be able to float their apples to the Portland market. The difficulty is that an apple traveling that distance through that hot, bleak area of eastern Washington would not be edible by the time it reached Portland.

Be that as it may, the Corps would never be building Benjamin Franklin Dam if it had any conservation standards.

This section of the river is the last natural piece of the river left. The spring and summer run of salmon enter *the tributaries* of the Columbia for spawning. But the fall run of the Chinook salmon spawn *in the main bed;* and upstream from Richland are the last spawning grounds left in the main river. Due to the disappearance of other spawning areas, this stretch of the river has become increasingly important. The 20-year average of spawning beds is 902; in 1965, there were 1770 spawning beds; in 1966, 3100; in 1967, 3267. This area now accounts for about 30 percent of all the fall Chinook production. Where they will go if the river becomes a lake, no one knows.

This stretch of the river is also an important breeding ground for smallmouthed and largemouthed bass, white sturgeon and whitefish.

It is also a natural spawning ground for steelhead trout, an operation greatly aided by a state hatchery. At least 30,000 steelhead trout a year are produced here; and the summer run is so excellent that sportsmen now catch 11,000 there.

The Benjamin Franklin Dam would wipe out 20 natural islands that are breeding grounds for the Canada goose and for several species of gulls, including the California and the ring-billed. The nesting geese number about 300 adult pairs and they produce about 1000 goslings a year. The dams with their resultant impoundments have greatly reduced, in all of the upper Columbia, the goose population from 13,000 to less than half. With all the dams being completed, the upper Columbia will have fewer than 3500 geese.

The river above Richland accommodates as many as 200,000 wintering waterfowl on a single day. Most of the facilities for these wintering inhabitants will be destroyed by the Benjamin Franklin Dam.

The destruction of these spawning grounds and breeding areas is a form of official vandalism. No federal agency with any concern for the values of conservation would be implicated in such a senseless plot.

Much of the river to be destroyed is now a part of a reservation of the Atomic Energy Commission, which uses the river to run its plutonium reactors. The AEC knows enough to realize how destructive the plans will be to the Columbia's natural wonders. But the AEC will not promote the dam nor oppose it. It is on the Corps' payroll and, like other similar federal agencies, it is beholden.

The conservation cause is therefore handicapped. A stalwart group is fighting the dam. But public opinion is difficult to muster, as only a few people can enter the sacred precincts of the AEC reservation. So the river has few knowledgeable friends.

The Corps is now starting a vast internal canal-building project to build waterways into the dry, desert-blown parts of America. What chamber of commerce does not long to make its forgotten city a great port?

Will Rogers used to joke that the best thing to do with the Trinity River at Fort Worth, Texas, was to pave it, the stream being a bare trickle at times. That wild idea is now a reality. Construction of a 370-mile canal from Fort Worth to Houston is under way, with 20 new dams (multipurpose) and 20 locks.

Rogers used to twit the Corps about getting him "a harbor on the Verdigris at Oologah" in Oklahoma. That 1.2-billion-dollar project is now under way—a 539-mile canal reaching into the heart of Oklahoma. The plan includes 18 locks and dams that will lift river traffic 530 feet from the Mississippi to the level of Catoosa, the head of navigation.

In 1967, the Corps approved a $316,000,000 Tennesee-Tomlingbee waterway as justified by a benefit-cost ratio of 1.24 to 1. The secretary of the army, Stanley Resor, sent the report to Congress with his own contrary conclusion that the project did not have the requisite "margin of economic safety." But the interested Congressmen ignored Resor's conclusion, did not take the issue to Congress, but in committee ordered the Engineers to start the controversial canal that is to run 253 miles.

The most brazen project of all is known as Mike Kirwan's Big Ditch, linking Lake Erie with the Ohio River. Kirwan is chairman of the subcommittee of the House Appropriations Committee on Public Works. Eighty-year-old Kirwan has long been a stern opponent of national-park development. "The U. S. owns too much land" is his position. A member of his subcommittee who opposes him is in a perpetual doghouse, never getting any favors of his own. So they all —mostly all—meekly fall into line.

Kirwan's Big Ditch would be 120 miles long, with a 35-mile reservoir to supply the canal with Erie's sewage water. Nearly 90,000 acres of the nation's finest dairy farms would be inundated and more than 6000 people would lose their homes.

The idea is an old one, going back to George Washington; but today the experts think it is utterly worthless.

The Corps benefit-cost ratio was juggled to suit its needs; obvious costs to the tune of at least $170,000,000 were left out. Benefits were rigged. Thus, "recreation" was valued at $17,000,000 a year—a sum that could be reached only if 500,000 sportsmen descended on this stinking sewage water on a normal Sunday.

The Corps approved the project, estimating the cost at over a billion dollars. It let Kirwan make the announcement. Kirwan managed it through the House; and the Senate—without a roll call—approved.

Two million of the needed one billion dollars plus for Mike Kirwan's Big Ditch was in L. B. J.'s budget, a budget in which L. B. J. said, "Waste and nonessentials have been cut out. Reductions or postponements have been made wherever possible."

And so the skids were greased. But the voice of Pennsylvania spoke up in opposition; and the Big Ditch has been delayed. Yet the momentum is so great in Washington, that if Texas and Oklahoma can have their worthless canals, so can Ohio.

The truth is that our waterways present staggering problems demanding money, engineering skills and ecological insights. These critical problems are not being managed by the Army Engineers.

Instead, the Corps is destroying free-flowing streams to make unnecessary dams. It is trying to turn natural rivers into sluiceways; it is destroying our estuaries. Having no conservation standards, the Corps can easily destroy the Everglades in favor of get-rich real-estate promoters.

The Corps, presently headed by the efficient General William F. Cassidy, has a long and illustrious record, completely free of fraud, mismanagement or other types of scandal. By 1942, it had built two and a half billion dollars' worth of facilities in a year and a half; and during World War II, ten billion dollars' in four years. In terms of coverage, it has included navigation, flood control, hydropower, beach erosion, water supply, fish and wildlife preservation, hurricane protection and related subjects. Since 1824, it has built most of the nation's harbors and navigable waterways. From the beginning, it was active in flood control; and when the first national Flood Control Act was passed by Congress in 1917, it became very active, especially in the Mississippi Valley. One who tours America will see many great and useful structures built by the Corps. Certainly, the Corps is unlike the Mafia; it has no conspiratorial function. It is honest and aboveboard.

The difficulty is, however, that we are running out of free-flowing rivers and healthy estuaries. The traditional engineering functions no longer fit our needs. Our need is to preserve the few remaining natural wonders that we have and make them clean and sparkling and fit for use by humans and by the vast world of birds, fish, reptiles and crustaceans that possess our waters.

We need the Corps. But we need also to redefine its functions and change its focus.

We pay farmers not to plant crops, Let's pay the Corps not to build dams, dredge estuaries, convert rivers into sluiceways or build inland canals.

We can accomplish that goal by a few simple amendments to the Corps' basic statutory authority.

First, its projects for river improvement should now be conditioned by conservation standards. Will the project protect the marshlands? Will it provide the needed fresh water for sanctuaries such as the Everglades? Will it preserve the bottom lands sorely needed for ecological studies?

Second, the Corps' statutory authority should be enlarged to authorize it to construct sewage-disposal plants. It has no such authority. It can be busier at that than at dam building. Its large civilian staff, dependent on federal largess for salaries, can fatten on sewage as well as on flood control and navigation.

The Corps needs statutory redesigning to meet modern urban and technological needs.

One billion dollars is needed in the Lake Erie complex to restore that dead lake, so that swimming, boating and fishing are once more possible. Mike Kirwan would not get a Big Ditch under this new regime. But he might get a big sewage-disposal plant named for him.

These are rewards enough, even at the level of pork barrel, if the Corps concentrates on socially useful projects that are desperately needed. Now is the chance to save the rest of our rivers by proclaiming our love of the land and our determination to preserve its natural wonders, even against despoilers as professionally competent as the Army Corps of Engineers.

FRATRICIDE IN THE SIERRA CLUB

Robert A. Jones

I first heard of David Brower in the early 1960s. I was supposed to be restacking picture books in a college library in New York, but most of the time I thumbed idly through their pages. I sat down, safely buried in the long rows of stacks, and picked up a large picture book called *The Eloquent Light.* I went through the book once, then again. The photographs of the Sierra Nevada had been taken by a man named Ansel Adams and edited by David Brower at the Sierra Club. I had heard of neither the men nor the Sierra Club, and for a few months the book was a secret.

Then one day I saw *The Eloquent Light* in a college bookstore, and soon it was in every bookstore. The design, the beauty of the photographs, the plea for the preservation of the land the photographs described were contagious. The book, and others that followed it, were expensive, but for every person who bought the book, at least a hundred must have read it in the store. After several black-and-white books, the Sierra Club began publishing in color. Then posters appeared, huge things with color reprints from the books; then paperbacks; then wall calendars; then stationery. It seemed, by 1968, that

Robert A. Jones, "Fratricide in the Sierra Club," THE NATION, *May 5, 1969. Reprinted by permission.*

the Sierra Club had a talent second only to *Peanuts* for glutting the bookstore market. Behind them all was the name of David Brower.

In San Francisco, seven years after I saw *The Eloquent Light,* I watched Brower and Adams at a Sierra Club board meeting in October 1968. Brower sat at one end of a long directors' table, his head bent over almost to his knees and moving slowly back and forth. At the table, Ansel Adams was demanding that Brower be fired as executive director of the Sierra Club.

In the years between the first publishing of *The Eloquent Light* and the confrontation at the board meeting, the Sierra Club had become a particular success. After he was appointed the club's executive director in 1952, Brower began, slowly at first, to promulgate the club's conservationist-preservationist ideas through books. He was, after all, a former editor of the University of California Press. The idea was new to conservation and, at the first try, it worked with a book in 1954 titled *This Is Dinosaur,* a plea for the establishment of Dinosaur National Monument. But outside California the club remained relatively unknown until the publishing of *The Eloquent Light* began the series of large-format picture books in 1960.

Brower had managed to move conservation from garden clubs to the college campus and to large-scale publishing; in doing so he was to catch the scent of the sixties. Many of the thousands of volunteers the club attracted to testify at government hearings and to stuff envelopes and to write letters to congressmen had first learned of the club from seeing its books in their college bookstores. Brower's use of the books, his films, and his promotion advertising appealed to the growing activism of the decade, and his outrage at the rape of the land by big government and big business dovetailed nicely with its morality.

By 1966 the club had become large, powerful, but unwieldly. Using full-page advertisements in *The New York Times, The Washington Post, Los Angeles Times,* the *San Francisco Chronicle* and other newspapers, it had led, and would soon win, campaigns for a Redwood National Park and a North Cascade National Park. Fighting back from the destruction of Glen Canyon, flooded by the Army Corps of Engineers, it prevented a similar dam in the Grand Canyon. Although the club, and all conservationists, were still losing more bouts than they were winning, the gap was closing. After the Redwood National Park was gerrymandered by the logging companies of Northern California, the Arcata Redwood Company, one of the largest, announced that it would go out of business in five years. "But didn't you manage to keep most of your land *out* of the park?" asked a member of the press. "Do you really believe Brower's people won't come back next year and get it all?" the company official shot back.

But as the Sierra Club grew it became infinitely difficult to manage. It was a hybrid of the professional and the amateur, and the path of a conservation idea from birth to execution led from committee to committee to board of directors to president to executive director. Sometimes ideas could be lost for years. One of Brower's last schemes for the club, a book series dealing with international environment problems, was originally proposed five years before the first book was published.

To compound the difficulties, the two segments of the club had grown suspicious of each other's power. The volunteer and amateur board of directors ceaselessly reminded the professional Brower that he had been hired only to execute their policies, not to create policies of his own. Brower would shrug consent, return to work, and ignore the pleas of the board.

Brower's drive to innovate, to change, to surprise, and to do it all quickly could not be held in check by the board. When one club publication, the *Sierra Club Bulletin,* was taken from his control, he invented another, the *Sierra Club Explorer.* When he believed that club procedure would interfere with the timing of a $20,000 advertisement in *The New York Times,* he ignored protocol and bought the advertisement in secret. "They want," he said with disdain, "to run this place like a bank."

As Brower's plans for the future increased, so did the apprehensions of other leaders of the club. One of the board members told me: "There's a recklessness to Dave that's terrifying. It's like driving down a city street with a man who's going 90 miles an hour. For a couple of blocks you may be O.K., but pretty soon you're gonna hit something. Well, that scares the hell out of me. But you know what? I think Dave likes it."

Those who opposed Brower were, above all, reasonable men. They are doctors and lawyers from San Francisco's financial district, scientists from Berkeley and a judge from Oakland, men who have lived their lives in the spirit of compromise, not confrontation. They are men who ask, "How much does it cost?" and "How much will it buy?" They would never have created the exciting and compelling picture but neither would they bankrupt the club. They were not young men, they did not burn with Brower's self-righteous fire; they were careful, sure and sophisticated.

Members like Richard Leonard, a San Francisco corporate lawyer, Paul Brooks, vice president of Houghton Mifflin in Boston, or Edgar Wayburn, a San Francisco doctor, could not understand a man whose publishing program had lost almost $300,000 and who yet proposed to expand it in such a way that it would lose millions. They admitted that they feared a man who could propose not only the expanded book program but a television series, film documentaries and advertising campaigns.

For Brower, the plans for the future of the Sierra Club were like a vision, and his confidence in his own abilities to bring it off approached religious faith. Once I spent an afternoon discussing the vision with him, and his enthusiasm was so contagious that I left feeling that it could all very well happen.

The vision was a complex, coordinated network of conservation propaganda that would, Brower felt, eventually equal the propaganda of the dam builders, the loggers, the highway engineers, and the infinite variety of their species. The books would discuss not only the problems of the United States but of the whole world. (The unauthorized *New York Times* advertisement proposed an "Earth National Park.") The movements and plans of business and governments would be watched by teams of field representatives that could also coordinate local resistance. Brower had already approached Time-Life, Standard Oil of New Jersey, Xerox, and other large corporations to help finance television documentaries, and movie-house shorts on crises that could not wait for books. Brower's contact with the corporations termed their reaction "very enthusiastic."

Not even the most conservative members of the club's board could help but feel the temptation of such a vision. The power and glory that it would bring were titillating. But the old jealousies prevailed. What, they asked, would happen to the volunteers in such a program? William Siri, a member of the American Mount Everest expedition and club director, said: "We believe what Brower is doing, whether it makes money or not, is heading the club toward disaster. Brower's ideas leave no place for the amateur, and the Sierra Club is unique because it is an amateur, a volunteer organization."

When the attack was mounted against the vision, Brower was impaled on charges other than his threat to the amateurs. Obviously believing that personal charges against Brower would be more effective than attacks on his ideas, his enemies gathered an impressive list of misuse of funds. The most serious, they said, occurred in 1968 when

Brower signed contracts that would have paid him 10 percent of the 8 percent total royalties from three Sierra Club books. The leaders of the club, all once close friends, had seen their mutual respect and shared concern deteriorate to such an extent that they could now only shout at one another in rage. The following account of a closed meeting has been verified by several directors:

President Edgar Wayburn: Dave, the chairman of the Legal Committee reports to me that . . . to his surprise he finds that 10 percent of the gross royalty is to you. What is your explanation?

Brower: The royalty is for creativity. It takes a great deal of skill to make those books as successful as they have been.

Wayburn: Well, you are paid for that. It is part of your job.

Brower: I am not paid for it! I am badly underpaid.

Wayburn: Your action is unilateral. Neither the president nor the board of directors has heard of this. Mr. Treasurer, were you consulted?

Treasurer: No.

Wayburn: I agree that salary readjustments for fine work should be . . . reviewed frequently, but that is an entirely different matter from this unilateral action.

Brower: It is not extra pay! Every one of those royalty checks will be paid back to the Sierra Club.

Director Richard Leonard: But then you are going in a circle. If the Sierra Club pays it to you and you pay it back, what is the purpose?

Brower: The purpose is to provide a discretionary fund for the use of the executive director.

Treasurer: But you already have a discretionary fund of $25,000. . . .

Brower reacted furiously to the attack. He countercharged that Wayburn and Leonard were jealous of his talents and success, and even hinted that they might be in the pay of the lumber companies or big utilities.

Neither side would recognize how badly it needed the other. The doctors and lawyers needed, and would always need, the ideas and the style of a man like Brower. Instead of making that admission, they rationalized that a "time for a change" had come within the club. Maynard Munger, a long-time club leader in Oakland, even theorized on the club's development: "From 1952, when Dave took over, until now, the club has been a charismatic organization. It operated on the spirit and impetus of one man. But now, in order to return the club to the idea on which it was founded, that is, a volunteer club, it must become a rational organization, and the charisma of the one-man leadership must disappear."

Blind as the opposition directors were to their needs, Brower was worse. As a visionary he could not accept serious criticism, and as the administrative conservation leader he could not accept even a small defeat by the board. In the modern corporate life, when every presiding genius needs a good accountant behind him, Brower's greatest failing was his refusal to be financially controlled. Films and books were contracted for that no one but Brower had considered. Donations were made to other organizations without explanation. When the club feared revocation of its tax-exempt status because of its legislative activities, it formed a separate Sierra Club Foundation, also tax exempt, to minimize the loss. Because he failed to consult the club's own legal advisers, Brower later jeopardized this safety move by including the foundation's name in a strongly worded advertisement that appeared in *The New York Times.*

Throughout the battle, which lasted for more than three years, there were few differences between Brower and his opponents over conservation policy itself. Although his opponents feared that Brower's vision might eventually run the club to bankruptcy, none of them questioned its potential scope or power. And Brower, who reminds reporters that he "was a volunteer for almost twenty years," claimed he had always supported the volunteer phases of the club.

But the battle had become a personal one between proud men, none of whom could lose gracefully. In January, when Brower placed a $20,000 advertisement in *The New York Times* without approval from the board or the president of the club, he was both precipitating a crisis that would leave no hope of compromise and rallying his supporters. When Wayburn suspended him the next day, the dare had been taken. The coming elections of the board of directors would decide whether Brower would rule with almost no support from thousands of Sierra Club volunteers, or whether the volunteers would control an organization deprived of the directing skill that had made it famous.

Because Brower's campaign within the club carried the same self-righteous tone that characterized his campaigns against government and business, and because the accumulated charges against his years of free spending could not be well defended, Brower lost badly. Of five positions open on the board, Brower lost all five to men who vehemently opposed him. The day after the election results were announced, I called Richard Leonard, a director of the opposition, and asked him what he thought would be done with Brower. "Dave Brower," he said, "will be fired at the May 3 meeting of the board of directors for his gross crimes against the Sierra Club."

What will thus be lost is not so much the "policies" of David Brower as the spirit he infused into the offices of the club. Maynard Munger's prediction will have become a fact: the Sierra Club will cease to be a charismatic organization and will become a rational one, but to have rationality at the total expense of vision and drive is a tragedy that should never have happened.

When the press writes of the Sierra Club, it usually feels an obligation to tack an adjective ahead of its name, as "prestigious" or "abrasive" or just "powerful." The Sierra Club, throughout its history, has not always been granted such respect and the question is whether it will continue to do so now. It will not become, as Brower predicts, a "hiking club." It will remain extremely active. But much more than activity is required to maintain an institution that fights for the faith and ideals of many people. The press rarely refers to an "abrasive" Audubon Society or a "powerful" Izaak Walton League.

The real question is whether the club will be able to sustain the force and clarity, the feeling of being so recklessly right in spite of all odds that Brower gave it. The men who won the election seem willing to chance it, but to those who sneaked back in the stacks for one more look at *The Eloquent Light,* the odds seem long.

THE NEW ECONOMICS OF RESOURCES

Nathaniel Wollman

The premise that there is a "new economics of resources" is itself subject to debate, but if there is, it differs from the "old" in that it pays greater attention to constraints within which economizing behavior is observed and gives greater weight to so-called "intangibles." It is an economics for which the "proper" supply of nonmarketed goods and services is a question of considerable moment, as is the design of the machinery by which the proper supply can be ascertained.

The natural environment—its various dimensions and qualities—is an especially apt subject for the new economics. I shall assume that we all agree on the fact of environmental deterioration, and argue that the low value we put on the environment reflects deeply imbedded philo-

Nathaniel Wollman, "The New Economics of Resources," DAEDALUS, *Fall 1967. Reprinted by permission from* DAEDALUS, *Journal of the American Academy of Arts and Sciences, Boston, Massachusetts, Volume 96, Number 4.*

sophic principles and historic sequences. The disregard of aesthetic factors and the dominating influence of the "economic man" were joint results of common causes. We still have no scientific way of determining how much "should" be spent on environmental quality, nor do we know what relationships, if any, exist between environmental quality and productivity. The knowledge we have of consumer preferences is inadequate, and we do not know how much weight should be attached to those consumer preferences that we can identify. Since environmental changes frequently trigger a sequence of irreversible effects, we cannot expect decisions to be both "correct" and based upon democratic authority unless the electorate is well informed and aesthetically sensitive. Lacking these qualities but aware of the deficiency, the electorate can proceed with confidence if there is a qualified body to whom it can delegate responsibility. Since all levels of government have environmental problems to solve, there is need for a corresponding hierarchy of environmental boards of experts. These boards should possess the power and authority that is now accorded the military establishment, not only because the penalty of inexpert decisions may be just as disastrous for the human race as the effect of military weapons, but because the ability of most of us to make expert decisions is no greater in the field of ecology, broadly conceived, than in warfare.

In advising or manning a board of experts, the economist functions as a member of a team. The economic task of "optimizing" resource use consists of bringing into an appropriate relationship the ordering of preferences for various experiences and the costs of acquiring those experiences. Preferences reflect physiological-psychological responses to experience or anticipated experience, individually or collectively revealed, and are accepted as data by the economist. A broad range of noneconomic investigations is called for to supply the necessary information.

Economists, as Tibor Scitovsky has pointed out, tend to think in terms of money. "Exactness, precision, and rational calculation hinge on the use of money. In the words of Georg Simmel, 'money economy and the dominance of the intellect are intrinsically connected. They share a matter-of-fact attitude in dealing with men and with things'." Thinking in terms of market prices, continues Scitovsky, yields a "consciousness of society's valuations; and when a person's actions are influenced by market prices, they conform that much more closely to society's needs and limitations."[1]

---

[1] T. Scitovsky, "External Diseconomies in the Modern Economy," *The Western Economic Journal* (Summer 1966), pp. 197-202.

Scitovsky then goes on to discuss the deficiencies in the price system that grow out of its failure to account for all aspects of money transactions. The price system fails to account adequately for benefits or costs that are enjoyed or suffered by people who were not parties to the transaction. These "extra-party" costs and benefits are the "externalities" of economic analysis. (Familiar examples are the disfigurement of the landscape by billboards, the sulfuric odors that surround a paper mill, or the pleasure of a neighborhood in a well-landscaped front yard.) Economists have long recognized their existence, but have usually treated them as side effects of uncertain magnitude rather than as central points of interest. In general, these externalities have no monetary valuations because the machinery by which valuations are created—that is, a market—does not exist for them. The markets do not exist because the benefits that are gained or lost are not exclusive or appropriable, and, until recently, the costs have not imposed such a burden that society saw fit to make an issue of them.[2]

The market malfunctions not only when it fails to register third-party effects, but also when participants in the market fail to act in accordance with their own interests. We infer that market action is *per se* welfare maximizing, but this inference rests upon the prior assumption of adequate knowledge and foresight. To the extent that people act on the basis of restricted information and inadequate understanding of the consequences of their acts, market transactions fail to achieve maximum human welfare.[3] Reliance upon consumer sovereignty has its limitations.

The past's low regard for careful preservation of the environment stemmed from several circumstances. Those controlling the use of resources could usually avoid permanent contact with dirt and ugliness. Moreover, environmental control required collaborative action. One man could blight a region, but collective action was needed to prevent this. Furthermore, levels of income were not high enough to suggest a substitution of beauty for physical goods, and those in the business of developing and disseminating good taste and sensitivity to beauty usually had as clients not the public, but the wealthy. The classic examples of blight—polluted air, polluted water, and scarred hillsides—

[2] See papers by R. Turvey and R. N. McKean in *Environmental Quality,* ed. Henry Jarrett (Baltimore, 1966); also J. M. Clark, *Economic Institutions and Human Welfare* (New York, 1957).

[3] "Maximization of welfare" by market transactions is assumed to be constrained by the distribution of wealth, the availability of natural resources, and science and technology. There also are other reasons why a market may not function "efficiently": presence of monopoly, immobility of resources, and discontinuities that result from large fixed capital investments.

were more often than not concomitants to the process of accumulating private fortunes. Today's interest in public beautification stems in part, perhaps in large part, from the fact that those professionally concerned now have the public as a client. Interest has also grown because we find it increasingly difficult to escape, and because sectors of the society —the upper-middle class particularly—have become saturated with goods and services.[4]

The foregoing catalogue does not exhaust the explanations of why we inured ourselved to environmental decay. Several additional, perhaps more fundamental, reasons can be advanced. Blight was an inescapable part of the industrial revolution, which began, in Lewis Mumford's phrase, with the paleotechnic age—an age dependent upon coal and iron and, consequently, the disfigurement of the landscape.

After technological developments made the home inadequate as a production center, laborers began to concentrate in factories. These were probably related, aesthetically, to problems of pauperism and public charity. As a manufacturing center, the factory appeared late in the history of cities and was, therefore, relegated to the periphery. "The operators of workhouses [factories] first found their labor supply not from within the city, but among runaway serfs and country yokels. . . . [Industrial plants] are still striving for a rational place in the body of the urbanized region."[5] The aesthetic decline of the city to the level of the workhouse had greater force than the elevation of the aesthetic quality of the factory to the level that had been attained by the medieval city.

The Anglo-American understanding of man's nature, based upon epistemological questions raised by Galilean and Newtonian physics, focused attention on man as a thinking rather than a feeling being. F. S. C. Northrop points out that "when Locke made explicit the complete consequences of his friend Newton, this experimentally verified physics was found to provide a theory not merely of physical nature but also of conscious man."[6]

Northrop's explanation, dealing as it does with man's conception of man and with the elemental units which together comprise the comprehension of reality, is the closest we can come to fundamentals. The Lockean person was a "mental substance . . . a completely local, independent thing having nothing in common with all other persons

[4] See M. Gaffney, *Environmental Quality*, p. 101.

[5] R. Neutra, *Survival through Design* (New York, 1954), p. 374. See also L. Mumford, *Technics and Civilization* (New York, 1934).

[6] F. S. C. Northrop, *The Meeting of East and West* (New York, 1946), p. 81.

and things." In his view of man, Locke erred in failing to recognize that, in addition to the "theoretic continuum, ... there is an all-embracing indeterminate continuum of feeling common to all creatures in their aesthetic immediacy. ... All these aesthetic materials, including the all-embracing aesthetic continuum, are the kind of thing which can be known only by being immediately experienced. No syntactically formulated, mathematically or logically abstract, indirectly and experimentally verified theory can ever designate them."

Northrop points out that Hume and his positivistic followers used the aesthetic materials mainly to develop a "mathematical, deductively formulated theory in the science of economics" and ignored the "purely empirical aesthetic factor in things for its own sake." Hume, Bentham, Mill, and Jevons erected the body of doctrine that has dominated our culture on the Lockean view of man. Northrop's quotation from Gautier's preface to his *Mlle. de Maupin* is worth repeating both because it reveals the deep sense of frustration felt by those whose aesthetic sensibilities were deeply scarred by what they saw, and because the attack on Hume and the economists who followed him was somewhat unfair.

Poor fellows! Their noses are too short to admit of their wearing spectacles, and yet they cannot see the length of their noses.

If an author threw a volume of romance or poetry on their desk, these gentlemen would turn round carelessly in their easy chair, poise it on its hinder legs, and balancing themselves with a capable air, say loftily—"What purpose does this book serve? How can a man, instead of making the great synthesis of humanity, and pursuing the regenerating and providential idea through the events of history, how can he write novels and poems which lead to nothing, and do not advance our generation on the path of the future? How can he busy himself with form, and style, and rhyme in the presence of such grave interests? What are style, and rhyme, and form to us? They are of no consequence (poor foxes! they are too sour). . . ."

No, fools, no, . . . a book does not make gelatine soup; a novel is not a pair of seamless boots. . . . There are two sorts of utility, and the meaning of the vocable is always a relative one. What is useful for one is not useful for another. You are a cobbler, I am a poet. . . . You will object that a cobbler is far above a poet, and that people can do with the one better than without the other. Without affecting to disparage the illustrious profession of cobbler, which I honour equally with that of constitutional monarch, I humbly confess that I would rather have my shoe unstitched than my verse badly rhymed, and that I should be more willing to go without boots than without poems. . . . I know that there are some who prefer mills to churches, and bread for the body to that for the soul. To such I have nothing to say. They deserve to be economists in this world and also in the next.

For my own part, may it please these gentlemen, I am one of those to whom superfluity is a necessity—and I like things and persons in an inverse ratio to the services that they render me. I prefer a Chinese vase, strewn with dragons and mandarins, and of no use to me whatever. . . . Of my talents the one I esteem the most is my incapacity for guessing logogriphs and charades.

Northrop comments that there is nothing in utilitarian economics "which requires that its basic concept of 'utility' be restricted to eliminate the aesthetic object in the manner which [Gautier] has suggested. The Chinese vase is as much an 'economic good' as is a jar of mustard or a ton of coal." He goes on to add:

Nevertheless, in their actual handling and use of the emotional and aesthetic materials given in the purely empirical component of human knowledge, the modern British empirical philosophers and economists did actually neglect the aesthetic and emotional values, which these empirical materials, pursued in and for themselves for their own sake, provide, and did tend to turn them into mere counters, entering them into theoretical scientific relations, for understanding and computing the course of prices in the market place. Thus the equally important aesthetic values which their purely empirical knowledge could have given modern Western mankind were lost, and the modern Western world fell into the very serious fallacy, to which the Marxians as well as the Anglo-Americans are heirs, of tending to identify the whole human value with nothing but restrictedly utilitarian economic value.[7]

If Northrop is right, we still lack the bridge in economics that links the aesthetic and theoretic continuums. We have no way of incorporating into the body of the state's "rational" economic behavior (or even into theoretical economic models of the state) the clues to collective action that are yielded by what is directly sensed. Economists have clearly avoided any calculation that depends upon a cardinal measure of sense perceptions and any scientific judgment regarding human welfare where, in the economist's phrase, an interpersonal comparison of states of satisfaction has to be made.

A completely puristic view on this question would have severely restricted the usefulness of economics in coping with real problems.[8] By limiting himself to situations in which no interpersonal utilities are compared, the economist is reduced to the conclusion that an act is good if no one loses and at least one party gains. This criterion does not let us go very far. For example, progressive income taxes (in fact, any kind of tax protested by one individual), agricultural price supports, Medicare, public education, interstate-highway programs, and

[7] Ibid, pp. 307-10.
[8] Note the asperity with which Turvey refers to the turn that theoretical welfare economics occasionally takes. *Environmental Quality,* p. 49n.

most of our past military expenditures could never be supported on economic grounds in the context of a full-employment economy.

Economic decisions are being and will continue to be made by both economists and noneconomists, unrestrained by knowledge that interpersonal comparisons of utility cannot be scientifically made.[9] We should, therefore, be aware of what we can do in addition to balancing intuitively gains and losses that cannot be measured objectively. Occasionally we can bolster our conclusion with relatively well-supported arguments. For example, a reduction in bacterial contamination of water will reduce morbidity, raise life expectancy, and result in an increase in Gross National Product in excess of the resources absorbed by improving the water supply. Unfortunately, such arguments cannot be used for most of the problems we face. We cannot support a program of atmospheric-pollution abatement on productivity grounds.[10] If in fact, there is a correlation between Gross National Product and atmospheric pollution, or between GNP and any other deficiency, such as lack of urban recreational facilities, congested living conditions, or failure to preserve adequate wilderness areas, we do not yet have the supporting data.

Does our ignorance mean that we should do nothing? There are two answers that support action. The first is that when in doubt, the burden of proof ought to be put on the backs of those who are responsible for deterioration. Let them demonstrate that no one's productivity is impaired. The other answer is that the value of the environment is measured less by changes in man's productivity than by man's direct sensual response—delight, repugnance, or unconcern. Measuring direct sensual response is more difficult than measuring productivity, but the validity of the thing measured, human satisfaction, is more compelling. After one has demonstrated that the improvement has raised GNP, one would still be faced with explaining why an increase in Gross National Product serves as grounds for saying that welfare is increased; measurement of satisfaction can end the matter.

[9] R. B. Brandt, "The Concept of Welfare," and C. W. Churchman, "On the Intercomparison of Utilities," *The Structure of Economic Science,* ed. S. R. Krupp (Englewood Cliffs, N.J., 1966). Both Brandt and Churchman argue that the "purist" position taken by economists is extreme and cannot be sustained without being exposed to weakness. Brandt asks whether we cannot make some assertions about the consciousness of others: that, for example, a proctoscopic examination will hurt more than a mosquito bite; and that the economist will want his child to be anesthetized for an operation. For an excellent essay on "Values and Value Theory in Economics," see Jerome Rothenberg's paper in the same volume.

[10] A. Kneese, *Environmental Quality;* also R. Revelle, "Pollution and Cities," in *The Metropolitan Enigma* (Washington, D.C., 1967), pp. 78-128.

Putting the burden of proof on the polluter, and thereby compelling him to bear all costs of abatement, does not serve as a guide for such questions as the adequacy of recreational facilities. The only rules we have are those that treat man as either a producer or a consumer. If man is considered to be solely a producer, we should have that quantity of recreational facilities for which the marginal dollar spent adds as much to national product as any other expenditure would add. Since this point of view conceives of man as something less than a dog, which is well treated on humanitarian grounds, we may seek to substitute a criterion based on human satisfaction, on the sense of well-being and fulfillment. (Any objective other than productive capacity can be specified.) We face the same problem in this area as in environmental quality: we possess no criterion other than our preference. Someone in authority has to make the decision on the basis of whatever information he can gather regarding the relative strength of our respective preferences.

The overriding importance Anglo-American culture attaches to the theoretic component at the expense of the aesthetic is partially matched by its view of "work" as a source of "negative satisfaction." Work is a duty rather than a privilege, a punishment imposed by God on man rather than an activity that is sought for its own sake. If work is negative utility, idleness is utility. But this is false. We know that man must be engaged in meaningful activity if his mental health is to be sustained. Throughout man's history, this need has been met by the production of goods and services. Now that we are faced with the prospect that man's involvement in the production process will be substantially reduced by the cybernetic revolution, his deep-seated psychological requirement for productive activity will have to be met by activities that now come under the heading of "recreation." (Income will no longer be a necessary inducement for work, nor will income differentials necessarily reflect differences in the ratios of the demand for and supply of various occupations or activities.[11])

An alternative proposition, or at least one that modifies the impact of increased productivity, argues that part of the labor force released from the production of food, shelter, clothing, and equipment will be available for other purposes. We can, therefore, polish up the environment without "sacrificing" any of the goods and services we now consider essential. Increases in labor productivity in the past were met by a general rise in the level of consumption of "necessities," a proliferation in the variety of goods and services, and an increase in leisure—

[11] See M. Harrington, *The Accidental Century* (Baltimore, 1966); especially chap. 8, "The Statues of Daedalus."

all at the expense of a decay in environmental quality. Given a positive desire for work and the probable reduction in per-capita effort needed to supply goods and services, the necessary outlay on environmental improvement for daily living could be costless. In other words, the effort required to improve the environment may itself yield satisfaction that would not be enjoyed otherwise. On top of the positive pleasure of the work, we would have the pleasure of the improved environment.

If human needs for work could be filled in part through opportunities to improve the environment, the burden on recreation to supply the satisfactions of meaningful activity would be lightened. To the extent that we reduce the need for recreation, we reduce those environmental pressures that are hardest to meet, namely, broadly based access to outdoor facilities of high quality. (Compare the ease with which we meet recreational demand for bowling alleys with the difficulty of meeting a demand for lonely contact with nature.) Furthermore, as we devote more work to environmental improvement, we expand man's contact with nature and thereby satisfy those recreational needs that are uniquely dependent upon nature.

I shall assume that in a democratic society we do as well as we can in selecting responsible public officials. In coming to a decision with regard to environmental quality, these officials face a double-barrelled question: what do the people want—how much of other things (measured as a sum of money) are they willing to give up to enjoy these benefits of nature? And do we accept the idea that the people's judgments truly reflect their welfare?

We can find out what people want in various ways: directly, by asking them; indirectly, by inferring preferences from observed action; and, combining the direct and the indirect methods, by exposing people experimentally to alternative situations and asking their reaction as well as observing their behavior. Gilbert F. White has concluded that attitudes toward the environment vary widely, and that we do not fully know how to elicit and interpret information regarding what people think they want.[12] I assume that we shall learn more about what people want, and that knowledge of consumer preferences will help us reduce guesswork.

Better knowledge of what people want leaves unsettled the question of how much reliance should be placed upon expressed preference. The question does not arise in market transactions merely because we

[12] See the paper by G. F. White, "Formation and Role of Public Attitudes," *Environmental Quality.*

choose that it be suppressed: by hypothesis, each consumer is free to
act as he chooses in the market, and therefore he acts in his best interest. So long as transactions are no more consequential than picking
tonight's soup, the consumer is able to survive poor decisions and learn
to make better ones. In the private sector, most decisions are perhaps
marginal and reversible. The opposite is likely to obtain in the public
sector; for this reason, there is less rationale for reliance upon consumer preference. Only if we are also assured that preferences are
based upon adequate information, adequate exposure to and experience of alternatives, and adequate appreciation of the future consequences of present actions, will expressed preferences be consistent
with maximum welfare. A broad "base of citizens who have the
maturity to deal with complex and probabilistic conditions" will, as
White points out, allow us to reduce our reliance upon a technical elite
for making the correct decision. But, as David Lowenthal remarks in
commenting on White's paper, many attitudes are formed and can only
be stated "*after* an environmental decision has been acted on." [13]
Richard Neutra has observed:

Plans for public garbage collection, incineration, and elaborate sewage
disposal first appeared as doctrinary, idealistic dreams conceived in a
vacuum of any possible "financial facts" and altogether devoid of practical
sense. . . . The most ordinary sewer systems of today would have seemed
like black fantastic nightmares to the taxpayers of only one hundred years
ago. [14]

In short, transcendental guidance on the question—How much
should we spend on environmental improvement?—does not exist. The
economic guide that indicates a *minimum environmental quality control level* can be specified as those standards that yield the maximum
Gross National Product net of environmental control costs. [15] Apart
from the fact that we have little information that relates environmental
quality to productivity, this guide is limited because it excludes the
aesthetic factor—that is, consumer preference for high-quality environment at the expense of other goods and services.

Where does this leave us? I think that we are where we always have
been, namely, facing the questions of what we want and of what
machinery we can rely upon to reconcile conflicting individual and

[13] D. Lowenthal, "Assumption Behind the Public Attitudes," *Environmental Quality*.

[14] Neutra, *Survival through Design,* p. 372.

[15] This is tantamount to saying that we raise environmental standards to the
point where the marginal cost of any environmental improvement is equal to the
induced increase in Gross National Product.

social goals. Environmental quality, no less than food, shelter, clothing, and comic books, comes at a cost. In some instances, the cost is ours; in others, it is transferred to the future; in still others, it can be transferred to foreigners. Often there is no well-defined net social cost or social benefit, but rather a transfer of income (real or psychic or both) from one group to another at a given time. The way in which these conflicts are resolved is the stuff of economics, but their resolution is not the economist's responsibility. In fact, if we are to live in a world that is aesthetically and ecologically more satisfying than the one present trends promise, the responsibility is clearly on those whose aesthetic insights are clear and whose knowledge of ecological, physiological, and biological change can be communicated persuasively to society. Deciding what to do is only weakly an "economic" decision; the decisions once made, however, may have various economic impacts.

The most likely effect of a decision to upgrade the physical environment is a change in the pattern of goods and services produced, with no change in Gross National Product—at least in the short run. Long-run effects on Gross National Product will depend upon several different forces, about which we can only speculate. If we are faced with economic rootlessness and lack of purpose as a result of the technological destruction of the psychic importance of work, expenditures on environmental improvement that are economically justified on a long-term basis may be much greater than appear appropriate on the surface. Furthermore, *recreational* experiences may have to provide a psychic substitute for work; such need may justify much larger expenditures on the natural environment that anyone today believes reasonable.

The most significant aspect of the full-employment economy when viewed in a static perspective is that we can have more of A only by sacrificing some of B. Hence "costs" are impressive. For example, Allen Kneese has pointed out that if we were to adopt a standard of pristine purity for all effluents returned to a watercourse, it "might cost $20 billion a year—about as much as we spend for primary and secondary education. I am sure that most people would find such an undertaking ridiculous." [16]

If we shift to a dynamic perspective, the absurdity of absolutely pure

[16] Kneese, *Environmental Quality*, p. 71. See also H. H. Landsberg, "The U.S. Resource Outlook: Quality and Quantity," a paper presented at Swarthmore College, Feb. 1966, for a valuable discussion of economic issues concerned with environmental quality.

water in all our streams diminishes. Twenty billion dollars a year is roughly one third to one half the amount by which one year's GNP exceeds the previous year's GNP at current rates of output. Should we decide, therefore, to restore our streams to purity, the cost is a delay by four to six months of the expected *increase* in all other goods and services that we would otherwise enjoy. (One could argue with equal validity that a doubling of the outlay on primary and secondary education would have a similar effect and would be of even greater merit.)

Another dynamic problem about which we know little but which we should approach optimistically is the impact of alternative environmental standards on technology. The direction of research and development and the flow of new goods and services would be modified in proportion to the rigor of the standards. We can imagine the effect on Du Pont: instead of devoting technical know-how to developing new yarns from petroleum and adding thereby to the industrial waste problem, it would be developing low-cost tertiary treatment of sewage. Changes in other policies would also affect environmental quality. If highway programs were reduced sufficiently, automotive traffic would become so snarled that cities would be compelled to turn to mass-transportation systems, thereby reducing air pollution and releasing land for other uses.

Outlays to improve the environment cannot be described wholly as "consumption" or "capital" expenditures, since both are involved. As a consumption outlay, the effect on GNP of increased expenditure on environment would probably be imperceptible, provided it was offset by reduced expenditure on other forms of consumption. If the offset were a reduction of investment, the net effect would probably be a reduction in the rate of economic growth. Increased outlays by government on natural resources would most likely have a negligible effect on savings and investment if they were financed by consumer charges rather than by taxes. The fee to enter a national park, for example, is likely to compete against other travel items in the family budget. At the same time, changes in outlays on environment made without regard to revenue collected from users serve as an extremely desirable anti-cyclical device. Furthermore, should we ever be serious about the abolition of poverty, large outlays on environmental improvement would serve as an appropriate vehicle for employment of unskilled and other disadvantaged labor classes.

Some forms of blight can be corrected at practically no cost, if we exclude heightened emotions, short-run dislocations, and some income redistribution. In fact, the improvement would be accompanied by a net release of resources to other uses, hopefully less injurious to aesthetic standards. I refer here, of course, to the eyesore created by outdoor advertising—highway and urban. We have generated some momentum toward improving conditions along federal highways. Measured by man-hours of impact, highway beautification will achieve negligible results, since most of us spend most of our time in the city. Efforts to improve conditions are even weaker in town than in the country.

All effects that fall under the heading of "external costs"—that is, all cases where marginal social costs exceed marginal private benefits— imply that there has been a transfer of income from one group to another. The incidence of this income transfer has probably been regressive; the poor have suffered for the benefit of the rich. As we examine alternative ways of financing environmental uplift, our eyes naturally fall upon the polluter. Costs imposed on the polluter will, in the course of events, probably appear in the market price of the goods that are responsible for the pollution. Since products that are a serious threat to environmental quality are likely to be produced and consumed on a large scale, the ultimate incidence of the costs of pollution control is also likely to be "regressive," but no more so than the costs of any widely consumed product. Only if we start with the premise that we have a "natural right" to use the environment for "free" waste disposal would a different incidence of pollution-abatement costs be appropriate.

The "appropriate level" of expenditure on environmental quality is not a figure that can be ascertained any more accurately than the appropriate level of expenditure on education, national defense, or television entertainment. The cost of doing nothing in the face of environmental decline is itself quite high. Only by continuous negotiation, via political and market mechanisms, between those who have demands and those who have resources or control over resources can we determine what we should spend. The "new economics" can help in these negotiations by bridging the aesthetic gap—by developing new methods of analysis that will show us how to incorporate into a measured system the direct sensual responses that up to now have figured solely as intuitively valued side conditions. For what is now measurable, the "old economics" is good enough.

One task of the new economics is to decide when things should *not* be done. For example, new roads into places now accessible only by trail constitute the main threat to continued existence of the relatively small amount of undisturbed country still left. To protect against this, strong industrial and bureaucratic interests must be opposed. There is no bureaucracy or industry organized to prevent unspoiled areas from encroachment, only organizations of amateurs. Perhaps the best immediate solution is a merger of existing like-minded private groups into a national federation that would adequately reflect the growing interest in a primitive natural base.

Most environmental needs can be satisfied only collectively. In order to generate public awareness, expert findings must be broadly disseminated. Occasionally environmental problems are dramatic enough to stimulate a spontaneous response, but more often they reflect, in Secretary Udall's phrase, a "quiet crisis," recognized by relatively few people. For this reason, a network of citizen groups is needed to serve as a link between the experts and the electorate. A wide variety of groups would be desirable: urban, rural, county, state, regional, federal, landscape, air, water, wildlife, architectural, beach, mountain, and so forth. Citizen involvement can be facilitated by a modest federal matching-grant program to finance costs. In addition, a staff position of aesthetician should be created in all agencies concerned with use of resources, public construction, and zoning. The plan of study of the North Atlantic Regional Water Resources Study Coordinating Committee prepared by the North Atlantic Division of the Corps of Engineers includes an appraisal of "aesthetic and cultural values," a step that should be taken as a matter of course in all projects.

If we accept the solutions offered by existing market forces, we shall probably waste and misuse part of our resources. This conclusion rests upon the probability that there is a bias in the "old economics" in favor of underestimation rather than overestimation of needs met by non-marketed goods and services.

A partial cure for underestimation of the importance of non-marketed goods and services is an extension of the price system to activities now excluded. This can be achieved by encouraging the growth of co-operatives and profit-making enterprises into new areas (tax benefits and other subsidies can be conferred), and by extension of user charges by governmental agencies. Such charges can be employed to measure demand as well as to provide a source of funds for the acquisition of new facilities. User charges are an especially attractive way of financing new and better facilities, since the consumer can usually find the funds by reducing outlays on complementary resources or other forms of consumption. So long as access to water is "free," the fisherman can afford to buy a more expensive trout rod. As a consequence, we tend to have better trout rods and poorer fishing waters than a different pricing arrangement would warrant—a condition analogous to the disparity between expenditures on automobiles and highways noted by John Kenneth Galbraith.

To the economist, a user charge also makes possible a more efficient allocation of existing scarce resources. In the absence of a charge, each user employs the resource up to the point where the last unit of use yields a zero benefit. This is socially justifiable only if there is such a large quantity of the resource in question that everyone has as much as he wants, which is patently not the case for most natural resources—such as wilderness, fishing streams, camping facilities, and national parks.

The "new economics" of natural resources and environmental quality will, one hopes, be concerned with deciding which choices should be made by the market and which by other devices, and with increasing the "efficiency" of the market not so much by removing frictions introduced by monopoly and oligopoly, as by improving the connection between aesthetic response and market response. But the economist will need help. Consumer preferences can be formulated sharply only if consumers have an understanding of alternatives. In order to help develop such understanding, the consumer must be exposed to a wider variety of experiences than he now enjoys. Expenditures for environmental improvement on the order of those now going into education are not unreasonable, especially since the needs to be met are not dissimilar.

Rather than question our ability to achieve a high-quality environment, we should ask whether we want it badly enough to pay for it. The costs are not likely to be so great as to absorb resources needed for adequate diet, shelter, clothing, education, medical care, national defense, and whatever else we are likely to include under the heading of "necessities." The debate will be over the kinds of luxuries we want. Yesterday's economics, overwhelmed as it was by the widespread incidence of poverty, malnutrition, slums, unemployment, and severely restricted health facilities, was preoccupied with the need for widespread distribution of necessities. Alfred Marshall has pointed out that not until low-cost coal was available could the poor heat their houses and enjoy decent ventilation at the same time. How many victims of the paleotechnic age would sacrifice a well-ventilated hearth for a more sightly countryside? Today such choices need not be made in the more prosperous countries of Western Europe and certainly not in the United States. If anything, the choices to be made in the United States may have an aesthetic multiplier effect: outlays on environmental improvement not only yield direct satisfaction, but absorb resources that if used otherwise would contribute to environmental decay.

BRINGING SCIENCE UNDER LAW

Harvey Wheeler

In referring to science and technology here, I am invoking the distinction Linus Pauling once made between "developmental" science and what is usually called "pure" science. By developmental science Pauling did not mean merely technology nor did he mean only bureaucratized science, i.e., the mass cooperative endeavor that takes place in great institutes and business corporations. Rather, he had in mind the day-to-day work of the brilliant men who are exploring the implications of the breakthroughs made by first-magnitude geniuses.

One distinctive feature of developmental science is its rapid technological transformation. In fact, the pace of technological application is such that developmental science these days is almost immediately converted into technology. In speaking of science in this article, I have this in mind. I am not, in a word, concerned with the basement-and-garret science of the lonely pioneering genius.

—H. W.

A shock reverberated through the intellectual establishment of the West in the mid-twentieth century when it became apparent that science was not necessarily incompatible with totalitarianism. The West had previously "proved" on paper that science required the so-called free market in ideas, a John Stuart Mill type of liberal democracy, in order to flourish. This, it now became clear, was simply not true.

There had been an even more disturbing revelation earlier. Nazi Germany had shown that even the most "ethical" of the professions, medicine, was capable of turning its humanitarian code into a license to perform gruesome experiments on living people. While this was chilling, it also seemed at the time to be too perverse to be a threat elsewhere. Now, however, with authoritarianism increasing throughout

Harvey Wheeler, "Bringing Science under Law," THE CENTER MAGAZINE, *March 1969. Reprinted by permission.*

the West, and with organ transplants becoming commonplace, we are beginning to have vague fears that something similar to the Nazi corruption of medical science might be looming for all of us.

A third shock occurred after World War II when we learned that our own American scientists had eagerly produced history's most awesome weapons, hardly stopping to consider that moral issues might be involved in their decision to do so. Science, these eminent men insisted, was ethically neutral.

Recently, a technological development renewed our concern. Dramatic developments in mathematical logic, cybernation, systems analysis, and the planning-programming-budgeting approach to administrative control have been giving us reason of late to believe that a science-spawned managerial revolution may yet be in the offing. During the past twenty years or so, it has begun to appear that management may gain access to techniques and tools that could be used to achieve their managerial ends without concern for the public good.

The appearance of a new technology, of course, need not necessarily be a matter of concern unless another factor is present; that is, the new technology and its practitioners must be engaged in doing something that intimately affects the public interest. When this happens there are grave potentials for harming, as well as benefiting, society. The question, then, arises as to whether or not we can or should act collectively to inhibit the harmful effects that may result from the bad uses of science and technology. This is our present problem.

Currently many solutions are being offered. One is to find some way of revivifying the classical idea of the profession. Another is to create some sort of government agency charged with coordinating science policy. Both solutions strike me as seriously deficient. Nothing less than an entirely new look at science will suffice. This requires discussion of what has come to be known as the scientific revolution.

The process by which the A-bomb was created pointed up the inner political logic of that revolution. It also laid bare the corrosive impact developmental science is having on our traditional liberal democratic dogmas and practices. The birth of the bomb demonstrated once and for all that neither the people, their elected representatives, nor even bureaucratic experts are competent any longer to "legislate" about scientific problems. The traditional deliberative processes of Western democracy, it is clear, were undermined when it became apparent that they could not cope with the implications of contemporary science for public policy.

But there was also a positive side. The implications of the new science ranged far beyond the interests and activities of the scientific establishment itself; fundamental scientific innovations, such as those relating to atomic energy and solid-state physics, furnished the foundations on which the very shape of society would be built in the future. Important scientific discoveries had always brought about profound social changes, of course. But as long as these discoveries occurred infrequently and without conscious anticipation, much less design, one could not say that they were called forth politically. However, with the maturity of the sciences, Francis Bacon's *New Atlantis* became a prescription for the present rather than a fanciful vision of the future. The time, then, had arrived when science made it possible to "legislate" the shape of the future.

This shifted politics to a new plane. Those who had produced the atom bomb were actually the first to see that they had wrought not only a scientific but a political revolution—legislatures might continue to operate in their accustomed fashion, politicians might continue to campaign for office as of old, but those who were really determining the outlines of the future belonged to the scientific, rather than the political, establishment. As a consequence of these developments, the significance of today's scientific revolution can be summarized simply: the revolution has brought about social transformations; relationships between theory and practice that seemingly had been firmly established by the Industrial Revolution were reversed. This change means, among other things, that in the world created by the scientific revolution the critical force in society will no longer be the flow of capital but scientific and technological innovation. The most fateful struggles in that society will be fought over the efforts to direct and control these innovations. This is where constitutionalization comes in.

Our notion of legislation and/or constitutionalization has long been built on two assumptions, neither of which is now acceptable. The first was that men of common prudence and wisdom are capable of understanding every political problem that needs to be understood. The second was that such men could make laws to deal with these problems. The scientific revolution is undermining the first of these assumptions by posing problems too technical for laymen to fathom. It is undermining the second by making it impossible for legislatures to lay the foundation for the future. The result is already evident; we either have to invent new procedures for handling science policy or be ruled by technology.

How do we deal with the problem? At first blush, it might seem enough merely to strengthen our governing institutions with more scientific advisers. But this is not enough; it won't do. The reason is that the scientific expert has to be such a narrow specialist he cannot acquire the general knowledge necessary to grasp the social and philosophical implications of even those technical matters on which he is an acknowledged expert. The same thing applies in reverse. The generalist's knowledge of any one specialty is not thorough enough for him to master the complex problems now associated with science and technology.

There is a philosophical issue here. It turns on a very old argument about science—one as old as the temptation of Adam and Eve, the curiosity of Pandora, or Prometheus' defiance of the gods. Perhaps of all such myths, the Doctor Faustus story is the most pertinent.

That myth embodied the essential ethic of medieval science—something the men of the Middle Ages took very seriously. Remember they did not look upon science as ineffectual. On the contrary, everyone believed in its power—black magic it was called—just as everyone believed in white magic, the power of miracles. But one magic was satanic and the other godly. One defied God and incurred His wrathful retribution; the other entailed His bountiful intervention.

The war between the two varieties of magic was carried over into attacks on magicians who practiced the black arts of alchemy and astrology and employed spells, secret words, cabalistic designs, talismanic charms, and amulets to gain power over the spirits who—it was widely believed—were in control of human events. As the various departments of magic matured into the post-medieval sciences, the pioneers were anxious to purge science of this reliance on supernatural forces. At the same time they were eager to proclaim their own religious orthodoxy. Such, at least, was the aim of Copernicus, Galileo, Brahe, and Vesalius. It was also the later concern of Descartes, Bacon, Newton, and Leibnitz. But, though science was changing the face of the earth, the theologians still looked at the world in the old manner. As a result, the old war between black and white magic turned into a new war between science and religion.

The leading early apologist for the new view of science was Francis Bacon. Bacon claimed that science had no theological significance; like heaven and earth, theology and science were simply different realms of truth. To make his case, Bacon and his followers invoked the Biblical text that distinguished between the things owing to Caesar and those owing to God. They argued from it that a man could be faithful to one and yet serve the other. Beyond this, Bacon held that there was something intrinsically humanistic about science. It advanced human knowledge, which in turn contributed to human progress. The only thing necessary, then, was to keep science free of dogma and authority.

Bacon's position in time became the professional ideology of science, to such an extent that it seemed to be a self-evident truth. All seemed to be going well—the ideology went largely unchallenged—until the contemporary scientific revolution reopened certain ethical issues that had remained closed since the seventeenth century. We are in a sense, then, back to Doctor Faustus.

Recall that the Faustian legend was informed with a view that had science dependent on the special intervention of supernatural forces. Medieval science had sought for ultimate power and knowledge—omnipotence and omniscience, the attributes of God. The scientists of that period, in a word, had pursued the most fundamental quests. They tried to plumb directly to the secrets of the creation of life. They sought the magical elixir that would bring everlasting youth, searched for the philosopher's stone that would convert the baser metals into the finer, puzzled over the secret "signatures" of events that would unlock the mysteries of past and future and produce control over the paths of the planets and the vagaries of the weather. They propitiated spirits who could empower them to move mountains, change men into different shapes, and permit moving about through space and time at will. With such goals, the prospects for science were more revolutionary, and the risks incurred by its practitioners far more dangerous, than what was to come later. Medieval science, then, faced up to the questions about men who would play God. The advent of the early-modern sciences required a new informal "contract" in place of the older one Faustus had negotiated with Satan. According to the new pact, scientists would abandon all the quests that were disturbing to theologians in return for freedom to work without interference. As scientists they would stay out of God's province, concerning themselves only with the problems of this world. Theologians and philosophers for their part would stop pillorying science. Francis Bacon drafted this "contract" for the Anglo-Saxon world; it was also described by Descartes and Leibnitz.

Although modern science abandoned an over-all ethic, it did adopt a kind of internal code. The scientist was supposed to maintain his methodological and intellectual honesty, but that was all. Hence, from a deeper standpoint, early-modern science was ethically barren, and proud of it. This, however, will no longer do. Science today is once more delving into something like the quests pursued by medieval magic. For example, the deliberate synthesis of miracle fabrics, exotic metals, and precious stones has become an everyday occurrence. The genetic code through which the rudimentary substances of life are ordered into their distinctive shapes and functions has been deciphered. The French physicist Pierre Auger has even suggested that molecular biologists may succeed in recalling previously extinct animal forms from the burial grounds of history. The contemporary scientist must, then, face the ethical problem Doctor Faustus confronted. Unfettered freedom for developmental science is no longer tolerable. Scientists themselves recognize it, as was evident in the bad consciences of some of those who built the atom bomb.

The distinguished physicist Max Born has pointed to a source for the ethical corrosion in modern science. For men to be ethical they must perceive the moral implications of the alternative actions open to them. This is not necessarily a pragmatic or utilitarian view of ethics, for even if one holds that such things as murder are evil the hard question comes when we have to decide in a given case exactly what constitutes "murder" and whether or not there are circumstances that might justify it. Ordinarily, ethical judgements of this kind are not too difficult. If a military commander orders a subordinate to commit a crime against humanity, the soldier may decide he has no alternative but to obey. However, he cannot claim ignorance of the ethical issue. The case of the scientist, though, is somewhat different. When a scientist sets out to produce atomic bombs or death rays, the preliminary research may be on such an abstract level that the connection between pure science and the purpose for the research effectively disappears. The scientists working on such projects can dispel any ethical qualms they might have by intoning the traditional ideology: any augmentation of knowledge must be good. In short, ethical judgments require making a connection between actions and effects, and it is this connection that science dissolves. Moreover, the full implications of a scientific discovery may not become completely apparent for many years. A scientist may work in full innocence only to learn years later that he helped produce a horror.

It has always been true, of course, that an action in the present may have unforeseeable harmful effects in the distant future. The invention of the automobile is an all too familiar illustration. A similar separation—not in time but in function—accompanies bureaucratization. Bureaucracy transforms people into impersonal functionaries. This was one reason Nazi concentration-camp executives could go about their duties seemingly detached from the atrocities they administered. A similar effect occurs when science becomes bureaucratized—the individual scientist deals with so minute a segment of the over-all project that he becomes almost as detached from the implications of his work as Adolf Eichmann alleged he was. Now contemporary science is raising this separation between actions and their effects to a new level. The more profound a scientific innovation, the more universal its potential applications—and the more difficult it becomes to foresee its extended effects. Professor Born's mournful conclusion was that the contemporary scientific revolution has destroyed ethics, ushering mankind into a new world that is not only post-industrial but post-ethical.

Ethics is philosophical but practical; science is logical and mathematical in form. The result is that scientific knowledge accumulates from generation to generation like the compound interest on savings deposits. Each new scientist stands on the shoulders of those who have gone before, leaving behind him a hundred more who will do the same in turn. Each fledgling scientist begins his career by mastering the distilled essences of the work of his predecessors; his lifetime is devoted to adding elements to the accumulated scientific edifice. He need not, indeed, start out by retracing all the laborious steps that have brought science from its earliest beginnings to its present elevated state. If that were necessary, the progress of science would be limited to how much of it could be assimilated anew by each successive neophyte: science could not develop beyond the limits of scientific powers one man could bring to bear in the course of a single lifetime.

This latter condition, however, was roughly the case before the advent of modern science. Prior to that, the quest for both scientific and ethical knowledge proceeded in much the same way. Both were subject to similar limitations and neither could systematically develop and accumulate its findings. Bacon, realizing this, was right in seizing upon augmentation as the trademark of early-modern science.

When, in the seventeenth century, science acquired this power of augmentation, the growth of scientific knowledge shot up at an exponential rate, while ethical knowledge remained, and remains to this day, much as before. The social effect of such knowledge—that is, its capacity for good—is limited by the amount of wisdom individual men can acquire during their lifetime, for one does not assimilate the truth of an ethical precept the way one grasps the truth of a mathematical solution. On the contrary, one must first become a philosopher to perceive the validity of the teachings of the wise men who have gone before. Coué was wrong, with his doctrine that every day in every way we are getting better and better. His error, and that of the doctrine of progress, was in assuming that the augmentation observable in the sciences was applicable to moral philosophy. On the contrary, moral philosophy has progressed but little during its entire twenty-five hundred years of history.

Each man must learn and apply ethical truths for himself. This is an additional basis for the contemporary separation between science and ethics. As science progresses cumulatively the problems it poses become progressively more numerous and complex. The gap between science and ethics widens with each passing hour. Some relief might develop were science able to extend human longevity, permitting us to devote more time to the quest for wisdom. Short of this, however, the only solution would appear to lie in a concerted effort to constitutionalize science, so that its progress and development can be subjected to planning and control. A new ethic of science must be developed. We face a genuine culture crisis. This would be true even if, improbably, science were to grind to a halt and technological developments based on it were to cease. If today's life scientists are correct, the present crisis will shortly take an even more ominous turn.

The life sciences—biology, genetics, and so forth—are on the brink of a revolutionary development that will usurp the primacy that the physical sciences have enjoyed for over three hundred years. But note one difference: tampering with life processes demands ethical norms. Sciences that deal with life processes cannot avoid questions concerned with the goals, ends, and purposes of life. The tragedy, however, is that such questions do not interest most scientists, while philosophers by and large are not interested in what science is doing. Nonetheless, anything connected with the life processes involves ethics. It is *there,* unavoidable, lying at the heart of the life sciences. Yet, the biological sciences matured under the hegemony of the physical sciences—and, more's the pity, their recent spectacular advances have come from molecular biology, whose operating assumption is that life processes can be reduced to the principles of physics. The life sciences, then, have reached maturity with the amoral pursuit of "objectivity" that long characterized the physical sciences. Inasmuch as life is intrinsically normative, the contemporary ethical poverty of biology must be due to some more fundamental development that made this distortion seem plausible. I suggest it was the ancient maneuver whereby all nature, life as well as inert matter, was made profane. The maneuver predated modern science by nearly sixteen hundred years. It can be traced back to that point in the Western tradition when both nature and society were secularized. The striking fact is that not science but Christianity turns out to be the culprit.

Prior to the advent of Christianity there had been no secular society and there had been no secular view of nature in Western tradition. On the contrary, as with practically every other known culture, society and nature were regarded as intrinsically sacral. This, of course, was the point at issue between the early Christians and the ancient Romans. The Christians' way of stating this was that the one true God forbade their participation in the rituals of any other god. Viewed in the light of today's enlarged perspective, this commandment was preposterous. Worse, it smacked of the colossal effrontery of the unlettered. The urbane Romans, ironically destined to be known as pagans (peasants), pointed out that what Christians overdramatically objected to as Emperor worship was but the ritual celebration of the social order. That occurred in almost every society. Similar Roman rituals also celebrated the natural order. But the early Christians—today's Jehovah's Witnesses make much the same point—narrowly restricted the sacral to the attributes of their own remote triune God.

The issue was brought to a head four centuries later in the dramatic showdown between Saint Augustine and Bishop Faustus. Bishop Faustus represented the West's last chance to reject the hard-shell eschatology of the Christian extremists. But Augustine won that momentous battle and proceeded to establish the dualistic doctrine of the divine heavenly city and the corrupt city of this world as the official world view of the Western tradition. What Augustine wrought was, in effect, the birth of an ideology that ultimately permitted Western science to take an amoral approach to nature. In the light of the scientific revolution of our times, the Augustine-Faustus debate must be revived, overturned, and an ethical view of man, society, and nature reëstablished.

How would the control of developmental science, what I call constitutionalization, work? Perhaps the A.E.C., Telstar, and the T.V.A. can serve as examples. A public corporation for developmental science can be chartered and given its constitution. Civilian control can be installed and charged with the responsibility for several functions that are now not being performed at all. Most obvious is the need for an ombudsman to process public complaints as well as complaints from scientists inside the Establishment. The ombudsman should have positive, as well as negative, or corrective, functions. That is, in addition to investigating alleged evils he should also see that the scientific enterprise achieves its publicly approved goals. This would require a special court system of adjudication, complete with appeal procedures.

To approach science in this way requires a new conception of constitutional theory—an architectonic approach to the politics of science. In such a framework, intellectual endeavors would be thought of in broad political terms, rather than merely in terms of the narrow desires of those who wish to pursue knowledge for its own, or their own, sake. It would also require fresh thought about problems such as representation, which we thought the eighteenth century had put to rest for all times. If there is to be a new kind of public corporation for science, if it is to be under civilian control, and if the public will is to make its voice heard, then there must be some way for that will to find expression. This raises the "legislative" question of how to furnish science with responsible policy-forming and goal-establishing functions. We know that the scandalous scientific boondoggling of the recent past must be prevented. Scientists themselves have publicized certain unsavory aspects of "big science"—the space program and the Mohole project are examples. In addition to the fact that science may harm us, scientists sometimes make incredibly bad judgments about the conduct of their own affairs. Hence, science must be provided with a specially designed legislature, and, for civilian control to work, there must be participation by citizens as well as by professional scientists.

It may be that the envisioned public corporation should have a bicameral legislature, one house composed of scientists and the other of public members. One way to conceive of this would be to follow our traditional Constitutional wisdom and put financial controls and ratification powers in the public chamber and reserve the responsibility for initiating projects for the scientific chamber, with special provision for joint sessions. The proposal for a bicameral approach to science planning and policy formation immediately raises the question of a separation of powers, a checks-and-balances feature. Each house would exercise restraint on the other; concerted action would require the cooperation of both. Obviously, this new constitutionalized scientific order should not slavishly follow the established American Constitutional separation-of-powers mechanism, but certain analogues do seem promising.

This raises the question of federalism. The general Constitutional idea of federalism is "subsidiarity." It means a preference for the local over the centralized solution to problems. There may be a need in the scientific order for a special version of this principle. This should be considered in the context of a proposed bill of rights for science. Subsidiarity dictates that every possible scientific issue be dealt with at decentralized levels, rather than being disposed of in centralized institutions. One of the big chief sources of the evils we now observe in "big science" derives primarily from its centralization. Perhaps something like an anti-trust approach to science ought to be provided for. This might be the best way to protect local autonomy for our centers of scientific research.

This brings us to the necessity of educating the general public about leading scientific issues. Each sector could serve this need in its own characteristic manner. Representatives from the public sector would have to qualify for office in some way and the best way would be for them to stand for election on the basis of general programs for the development of science. Scientists, in qualifying themselves for selection by their peers, would be required to address themselves to more technical issues. Their educational role would be to uncover the extended social implications of the scientific matters at issue. A useful example was the Pauling-Teller debates a few years ago. These debates brought about a widespread public discussion of complex scientific issues. What I have proposed would regularize such public debates about the basic issues of science policy, conducted regularly by leading scientists.

There is a danger that in democratizing science we may submit it to the whims of public opinion. Many feel this would be better than leaving it to the scientists, but, of course, neither is ideal. Science is not the private property of scientists any more than the economy is the private property of businessmen, or the government the private property of politicians. Corruption occurs when scientists forget this. Actually, a scientist is much like a real-estate investor who has bought property in the path of an expanding city. When the value of his possession rises he begins to talk and act as if *he* were responsible for it. However, the individual scientist is merely the one who happens to be "in possession" at the time that knowledge is provided by massive institutional, economic, and political forces of his day. Perhaps we need a new Henry George to point out that if anybody "owns" science, it is the people themselves.

In setting our own house in order, we must face the serious problem that concerns our universities and the relationships between developmental science and the proper approach to higher education. Revelations about Project Camelot and defense-oriented university research programs have made it obvious that developmental science has already distorted our educational processes and corrupted the idea of the university. The constitutional approach allows us to correct this by separating the big developmental scientific institutes and laboratories from the universities, placing them instead under public corporations. Indeed, *all* our present professional and technical schools should properly be transferred to some such public corporation, freeing the university to safeguard the philosophic needs, the theoretical integrity, and the educational proprieties of the pursuit of knowledge without the contamination that political, financial, and practical needs now impose.

Two things that have corrupted the sciences and professions, of course, are money and power. Whenever an endeavor becomes extremely powerful or highly profitable, its moral integrity is threatened. This would make it appear that the only people capable of maintaining an ethic for a profession are the young, before they have used it to become rich and influential. We might recall a proposition once put forward by Harold Laski. He claimed that the effective regulators of the American judiciary were the law journals, which are run by the young before they have made any money practicing law. Perhaps we can somehow institutionalize the critical and ethical talents of youth and focus them on the conduct of the sciences, as is now done for the judiciary by the law journals. Perhaps what we need, among other things, is a number of science review journals devoted primarily to the social, political, and ethical implications of developmental science.

There must be some way of protecting the integrity of the scientific enterprise from corruption by either scientist or non-scientist. Traditionally such aims have been achieved through bills of rights. We are concerned here with matters such as academic freedom, the rights of students and teachers, the needs of the new Linus Paulings, the Oppenheimers, the Thorstein Veblens, and all who aspire to similar status. We are reminded once again that intellectuals are not necessarily those best qualified to understand the true needs of their own enterprise— just as businessmen are not necessarily those best qualified to understand the true needs of the economic order. Yet today's bureaucratic scientist continues to echo the nineteenth-century businessman's individualist ideology. A hundred years ago the laissez-faire ideology may have been adequate for the needs of both scientists and society. Today, however, the arguments for unhampered science are as irrelevant as the arguments for free private enterprise by mammoth corporations, or the arguments for an unregulated press by the mass-media monopolies. Three-quarters of research and development grants are for directed research. A monopoly already exists in science, and scientific freedom is largely a myth. Already, grave issues concerning intellectual freedom have arisen. Are there any projects the scientist has a right to refuse to work on? Lewis Branscom has made it clear that even if present trends continue unhampered some kind of bill of rights for science and letters will have to be instituted. The archaic ideology of science and the overweening hubris of the scientist must somehow be brought down to size. The most obvious way to do this is to provide for the constitutionalization of science in a special polity combining principles of both democracy and the rule of law. Within this context the liberties appropriate to intellectual endeavors can find proper expression and preservation.

A bill of rights reenforces the aforementioned need for a special court system. It would be necessary to provide for a prosecutor, subpoena power, and trial-like hearings. It is not possible for the common law side of our judicial system to assimilate easily these novel problems of adjudication. We will need a new jurisprudence of science, comparable to that we have developed for administrative law.

Policy formation for science means planning. It may well be that the essential nature of planning in the future will become subsumed under science policy—any other outcome would be almost inconceivable. No matter what problem we come up against—planning for the city of the future, demographic planning, resource conservation and development planning, or transportation planning—each begins from a scientific foundation and all have to be integrated into an over-all developmental program for the scientific enterprise. This requires Constitutional provision for science planning—a need that underscores the failure of our present Constitution to provide for planning of any kind. Even if science as such were to present no Constitutional issue, the need for planning should. A number of additional problems would remain even if all the innovations proposed above were to work perfectly. One of these is the relationship between the scientific and the military establishments. Three supplementary control devices may be required. One is a post-audit. This should be thought of in two ways: first, as a simple technical and financial post-audit to find out how appropriations were spent and whether irregularities occurred. But there must also be a *substantive* post-audit to inspect what actually was done in carrying out stated policies. This can be thought of as a retrospective application of planning-programming-budgeting techniques. We need to know whether space-program research and development was diverted into electronics R & D with commercial marketing potentials; whether funds for molecular biology were diverted into pharmacological research; and on down the line. Institutionalized post-audit devices are not sufficient because, as with the Army Inspector General and the federal regulatory agencies, the inspector tends to become a part of the system he inspects. Something similar to the British Commission of Inquiry is needed as well, and its quadrennial reports could coincide with the planning process and electoral campaigns. Such a commission, if staffed by men of eminence and independence, would guarantee a quality to its reports so often produced by presidential commissions.

Another issue of major importance is the larger ecological aspect of the scientific order. What is this scientific order? What are its boundaries? Taken most broadly, its boundaries are those of the universe itself. This means no nation by itself can constitutionalize its own science. Suppose America had decided to develop solid-state physics and transistor applications to maximize their usefulness to the public good and avoid the dislocations too rapid exploitation brings. Similar questions concerning the computer are actually before us. It may be that intensive research on the cultural implications of the computer should be carried out before we start using it to make everything from shoes to teaching machines, flooding the consumer market with hastily conceived gadgetry. In Russia, there was insufficient hardware for immediate application when the computer first appeared. As a result, the Russians were forced, as they had been earlier in the field of rocketry, to address themselves first to the theoretical implications of the computer while they waited for the hardware to become more widely available. It may be that this simple technological lag permitted them to take a wiser view of the role of the computer than we had in this country, where it seeped through the technological order as a result of the extension of ballistics-control devices to industrial and administrative processes. But the Russian example also makes clear that no one country, not even a dictatorship, can really plan in the realm of developmental science. The history of the transistor shows that Japan, or some other country, may come along and flood the world market. Ultimately what is needed, then, is a concerted effort on a world level. It makes little difference what one nation decides to do about the transistor if any other is able to do the contrary.

So it is apparent that there is an international, or transnational, aspect to the problem of constitutionalizing science. We already have transnational industrial corporations. Perhaps the scientific order in its constitutional mode must follow the example of the transnational industrial combine. Perhaps both in unison will provide us with avenues leading toward world order. In any case, the problem of world order is here, built into contemporary developmental science. There is no way to avoid it, and we must recognize that efforts to control science must be integrated throughout the world.

POLLUTION CONTROL: AN INTERNATIONAL PERSPECTIVE

Dennis Livingston

To many of the increasing numbers of scientists and laymen concerned with the disruptive effects on life resulting from the growth of industrial civilization, the proper strategy for reversing the undesirable trends has appeared to be a combination of alerting the public to the dangers of environmental pollution, accelerating research and development of pollution abatement technology, and pressuring federal, state, and local legislative bodies for the passage of effective anti-pollution laws. I believe this strategy must be supplemented by awareness of the fact that appropriate legal remedies are also available on the international level. Indeed, given that any large-scale environmental hazards are international in their effects on the future development of humanity, it seems logical to study the possibility of corrective legal action in the same international perspective.

To those unacquainted with postwar developments in international law, it might seem at first that there is little to hope for from this area. However, states have a reasonably good record of adhering to standards seen to be in their mutual self-interest and convenience; the obvious desirability of such standards makes less serious the absence of any permanent international police force available for enforcing them by threat of coercion. In addition, international law has been expanding from its traditional concern with regulating the diplomatic and military relations of states into such new concerns as the setting of guidelines for the exploitation of the resources of the continental shelf and the

Dennis Livingston, "Pollution Control: An International Perspective," SCIENTIST AND CITIZEN, *September 1968. Reprinted by permission.*

exploration of outer space, the elaboration of basic human rights applicable to all individuals, and the evolution of rules applicable to relations among the proliferating number of international organizations.

There is as yet, unfortunately, nothing as firm as an international ecological law, equivalent in its elaborateness of doctrine to, say, the centuries-old law of the sea. This reflects the fact that attention to the widely varying hazards of environmental contamination is itself relatively recent. In any case, the beginnings of such an international ecological law may be gleaned from an overview of the standards the international community has elaborated to date in various fields relevant to pollution abatement and prevention.

POLLUTION IN AREAS UNDER TERRITORIAL JURISDICTIONS

Oil Pollution of the High Seas. As one might expect, states have most readily come to agreement on some sort of anti-pollution standards written into binding treaty form with regard to areas not within the jurisdiction of any single state. The high seas comprise such an area. It includes that portion of the oceans beyond the offshore territorial waters (usually three to twelve miles) of states. Those working for the abatement and prevention of the pollution of the seas by oil and radioactive waste, the primary focuses of such efforts to date, have the additional advantage of building on long tradition that holds the high seas to be the common property of mankind, to be used by each state in a manner that takes into account the reasonable interest of other states.

States adhering to the Geneva Convention on the High Seas of 1958 are required, in general terms, to pass laws aimed at preventing the oil pollution of the seas that can result from the various uses made of these waters, the seabed, and the seabed's subsoil.[1]

The only detailed treaty to date on this subject is the Convention for the Prevention of Pollution of the Sea by Oil of 1954, amended in 1962.[2] The amended treaty, now in force, forbids the discharge from

---

[1] Geneva *Convention on the High Seas*, Apr. 29, 1958–Sept. 30, 1962, 13 UST 2312 (TIAS 5200). UST refers to United States Treaties and other International Agreements series (each treaty has a TIAS number); the first date given for a treaty is the date it was signed, the second, if any, the date it came into force.

[2] London *International Convention for the Prevention of Pollution of the Sea by Oil,* May 12, 1954–July 26, 1958, 12 UST 2989 (TIAS 4900). *Amendments of the . . .*, Apr. 11, 1962–May 18, 1967. The latter may be found in Senate Committee on Commerce, *Treaties and Other International Agreements Containing Provisions on Commercial Fisheries, Marine Resources, Sport Fisheries, and Wildlife to Which the Untied States Is Party* (Washington, D.C.: U.S. Government Printing Office, 1965), pp. 327-42.

tankers of over 150 tons gross tonnage of oil or oily mixture into a prohibited zone comprising all marine waters within fifty miles of the nearest land; provisions are made for specific zones of even greater distance (for instance, 100 miles off the northeastern United States). After May 1970, the anti-discharge rule will apply to virtually all other ships of over 500 tons gross tonnage. Discharge of any oil *anywhere* is also prohibited to ships of 20,000 tons gross tonnage or more if their building contract was placed after May 1967, although such ships' masters may discharge oil outside the prohibited zones if they believe "special circumstances" make this necessary. The government of each state signing the treaty must promote the provision of facilities that can receive the oily wastes remaining for disposal aboard ships and tankers at those of its ports, oil loading terminals, and ship repair ports it deems most suitable. On their part, ships and tankers to which the convention applies must maintain oil record books, readily available for inspection, in which are recorded oil discharge operations. Any violation by a vessel of these rules is punishable under the laws of the state in which it is registered. Penalties imposed are to be severe enough to discourage unlawful discharge and are not to be less than those the state imposes for equivalent violations within its territorial seas. Any signatory government may furnish evidence to another government that one of the latter's ships has violated the convention.

The convention, while not the last word on the subject, is a good start toward the goal of making it economically and technologically feasible to prohibit the discharge of persistent oils anywhere on the high seas. It has given an impetus to research in the technology of oil pollution abatement and detection, and has impelled governments to reevaluate their national oil pollution prevention laws. The U.S. Congress has been considering the revision of present federal oil pollution legislation, whose enforcement recent amendments have made somewhat difficult.

The most obvious problem with the convention is that vessels registered in states which have not signed it remain controlled on the high seas only to the degree required by their national laws, which may be quite lax. A weak link within the convention itself is the necessity of gathering vital evidence of an unlawful discharge from the oil record book of the alleged wrongdoer himself; clearly, advances are mandatory in the techniques of detecting discharges and tracing them back to particular ships. Finally, the prohibitions of the convention do not apply in cases of oil discharged from a ship in order to secure the safety of the cargo and of those on board, or in cases of oil which escapes from a ship due to damage or unavoidable leakage, provided reasonable efforts have been made to minimize the escape. All this leaves a rather big liability loophole, and indeed, there is nothing known to me in present international law that could cope with or prevent large-scale disasters like the *Torrey Canyon* incident (the basis of Great Britain's suit for damages is the occurrence of this accident in her territorial waters).

Faced with such issues, as well as proposals for setting aside specified sea lanes for oil tankers and international certification for the senior officers of large tankers, the assembly of the Intergovernmental Maritime Consultative Organization, a United Nations specialized agency, will hold an extraordinary session in November to discuss the oil pollution question.

Radioactive Pollution of the High Seas. The Geneva Convention on the High Seas contains an article with regard to radioactive pollution similar to its general statement on oil pollution; each state is to take into account relevant international standards in preventing pollution of the seas from the dumping of radioactive waste.

In contrast to the case of oil pollution, there is to date no more detailed international treaty setting forth standards with reference to the dumping into the high seas of radioactive waste material from land-based nuclear reactors. This matter is still largely in the hands of the relatively few states who use the seas for disposal, with relevant national regulations varying in their concern and effectiveness. However, at a minimum, it could be argued that any state, or operator licensed by it, whose waste-disposal methods were so unreasonable and unsafe, as judged by the standards of the scientific community or such private groups as the International Commission on Radiological Protection (ICRP), as to endanger the reasonable uses of the seas made by other states would be guilty of violating the freedom of seas enjoyed by the international community in general; harm to life or property resulting from the wrongful activity might then give rise to an international liability on the part of the licensing state.[3] As it happens, the International Atomic Energy Agency (IAEA) is working on a radioactive disposal treaty, and the Agency, as well as those of its members who practice disposal into the sea, will surely be influenced by the recommendations of an IAEA Ad hoc Panel which issued a report on this matter several years ago.[4] The panel recom-

[3] M. S. McDougal and W. T. Burke, *The Public Order of the Oceans: A Contemporary International Law of the Sea* (Yale, 1962), pp. 852-68.

[4] Report of the Ad hoc Panel, *Radioactive Waste Disposal into the Sea,* IAEA Safety Series no. 5 (1961), pp. 77-79. Recommendations and resolutions of such groups often take on the force of law when concerned states habitually put the proposals into practice, even in the absence of binding treaty obligations.

mended against the release into the sea of highly radioactive wastes, but suggested that under controlled conditions wastes of low and intermediate activity could be deposited into the sea at designated disposal sites, using ICRP and IAEA standards for guidelines.

These recommendations, along with the relevant national laws, would also apply to the disposal of radioactive waste from nuclear-powered ships. In addition, there does exist the Brussels Convention on the Liability of Operations of Nuclear Ships of 1962.[5] While this convention is not directly concerned with waste disposal methods or standards, it is relevant in that the deterrent liability system it establishes for nuclear ship operators in the event of nuclear damage should further stimulate the safest possible operation of such ships whose flag states sign the convention. Basically, the convention charges the operator of a nuclear ship with liability regardless of his fault or negligence (absolute liability) for any damage to life or property, anywhere in the world, which it can be proved was caused by an incident involving the nuclear fuel or waste products of such a ship. But the liability for damage is not absolutely absolute; no liability results from harm due directly to acts of war, and the operator may be exonerated in whole or part if he can prove that the nuclear damage suffered by the claimant resulted from something done by the latter with intent to cause damage. Liability is limited to 100 million for one nuclear ship regarding any one nuclear incident. Further provisions specify maintaining insurance, time limits for bringing action, and the national courts before which action for compensation may be brought.

The United States has not signed this treaty, as it includes warships within its terms. However, apart from national safety regulations applying to its nuclear ship *Savannah,* the United States has negotiated bilateral agreements with the countries whose ports the ship visits. A typical agreement with Norway specifies that the U.S. Government ensures that no disposal of radioactive wastes from the ship will occur while it is within Norwegian territorial waters without prior approval of Norwegian authorities.[6]

[5] Brussels *Convention on Liability of Operators of Nuclear Ships,* May 25, 1962– . This may be found in Joint Atomic Energy Committee, *Selected Materials on Atomic Energy Indemnity Legislation,* (Washington, D.C.: U.S. Government Printing Office, 1965), pp. 302-11. Also relevant is Annex C to the *Final Act of the International Conference on Safety of Life at Sea* (1960) concerning "Recommendations Applicable to Nuclear Ships," 16 UST 185. See, in general, L. M. Hydeman and W. H. Berman, *International Control of Nuclear Maritime Activities,* (Michigan, 1960).

[6] *Maritime Matters: Use of Norwegian Ports and Territorial Waters by the N.S. Savannah,* Mar. 1, 1963–May 8, 1964, 15 UST 434 (TIAS 5576).

Regarding its nuclear submarines, the U.S. prohibits the discharge of radioactive coolant water within port; on the high seas, such water must be below one-tenth the radioactive level accepted as safe by international organizations before discharge. A good illustration of the problems that can arise when such unilateral standards fall under suspicion by other states, and of continuing public sensitivity to the issue of radioactivity, was recently provided in the *Swordfish* incident. During the period last May while this submarine was visiting the harbor of Sasebo, Japan, Japanese monitoring devices detected a brief rise in the radioactivity of harbor waters. A team from the U.S. Atomic Energy Commission investigated and reported that the submarine was not responsible for the radioactivity increase. Apparently, this decision has not been entirely satisfactory to a part of the Japanese public and some Japanese scientists, especially as the latter, in their own studies, were not permitted access to all the information available from the *Swordfish*.[7]

It is possible that the future will see the recommendations of the IAEA Panel put into practice, as states either turn over entirely to an international organization responsibility for dumping their radioactive waste into the seas or themselves continue to carry out such dumping, but under the control and regulations of an international organization. In this regard, the European Nuclear Energy Agency, an organ of the Organization for Economic Cooperation and Development, recently supervised the dumping of packaged solid radioactive waste into the eastern Atlantic.

Pollution of Antarctic Waters. One region singled out for special attention has been the Antarctic. According to the Antarctic Treaty of 1959, signatory states laying claim to that continent suspend, but do not give up, these claims for the duration of the treaty. In the context of preserving wildlife inhabiting this international scientific territory, states must take reasonable steps to alleviate pollution of waters lying off the coast and ice shelves. The treaty specifically prohibits both the carrying out of nuclear explosions and the disposal of radioactive waste material on the continent.[8]

Rocket Exhaust Pollution of the Upper Atmosphere.   In response to fears expressed in the early 1960s that the exhaust from space vehicles might influence the gaseous composition of the upper atmos-

[7] *The New York Times,* May 15, 1968, May 26, 1968, June 3, 1968; *Christian Science Monitor,* May 28, 1968.
[8] *Antarctic Treaty,* Dec. 1, 1959–June 23, 1961, 12 UST 794 (TIAS 4780).

phere, with far-reaching climatologic consequences, the International Council of Scientific Unions in 1962 requested its Committee on Space Research (COSPAR) to study the matter. The latter in turn passed the issue to its Consultative Group on Potentially Harmful Effects of Space Experiments, which reported in 1964 that anything like a large-scale alteration in the atmosphere that affected man's environment had not occurred and seemed most unlikely.[9] The Consultative Group recommended further quantitative studies be made.

While no questions of treaty violation were raised here, the swift reaction of the scientific community to the potential danger might indicate growing sensitivity to a postulated, evolving norm of customary international law which would limit, or even prohibit, certain activities of states, such as large-scale scientific experiments, whose cumulative effects were to seriously pollute the environment. It is also intriguing to speculate whether or not the launching states would have been charged with an international, absolute liability had the COSPAR Group found evidence of contamination, and therefore a violation of the presumptive norm. That this issue remains of continuing relevancy is revealed by the concern now being raised at the prospect of possibly deleterious climatologic and economic alterations in the environment resulting from the operation of the supersonic transport planes now under development. I know of no specific legislative plans being considered at this time by the states constructing SST's that would restrain the use of these airplanes in their future operations to avoid such dangers; but there has been discussion in the U.S. Congress, in relation to the sonic boom issue, about restricting flights at supersonic speeds to ocean areas.

Extraterrestrial Contamination of the Earth.   While much attention has been paid to the problem of sterilizing spacecraft launched to the moon and planets in order to avoid their contamination with earthly organisms, an equally serious matter is the possibility of the transport of alien organisms to Earth by returning vehicles and astronauts. In this case, the Treaty on Outer Space of 1967 requires its signatories engaged in outer space activities to adopt appropriate measures against the introduction of extraterrestrial matter to the

[9] *Statement on Upper Atmospheric Pollution by Rocket Exhaust and Chemical Injection Experiments by the Cospar Consultative Group on Potentially Harmful Effects of Space Experiments,* May 16, 1964, in Senate Committee on Aeronautical and Space Sciences, *International Cooperation and Organization for Outer Space,* (Washington, D.C.: U.S. Government Printing Office, 1965), pp. 394-96.

environment of the Earth.[10] NASA has, in fact, established a Lunar Receiving Laboratory at the Manned Spacecraft Center, at which the Apollo space ship, astronauts, and whatever samples they bring back from the moon will undergo biologic quarantine and testing for a period of time after their return to the Earth.

POLLUTION IN AREAS UNDER TERRITORIAL JURISDICTION

Before examining the specific international legal status of air, water, and radioactive pollution of the environment originating within states, I must note the existence of several general international legal principles that may be interpreted as relevant to the issue of how a state treats the environment it shares with its neighbors.

First, and most important, it is a fundamental ordering principle of the international system that a state is *not* completely free to do as it wishes within its territorial sphere. This dictum was stated in a form of particular importance for the subject matter of this article by one of the foremost scholars in international law as follows: "A State, in spite of its territorial supremacy, is not allowed to alter the natural conditions of its own territory to the disadvantage of the natural conditions of the territory of a neighbouring state. . . ."[11] Many cases and official statements back up this view. For instance, in a case involving damage done to British destroyers by mines while the ships were passing through Albanian waters in the Corfu Channel, the International Court of Justice (ICJ), in assessing Albanian responsibility for the harm, held that every state was obliged "not to allow knowingly its territory to be used for acts contrary to the rights of other States."[12] A U.S. State Department memorandum of 1958 dealing with the use of international rivers further reflected the principle, declaring that a state bordering such a river has the right to make maximum use of that part of the river system coming within its jurisdiction, consistent with a similar right adhering to other states through which the river flows.[13]

---

[10] *Treaty on Principles Governing the Activities of States in the Exploration and Use of Space, Including the Moon and Other Celestial Bodies,* Jan. 27, 1967–Oct. 10, 1967, in Senate Committee on Aeronautical and Space Sciences, *Treaty on Principles . . .*: Analysis and background data, (Washington, D.C.: U.S. Government Printing Office, 1967), pp. 21-41.

[11] L. Oppenheim, *International Law: A Treatise,* ed. H. Lauterpacht, vol. 1— *Peace* (McKay, 1955), p. 290.

[12] 4 *International Court of Justice Reports* 22 (1949).

[13] W. L. Griffin, *Legal Aspects of the Use of Systems of International Waters,* State Department Memorandum, State Document 118 (1958).

Second, and close corollary of the above, there is the traditional, customary international rule prohibiting, in general, intervention by states in each other's internal affairs. The connotation here of "intervention" is an act of a forceful, dictatorial nature. In this regard, I do not think it too far-fetched to speak of a prohibition of ecologic intervention, as a modern addition to this principle; a state which allows some part of its environment to so deteriorate, whether intentionally or not, as to result in deleterious consequences to the environments of its neighbors has engaged in impermissible coercion in their affairs.

Third, while treaty and custom are the most important sources of international law, the Statute of the ICJ also refers, as a source, to "the general principles of law recognized by civilized nations." This means that some of the international legal obligations binding states may be drawn from an examination of the municipal laws of the various members of the international community; insofar as particular national laws from different countries can be shown to illustrate, in regard to their common subject matters, definite trends, one may deem the latter "general principles of law. . . ." It is my belief that the growing number of pollution abatement laws enacted by states are evocative of a general trend in this direction, which further strengthens the principles of reasonable use of national territory and ecologic nonintervention.

Fourth, one of the rapidly growing sub-fields of international law deals with the human rights of the individual. Again, I do not think it far-fetched to regard freedom from pollution as a basic human right. Very much to the point here is Article 12 of the U.N.-sponsored International Covenant on Economic, Social and Cultural Rights in 1966, not yet in force, which obligates signatories to improve all aspects of environmental and industrial hygiene as one step toward the realization of everyone's right to enjoy the highest attainable standard of physical and mental health.[14]

Given the above general rules that oblige each state to act in its territory with a decent respect for the ecologic opinions of mankind, there are, as yet, no multilateral treaties regarding air or water pollution that would serve to spell out the specific consequences of the general obligation. For indications of international legal trends regarding air and water pollution, one must rely on a handful of international judicial decisions, bilateral treaties, and resolutions and reports of

[14] *International Covenant on Economic, Social and Cultural Rights,* Dec. 16, 1966– , in 4 U.N. *Monthly Chronicle* 5 (Feb. 1967).

international organizations. There do exist several actual and proposed multilateral treaties relevant to radioactive contamination.

Air Pollution   The one major international case in the air pollution field is the *Trail Smelter Dispute* between the U.S. and Canada. This issue involved complaints by farmers in Washington State that sulphur dioxide fumes emitted by an iron ore smelter located in Trail, British Columbia, were drifting across the border with consequent harm to their agricultural produce and livestock. The problem was settled through the decisions handed down by an arbitration tribunal established under the Trail Smelter Convention negotiated by the two states in 1935.[15] The tribunal in 1938 awarded a cash indemnity to the U.S. for damage to cleared and uncleared land caused by the smelter; in order to prevent future significant fumigations in the U.S. without unreasonably restricting the output of the smelter, the tribunal in 1941 adopted detailed regulations for the future operation of the smelter drawn up by two scientists appointed by the court as technical consultants.[16] Although the tribunal used for its guideline on deciding damages appropriate U.S. laws and court decisions, it could find nothing in them that countered the general rules of international law. In addition, although decisions of international courts technically are not binding on future cases, in practice they may have great influence on the reasoning of later judges. In this regard, the tribunal stated the important dictum, reflective of the principle described earlier, that according to international law, no state may let its territory be used in such a way as to cause injury by fumes to the territory or inhabitants of another state, when the incident is serious and the injury clearly established.

In September 1966, the U.S. and Canada asked their International Joint Commission to study air pollution along the border. The U.S. also has Natural Resource Programs with Japan and Germany, part of which involve data and personnel exchanges in air and water pollution, while such international organizations as the World Health Organization and the Economic Commission for Europe have been studying air pollution for several years—all of which adds thrust to the growing realization of states that air pollution is no longer a local or even a national problem exclusively.

---

[15] *Convention for Settlement of Difficulties Arising from Operation of Smelter at Trail, B.C.,* Apr. 13, 1935—Aug. 3, 1935, 30 *American Journal of International Law Official Documents* 163 (Oct. 1936).

[16] First Decision, 33 *American Journal of International Law* 182 (Jan. 1939); Final Decision 35 *American Journal of International Law* 684 (Oct. 1941).

Such realization is already apparent in Europe, as one would expect, given the high density of industrialization superimposed on the traditional nation-state structure of that continent. After a conference called by the Council of Europe in 1964 on air pollution, a group of experts reporting to the Council's Committee of Ministers drew up a declaration of principles on air pollution control; this declaration, now pending adoption by the committee, covers industrial, domestic thermal, and vehicular sources of pollution, and is intended to guide national anti-pollution policies of council governments. As noted earlier, such recommendations often achieve as much obedience in practice as states usually give to more formal treaties.

Water Pollution of International Rivers. The pollution of fresh waters is most directly of concern to international law when international rivers are involved; these are rivers (or lakes) that form the boundary between states or that flow from one state into another. The experience of the international community with regard to pollution of such rivers is somewhat more extensive than its experience in air pollution matters.

Regarding decisions of international courts, one interesting case was the *Lake Lanoux Arbitration* between France and Spain in 1957.[17] Spain complained that France's diversion of water from the lake for hydroelectric purposes diminished the flow that had previously entered Spain; the tribunal decided in favor of France, which was sending the water it had used back into the river flowing into Spain. Although Spain did not raise the issue of pollution of the water thus returned to it, and the court found the returned waters unpolluted in any case, the court did say that Spain might have brought up the question of whether the waters would have had some harmful characteristic which could injure her interests.

Several important bilateral treaties deal with water pollution. Under the United States-Mexican Water Treaty of 1944,[18] the U.S. guaranteed the delivery to Mexico of 1.5 million acre-feet of water annually from the Colorado River; although the quality of this water was not specified, Mexican complaints that U.S. use of the river after 1961 for irrigation resulted in the delivery to her of water high enough in saline content to harm crops in the Mexicali Valley compelled the U.S. to negotiate an agreement with Mexico in 1965, under which

[17] 53 *American Journal of International Law* 156 (1959). See, in general, A. P. Lester, "River Pollution in International Law," 57 *American Journal of International Law* 828 (1963).

[18] 59 Statute 1219 (ts 994).

the U.S. agreed to build at its own expense an extension of a drainage canal on the U.S. side of the border that would divert the polluted water. The U.S.-Canadian Boundary Water Treaty of 1909[19] declared that the waters under its purview would not be polluted by either side so as to injure the inhabitants or property of the other, and established the International Joint Commission to keep watch over the uses made of these waters. The Indus Waters Treaty of 1960[20] between India and Pakistan contains a declaration of intention on the part of each party to prohibit, as far as practicable, such undue pollution of the waters as could harmfully affect uses equivalent to those to which the waters were being put on the date the Treaty entered force, and to agree to take reasonable measures ensuring that any sewage or industrial waste allowed to flow into the river system would be treated first, if necessary, so as not to materially affect uses being made of the waters. Other relevant documents include a convention regarding Lake Constance (Germany, Austria, Switzerland) worked out by the International Water Preservation Commission established by the three riparian states in 1959; the 1963 agreement setting up the International Commission for the Protection of the Rhine against Pollution; the World Health Organization's International Standards for Drinking Water; and the European Water Charter published by the Council of Europe in May 1968, which it is hoped will lead to the signature of a council convention on the control of fresh water pollution.

The brunt of this activity would seem to uphold the conclusion reached by the U.N. Economic Commission for Europe in 1961 that ". . . in accordance with established principles of customary international law no state should pass on its waters to its neighbouring states in such a polluted condition that this water would seriously damage the interest of its neighbouring states."[21] I would add that riparian states may well also have the obligation to cooperate in cleaning up such pollution as already exists, and the responsibility for being held internationally liable if they do not engage in effective abatement activities. These issues, plus the related ones of fairly apportioning abatement costs among coriparians and of establishing international bodies with the power of administering and enforcing water quality standards

[19] 36 Statute 2448.

[20] *Indus Waters Treaty,* Sept. 19, 1960–Jan. 12, 1961, 55 *American Journal of International Law* 797 (July 1961).

[21] Economic Commission for Europe, *Conference on Water Pollution Problems in Europe,* Mar. 17, 1961, p. 7.

for international drainage basins, have been under study by such groups as the ECE, the Council of Europe, and the private International Law Association.[22]

Radioactive Pollution of International Rivers. Regarding the general disposal of radioactive waste into territorial fresh waters, safety and health standards involved are still largely the task of national atomic energy regulatory bodies. However, an International Atomic Energy Agency panel of experts, while pointing out that details of such disposal were completely in the hands of national governments, further stressed that the disposal should be done by a country in such a way that harmful effects would not be felt in marine waters or in other countries.[23] In addition there are two international conventions on liability for nuclear damage analogous to the Brussels Convention on nuclear ships: these are the Paris Convention on Third Party Liability in the Field of Nuclear Energy of 1960,[24] now in force, which is restricted in its application to Europe, and the world-wide Vienna Convention on Minimum International Standards Regarding Civil Liability for Nuclear Damage of 1963.[25] Both treaties apply to such nuclear installations as nuclear reactors, reprocessing factories, and nuclear storage facilities; definitions of nuclear damage and the absolute liability of operators are similar to those in the Brussels Convention, while equivalent provisions are included regarding location of suits brought, time limits for instigating suits, maximum monetary limits of liability, and insurance responsibilities of operators.

All these standards would, of course, apply to the direct disposal of radioactive waste into international fresh waters. The IAEA Panel of Experts further recommended in this regard that states might choose either to negotiate a convention establishing certain specific quality criteria for water passing from one country into another or to establish international organizations for particular drainage basins which would then specify conditions for the discharge of wastes. I know of no groups of this latter type set up to date.

[22] *Final Report of the Committee on the Uses of the Waters of International Rivers,* 1966, Helsinki Conference of the International Law Association.

[23] Report of an Ad hoc Panel of Experts, *Disposal of Radioactive Wastes into Fresh Water,* IAEA Safety Series no. 10 (1963), pp. 33-34.

[24] Paris, *Convention on Third Party Liability in the Field of Nuclear Energy,* July 29, 1960–Apr. 1, 1968, in Joint Atomic Energy Committee, op. cit., pp. 256-301.

[25] *Vienna Convention on Minimum International Standards Regarding Civil Liability for Nuclear Damage,* May 22, 1963– , in Joint Atomic Energy Committee, op. cit., pp. 312-22.

Radioactive Pollution from Weapons Testing. The partial Nuclear
Test Ban Treaty of 1963[26] can be considered part of the list of anti-
pollution international legislation, in that it effectively eliminated one
major source of radioactive fallout. Be it noted the treaty forbids the
carrying out not just of any nuclear weapon test explosion, but "any
other nuclear explosion" as well in the atmosphere, outer space, underwater, and underground (where "radioactive debris" from such
underground test drifts beyond the territory of the testing state). A
comprehensive test ban treaty, which has been discussed at Geneva
for several years, would close off the last loophole that allows states
to test nuclear weapons underground when the radioactivity is wholly
contained within their borders. The amount of radioactive debris
venting beyond national territory that would make a state guilty of
violating the 1963 treaty is nowhere defined in this treaty, and no
state has yet made an issue of the possible international liability of
another state for releasing such debris, although it has been detected
on several occasions in Japan, Finland, by the U.S. in the atmosphere
over the Pacific, and by Mexico near the U.S. border.[27]

In similar vein, the Treaty on Outer Space prohibits the placing
into earth orbit of "any objects carrying nuclear weapons" (as well as
any other weapons of mass destruction). However, this does not forbid
research and development on such weapons, nor does it, strictly speaking, forbid the launching of low flying missiles that return to earth
before completing one orbit (the Fractional Orbital Bombardment
System).

CONCLUSIONS

While it seems safe to say that the future will see the further elaboration and codification on the international level of rules and adminis-

---

[26] *Treaty Banning Nuclear Weapon Tests in the Atmosphere, in Outer Space
and under Water,* Aug. 5, 1963–Oct. 10, 1963, 14 UST 1313 (TIAS 5433).

[27] An underground test of about 200 kilotons was detonated by the U.S.S.R.
on January 15, 1965. Traces of radioactivity were picked up by U.S. air sampling
planes over the northern Pacific on January 18 and 19 (*The New York Times,*
Jan. 20, 1965). Niigata University in Japan recorded a rise of radioactivity in
the air the following day (AP story in *St. Louis Globe-Democrat,* Jan. 21, 1965).
Fresh fallout was detected in Finland on December 21, 1966, and was attributed
by Finnish and Swedish newspapers to an underground test in the U.S.S.R. on
December 18. Higher than normal radioactivity was detected at Mexican monitoring stations near the U.S. border after a U.S. underground test on January 19.
1968 (letter from Ing. Manuel Vasquez Barete, Director of Radiological Security, C.N.E.N., of the Mexican Nuclear Energy Commission to Dr. Meyer Chessin
of the Western Montana Scientists' Committee for Public Information).

trative regulations dealing with environmental pollution, this process is not likely to develop as rapidly as an objective evaluation of the need would indicate. Hindering speedy action on the international level are factors similar to those blocking action within states—lack of an organized constituency to press for anti-pollution laws, fear by some businesses of the economic cost of pollution abatement techniques, and bureaucratic conservatism. Additionally, at the international level one faces the delays inherent in getting a large number of states, jealous of their legal, if technologically obsolete, sovereign prerogatives, to agree on complex legislation for a subject whose full ramifications may not yet be completely understood. It is virtually self-evident that prevention of pollution of global environments such as the high seas, the atmosphere, and international rivers, requires effective international cooperation, yet states remain generally reluctant to endow international organizations with the authority and power that would make them efficient anti-pollution agencies.

On the other hand, one notices a certain gathering momentum here that may justify a guarded optimism. Two recent, parallel events at the national and international levels are good illustrations. In this country, twelve congressmen have introduced a resolution into the House of Representatives that would add a Conservation Bill of Rights to the Constitution; this document asserts the right of the people to a clean and aesthetically pleasing environment, requires Congress to make an inventory every ten years of America's natural and aesthetic resources and to stake steps for their protection, and requires any federal or state agency to first hold a public hearing before engaging in public work that would harm such resources.[28] To my knowledge, Congress has not yet taken action on the resolution. Internationally, during the summer Sweden suggested that the United Nations call a conference in 1971 dealing with the effects of man's industrial, urban civilization on the environment. This issue was taken up by the U.N. Economic and Social Council, which, in July 1968, passed a resolution that did not directly recommend the holding of such a meeting, but requested that the next General Assembly consider this possibility in the context of its discussion on how to protect the environment.[29]

As for the future, one can envision a scenario along the following lines: international anti-pollution norms will continue to emerge slowly from the varied sources of modern international law—the negotiation of bilateral and multilateral treaties; the development of custom evolv-

[28] *The New York Times,* Sept. 14, 1968.
[29] *The New York Times,* July 31, 1968.

ing from the behavior and national laws of states; decisions of national and international courts; the passage of resolutions and declarations by international organizations; the statement of authoritative views by scientific and legal experts; and the presentation over time by states of claims and counterclaims disputing the allocation and use of the resources of the natural environment. There may also be advances in detailing the penalties applicable to those directly responsible for pollution, and the international, absolute liability that may be vested in their states in cases of large-scale damage or injury resulting from ultra-hazardous activities; indeed, one can already trace the beginnings of a norm which would require states to consult with their neighbors and with authoritative scientific bodies before engaging in operations that are potentially dangerous for the regional or global community,[30] although it will no doubt be harder to come to agreement on the economic or diplomatic penalties to be levied against a state which violates international pollution standards.

The next step in this process would appear to be the establishment of international anti-pollution bodies, on a functional and regional basis, with real administrative, and not just recommendatory, powers, although one can well foresee the bureaucratic tangles that might arise, given the overlapping interests between such groups and their national counterparts. In any case, already in 1959, the Economic Commission for Europe suggested the formation of international river pollution control groups in Europe that would carry out such tasks as making reports on pollution prevention based on surveys and investigations; advising national and local authorities on particular technical, financial, and administrative pollution problems; establishing, after hearings, quality standards for each use of water; and issuing, after hearings, instructions setting a date on or before which sewage discharge is to be disposed of as specified (the instructions would become national regulations in the countries concerned, as would penalties). Important policy decisions relevant to a country would not be binding without the consent of its representative on the control body.[31] Such organizations might also follow the U.S. federal model in leaving it to the states in each region to set their own specific

[30] C. W. Jenks, "Liability for Ultra-hazardous Activities in International Law," *Recueil des Cours,* vol. 117 (Sijthoff: Hague Academy of International Law, 1967).

[31] Economic Commission for Europe, *Tentative Suggestions for the Establishment of International River Pollution Control Bodies in Europe,* Annex 3 of Document E/ECE/340 (Mar. 6, 1959), pp. 1-3.

standards, based on minimum requirements and guidelines enforced by the international body.

Ultimately, it is barely possible that the first tentative international and national steps described above may evolve and coalesce into a sophisticated and flexible world ecologic law, of which international anti-pollution regulations would form a vital part.

NATURE AND HUMAN NATURE

When we begin to look at environmental problems with the breadth of vision they require, we will have to go beneath political-economic conceptualizations to psychological ones, finding out how men are influenced emotionally by the environment and what causes them to alter it in the ways they do. Furthermore, we will have to go beneath mere studies of behavior to a deep feeling-out of the ways human beings experience the universe, to inquiries into realms which are generally fenced off as matters of religious faith. Nothing less than this will enable us to understand why we create the kinds of institutions we have and use the world as we do, but this is an area which today's leading academicians are not eager to explore; in political science, if nowhere else, the separation between church and state is perfect and complete. The contemporary hardnosed analyst does not deal with concepts of a religious nature, however relevant they might be to the problem at hand.

The kinds of concepts which might be brought out in such inquiry are suggested in the essay by Lynn White, Jr., a professor of history at the University of California at Los Angeles. In an impressive synthesis of data White gives some idea of the effects previous civilizations have had upon their natural environments, and raises an important question about the mystical foundations of contemporary science when he asserts that "modern technology is at least partly to be explained as an Occidental, voluntarist realization of the Christian dogma of man's transcendence of, and rightful mastery over, nature."

In the second essay, Margaret Mead tells something of how human beings first learn to piece together their view of themselves in nature in other cultures and then applies that notion to the question of how modern man can sanely learn to live with his enormous and still-growing capacity to change his environment. Her conclusion is that what is most necessary for us now is a forward leap in intellectual control, a heightened ability "to conceptualize, to make conscious and amenable to imagination and reason the paths by which we have come and what they mean in the places where we now are, and the directions we may take."

In the third selection Alan Watts, a philosopher and theologian whose main work has been in tracing the relationships between Oriental philosophies and Western ways of thinking, also looks at the present ecological crisis and suggests a way out—but his solution, although not incompatible with that offered by Margaret Mead, has an important difference in its emphasis. Watts goes to the prevailing attitude toward environment—the attitude which is revealed in commonplace phrases such as "man's conquest of nature"—and then isolates the philosophical assumption which underlies it: the assumption that it is ever possible in reality of separate man from nature, controller from controlled, figure from ground. Watts argues that no such separation is logically possible, but that the attempt to make such a separation dominates Western thought and action. Like Margaret Mead he sees the need for greater ability to conceptualize, but the kind of conceptualization he advocates is clearly more than an intellectual experience. It is not hard to extrapolate from his view of science a conviction that scientists in the future must cultivate not objectivity and rigorous dispassion but rather a frankly mystical sense of human participation in the universe. In a society dominated by the cult of objectivity, this is a truly revolutionary idea.

THE HISTORICAL ROOTS OF
OUR ECOLOGIC CRISIS

Lynn White, Jr.

A conversation with Aldous Huxley not infrequently puts one at the receiving end of an unforgettable monologue. About a year before his lamented death he was discoursing on a favorite topic: man's unnatural treatment of nature and its sad results. To illustrate his point he told how, during the previous summer, he had returned to a little valley in England where he had spent many happy months as a child. Once it had been composed of delightful grassy glades; now it was becoming overgrown with unsightly brush because the rabbits that formerly kept such growth under control had largely succumbed to a disease, myxomatosis, that was deliberately introduced by the local farmers to reduce the rabbits' destruction of crops. Being something of a Philistine, I could be silent no longer, even in the interests of great rhetoric. I interrupted to point out that the rabbit itself had been brought as a domestic animal to England in 1176, presumably to improve the protein diet of the peasantry.

All forms of life modify their contexts. The most spectacular and benign instance is doubtless the coral polyp. By serving its own ends, it has created a vast undersea world favorable to thousands of other kinds of animals and plants. Ever since man became a numerous species he has affected his environment notably. The hypothesis that his fire-drive method of hunting created the world's great grasslands and helped to exterminate the monster mammals of the Pleistocene from much of the globe is plausible, if not proved. For 6 millennia at least, the banks of the lower Nile have been a human artifact rather than the swampy African jungle which nature, apart from man, would have made it. The Aswan Dam, flooding 5000 square miles, is only the latest stage in a long process. In many regions terracing or irrigation, overgrazing, the cutting of forests by Romans to build ships to fight Carthaginians or by Crusaders to solve the logistics problems

"The Historical Roots of Our Ecologic Crisis," Lynn White, Jr., SCIENCE, *Vol. 155, pp. 1203-1207, 10 March 1967. Copyright 1967 by the American Association for the Advancement of Science. Reprinted by permission. This essay is also included in Lynn White, Jr.,* MACHINA EX DEO: ESSAYS IN THE DYNAMISM OF WESTERN CULTURE *(Cambridge, Mass.: M.I.T. Press, 1969).*

of their expeditions, have profoundly changed some ecologies. Observation that the French landscape falls into two basic types, the open fields of the north and the *bocage* of the south and west, inspired Marc Bloch to undertake his classic study of medieval agricultural methods. Quite unintentionally, changes in human ways often affect nonhuman nature. It has been noted, for example, that the advent of the automobile eliminated huge flocks of sparrows that once fed on the horse manure littering every street.

The history of ecologic change is still so rudimentary that we know little about what really happened, or what the results were. The extinction of the European aurochs as late as 1627 would seem to have been a simple case of overenthusiastic hunting. On more intricate matters it often is impossible to find solid information. For a thousand years or more the Frisians and Hollanders have been pushing back the North Sea, and the process is culminating in our own time in the reclamation of the Zuider Zee. What, if any, species of animals, birds, fish, shore life, or plants have died out in the process? In their epic combat with Neptune have the Netherlanders overlooked ecological values in such a way that the quality of human life in the Netherlands has suffered? I cannot discover that the questions have ever been asked, much less answered.

People, then, have often been a dynamic element in their own environment, but in the present state of historical scholarship we usually do not know exactly when, where, or with what effects man-induced changes came. As we enter the last third of the 20th century, however, concern for the problem of ecologic backlash is mounting feverishly. Natural science, conceived as the effort to understand the nature of things, had flourished in several eras and among several peoples. Similarly there had been an age-old accumulation of technological skills, sometimes growing rapidly, sometimes slowly. But it was not until about four generations ago that Western Europe and North America arranged a marriage between science and technology, a union of the theoretical and the empirical approaches to our natural environment. The emergence in widespread practice of the Baconian creed that scientific knowledge means technological power over nature can scarcely be dated before about 1850, save in the chemical industries, where it is anticipated in the 18th century. Its acceptance as a normal pattern of action may mark the greatest event in human history since the invention of agriculture, and perhaps in nonhuman terrestrial history as well.

Almost at once the new situation forced the crystallization of the novel concept of ecology; indeed, the word *ecology* first appeared in the English language in 1873. Today, less than a century later, the impact of our race upon the environment has so increased in force that it has changed in essence. When the first cannons were fired, in the early 14th century, they affected ecology by sending workers scrambling to the forests and mountains for more potash, sulfur, iron ore, and charcoal, with some resulting erosion and deforestation. Hydrogen bombs are of a different order: a war fought with them might alter the genetics of all life on this planet. By 1285 London had a smog problem arising from the burning of soft coal, but our present combustion of fossil fuels threatens to change the chemistry of the globe's atmosphere as a whole, with consequences which we are only beginning to guess. With the population explosion, the carcinoma of planless urbanism, the new geological deposits of sewage and garbage, surely no creature other than man has ever managed to foul its nest in such short order.

There are many calls to action, but specific proposals, however worthy as individual items, seem too partial, palliative, negative: ban the bomb, tear down the billboards, give the Hindus contraceptives and tell them to eat their sacred cows. The simplest solution to any suspect change is, of course, to stop it, or, better yet, to revert to a romanticized past: make those ugly gasoline stations look like Anne Hathaway's cottage or (in the Far West) like ghost-town saloons. The "wilderness area" mentality invariably advocates deep-freezing an ecology, whether San Gorgonio or the High Sierra, as it was before the first Kleenex was dropped. But neither atavism nor prettification will cope with the ecologic crisis of our time.

What shall we do? No one yet knows. Unless we think about fundamentals, our specific measures may produce new backlashes more serious than those they are designed to remedy.

As a beginning we should try to clarify our thinking by looking, in some historical depth, at the presuppositions that underlie modern technology and science. Science was traditionally aristocratic, speculative, intellectual in intent; technology was lower-class, empirical, action-oriented. The quite sudden fusion of these two, towards the middle of the 19th century, is surely related to the slightly prior and contemporary democratic revolutions which, by reducing social barriers, tended to assert a functional unity of brain and hand. Our ecologic crisis is the product of an emerging, entirely novel, democratic culture.

The issue is whether a democratized world can survive its own implications. Presumably we cannot unless we rethink our axioms.

THE WESTERN TRADITIONS OF TECHNOLOGY AND SCIENCE

One thing is so certain that it seems stupid to verbalize it: both modern technology and modern science are distinctively *Occidental*. Our technology has absorbed elements from all over the world, notably from China; yet everywhere today, whether in Japan or in Nigeria, successful technology is Western. Our science is the heir to all the sciences of the past, especially perhaps to the work of the great Islamic scientists of the Middle Ages, who so often outdid the ancient Greeks in skill and perspicacity: al-Razi in medicine, for example; or ibn-al-Haytham in optics; or Omar Khayyám in mathematics. Indeed, not a few works of such geniuses seem to have vanished in the original Arabic and to survive only in medieval Latin translations that helped to lay the foundations for later Western developments. Today, around the globe, all significant science is Western in style and method, whatever the pigmentation or language of the scientists.

A second pair of facts is less well recognized because they result from quite recent historical scholarship. The leadership of the West, both in technology and in science, is far older than the so-called Scientific Revolution of the 17th century or the so-called Industrial Revolution of the 18th century. These terms are in fact outmoded and obscure the true nature of what they try to describe—significant stages in two long and separate developments. By A.D. 1000 at the latest—and perhaps, feebly, as much as 200 years earlier—the West began to apply water power to industrial processes other than milling grain. This was followed in the late 12th century by the harnessing of wind power. From simple beginnings, but with remarkable consistency of style, the West rapidly expanded its skills in the development of power machinery, labor-saving devices, and automation. Those who doubt should contemplate that most monumental achievement in the history of automation: the weight-driven mechanical clock, which appeared in two forms in the early 14th century. Not in craftsmanship but in basic technological capacity, the Latin West of the later Middle Ages far outstripped its elaborate, sophisticated, and aesthetically magnificent sister cultures, Byzantium and Islam. In 1444 a great Greek ecclesiastic, Bessarion, who had gone to Italy, wrote a letter to a prince in Greece. He was amazed by the superiority of Western ships, arms, textiles, glass. But above all he was astonished by the spectacle of waterwheels sawing timbers and pumping the bellows of blast furnaces. Clearly, he had seen nothing of the sort in the Near East.

By the end of the 15th century the technological superiority of Europe was such that its small, mutually hostile nations could spill out over all the rest of the world, conquering, looting, and colonizing. The symbol of this technological superiority is the fact that Portugal, one of the weakest states of the Occident, was able to become, and to remain for a century, mistress of the East Indies. And we must remember that the technology of Vasco da Gama and Albuquerque was built by pure empiricism, drawing remarkably little support or inspiration from science.

In the present-day vernacular understanding, modern science is supposed to have begun in 1543, when both Copernicus and Vesalius published their great works. It is no derogation of their accomplishments, however, to point out that such structures as the *Fabrica* and the *De revolutionibus* do not appear overnight. The distinctive Western tradition of science, in fact, began in the late 11th century with a massive movement of translation of Arabic and Greek scientific works into Latin. A few notable books—*Theophrastus,* for example—escaped the West's avid new appetite for science, but within less than 200 years effectively the entire corpus of Greek and Muslim science was available in Latin, and was being eagerly read and criticized in the new European universities. Out of criticism arose new observation, speculation, and increasing distrust of ancient authorities. By the late 13th century Europe had seized global scientific leadership from the faltering hands of Islam. It would be as absurd to deny the profound originality of Newton, Galileo, or Copernicus as to deny that of the 14th century scholastic scientists like Buridan or Oresme on whose work they built. Before the 11th century, science scarcely existed in the Latin West, even in Roman times. From the 11th century onward, the scientific sector of Occidental culture has increased in a steady crescendo.

Since both our technological and our scientific movements got their start, acquired their character, and achieved world dominance in the Middle Ages, it would seem that we cannot understand their nature or their present impact upon ecology without examining fundamental medieval assumptions and developments.

MEDIEVAL VIEW OF MAN AND NATURE

Until recently, agriculture has been the chief occupation even in "advanced" societies; hence, any change in methods of tillage has much importance. Early plows, drawn by two oxen, did not normally turn the sod but merely scratched it. Thus, cross-plowing was needed and fields tended to be squarish. In the fairly light soils and semiarid climates of the Near East and Mediterranean, this worked well. But such a plow was inappropriate to the wet climate and often sticky soils of northern Europe. By the latter part of the 7th century after Christ, however, following obscure beginnings, certain northern peasants were using an entirely new kind of plow, equipped with a vertical knife to cut the line of the furrow, a horizontal share to slice under the sod, and a moldboard to turn it over. The friction of this plow with the soil was so great that it normally required not two but eight oxen. It attacked the land with such violence that cross-plowing was not needed, and fields tended to be shaped in long strips.

In the days of the scratch-plow, fields were distributed generally in units capable of supporting a single family. Subsistence farming was the presupposition. But no peasant owned eight oxen: to use the new and more efficient plow, peasants pooled their oxen to form large plow-teams, originally receiving (it would appear) plowed strips in proportion to their contribution. Thus, distribution of land was based no longer on the needs of a family but, rather, on the capacity of a power machine to till the earth. Man's relation to the soil was profoundly changed. Formerly man had been part of nature; now he was the exploiter of nature. Nowhere else in the world did farmers develop any analogous agricultural implement. Is it coincidence that modern technology, with its ruthlessness toward nature, has so largely been produced by descendants of these peasants of northern Europe?

This same exploitive attitude appears slightly before A.D. 830 in Western illustrated calendars. In older calendars the months were shown as passive personifications. The new Frankish calendars, which set the style for the Middle Ages, are very different: they show men coercing the world around them—plowing, harvesting, chopping trees, butchering pigs. Man and nature are two things, and man is master.

These novelties seem to be in harmony with larger intellectual patterns. What people do about their ecology depends on what they think about themselves in relation to things around them. Human ecology is deeply conditioned by beliefs about our nature and destiny—that is, by religion. To Western eyes this is very evident in, say, India or Ceylon. It is equally true of ourselves and of our medieval ancestors.

The victory of Christianity over paganism was the greatest psychic revolution in the history of our culture. It has become fashionable today to say that, for better or worse, we live in "the post-Christian age." Certainly the forms of our thinking and language have largely ceased to be Christian, but to my eye the substance often remains amazingly akin to that of the past. Our daily habits of action, for example, are dominated by an implicit faith in perpetual progress which was unknown either to Greco-Roman antiquity or to the Orient. It is rooted in, and is indefensible apart from, Judeo-Christian teleology. The fact that Communists share it merely helps to show what can be demonstrated on many other grounds: that Marxism, like Islam, is a Judeo-Christian heresy. We continue today to live, as we have lived for about 1700 years, very largely in a context of Christian axioms.

What did Christianity tell people about their relations with the environment?

While many of the world's mythologies provide stories of creation, Greco-Roman mythology was singularly incoherent in this respect. Like Aristotle, the intellectuals of the ancient West denied that the visible world had had a beginning. Indeed, the idea of a beginning was impossible in the framework of their cyclical notion of time. In sharp contrast, Christianity inherited from Judaism not only a concept of time as nonrepetitive and linear but also a striking story of creation. By gradual stages a loving and all-powerful God had created light and darkness, the heavenly bodies, the earth and all its plants, animals, birds, and fishes. Finally, God had created Adam and, as an afterthought, Eve to keep man from being lonely. Man named all the animals, thus establishing his dominance over them. God planned all of this explicitly for man's benefit and rule: no item in the physical creation had any purpose save to serve man's purposes. And, although man's body is made of clay, he is not simply part of nature: he is made in God's image.

Especially in its Western form, Christianity is the most anthropocentric religion the world has seen. As early as the 2nd century both Tertullian and Saint Irenaeus of Lyons were insisting that when God shaped Adam he was foreshadowing the image of the incarnate Christ, the Second Adam. Man shares, in great measure, God's transcendence of nature. Christianity, in absolute contrast to ancient paganism and Asia's religions (except, perhaps, Zoroastrianism), not only established a dualism of man and nature but also insisted that it is God's will that man exploit nature for his proper ends.

At the level of the common people this worked out in an interesting way. In antiquity every tree, every spring, every stream, every hill had its own *genius loci*, its guardian spirit. These spirits were accessible to men, but were very unlike men; centaurs, fauns, and mermaids show their ambivalence. Before one cut a tree, mined a mountain, or dammed a brook, it was important to placate the spirit in charge of that particular situation, and to keep it placated. By destroying pagan animism, Christianity made it possible to exploit nature in a mood of indifference to the feelings of natural objects.

It is often said that for animism the Church substituted the cult of saints. True; but the cult of saints is functionally quite different from animism. The saint is not *in* natural objects; he may have special shrines, but his citizenship is in heaven. Moreover, a saint is entirely a man; he can be approached in human terms. In addition to saints, Christianity of course also had angels and demons inherited from Judaism and perhaps, at one remove, from Zoroastrianism. But these were all as mobile as the saints themselves. The spirits *in* natural objects, which formerly had protected nature from man, evaporated. Man's effective monopoly on spirit in this world was confirmed, and the old inhibitions to the exploitation of nature crumbled.

When one speaks in such sweeping terms, a note of caution is in order. Christianity is a complex faith, and its consequences differ in differing contexts. What I have said may well apply to the medieval West, where in fact technology made spectacular advances. But the Greek East, a highly civilized realm of equal Christian devotion, seems to have produced no marked technological innovation after the late 7th century, when Greek fire was invented. The key to the contrast may perhaps be found in a difference in the tonality of piety and thought which students of comparative theology find between the Greek and the Latin Churches. The Greeks believed that sin was intellectual blindness, and that salvation was found in illumination, orthodoxy—that is, clear thinking. The Latins, on the other hand, felt that sin was moral evil, and that salvation was to be found in right conduct. Eastern theology has been intellectualist. Western theology has been voluntarist. The Greek saint contemplates; the Western saint acts. The implications of Christianity for the conquest of nature would emerge more easily in the Western atmosphere.

The Christian dogma of creation, which is found in the first clause of all the Creeds, has another meaning for our comprehension of today's ecologic crisis. By revelation, God had given man the Bible, the Book of Scripture. But since God had made nature, nature also must reveal the divine mentality. The religious study of nature for the better understanding of God was known as natural theology. In the early Church, and always in the Greek East, nature was conceived primarily as a symbolic system through which God speaks to men: the ant is a sermon to sluggards; rising flames are the symbol of the soul's aspiration. This view of nature was essentially artistic rather than scientific. While Byzantium preserved and copied great numbers of ancient Greek scientific texts, science as we conceive it could scarcely flourish in such an ambience.

However, in the Latin West by the early 13th century natural theology was following a very different bent. It was ceasing to be the decoding of the physical symbols of God's communication with man and was becoming the effort to understand God's mind by discovering how his creation operates. The rainbow was no longer simply a symbol of hope first sent to Noah after the Deluge: Robert Grosseteste, Friar Roger Bacon, and Theodoric of Freiberg produced startlingly sophisticated work on the optics of the rainbow, but they did it as a venture in religious understanding. From the 13th century onward, up to and including Leibnitz and Newton, every major scientist, in effect, explained his motivations in religious terms. Indeed, if Galileo had not been so expert an amateur theologian he would have got into far less trouble: the professionals resented his intrusion. And Newton seems to have regarded himself more as a theologian than as a scientist. It was not until the late 18th century that the hypothesis of God became unnecessary to many scientists.

It is often hard for the historian to judge, when men explain why they are doing what they want to do, whether they are offering real reasons or merely culturally acceptable reasons. The consistency with which scientists during the long formative centuries of Western science said that the task and the reward of the scientist was "to think God's thoughts after him" leads one to believe that this was their real motivation. If so, then modern Western science was cast in a matrix of Christian theology. The dynamism of religious devotion, shaped by the Judeo-Christian dogma of creation, gave it impetus.

AN ALTERNATIVE CHRISTIAN VIEW

We would seem to be headed toward conclusions unpalatable to many Christians. Since both *science* and *technology* are blessed words in our contemporary vocabulary, some may be happy at the notions, first, that, viewed historically, modern science is an extrapolation of natural theology and, second, that modern technology is at least partly to be explained as an Occidental, voluntarist realization of the Christian dogma of man's transcendence of, and rightful mastery over, nature. But, as we now recognize, somewhat over a century ago science and technology—hitherto quite separate activities—joined to give mankind powers which, to judge by many of the ecologic effects, are out of control. If so, Christianity bears a huge burden of guilt.

I personally doubt that disastrous ecologic backlash can be avoided simply by applying to our problems more science and more technology. Our science and technology have grown out of Christian attitudes toward man's relation to nature which are almost universally held not only by Christians and neo-Christians but also by those who fondly regard themselves as post-Christians. Despite Copernicus, all the cosmos rotates around our little globe. Despite Darwin, we are *not,* in our hearts, part of the natural process. We are superior to nature, contemptuous of it, willing to use it for our slightest whim. The newly elected governor of California, like myself a churchman but less troubled than I, spoke for the Christian tradition when he said (as is alleged), "when you've seen one redwood tree, you've seen them all." To a Christian a tree can be no more than a physical fact. The whole concept of the sacred grove is alien to Christianity and to the ethos of the West. For nearly 2 millennia Christian missionaries have been chopping down sacred groves, which are idolatrous because they assume spirit in nature.

What we do about ecology depends on our ideas of the man-nature relationship. More science and more technology are not going to get us out of the present ecologic crisis until we find a new religion, or rethink our old one. The beatniks, who are the basic revolutionaries of our time, show a sound instinct in their affinity for Zen Buddhism, which conceives of the man-nature relationship as very nearly the mirror image of the Christian view. Zen, however, is as deeply conditioned by Asian history as Christianity is by the experience of the West, and I am dubious of its viability among us.

Possibly we should ponder the greatest radical in Christian history since Christ: Saint Francis of Assisi. The prime miracle of Saint Francis is the fact that he did not end at the stake, as many of his left-wing followers did. He was so clearly heretical that a general of the Franciscan Order, Saint Bonaventura, a great and perceptive Christian, tried to suppress the early accounts of Franciscanism. The key to an understanding of Francis is his belief in the virtue of humility—not merely for the individual but for man as a species. Francis tried to depose man from his monarchy over creation and set up a democracy of all God's creatures. With him the ant is no longer simply a homily for the lazy, flames a sign of the thrust of the soul toward union with

God: now they are Brother Ant and Sister Fire, praising the Creator in their own ways as Brother Man does in his.

Later commentators have said that Francis preached to the birds as a rebuke to men who would not listen. The records do not read so: he urged the little birds to praise God, and in spiritual ecstasy they flapped their wings and chirped rejoicing. Legends of saints, especially the Irish saints, had long told of their dealings with animals but always, I believe, to show their human dominance over creatures. With Francis it is different. The land around Gubbio in the Apennines was being ravaged by a fierce wolf. Saint Francis, says the legend, talked to the wolf and persuaded him of the error of his ways. The wolf repented, died in the odor of sanctity, and was buried in consecrated ground.

What Sir Steven Ruciman calls "the Franciscan doctrine of the animal soul" was quickly stamped out. Quite possibly it was in part inspired, consciously or unconsciously, by the belief in reincarnation held by the Cathar heretics who at that time teemed in Italy and southern France, and who presumably had got it originally from India. It is significant that at just the same moment, about 1200, traces of metempsychosis are found also in western Judaism, in the Provençal *Cabbala*. But Francis held neither to transmigration of souls nor to pantheism. His view of nature and of man rested on a unique sort of pan-psychism of all things animate and inanimate, designed for the glorification of their transcendent Creator, who, in the ultimate gesture of cosmic humility, assumed flesh, lay helpless in a manger, and hung dying on a scaffold.

I am not suggesting that many contemporary Americans who are concerned about our ecologic crisis will be either able or willing to counsel with wolves or exhort birds. However, the present increasing disruption of the global environment is the product of a dynamic technology and science which were originating in the Western medieval world against which Saint Francis was rebelling in so original a way. Their growth cannot be understood historically apart from distinctive attitudes toward nature which are deeply grounded in Christian dogma. The fact that most people do not think of these attitudes as Christian is irrelevant. No new set of basic values has been accepted in our society to displace those of Christianity. Hence we shall continue to have a worsening ecologic crisis until we reject the Christian axiom that nature has no reason for existence save to serve man.

The greatest spiritual revolutionary in Western history, Saint Francis, proposed what he thought was an alternative Christian view of nature and man's relation to it: he tried to substitute the idea of the equality of all creatures, including man, for the idea of man's limitless rule of creation. He failed. Both our present science and our present technology are so tinctured with orthodox Christian arrogance toward nature that no solution for our ecologic crisis can be expected from them alone. Since the roots of our trouble are so largely religious, the remedy must also be essentially religious, whether we call it that or not. We must rethink and refeel our nature and destiny. The profoundly religious, but heretical, sense of the primitive Franciscans for the spiritual autonomy of all parts of nature may point a direction. I propose Francis as a patron saint for ecologists.

A WORKING PAPER FOR MAN AND NATURE

Margaret Mead

Each human being embodies his culture whether the culture is that of a small, isolated, primitive tribe or of a modern city like New York, London, or Peiping. And he embodies all of it: a male child embodies the behavior of the mother whom he can never be like, just as the female child embodies her mother's behavior, which will be hers, and the behavior of her father and brother, which cannot be hers. In traditional caste societies, the members of each caste embody not only their own caste behavior but also the behavior of the other castes to which they do not and cannot belong. If a child belongs to a group whose total membership is a few hundred people, the size of the group will also be expressed in the way those about him treat him, in the certainty, for example, that all adults know who he is. So a mother in the isolated mountains of Kentucky places her child with his back against her body, facing out, toward a circle of known kin, but as she moves away from this small, intimately known world, she turns the child around, facing in, toward her protecting body, away from the strangers whose gaze will reinforce her gesture; and from both gaze and gesture, the child will learn about a different kind of world, a world in which most human beings are strangers. Among the seagoing Manus of New Guinea, a mother lifts her baby onto her back. She includes in the tension of her arm the way the baby must hold on, so that her arms will be free to punt or paddle, and the distances over which her eye will range as she does so. Wide horizons of sea or snow or the closed walls of the jungle or the mountain valley are included in every touch the child experiences. The Greek peasant who names his son Daedalus includes the era of the old gods, while the name Constantine, which is given his other son, includes the era after the gods had left Greece and Christianity had come.

If we speak in terms of conscious educational processes, then we can discuss the moment when a child learns geography or the metric system, the meaning of the secret ballot or the graduated income tax. Formal education proceeds along these lines of consciousness; what the school is believed to teach is labeled and compartmentalized, not known until it is encountered in a classroom or in a book. But this applies only to learning that has been identified and tagged. Actually the child in a culture in which arithmetic and geometry are so recognized, encounters them both, early on, in the way in which his parents and brothers and sisters play with him—"one, two, buckle my shoe; three, four, shut the door"—and in the square corners of the room, the sharp angles of his crib, and the bouncing of a rubber ball that is a perfect sphere. The father's arm lifting the child high, lifts him up as high as the tallest palm tree, as high as the flight of one of the eagles of Zeus, as high as the recently scaled Mount Everest, as high as a balloon, a jet, a satellite, or tosses him toward the moon.

The grandmother who sings to the child on her lap, includes all that she knows of time, since her ancestors came out of a hole in the ground near the headwaters of the Sepik River, since the gods walked among men, since Jehovah led the children of Israel through the sea, or since Sheridan's riders burned and plundered a hundred years ago. The child in her arms receives, as she holds him, all of time and space that she herself grasps, or knows that she does not grasp. He receives her knowledge and her ignorance, as cloth receives a pattern in which the empty, undyed spaces are as much a part of the pattern as the filled squares. Today the physicist father preoccupied with problems too abstruse to share, he believes, with anyone except perhaps three colleagues and two or three favored students, nevertheless, gives his infant son a sense of a world in which so few men know so much. And the poorly educated taxi driver who says to the physicist, "It must be wonderful to understand so much. I have stopped reading the newspapers because there is so much that I do not understand," conveys his bewilderment to his son. But the physicist, turning away slightly abashed by the honesty and innocence of the other, will also convey this to his own son as he watches him arrange knives and forks into categories on the floor. The son's first steps in learning will look different to his father because of the innocence and ignorance of the taxi driver. If the physicist also knows, and feels, that for a hundred thousand years men knew far less than the wistful driver, this too will enter in, as he watches his son traverse a path of growth bounded by such different limits than the path his human ancestors trod; as he realizes that the number *one,* when one can only count to twenty, is the same *one*—with its overtones of individuality and singleness—to himself, his child, and to all their ancestors but is also a *one* that is almost incredibly different. And he will realize that he can no more wrench his mind back to the state of the man who lived in a world where no one counted to more than twenty than his forebears could project forward to the simplest of the mathematics that he knows. This recognition, in turn, becomes part of the way he watches his child, part of the tonus of his hand when he lifts him up, part of the relaxation when he sets him down.

In every culture, no matter how simple, no matter how complex, no matter how impoverished or decayed, how exuberant and efflorescent, the children receive a total impression. The deepest ignorance and the state of the most esoteric knowledge is conveyed to them, inarticulately, by the way they are held and sung to, fed and punished, permitted to wander or kept close to home. But in complex societies like our own they share it very differently; some children receive as their birthright the sense of tremendous knowledge and power over nature that so informs the modern Western world; other children receive it as a sense of power and mastery that they themselves will never have. For some a ride through the stars becomes an easy expectation; for others a daydream, which can be indulged even more freely because it is manifestly unrealizable. As such children grow older, the differences in the way in which they receive the same knowledge in turn generates other kinds of beliefs. And so we get a conversation between two students, one black and one white, in which the black girl says: "Things aren't the same to you that they are to me. You don't see what I see, and I don't see what you see. If you think of an apple, you think of it on a silver platter, while I think of it falling to the ground from a tree." Yet the white girl has never been served an apple on a silver platter, and she, too, grew up in the country and gathered fallen apples from the high grass in the orchard. The experience of each has been screened through the imagined experience of the other, a different pattern laid on each. But both embody the same culture, though in such different ways.

We are on the verge of a tremendous change in the nature of man, a change as far reaching as the great changes of the past, when man's precursors learned to use tools, to speak, to plant seeds, to build cities, and to write. Perhaps an even greater change. One component of that change is the kind of knowledge and the kind of understanding we have about earlier man. It is not only that the complex tools that man uses today, as he moves huge weights or builds a spaceship, are the lineal descendants of earlier tools, or that speech preceded writing; writing, printing; and printing, video. It is not only that the earlier behaviors are included with the later operations we perform so that we simultaneously depend upon techniques that appeared at intervals of thousands of years. This simultaneity gives to all our learning a strange, discrepant, clumsy character, as we use old gestures on new machines, old safeguards where they are not needed, old audacities where they are deadly inappropriate. But perhaps more important still is the question of whether we are able to conceptualize, to make conscious and amenable to imagination and reason the paths by which we have come and what they mean in the places where we now are, and the directions we may take. Our lack of ability to teach the kind of precision and responsibility that is essential for the machine age, has cost, and is costing, millions of lives. Our inability to develop new and different centers of decision and authority (for example, for international air travel and control of nuclear weapons) is endangering mankind and the planet itself. Much of this can be attributed to the survival of old forms into a new age, to the persistence of old forms of learning when they are no longer appropriate. Much of it is due to our inability to use the older forms of learning constructively, so they become hindrances rather than helps.

But there are dangers in stressing the usefulness and the beauty of the old forms of learning, just as there are dangers in stressing those that are no longer relevant. It has been found that children who depend overmuch on touch, may lose out in a world in which sight and sound have replaced touch and taste and smell as major sensory pathways. But there are different ways in which we may respond to this knowledge. We may say: "We have lost something extremely precious and we must get it back, learn to use every sense, restore the senses to their once undisputed immediacy, construct a world in which there is less dependence upon reason and more dependence upon sense and feeling." This is one response to the recognition of discrepancy, to glimpses of the life of fisherfolk or mountaineers, to endearing glimpses, from the safety of a good supply of modern biotics, of the life of Indians in the South American jungle. Or we can recognize that these ways of our forebears are ways to which we can never return, but that the more we can recapture of this earlier wisdom, in a form we can understand, the better we can understand what is happening today, when a generation almost innocent of a sense of history has to learn how to cope with an unknown future, one for which they were not reared.

THE INDIVIDUAL AS MAN/WORLD

Alan Watts

There is a colossal disparity between the way in which most individuals experience their own existence, and the way in which the individual is described in such sciences as biology, ecology, and physiology. The nub of the difference is this: the way the individual is described in these sciences is not as a freely moving entity within an environment, but as a process of behavior which *is* the environment also. If you will accurately describe what any individual organism is doing, you will take but a few steps before you are also describing what the environment is doing. To put it more simply, we can do without such expressions as "what the individual is doing" or "what the environment is doing," as if the individual was one thing and the doing another, the environment one thing and its doing another. If we reduce the whole business simply to the process of doing, then the doing, which was called the behavior of the individual, is found to be *at the same time* the doing which is called the behavior of the environment. In other words, it is quite impossible to describe the movement of my arm except in relation to the rest of my body and to the background against which you perceive it. The relations in which you perceive this movement are the absolutely necessary condition for your perceiving at all. More and more, a "field theory" of man's behavior becomes necessary for the sciences.

Yet this is at complete variance with the way in which we are trained *by our culture* to experience our own existence. We do not, generally speaking, experience ourselves as the behavior of the field, but rather as a center of energy and consciousness which sometimes

Alan Watts, "The Individual as Man/World," PSYCHEDELIC REVIEW, *June 1963. Reprinted by permission.*

manages to control its environment, but at other times feels completely dominated by the environment. Thus there is a somewhat hostile relationship between the human organism and its social and natural environment, which is expressed in such phrases as "man's conquest of nature," or "man's conquest of space," and other such antagonistic figures of speech.

It would obviously be to the advantage of mankind if the way in which we feel our existence could correspond to the way in which existence is scientifically described. For what we feel has far more influence upon our actions than what we think. Scientists of all kinds are warning us most urgently that we are using our technology disastrously, eating up all the natural resources of the earth, creating incredibly beautiful but wholly non-nutritious vegetables by altering the biochemical balances of the soil, spawning unbelievable amounts of detergent froth which will eventually engulf cities, overpopulating ourselves because of the success of medicine, and thus winning our war against nature in such a way as to defeat ourselves completely. All this advice falls on deaf ears, because it falls on the ears of organisms convinced that war against nature is their proper way of life. They have to be unconvinced, and can be, to some extent, by intellectual propaganda, scientific description, and clear thought. But this moves relatively few people to action. Most are moved only if their feelings are profoundly affected. We need to *feel* this view of our individual identity as including its environment, and this must obviously concern scientists who are trying to find ways of controlling human feelings.

This problem has an important historical background. It is curious how the ancient philosophical debates of the Western world keep coming up again and again in new forms. Any question of the definition of the individual always becomes involved with the old argument between nominalism and realism. The realistic philosophy of the Middle Ages and of the Greeks was not what today we call realism. It was the belief that behind all specific manifestations of life such as men, trees, dogs, there lies an archetypal, or ideal, form of Man, of Tree, of Dog, so that every particular man is an instance of that archetypal form, and that behind all men is something which can be called Man with a capital M, or the "substance" of man, of "human nature."

The nominalists argued that this was a mere abstraction, and that to regard Man (capital M) as possessing any effective existence was to be deluded by concepts. There are only specific, individual men.

This idea is carried on in one of the most remarkable forms of modern nominalism, General Semantics, which argues that such abstractions as "The United States," "Britain," or "Russia," are so much journalistic gobbledygook.

Most people working in the sciences tend to be nominalists. But if you carry nominalism to its logical conclusion, you are involved in awkward problems. Not only would there be no such thing as Man, Mankind, or Human Nature, but it would also follow that there are no individual men, because the individual man is an abstraction, and what really exists is only an enormous amalgamation of particular molecules. If you pursue this further and inquire about the individual entities composing the molecules, there is an interminable array of nuclear and sub-nuclear realities, and if *these* in turn are to be regarded as the only realities, then the reality which we call a man is simply the association of discontinuous particles. This is the *reductio ad absurdum* of nominalism carried too far. The nominalist and realist viewpoints are actually *limits*—to borrow a term from mathematics. I have often thought that all philosophical debates are ultimately between the partisans of structure and the partisans of "goo." The academic world puts a heavy emphasis on structure: "Let's be definite, let's have rigor and precision, even though we are studying poetry." But the poets will reply: "We are for goo, and you people are all dry bones, rattling in the wind. What you need is essential juices, and therefore more goo is necessary to liven you up." But when we want to know what goo is, and examine it carefully, we eventually turn up with a structure, the molecular or atomic composition of goo! On the other hand, when we try to examine the structure itself to study the substance of its bones, we inevitably come up with something gooey. When the microscope focus is clear, you have structure. But when you reach beyond the focus and what confronts you is vague and amorphous, you have goo because you cannot attain clarity. Structure and goo are essential limits of human thought; similarly, the nominalist-structural and the realist-gooey will always be essential limits in our thinking. We must be aware that today, the particular academic and scientific fashion leans heavily in the direction of structure and nominalism.

To take a specific example, we all know that in modern medicine nominalism and structuralism hold the field. When you go to a hospital, you are liable to go through a process of examination by specialists working upon you from different points of view. They will treat

you as a non-person, from the very moment you enter. You are immediately put in a wheelchair—a symbol of the fact that you are now
an object. You will be looked at piecemeal, X-rays will be taken of
various organs, and special tests will be made of their functioning.
If anything is wrong, you will be taken to a medical mechanic, i.e.,
a surgeon, who will use his equivalents of wrenches, screwdrivers and
blowtorches to make certain mechanical alterations in your organism,
and it is hoped you will get along fairly well with these repairs!

But the opposite, minority school of medicine will say: "This is all
very well, and the services of the surgeon are sometimes greatly welcomed, but man must be considered as a whole. He has complicated
metabolic and endocrine balances, and if you interfere with him seriously at one point, you will affect him unpredictably at many others,
for man is an organic whole." Such are accused of being woolly-
minded, old-fashioned doctors, mostly from Europe, with a kind of
nature-cure background, who will use diet, complicated fasts, and
massage. The poor layman doesn't know whether to deliver himself
over to these old-fashioned naturalistic doctors or to Mr. Sawbones
with his very up-to-date qualifications.

Fortunately, precise science is coming to the rescue of our man-
as-a-whole. More recent studies are showing just how diseases formerly regarded as specific entities, or afflictions of a particular organ or
area, are actually brought about by responses of the central nervous
system, acting as an integrated whole. We are beginning to see how
man, as a complex of organs, is not an *addition* of parts, like an automobile. His various organs are not to be treated as if they were assembled together, but by seeing the physical body as a unified or integrated pattern of behavior—which is just what we mean when we talk
about an entity or thing. What happens when we have the feeling that
we understand something, when we say, "Oh, I see?" If a child asks,
"Why are the leaves green?" and you answer, "Because of the chlorophyll," and the child says, "Oh!" that is *pseudo*-understanding. But
when the child has a jigsaw puzzle and sees how it all fits together,
then the "Oh!" has a different meaning from the "Oh!" following the
chlorophyll explanation. To understand anything is to be able to fit
various parts into a system which is an integrated whole, so that
they "make sense."

As organic diseases are fitted into a whole, and problems of crime
or psychosis in individual behavior are fitted in with a pattern of social
behavior that makes sense, that is consistent with those kinds of
behaviors, we say "Aha!—*now* I see!"

Fascinating work is being done in studying the ways in which the individual as a system of behavior is related to his biological and social environments, showing how his behavior may be explained in terms of those environments. One of the people who has done very important work in this sphere is our distinguished colleague, B. F. Skinner. I cite his work because it brings out these ideas in a marvellously clear, crucial, and provocative way, and because it is evidence for conclusions which he himself does not seem to have realized. One of his most important statements is in his book, *Science and Human Behavior.*[1]

The hypothesis that man is not free is essential to the application of scientific method to the study of human behavior. The free inner man who is held responsible for the behavior of the external biological organism is only a prescientific substitute for the kinds of causes which are discovered in the course of a scientific analysis.

He is talking, of course, about the chauffeur inside the body, or what Wittgenstein called the little man inside the head: this is for him a pre-scientific substitute for the kinds of causes for behavior which are discovered in the course of scientific analysis. He continues:

All these alternative causes lie *outside* the individual. The biological substratum itself is determined by prior events in a genetic process. Other important events are found in the nonsocial environment and in the culture of the individual in the broadest possible sense. These are the things which *make** the individual behave as he does. For them he is not responsible and for them it is useless to praise or blame him. It does not matter that the individual may take it upon himself to control the variables of which his own behavior is a function or, in a broader sense, to engage in the design of his own culture. He does this only because he is the product of a culture which *generates** self-control or cultural design as a mode of behavior. The environment determines the individual even when he alters the environment.[2] [*Emphasis mine—A.W.W.]

I am not going to quarrel with this finding. I am not a clinical or experimental psychologist and am therefore unqualified to criticize Skinner's evidence. Let's take it for Gospel, simply for the sake of argument.

But there is a rather heavy emphasis upon the individual being the puppet. "All these alternative causes," i.e., the kinds of causes discovered in the course of scientific behavior, "lie outside the individual," i.e., outside this wall of flesh and bag of skin. The individual is therefore passive. This is psychology in terms of Newtonian physics.

[1] New York: The Macmillan Co., 1953, pp. 447-48.
[2] Ibid.

The individual is a billiard ball upon which other balls impinge, and his seemingly active behavior is only a passive response. Skinner admits the individual does and can alter the environment, but when he does so, he is *being made* to do so. This is put forth in such a way as to make the individual appear passive and the things *really* controlling his behavior outside him.

But the reciprocal relationship between the knower and the known, common to all the sciences, is set aside here although he mentions it elsewhere.

A laboratory for the study of behavior contains many devices for controlling the environment and for recording and analyzing the behavior of organisms. With the help of these devices and their associated techniques, we change the behavior of an organism in various ways, with considerable precision. But note that the organism changes our behavior in quite as precise a fashion. Our apparatus was designed by the organism we study, for it was the organism which led us to choose a particular manipulandum, particular categories of stimulation, particular modes of reinforcement, and so on, and to record particular aspects of its behavior. Measures which were successful were for that reason reinforcing and have been retained, while others have been, as we say, extinguished. The verbal behavior with which we analyze our data has been shaped in a similar way: order and consistency emerged to reinforce certain practices which were adopted, while other practices suffered extinction and were abandoned. (All scientific techniques, as well as scientific knowledge itself, are generated in this way. A cyclotron is "designed" by the particles it is to control, and a theory is written by the particles it is to explain, as the behavior of these particles shapes the nonverbal and verbal behavior of the scientist.) [3]

In one of his essays, he has a cartoon of one mouse saying to another "Boy, have I got that guy up there fixed! Every time I press this bar, he gives me some food!"

Although Skinner seems in general to be stressing heavily the point of view that the individual is the puppet in the field in which he is involved, he is nevertheless stating here the opposite point, that the individual organism, mouse, or guinea pig, in the experiment is nevertheless determining the environment even when, as in a laboratory, the environment is designed to control the specific organism. The environment of a rat running in a barn is not designed to control the rat, but the more it is so designed, the more the rat is involved in and shaping its environment. He writes elsewhere that what he has been saying

does not mean that anyone in possession of the methods and results of science can step outside the stream of history and take the evolution of

[3] "The Design of Cultures," *Daedalus*, Summer 1961, p. 543.

government into his own hands. Science is not free, either. It cannot interfere with the course of events; it is simply part of that course. It would be
quite inconsistent if we were to exempt the scientist from the account
which science gives of human behavior in general.[4]

Now we might well object: "Look, Professor Skinner, you say we are
completely conditioned behavior-systems. We cannot change anything. At the same time, you are calling upon us to embark upon the
most radical program of controlling human behavior. How can you
write *Walden II,* a utopia? Are you not a monstrosity of inconsistency
by calling for responsible human action and at the same time saying
that we have no freedom?" But is this actually a contradiction? He is
saying two things, both of which can be valid, but he does not provide
a framework in which the opposed points of view can make sense.
Similarly, the physicist says light can be considered as a wave or as a
particle system. These sound mutually exclusive to the non-physicist.
In the same way, the advocacy of a planned development of human
resources and potentials, coupled with the idea that the individual is
not a self-controlling, skin-encapsulated ego, needs some further concept to help it along. The following passage clinches the problem.

Just as biographers and critics look for external influences to account for
the traits and achievements of the men they study, so science ultimately
explains behavior in terms of "causes" or conditions which lie beyond the
individual himself. As more and more causal relations are demonstrated,
a practical corollary becomes difficult to resist: it should be possible to
produce behavior according to plan simply by arranging the proper conditions.[5]

There is the contradiction which necessarily arises in a psychology
with a language system which incorporates into present scientific
knowledge an outmoded conception of the individual—the individual
as something bounded by skin, and which is pushed around by an
environment which is not the individual. Skinner is naturally aware
that his emphasis on our passive relationship to conditioning causes is
rather unpalatable.

The conception of the individual which emerges from a scientific analysis
is distasteful to most of those who have been strongly affected by democratic philosophies . . . it has always been the unfortunate task of science
to dispossess cherished beliefs regarding the place of man in the universe.
It is easy to understand why men so frequently flatter themselves—why they
characterize the world in ways which reinforce them by providing escape
from the consequences of criticism or other forms of punishment. But

---

[4] *Science and Human Behavior,* p. 446.
[5] "Freedom and the Control of Men," *The American Scholar* 25, no. 1 (Winter 1955–56): 47.

although flattery temporarily strengthens behavior, it is questionable whether it has any ultimate survival value. If science does not confirm the assumptions of freedom, initiative, and responsibility in the behavior of the individual, these assumptions will not ultimately be effective either as motivating devices or as goals in the design of culture. We may not give them up easily, and we may, in fact, find it difficult to control ourselves or others until alternative principles have been developed.[6]

There the book ends, and there is no suggestion as to what those principles might be, even though they are implied in his conclusions.

When an individual conspicuously manipulates the variables of which the behavior of *another** individual is a function, we say that the first individual controls the second, but we do not ask who or what controls the first. When a government conspicuously controls its citizens, we consider this fact without identifying the events which control the government. When the individual is strengthened as a measure of counter-control, we may, as in democratic philosophies, think of him as a starting point. [*My emphasis—A.W.W.]

Isn't this political nominalism?

Actually, however, we are not justified in assigning to *anyone or anything** the role of prime mover. Although it is necessary that science confine itself to selected segments in a continuous series of events, it is *to the whole series** that any interpretation must eventually apply.[7] [*My emphasis— A.W.W.]

We are now listening to a man who represents himself as a behavioristically oriented, non-mystical, on-the-whole materialistic, hard-headed scientist. Yet this passage is the purest mysticism, which might have come straight from Mahayana Buddhism: "We are not justified in assigning to anyone or anything the role of prime mover." No segment, no particular pattern of integrated behavior within whatever universe we are discussing can be called the prime mover. Now this is the *Dharmadhatu* doctrine of Mahayana Buddhism, that the universe is a harmonious system which has no governor, that it is an integrated organism but nobody is in charge of it. Its corollary is that everyone and everything is the prime mover.

In Skinner's language, the popular conception of the inner self, the little man inside the head who is controlling everything, must be replaced by the whole system of *external* causes operating upon the individual, the whole network of causal relationships. But this language obscures a very simple thing: when there is a certain cause in the external environment whose effect is always a particular individual

---

[6] *Science and Human Behavior,* p. 449.
[7] Ibid., pp. 448–49.

behavior, you are using very cumbersome language for something you can describe more simply. For when you find these two things going together, you are actually talking about one thing. To say that Event A causes Event B is a laborious way of saying that it is one Event C. If I lift up this book by a corner, all the corners are lifted up at the same time. If I lift up an accordion, there is an interval between cause and effect. Similarly when we study the individual's behavior, we are studying a system of relationships, but we are looking at it too close up. All we see is the atomic events, and we don't see the integrated system which would make them make sense if we could see it. Our scientific methods of description suffer from a defective conception of the individual. The individual is not by any means what is contained inside a given envelope of skin. The individual organism is the particular and unique focal point of a network of relations which is ultimately a "whole series"—I suppose that means the whole cosmos. And the whole cosmos so focused is one's actual self. This is, whether you like it or not, pure mysticism. Skinner is saying that although science is a method of observation which, by reason of the blinkers of the head, is limited to our one-thing-at-a-time method of thought, science can only look at the world area by area. But science also becomes the method of understanding its own limitations. When you conduct any experiment, you must be careful to exclude variables you cannot measure. When you want to keep something at a constant temperature, you must put it into some kind of heat-and-cold-proof or shock-proof, or cosmic-ray-proof system. So by excluding variables and by having to do it rigorously, you begin to understand how really impossible it is to do except in very special cases. In this way, the scientist, by attempting to isolate events and by looking as rigorously as he can at one segment of the world at a time, becomes aware of the fact that this looking at things simply in segments, although it is a form of very bright, clear, conscious knowledge, is also a form of ignorance. For it is a form of "ignore-ance," ignoring everything that is not in that segment. Therefore he becomes aware of the fact that just this is *ultimately* what you can't do. You *can* do it only to discover you *cannot* do it.

I commend these observations to you simply to show how a scientific thinker whose whole stance is in the direction of mechanism, of regarding the human being as a kind of biological puppet, must be forced by the logic of his own thinking to conclusions of a rather different kind. He states these questions in veiled language, so that neither he nor his colleagues will see their disastrously unrespectable implications!

Suppose, then, it becomes possible for us to have a new sense of the individual, that we all become conscious of ourselves as organism-environment fields, vividly aware of the fact that when we move, it is not simply my self moving inside my skin, exercising energy upon my limbs, but also that in some marvelous way the physical continuum in which I move is also moving me. Would such an awareness be significant? Would it add to our knowledge? Would it change anything, make any difference? Seriously, I think it would; because it makes an enormous difference whenever what had seemed to be partial and disintegrated fits into a larger integrated pattern. It will of course be impossible finally to answer the question, "Why does that satisfy us?" because to answer this question exhaustively I would have to be able to chew my own teeth to pieces. In the pursuit of scientific knowledge, always watch out for that snag. You will never get to the irreducible explanation of anything because you will never be able to explain why you want to explain, and so on. The system will gobble itself up. The Gödel theory has roughly to do with the idea that you cannot have any system which will define its own axioms. An axiom in one system of logic must be defined in terms of another system, etc., etc. You never get to something which is completely self-explanatory. That of course is the limit of control, and the reason why all systems of control have ultimately to be based on an act of faith.

The problem confronting all sciences of human behavior is that we have the evidence (we are *staring* at it) to give us an entirely different conception of the individual than that which we ordinarily feel and which influences our common sense: a conception of the individual not, on the one hand, as an ego locked in the skin, nor, on the other, as a mere passive part of the machine, but as a reciprocal interaction between everything inside the skin and everything outside it, neither one being prior to the other, but equals, like the front and back of a coin.